TAX, PUBLIC FINANCE, AND THE RULE OF LAW

This book offers a key point of reference for reflective and thoughtful examinations of the rule of law in tax and related disciplines.

It features a stellar cast of established and early-career researchers from a variety of jurisdictions who have entered into conversations about the nature of the rule of law; its relevance to questions about tax, welfare, distribution and public spending; and the challenges involved in applying legal standards in these fields.

There is a particular focus on the interaction between the rule of law and the rapidly emerging world of cross-border tax avoidance, reforms influenced by the OECD's Base Erosion and Profits Shifting project and the evolution of EU-level governance over direct as well as indirect taxes. The book is accessible to those new to taxation and public finance as well as to experts, and to lawyers and non-lawyers alike.

Tax, Public Finance, and the Rule of Law

Edited by
Dominic de Cogan
Alexis Brassey
and
May Hen

•HART•
OXFORD • LONDON • NEW YORK • NEW DELHI • SYDNEY

HART PUBLISHING

Bloomsbury Publishing Plc

Kemp House, Chawley Park, Cumnor Hill, Oxford, OX2 9PH, UK

1385 Broadway, New York, NY 10018, USA

Bloomsbury Publishing Ireland Limited, 29 Earlsfort Terrace, Dublin 2, D02 AY28, Ireland

HART PUBLISHING, the Hart/Stag logo, BLOOMSBURY and the Diana logo are trademarks of Bloomsbury Publishing Plc

First published in Great Britain 2025

First published in hardback, 2025

Paperback edition, 2026

A catalogue record for this book is available from the British Library.

A catalogue record for this book is available from the Library of Congress.

Library of Congress Control Number: 2024950001

ISBN: PB: 978-1-50997-779-6
ePDF: 978-1-50997-782-6
ePub: 978-1-50997-783-3

Typeset by Compuscript Ltd, Shannon

For product safety related questions contact productsafety@bloomsbury.com

To find out more about our authors and books visit www.hartpublishing.co.uk. Here you will find extracts, author information, details of forthcoming events and the option to sign up for our newsletters.

CONTENTS

CONTRIBUTORS

Jo Badisco is a postdoctoral researcher at the Centre for Government and Law (CORe), Faculty of Law, Hasselt University.

Alexis Brassey is an affiliated lecturer at the Cambridge Law Faculty and Visiting Fellow of the Centre for Tax Law. He is course convenor for the Tax Law and Policy Seminar paper and researches tax, constitutional law, and political philosophy.

Previously, Alexis was managing partner of Cavendish Legal Group, after working in senior management at a number of investment banks including BZW, Lehman Brothers, Citibank, Sakura Bank and SMBC. He is currently Executive Director of the Waltham Forest Friendly Society.

Dirk Maarten Broekhuijsen has been an associate professor at the department for tax law of Leiden University since January 2024. He is interested in international tax law and the taxation of individuals. Prior to his appointment as associate professor, Dirk worked as a tax inspector at the Amsterdam office of the Dutch Tax and Customs Administration.

Tirza Cramwinckel is an assistant professor at Leiden University, the Netherlands, and a tax lawyer at Stibbe, the Netherlands.

Stephen Daly is a reader in Tax Law at King's College London. He holds degrees in law from University College Cork (BCL), University College London (LLM) and the University of Oxford (DPhil). He is also a CTA (Fellow). Dr Daly's research focuses on administrative law, technical tax law and EU law. He published his first monograph with Hart Publishing (HMRC Advice and the Public (2020)) and has published in leading generalist academic journals (*Law Quarterly Review, Modern Law Review*), in various edited collections and specialist tax journals (*British Tax Review, Bulletin for International Taxation, European Taxation, Fiscal Studies, Intertax, Tax Notes*). His commentary of issues of tax law and policy has featured in *The Observer, The Times*, specialist law and tax media (*Bloomberg Tax, Tax Journal, Tax Notes Today International, Politico, Law360*) as well as on the BBC World Service.

Dominic de Cogan is a professor of tax and public law at the Faculty of Law, University of Cambridge and assistant director of the Centre for Tax Law.

Stefanie Geringer is a postdoctoral researcher in the Department of Tax Law at the Faculty of Law at the University of Vienna and a certified tax adviser and manager at BDO Austria.

Rory Gillis is an assistant professor at the University of Western Ontario Faculty of Law in London, Ontario, Canada. His research focuses on tax law & policy. Rory holds a BA and JD from Yale Law School and a doctorate in law from the University of Toronto.

Helen Hodgson is an expert in taxation, based at the Curtin Law School. Her research is in the areas where tax and social policy intersect: superannuation; welfare and inequality. Professor Hodgson has contributed significantly to policy review in the areas of superannuation, the tax and transfer system and housing, specifically examining these systems through a gender lens. Helen holds qualifications in accounting, business law and taxation and has taught taxation law in business and law schools.

May Hen is a Leverhulme Trust Early Career Research Fellow, based at the Faculty of Law, University of Cambridge. She is also chair of the Cambridge Socio-Legal Group. She is a fiscal sociologist focused on offshore finance, blockchain, cryptocurrencies and digital assets.

Richard Krever is a professor in the law school of the University of Western Australia. He is the author of more than 100 articles and book chapters on taxation law. Professor Krever was made a member of the Order of Australia by the Australian government for his contributions to tax scholarship. As a consequence of his international scholarship, Professor Krever has worked with numerous international bodies including the International Monetary Fund, World Bank, United Nations and European Union and has been seconded to the Australian Treasury and Australian Taxation Office.

Giedre Lideikyte Huber is an assistant professor of tax law and vice-director of the Institute for Law and Economics at the University of St Gallen. Her research focus is tax law, with a particular focus on tax incentives, sustainable tax policies, and philanthropy. She was a visiting scholar at Massachusetts Institute of Technology (MIT), University of Oxford, University of Zurich, UC Berkeley School of Law and at Harvard Law School. Giedre also worked in both the private and public sectors.

Ira Lindsay is an associate professor at the University of Surrey where he serves as head of Surrey Law School and associate head of the School of Social Sciences. He holds a JD from Yale Law School and a PhD in Philosophy from the University of Michigan.

Michael Littlewood (BA/LLB(Hons), Auckland; PhD, HKU) is a professor at Auckland University Law School. He is admitted as a barrister and solicitor in New Zealand, as a solicitor in England and Wales and as a solicitor in Hong Kong. He is an authority on tax law, tax policy and tax history, and an occasional adviser to taxpayers and the governments of several jurisdictions. His work has been published in New Zealand, the US, the UK, Australia, China and Hong Kong.

Lynne Oats is emeritus professor, University of Exeter, UK. Prior to her retirement, she worked as a tax academic in Australia and the UK. In addition to publishing numerous journal articles and book chapters, Lynne is co-author of *Taxation Policy and Practice* (Fiscal Publications), author of *Principles of International Taxation* (Bloomsbury), and editor of *Taxation: A Fieldwork Research Handbook* (Routledge). She continues to research taxation as a social practice and is currently working on a new book, *Fiscal Belonging* (Palgrave).

Henry Ordower is professor of law at Saint Louis University School of Law, St Louis, MO, USA. Ordower, who has an extensive background in European Languages, holds a JD from the University of Chicago. He teaches and researches extensively concerning taxation and tax policy. Ordower is an elected fellow of the American College of Tax Counsel and an elected member of the European Association of Tax Law Professors and the International Academy of Comparative Law.

Rodrigo Ormeño-Pérez serves as an associate professor B in Taxation and Accounting at Kemmy Business School, University of Limerick, Ireland. He has previously held faculty positions at the University of Chile and the University of Birmingham, UK. His research focuses on the intersection of taxation, politics, policies, and sociology, with recent publications in prominent accounting journals including *Critical Perspectives on Accounting* and *The British Accounting Review*. Before embarking on his academic career, Rodrigo worked as a tax auditor for PwC and a risk auditor for Deloitte in his native Chile.

Katerina Pantazatou is an associate professor in tax law at the University of Luxembourg. She has been a visiting professor at the University of Bergamo and the University of Valencia and a visiting researcher at Harvard University and the Institute for Austrian and International Tax Law at WU.

Chetan Rao is an Officer of the Indian Revenue Service.

Kerrie Sadiq is a professor of taxation at Queensland University of Technology, Australia. She is an international tax scholar specifically known for her work in base erosion and profit shifting, transfer pricing, thin capitalisation, tax expenditures, and capital gains tax. Kerrie is co-editor of the *Australian Tax Review* and an author of publications in both Australian and international journals, edited books, and leading taxation texts. Throughout her career, she has contributed to Australian Government Senate Inquiries and Board of Taxation Reviews of tax policy.

Adrian Sawyer is professor of taxation at the University of Canterbury in New Zealand and extraordinary professor at the University of South Africa. He holds an SJD from the University of Virginia, and MCom(Hons), BCom and LLB degrees from UC. He is a FCA (CA-ANZ), FCPA (CPA Australia), and barrister and solicitor (NZ). Adrian is an editor of the *New Zealand Journal of Taxation Law and Policy*. His research interests include tax administration, compliance, policy, taxpayers' rights, and international taxation.

Suranjali Tandon is an associate professor at the National Institute of Public Finance and Policy, India.

Elly Van de Velde is a member of the Council of State of Belgium, professor of tax law at the Centre of Government and Law (CORe), Faculty of Law, Hasselt University, and a voluntary researcher at the University of Antwerp.

Bastiaan van Ganzen is a lecturer and PhD candidate at the Institute of Tax Law and Economics of Leiden University.

Jan Vleggeert is professor of tax law at Leiden University and head of the tax department since 1 February 2020. He defended his PhD thesis at Leiden University on 23 June 2009 entitled: 'Interest deduction restrictions in international tax law'. His research concerns the rules for the protection of the national (corporate income) tax base, and the prevention of tax avoidance.

Henk Vording is professor of tax law at Leiden University.

1

The Rule of Law and Taxation

DOMINIC DE COGAN, ALEXIS BRASSEY AND MAY HEN

Abstract

The rule of law cannot simultaneously fulfil all of the expectations that are placed on it within the tax and public finance fields. Nevertheless, it is a concept with powerful appeal that typically converges on the ideas that arbitrary government is undesirable and that individuals and businesses ought to be protected from it. Whilst commentators often accept the 'formal' rule of law values set out by theorists such as Lon Fuller and Joseph Raz, for some they are inextricable from wider theories of good fiscal governance which do not always fit comfortably within the formal-substantive spectrum that is conventional in the public law literature.

The Rule of Law

The rule of law is discussed widely in public finance contexts and has an obvious superficial appeal. Of course, tax, welfare and related fields should comply with the rule of law. At the same time, it does not require an especially deep reading of the literature to wonder whether all the advantages ascribed to the rule of law in these fields could possibly be achieved at once, and under the cover of the same legal concept. For example, it is plausible to say that the rule of law requires the substantive equality of taxpayers; it is also plausible that it requires the protection of settled expectations. However, it is trickier to argue that it requires both at once, at least in a way that is likely to offer clear guidance in a hard case such as an attempt by a taxpayer to enforce expectations of unequally favourable treatment. The point is not that legal systems are incapable of reconciling conflicting values or resolving difficult cases, but simply that the competing demands of substantive equality and taxpayer expectations cannot necessarily be settled by a simple appeal to the rhetorical force of the rule of law. The rule of law may indeed be a point of entry into a fuller examination of the merits of a difficult case rather than itself providing a solution.

A more worrying variant of the same problem arises when the rhetorical force of the rule of law is commandeered to lend a veneer of objectivity to self-interested, political and even party-political arguments that would otherwise be recognised immediately as controversial and contestable. Some commentators might respond that the rule of law is unavoidably and irreducibly political, so that any attempt to present it in neutral and legalistic terms is a form of obfuscation. Either way, the burden of convincing a reader of the value of an argument, political or otherwise, should be on its proponent. The intuitive appeal of the rule of law is not enough on its own to discharge this burden.

If asserting the rule of law can only ever be the beginning of a wider conversation about its meaning and content, the purpose of invoking it and its consequences, it would be going too far in the other direction to say that it is meaningless, devoid of content and ought to be ignored altogether in favour of more specific arguments about the rights and obligations of taxpayers, welfare recipients and others. In particular, there does seem to be a high degree of convergence on the idea that the rule of law involves a disapproval of arbitrary government and that it commits us to certain procedural protections for individuals and businesses in the face of potential arbitrariness: for instance, that legal rules should be generally applicable, well publicised, prospective, clear, non-contradictory, capable of compliance and reasonably stable.[1]

Of course, convergence of opinion is not identical to agreement; if anything the wide acceptance of these procedural standards of the rule of law tends to mask deeper disagreement about why they matter and how they might operate in real-life scenarios. To offer a well-known example, few would dispute the principle that legal rules should be applied consistently. However, things become more complicated when we ask what it would mean for the rule of law to demand consistent application of income tax to a non-disabled person who earns €100,000 and a disabled person who works much harder and incurs additional expenses to earn the same amount. On the one hand, the view could be taken that the rule of law merely requires the income tax legislation to be applied according to its terms. If the outcome is to discriminate against the disabled person, then this may be regrettable but is a matter for the legislature and is irrelevant to the rule of law as such. On the other hand, it could be argued that the principle of consistency is only worth pursuing if it reflects a coherent theory of substantive equality, in which case an income tax that fails to take account of the special burdens of disability can fairly be described as applying inconsistently and hence contravening the rule of law.

More could be said about this example, but the key point for now is that the convergence of opinion on certain aspects of the rule of law masks deeper disagreement, to the extent that it is difficult even to claim that we *agree* on certain core concepts even if there are peripheral areas of disagreement. The controversy just described was not about how the principle of consistency should be implemented but instead about what it is. Another way of putting the point is that a substantial number of observers, including some represented in the present volume,[2] would accept the principle of consistency as part of the rule of law but also argue that it only makes sense and can only be accepted as part of a wider theory of good law, taxation, politics or society. If asked to agree to the principle of consistency in isolation from their preferred theory, they would respond 'no, this no longer makes sense'. What has been described above as a convergence of

[1] These ideas are heavily emphasised in 'formal' or 'thin' conceptions of the rule of law: see further discussion in the text below, under the heading 'Part I: Fundamental Concepts' and Daly, Chapter 2 in this volume.

[2] See generally Part II of this volume.

opinion is therefore not really a zone of *consensus* but rather a *focal point* for very different ways of viewing the world and the role of law in tax and public finance.

The English-language public law literature tends to portray these dynamics within the framework of 'formal' or 'thin' versus 'substantive' or 'thick' conceptions of the rule of law, whereby authors in the former tradition restrict their account to a relatively conventional list of procedural principles, whilst authors in the latter tradition also include human rights protections and other principles which allow substantive outcomes as well as procedures to be evaluated. Though this formal-substantive division is instructive in its way, it provides an impoverished basis for understanding the many and various ways in which rule of law ideas are conceived by contributors to this volume and within communities of tax and public finance specialists more generally.[3]

An example of a strand in the literature that does not fit comfortably within the formal-substantive framework can be found in the contributions to this volume dealing with EU tax law, in which there is a sense that the rule of law requires coherent treatment of taxpayers not only in each jurisdiction but across the Union as a whole. This perspective, which engages questions of integration and reflects the EU's potentially constructive role in furthering high-quality legal standards across an entire continent, is an important one but does not align neatly with either formal or substantive versions of the rule of law. The question is more about who does what, that is, whether good procedural and/or substantive outcomes are best coordinated at EU or municipal level. Linking this with the discussion immediately above, the authors in this vein are likely to agree that procedural rule of law values are desirable but need to be seen in the context of a wider jurisdictional discussion about whether EU integration is to be preferred or resisted.

The mention of EU integration leads directly into another important point. A key insight in the EU tax literature is that coherent Union-wide rules might help not only to protect individuals but to support the achievement of high standards of governance across the Union.[4] The EU is not alone in holding this perspective, and, for example, the World Justice Project defines the rule of law as follows:

> The rule of law is a durable system of laws, institutions, norms, and community commitment that delivers four universal principles: accountability, just law, open government, and accessible and impartial justice.[5]

There is not much here about protecting individuals and businesses from arbitrary government. The emphasis is on institution-building and good governance. The UN's account of the rule of law, which is too long to quote in full, is more balanced and mentions good governance alongside the protection of individuals:

> The rule of law is fundamental to international peace and security and political stability; to achieve economic and social progress and development; and to protect people's rights and

[3] In any case, a strict distinction between procedure and substantive outcomes can be particularly difficult to maintain in the tax field: see D de Cogan, 'Public Law and Political Values in Tax Law' in L Parada (ed), *A Research Agenda for Tax Law* (Cheltenham, Edward Elgar, 2022), Part II.

[4] See also EU Charter of Fundamental Rights, Art 14 and the discussion of relevant caselaw in the Explanations. Available at: https://fra.europa.eu/en/eu-charter/article/41-right-good-administration.

[5] World Justice Project, 'What is the Rule of Law?' Available at: https://worldjusticeproject.org/about-us/overview/what-rule-law (accessed 26 August 2024).

> fundamental freedoms. It is foundational to people's access to public services, curbing corruption, restraining the abuse of power, and to establishing the social.

The UN's running together, if not exactly elision, of the benefits of rules-based good governance and the protection of individuals and businesses from arbitrary state power, is widespread in the tax and public law literature alike but is also often very reasonable. It is plausible to suggest that subjecting the tax authorities to certain rules and principles is likely to improve the quality of tax governance as well as to protect individuals and businesses from arbitrary conduct,[6] though of course this is a claim that would benefit from detailed empirical evidence. However, there are also situations in which the alignment between good governance and protection is not quite so obvious, or at least where there is a stronger emphasis on one side than the other.[7] An example is where a taxpayer has a particularly high level of bargaining power relative to a tax authority, perhaps a multinational mining enterprise dealing with the government of a least-developed country. The possible benefits of rules based good governance in this scenario are easy to imagine; the need for the mining enterprise to be protected against overweening state power is more obscure though doubtless not entirely absent.

To recap, the convergence of opinion around the importance of certain procedural rule of law values masks a series of deeper disagreements about whether a commitment to those values is capable of being separated from a wider theory of good law, taxation, politics or society. In turn, some of those theories focus on substantive outcomes and fit neatly into the conventional public law classification of 'formal' and 'substantive' conceptions of the rule of law, but others focus on different questions such as the location of responsibility for the rule of law (eg EU institutions) or the relative weight to be placed on good administration and the protection of individuals and businesses. The terminology of 'substantive' to refer to all of these varieties of opinion is compendious and vague, and it can be more informative – at least in the tax and public finance fields – simply to ask whether an author treats the procedural values of the rule of law as inseparable from a wider theory, and if so, what that theory is.

This discussion helps to provide a clearer response to the anxieties expressed at the outset about the coherence and usefulness of the rule of law in debates about tax and public finance. A useful parallel might be made here with ideas of fairness in taxation. Few would argue that it is pointless to aim for fairness in taxation, or that we ought to be indifferent whether tax systems are fair or unfair. Equally, if an author appeals to fairness, it is obvious, first, that much depends on exactly what they mean by fairness and, second, that this is likely to be shaped strongly by their wider beliefs. In turn, this close attention to the meaning and context of an author's presentation of fairness provides an opportunity for readers to challenge controversial claims about fairness without having to admit a partiality for unfairness. So it is with the rule of law. It expresses a valuable set of ideas that have normative as well as rhetorical force, yet anyone who asserts the rule of law can reasonably be expected to explain what they mean and to defend

[6] See Daly, Chapter 2 in this volume. See generally: DJ Galligan, *Discretionary Powers: a Legal Study of Official Discretion* (Oxford, Clarendon, 1990).

[7] A stronger version of this point is made in JNE Varuhas, 'The Public Interest Conception of Public Law' in J Bell, M Elliott, JNE Varuhas and P Murray (eds), *Public Law Adjudication in Common Law Systems: Process and Substance* (Oxford, Hart Publishing, 2016) 45–86.

their own conception against alternatives. Finally, whilst it has been argued that the broad convergence around the procedural values of the rule of law does not amount to true agreement on a core set of principles, even convergence is likely to be sufficient in gathering broad support for practical recommendations for improving tax and public finance arrangements. The rule of law, after all, is not only an intellectual construct but also a call for change, and in this role need not necessarily be defeated by underlying disagreement.

The Structure of the Volume

In the light of the discussion above, the structure of this volume is very straightforward. Part I deals with fundamental concepts surrounding the rule of law, predominantly in the tax field, whereas Parts II and III showcase debates about the extent to which the rule of law should be contextualised within a wider theoretical frame. Part II examines the potential links between the Rule of Law, social theory, ethics, a concern for social and racial inequalities and the borderlines between tax, welfare and public borrowing. Part III examines the opportunities and challenges of thinking about the rule of law across jurisdictional boundaries, with a particular focus on international and EU tax law.

Part I: Fundamental Concepts

The volume opens with Daly's exploration of fundamental ideas about the rule of law in the context of access to tribunals and courts by UK taxpayers. According to Daly, legal accountability is weakened by the obstacles placed in the way of taxpayers hoping to challenge tax decisions, especially at higher tiers of appeal than the First-tier Tribunal. These obstacles include the unavailability of legal aid in tax disputes but also deliberate restrictions that have been implemented in order to prevent the misuse of appeals processes and to pursue other policy objectives. Such restrictions may offend against the rule of law, but this depends critically on which account of the rule of law is preferred. In particular, the appeals system for UK taxpayers may be more or less consistent with the procedural principles set out in the 'formal' or 'thin' rule of law accounts of Fuller, Raz and Waldron. If those principles are to be supplemented by the wider concern for human and property rights that typifies 'substantive' or 'thick' accounts of the rule of law, however, it is likely that serious shortcomings will be identified in existing appeals arrangements and in particular in the mechanisms for restricting appeals.

If Daly shows that incorporating a wider respect for human and property rights into the rule of law can influence how we evaluate existing arrangements, Lindsay stands this argument on its head and shows that the quality of tax governance in a given jurisdiction might influence our understanding of the nature and significance of rule of law breaches. If tax administration is carried out competently and with due respect for human and property rights, limited breaches of what Lindsay terms the 'narrow scope' rule of law ('whether disputes are decided according to legal norms that are general, prospective and impartial')[8] may not be too objectionable, especially if they help to ensure equitable outcomes under the applicable legislation. Any potential criticism would be tempered by adhering to the 'wide scope' rule of law ('whether political authorities respect existing legal entitlements rather than conferring benefits and burdens on an ad hoc basis').[9] Conversely, if there are serious weaknesses in tax governance in a given jurisdiction, this might recommend a strict adherence to the narrow-scope rule of law even at the expense of loss of revenue or inequitable outcomes.

It can be seen immediately that these two portrayals of the rule of law are not strictly inconsistent yet aim at very different targets. Whilst Daly's chapter centres on a taxpayer who is seeking justice from the appeals system, Lindsay's chapter speaks more clearly to a government hoping to improve the standard of tax governance in its jurisdiction. It is not a coincidence that Lindsay's 'wide scope' rule of law closely resembles the 'discussion of the rule of law … by international organisations such as the World Bank and the United Nations'[10] who, of course, have a similar emphasis.

While Daly and Lindsay explore big-picture debates on the rule of law's content and its significance for taxpayers and governments, Gillis demonstrates that there is much to be said at the micro-level of particular requirements of the rule of law. In particular, how these requirements are interpreted can reveal much about the values held by the interpreter. Gillis illustrates the point by reference to the principle that legal rules should ordinarily be prospective rather than retrospective in application, and picks on a distinction made in Lon Fuller's *Morality of Law*[11] between retrospective changes to tax law that have the consequence of modifying *future* tax payment obligations and those that generate new obligations to pay tax *in the past* that are now impossible to perform. If one adopts Fuller's own preference in focusing attention on the latter type of retrospectivity, a consequence is to downplay the relevance of the rule of law to the disruption of settled expectations. Conversely, a commentator who places a higher priority on the protection of expectations is likely to take a wider interpretation of retrospectivity than Fuller's. Not uncharacteristically of the tax field more generally, a definitional question that initially seems straightforward turns out to conceal wider value disagreements.

This point becomes immediately apparent in the next chapter, in which Cramwinckel draws on communication theory and a 'citizens' perspective' in order to argue for the stronger protection of taxpayers' expectations. As she explains, this may involve prioritising some aspects of the rule of law over others, placing particular weight on *legal certainty* for those relying on information provided by the tax authorities as well as on the *comprehensibility* of this information, even at the expense of a strict *application of the published law*. The author illustrates the point with reference to the law of the Netherlands, in which *ultra vires* or '*contra legem*' legitimate expectations can already be asserted against the tax authorities in limited circumstances, and sets out a series of proposals outlining how the protection of expectations could be strengthened even further.

[8] See Lindsay, Chapter 3 in this volume.
[9] ibid.
[10] ibid.
[11] L Fuller, *The Morality of Law* (New Haven, Yale University Press, 1964) 59–60, cited by Gillis, Chapter 4 in this volume.

The question of certainty is also raised, but in a very different way, by Tandon and Rao's chapter on the Indian General Anti-Avoidance Rule and UK General Anti-Abuse Rule. GAARs are often criticised for undermining legal certainty, but, as the authors explain, this misses some key points. The first is the simple but obvious point that they are considered to be necessary in order to deal with certain kinds of unacceptable tax avoidance. Indeed, this could be phrased in rule of law terms, in the sense that the relatively stable, comprehensible and well-communicated system of rules described by many rule of law theorists, with which it is possible to comply, can tend to be undermined by tax avoidance activity. Conversely, anti-avoidance rules are not unvaryingly damaging to rule of law values but may in some circumstances help to support them.[12] The second point is that GAARs not only boast safeguards for taxpayers' rights, but have also been shaped from the outset by rule of law values. Indeed, the core of Tandon's and Rao's chapter is a detailed discussion of the development of Indian and UK GAARs over history and the role played in that development by rule of law reasoning.

This relative optimism about GAARs is balanced in the following chapter by a highly pessimistic portrayal by Sawyer of a tax system that is often praised for its strong adherence to rule of law values. The author examines the New Zealand government's conduct before, during and after the COVID-19 pandemic and points to a tendency to set aside or curtail long-established practices relating to the development and implementation of tax policy and legislation. The consequence is to degrade the quality of tax governance, to erode trust in the tax system and, ultimately, to damage even core rule of law values such as comprehensibility and consistent application of the law. In order to remedy the situation, Sawyer advocates far-reaching constitutional reforms that would aim to increase the protection of tax legislation and administration from considerations of urgency and expediency. These might include institutionalising expert input into tax policy, insulating the tax system from politics, entrenching legislation and even establishing an upper legislative house that would ensure greater scrutiny of tax policy.

Part II: Contextualised Theories

The authors in Part I present a wide range of views, bringing in formal and substantive accounts of the rule of law and varying degrees of emphasis on taxpayer protection and good governance, but all adopt taxation as their core subject matter, and all present the rule of law in ways that are readily recognisable from the public law literature. The authors in Part II broaden the focus even further and reposition the discussion within the context of social theory, moral philosophy, public expenditure, social welfare and public borrowing. As such, they typify the attitude described above, whereby the rule of law is thought only to make sense within the context of a preferred theoretical framework or field of enquiry.[13]

[12] Cf the cautious perspective on 'abuse' and related concepts in the tax field in W Schön, 'The Concept of Abuse of Law in European Taxation: A Methodological and Constitutional Perspective' in G Loutzenhiser and R de la Feria (eds) *The Dynamics of Taxation: Essays in Honour of Judith Freedman* (Oxford, Hart, 2020).

[13] For the avoidance of doubt, it is accepted that some chapters in Part I of this volume could be framed in this 'contextual' light and some chapters in Part II could be reconciled comfortably with the conventional public law literature. The division between the two Parts is adopted for convenience, and, it is hoped, explanatory power, but is acknowledged to be both porous and contestable.

An excellent example of this type of approach is Ormeño Perez and Oats' examination of the rule of law against the background of social theory and, in particular, the work of Pierre Bourdieu. From this perspective, taxation is best explained in the light of interplays between social and political power relationships. This means, in turn, that the rule of law might take on a very different complexion, depending on who is asserting it, in what way and in relation to whom. The point is illustrated by reference to recent Chilean history, in which a heavy emphasis was placed on property rights during the Pinochet period but substantive rights and even welfare have since come to greater prominence. There are potential parallels here with thin and thick versions of the rule of law, but the value of the chapter is to show how social theory can make help to sense of the complex shifts between different approaches to the rule of law – not only in the abstract but also in relation to policy design, legislative drafting, administration and the extent to which tax planning is considered legitimate.

Badisco and van de Velde also believe that the dynamics of the rule of law are best understood in theoretical context, and their preferred lens is that of virtue ethics. They explain that the rule of law takes shape within a framework of ethical values by which the conduct of actors within tax systems is both informed and evaluated. This applies not only to tax officials but also to taxpayers and advisors, so that, for instance, enjoying the benefits of a system underpinned by the rule of law could be said to presuppose a certain attitude to law that is consistent with others deriving the same benefits. This line of reasoning differs strikingly from those accounts of the rule of law which focus exclusively on the characteristics of legal rules rather than on the disposition of persons using the rules, and not everyone will agree with it. All the same, the authors' argument is not that it is impossible to rely on the rule of law without acting virtuously, but that it is better to do so. To use the virtues as a way of evaluating and interpreting rules is likely, not only to make more sense of those rules, but also to lead to better and fairer outcomes.

A different set of contextual factors is in play in the three subsequent chapters, namely the porous boundaries between tax and other aspects of public finance. Ordower deals with the vexed question of whether the rule of law can be asserted coherently in a tax setting without a sensitivity towards preexisting social divisions, a question that draws in not only the distribution of tax burdens but also how they are spent. His focus is on social security, an area in which the linkages between taxation, public expenditure and welfare entitlements can be especially close. He argues, first, that the equal respect promised by the rule of law cannot be satisfied without paying attention to deep social and racial inequalities that otherwise risk simply being replicated through the law. He points out, second, that the US social security tax regime does not take sufficient account of these divisions, and indeed exacerbates them by burdening labour income more heavily than capital income. A good start, it is contended, would be to unbundle social security benefits from payroll taxation, which would allow fairer outcomes to be pursued in both fields. Again, Ordower is putting forward a profoundly thick conception of the rule of law, but in a far from abstract manner – his view is influenced by a wider and unashamedly positioned understanding of fair taxation and the proper interaction of tax, welfare and spending.

Hodgson's chapter on the 'Robodebt' scandal in Australia draws on ideas already familiar from this Part II of the volume, but in a very different constellation. This scandal involved an automated fraud detection system for welfare benefits that was poorly designed, insensitive to contextual information, lacked consultation and appeal opportunities, tended to generate false positives and, in sum, caused untold misery for those suspected of fraud or over-receipt of benefits. There are obvious systemic lessons to be drawn from these events, especially in relation to the use by welfare or tax authorities of automated data, artificial intelligence or other forms of algorithmic systems. However, Hodgson does not stop at systemic observations but reintroduces a human angle that has echoes of Badisco's and van de Velde's discussion of virtue ethics. The observance of the rule of law in relation to the Robodebt claimants would have required not only a better system, but a commitment to professionalism, competence, good faith and good communication. The rule of law, in Hodgson's presentation, is therefore not simply about respect for the legal rights of taxpayers, but about good administration of welfare and tax systems alike.

In Brassey's chapter, the concern shifts from welfare claimants to the interests of those who finance government borrowing. This change of context produces some rather interesting results. When we consider the effects of rule of law breaches for welfare claimants or even individual taxpayers, our immediate focus is likely to be on the human distress caused to those individuals. However, when we turn our attention to rule of law breaches towards public lenders, our attention is likely to be directed less towards human distress than to the potentially negative consequences for a state if the lenders react with reduced willingness to provide finance. This is precisely where Brassey's analysis goes, and he draws on British and English history as well as comparative examples to demonstrate the importance of faithfulness to rule of law values for a state's credibility in the financial markets. In turn, a state's commitment to the rule of law can be supported, and advertised to potential lenders, with binding fiscal rules. These are not new to UK politics, with Gordon Brown's fiscal rules being particularly well-known, but the market reaction to the Truss-Kwarteng Budget illustrates the need for a more marked shift towards a rule-based approach to borrowing and spending in the UK.

Part III: The Rule of Law in EU and International Context

The contributions in Part II show that the nature and significance of the rule of law may depend heavily on context, whether that context consists of a preferred theoretical framework or the precise field of enquiry. The chapters in this final Part III of the volume consider the importance of context in jurisdictional perspective, and consider whether and to what extent our ideas of the rule of law must be modified in the light of EU law and international agreements.

A very clear sense that rule of law concepts applied to domestic law may not translate easily to an international setting is provided by van Ganzen, Broekhuijsen, Vording and Vleggeert. The authors conceptualise the rule of law as the expression of a narrower or wider range of legal values clustering around the idea of 'law as guidance', which carry weight in political, legislative and administrative processes though they may ultimately be outweighed by other considerations. Even where only one state is involved, it is difficult to make generalisations about how much priority governing institutions should give to rule of law values relative to other imperatives. It is trickier still in the context of cross border taxation that engages rules promulgated by multiple states and international organisations, to the extent that supposed rule of law arguments about clarity, stability, prospectivity and even human rights or democratic processes can be difficult to distinguish from any other expression of 'power, persuasion and politics'.[14] The recent criticisms of international tax initiatives on the basis that they violate certain rule of law values ought therefore to be taken with a degree of caution.

If there are conceptual problems with applying rule of law arguments in an international context, Littlewood shows that there are corresponding complexities in applying international standards in a domestic tax system subject to the rule of law. This is brought into clear focus by the decision in New Zealand to incorporate the OECD's Pillar Two Model Global Anti-Base Erosion (GloBE) Rules and Commentary into domestic law by reference. On the one hand, this approach helps to guarantee the close compatibility of New Zealand law with international standards, especially in those cases where the reference is 'ambulatory'. That is to say, domestic legal effect is given to the most recent version of the international standard from time to time, not merely the version in force at the date on which the reference was made. On the other hand, legislation by reference can tend to bypass the ordinary democratic procedures of a state, especially when the references are ambulatory so that the content of the law can change significantly without further input from the domestic legislature. In rule of law terms, the consequence may also be to dilute the state's usual ability to guarantee clarity, stability, non-retrospectivity and so forth. Littlewood considers the advantages and disadvantages of the New Zealand experiment and concludes that the former are likely to outweigh the latter.

The idea that pursuing rule of law values might be a different exercise internationally and domestically is extended to the EU in the two subsequent chapters. In Geringer's chapter, the focus is the procedural one of whether, and to what extent, the Court of Justice of the EU (CJEU) is institutionally suited to promoting the rule of law in the VAT field. The discussion has something of an integrationist flavour, for the simple reason that it may be insufficient for a cross-border taxpayer for individual jurisdictions to respect the rule of law, if the EU-wide experience is of a system that is unclear, unstable and poorly understood. Geringer accepts the CJEU's pivotal role in protecting the rule of law in this extended sense but points to various factors that limit its effectiveness. In particular, the court's capacity for additional workload is constrained, despite reforms that transfer some cases to the General Court. At the same time, the CJEU is not the only means of protecting the rule of law across borders. There is an entire arsenal of other mechanisms, including infringement procedures and state aid assessments at Union level, which can be very effective even in difficult cases involving systemic misconduct in Member States' application of VAT law. Equally, there are problems stemming from the poor coordination of Member State authorities and courts that cannot be dealt with by the judiciary and require action by the EU legislature. It would be a mistake in these cases for the CJEU to seek to act as a substitute.

The potential for EU institutions to provide meaningful protection to the rule of law in a cross-border setting is highlighted in a very different way in the following chapter.

[14] See van Ganzen et al, Chapter 13 in this volume.

Whereas Geringer's main focus is on procedural matters such as institutional capacity, Pantazatou asks the substantive question of whether the rule of law might help to justify the application of the 'single tax principle' in an EU context. This principle, drawn by the author from the work of Avi-Yonah, states that 'income from cross-border transactions should be subject to tax once',[15] which is to say that both double taxation and double non-taxation ought to be avoided. This principle, at the very least, coheres with the ambition that taxpayers ought to be able to carry out their affairs under a system of tax rules that is reasonably coherent, possible to navigate and that is applied equally to them as to other taxpayers. Is it possible to go further and to argue that the single tax principle is required by the rule of law? Pantazatou ultimately concludes that it is not. The difficulty in applying the principle across the EU is at least partially attributable to the fact that tax law is not fully harmonised; in turn, it is too much of a stretch to argue that the rule of law requires harmonisation even if it assists with single taxation.

The discussion by Geringer and Pantazatou of the CJEU's limitations and the single tax principle respectively indicate that the concerns of van Ganzen *et al* about the conceptual force of the rule of law in cross-border scenarios may persist even in an EU context. A much more extreme example is provided by Lideikyte-Huber in her discussion of the online pornography industry which, like other digital industries, is commonly structured in such a way that very little tax is paid in any jurisdiction. As the author shows, it is very difficult to know exactly how the rule of law is supposed to intersect with the tax position of these businesses, either from the perspective of the taxpayer or in terms of the establishment and proper administration of a tax system that is consistent with the rule of law. Some of the problems presented by the industry are common to digital businesses more generally; others are more peculiar to online porn and have tended to be sidelined in discussions despite the size and importance of the industry, whether on account of delicacy or the tendency of tax writing to focus on the most recognisable online businesses such as Google.

The volume concludes with a polemical chapter by Sadiq and Krever on another area of cross-border taxation in which there are deep challenges in asserting rule of law values, this time not a sector of business but the practice of using artificial transfer prices for transactions between different arms of integrated multinational enterprises to allocate the enterprise's profits to its constituent parts. As this practice presents opportunities to shift profits from high-tax to low-tax jurisdictions, tax systems commonly include mechanisms allowing authorities to challenge the supposed 'arms'-length' transfer prices nominated by taxpayers and to substitute alternative prices that the authorities claim would have been charged for transactions between two independent businesses. The authors argue that a system allowing taxpayers and administrators to build their cases on artificial hypotheticals, which bear no relation to what would, in fact, take place between independent taxpayers, is not only inconsistent with but inherently incompatible with rule of law principles. The authors suggest that rule of law principles will only be realised when the present profit allocation system, drawn from fictional hypotheticals with no real-world counterparts, is replaced by an objective formula that allocates

[15] RS Avi- Yonah, 'International Taxation of Electronic Commerce' (1997) 52 *Tax Law Review* 507, 517, cited in Pantazatou, Chapter 16 in this volume.

the profits of multinational enterprises to their constituent parts by reference to the factors that determine the genuine source of their profits.

The Contribution of this Volume

There are extensive constitutional law, administrative law and human rights literatures dealing with the rule of law. In the tax field, frequent recourse is made to the rule of law, but this is often done in an intuitive, rhetorical way in support of prior political beliefs, with inadequate or at most selective citation of relevant public law literature. In contrast, the literature looking in a more systematic way at the meaning and significance of the rule of law in a tax context is surprisingly and disappointingly sparse. The position is even less positive in other public finance fields such as social welfare, though there are occasional acknowledgements that the rule of law might be relevant, especially following scandals that involve conspicuous unfairness towards welfare claimants on modest means. Against this background, there are clear benefits to a more informed and rigorous approach to the rule of law in taxation and other public finance fields. It would encourage writers to clarify what they mean by the rule of law and allow their claims to be subjected to critical examination. This should, in turn, facilitate a more meaningful set of conversations about the rule of law, with the capacity, not only to convey anger at apparent shortcomings in existing arrangements, but to provide robust and relatively specific guidance on how the rule of law could be protected more effectively. The central aim of the present volume, then, is to provide a point of reference for different ways of imagining the rule of law and of how these visions might possibly relate to each other.

Although the literature is unexpectedly thin given the wide currency of rule of law arguments, there are, predictably, some honourable exceptions. A relatively systematic collection with which some of the contributors to the present volume were involved was *The Delicate Balance: Tax, Discretion and the Rule of Law*.[16] This book focused on the discretionary powers of tax authorities and many of the chapters engage closely with the statutory and constitutional basis of these powers in the respective jurisdictions of the authors. The book is methodologically diverse, with the coverage in each chapter tending to reflect the preoccupations of its own jurisdiction at the time, whether this be the separation of powers in Canada, the position of Treasury Regulations in the US or systems of binding rulings in Australia, the Netherlands and elsewhere. Nevertheless, there is some sophisticated coverage of the rule of law both within the jurisdictional chapters and the thematic overview chapter by Dourado. The theme of discretionary powers threatening the rule of law is also picked up by several contributions to the present volume, including those by Sawyer and by Krever and Sadiq. An older volume prepared along similar lines is *Tax Avoidance and the Rule of Law*,[17] in which a close focus on judicial and statutory anti-avoidance techniques is elevated by the editors into a broader discussion of what the rule of law might require in this context.

[16] C Evans, J Freedman and R Krever (eds) *The Delicate Balance: Tax, Discretion and the Rule of Law* (Amsterdam, IBFD, 2011).

[17] GS Cooper (ed), *Tax Avoidance and the Rule of Law* (Amsterdam, IBFD, 1997).

Several conferences of the European Association of Tax Law Professors have dealt with themes that are contiguous to the rule of law. The volumes that emerge from these conferences contain country-specific reports that are of varying quality and methodology, partly tied together by thematic reports that suggest overarching narratives based on the insights drawn from each jurisdiction. This approach means that the EATLP volumes tend to be quite loosely organised, with nothing like the degree of editorial involvement or coordination that is possible in a conventional edited volume. Nevertheless, they provide an extremely useful collection of information on topics on which it can be quite difficult to find more developed literature. A closely relevant example is *Retro-Activity of Tax Legislation*,[18] in which the skill of the editors allows them to transcend the sometimes rather formulaic EATLP approach and to engage deeper questions, not only relating to non-retroactivity but also legal certainty, procedural fairness and government by press release. A similarly high level of editorial skill is brought to *Separation of Powers in Tax Law*,[19] in which the discussion ranges more widely than the immediate brief to cover matters such as indeterminacy and vagueness which are of clear relevance to the rule of law.

In addition to these loosely comparative volumes, there are several more idiosyncratic literatures on tax and the rule of law that reflect the particularities of their respective authors and jurisdictions. A good example is *Politics, Taxation, and the Rule of Law: The Power to Tax in Constitutional Perspective*.[20] This is a self-conscious expression of US fiscal conservatism that draws heavily on the work of James Buchanan, John Locke and on a certain mindset about what is required by the US Constitution. It starts with a forceful statement that the function of government is to preserve pre-existing rights over 'persona and property' and conversely that government cannot be properly regarded as the origin of these rights. The rule of law, and indeed the rest of the book, consists of a working through of this starting point in relation to a range of issues such as taxpayer rights, referenda, interest group influence, complexity, single taxation of site values and tax neutrality. The volume is interesting but will not be accepted by those who dispute its starting point.

There is also a cluster of books on the rule of law in Chinese taxation. The editors lack the language skills to assess much of this literature, but a recent example that has been translated into English is *Improving the Tax System Amid the Rule-of-Law China*.[21] A pessimistic attitude towards some of the writing this in style is taken by Wei Cui, who criticises the adoption of 'stylized discourse' around the rule of law as limited in relevance in a context where officials adhere to certain formal elements of legal rationality but often achieve results by bypassing legal mechanisms altogether. It would be better, he argues, to focus on ways in which 'the Chinese bureaucracy can incorporate elements of meritocracy and even autonomy'[22] that are sensitive to the reality of governance in

[18] H Gribnau and M Pauwels (eds) *Retro-Activity of Tax Legislation* (Amsterdam, EATLP, 2013).

[19] AP Dourado (ed), *Separation of Powers in Tax Law* (Amsterdam, EATLP, 2010).

[20] DP Racheter and RE Wagner (eds), *Politics, Taxation, and the Rule of Law: The Power to Tax in Constitutional Perspective* (Dordrecht, Springer, 2002).

[21] Q Wang and W Xi, *Improving the Tax System amid the Rule-of-Law China* (Singapore, Springer, 2022).

[22] W Cui, *The Administrative Foundations of the Chinese Fiscal State* (Cambridge, Cambridge University Press, 2022) 25.

China. In a very different context, a similar concern with the social and political underpinnings of the rule of law is exhibited by Marcelo Bergman in *Tax Evasion and the Rule of Law in Latin America*,[23] in which he unpicks why tax compliance is much more robust in Chile despite formal similarities with Argentine institutions. A similar insight is demonstrated by Hart Publishing's series on *The Rule of Law in Context* of which Paul Gowder's recent monograph, *The Rule of Law in the United States: An Unfinished Project of Black Liberation*,[24] is drawn upon heavily by at least one contributor to the present volume.

In spite of the depth and quality of some of the work represented in all of these volumes, there is an urgent need for a more sustained exploration of what the rule of law might involve in a tax context (whether nationally, internationally or supranationally); what level of weight can be placed on it in the course of understanding desirable and undesirable features of a tax system; the extent to which our answers might depend on underlying political and social phenomena; and the relevance of the discussion to other fields of public finance such as social welfare, public spending and public borrowing. The present volume will not provide the final word on these questions, but our hope is that the contributions of our outstanding colleagues will inspire an elevation of the debate on the rule of law, taxation and public finance, as well as providing future scholars and policymakers with a wealth of ideas on how the concept might be used effectively.

Acknowledgements

As with any of these projects, the present volume is the product of the untold effort and generosity of colleagues. We are particularly grateful to the contributors to the volume for their work, insight and patience with what has perhaps been an unusually intrusive editorial process; to Dr Geringer for her detailed comments on an earlier version of this chapter; to colleagues at Hart Publishing for their unwavering support and guidance; and to the administrative and catering staff at the Faculty of Law and Clare College in Cambridge for their support of the conference at which the work contained within the volume was presented and discussed. We hope that we have done justice to all of your efforts.

[23] M Bergman in *Tax Evasion and the Rule of Law in Latin America: The Political Culture of Cheating and Compliance in Argentina and Chile* (University Park, PA, Penn State University Press, 2009).

[24] P Gowder, *The Rule of Law in the United States: An Unfinished Project of Black Liberation* (Oxford, Hart, 2021).

PART I

Fundamental Concepts

2

The Rule of Law, Accountability and Tax Administration

STEPHEN DALY

'At the heart of the concept of the rule of law is the idea that society is governed by law ... Courts exist in order to ensure that the laws ... are applied and enforced. That role includes ensuring that the executive branch of government carries out its functions in accordance with the law. In order for the courts to perform that role, people must in principle have unimpeded access to them. Without such access, laws are liable to become a dead letter.'[1]

Abstract

This chapter investigates how HMRC is held to account through law. It argues that UK administrative tax law takes seriously the importance of accountability through law in respect of first instance appeals. This is to be contrasted with judicial review where there are significant barriers which operate generally, and specifically in the case of the exercise of HMRC's collection and management powers. Further, HMRC's collection notice powers are found to be coercive settlement powers which deliberately oust the role of the tribunals and courts. These findings are understood in light of the distinction between thin and thick rule of law accounts and Marmor's account of the rule of law. Marmor distinguishes between practical barriers which can be considered compatible with the rule of law – such as court fees, the narrowing scope of appeal and the *solve et repete* principle – and those instances where policy considerations trump access to the tribunals and courts. The latter serves as a reminder that while accountability through law is an important demand of the rule of law, it is only one ideal which it might be necessary to undermine to realise other ideals or important goals. Thick and thin accounts of the rule of law will differ as to the acceptability of such trade-offs.

[1] *R (UNISON) v Lord Chancellor* [2017] UKSC 51, [68].

Introduction

The structuring and content of a given legal system will express the rule of law in that system – we can learn how the rule of law informs the legal system, and conversely how our understanding of the rule of law should be informed by it. Tax, meanwhile, constitutes the State[2] and is the one area of public administration which is essentially unavoidable.[3] Thus, administrative tax law, those legislative rules (as informed by general public law principles) that are peculiar to the execution of the functions assigned to a given tax authority, is a good corpus of laws which can be used to evidence these insights.

There is insufficient space here to fully answer the question as to how the rule of law is reflected in, and expressed by, UK administrative tax law. But there is space to look at one particular demand of the rule of law and to make findings which are qualified insofar as they are only partial answers to that broader question. To that end, this chapter investigates how HMRC is held to account through law. It argues that UK administrative tax law takes seriously the importance of accountability through law in respect of first instance appeals. This is to be contrasted with judicial review where there are significant barriers which operate generally, and specifically in the case of the exercise of HMRC's collection and management powers. Further, HMRC's collection notice powers are found to be coercive settlement powers which deliberately oust the role of the tribunals and courts. These findings are understood in light of Marmor's account of the rule of law[4] (which is mapped on to the distinction between thin and thick rule of law accounts). For Marmor, not all deviations from the ideal should be regarded as deficiencies – court fees, the narrowing scope of appeal and the *solve et repete* principle can be characterised as compatible with the rule of law. Where there are deficiencies, such as where policy considerations trump access to the tribunals and courts, these serve as a reminder that while accountability through law is an important demand of the rule of law, it is only one ideal which it might be necessary to undermine to realise other ideals or important goals. Thick and thin accounts of the rule of law will differ as to the acceptability of such trade-offs.

The chapter is broken down into five parts. Part I explains the rule of law's demand for accountability through law. This analysis is infused with the thin/thick distinction and Marmor's account. Part II fully articulates the meaning of accountability through law in a tax administration context. Parts III, IV and V consider the intensity of the mechanisms holding HMRC accountable through law for their conduct.

The Rule of Law

The rule of law is an ideal of political morality which has the effect of elevating the importance of law and legal infrastructure in any system of governance.[5] Although

[2] D de Cogan, *Tax Law, State-Building and the Constitution* (Oxford: Hart, 2020).
[3] A Mehrotra, 'Reviving Fiscal Citizenship' (2015) 113 *Michigan Law Review* 943, 949, fn 24.
[4] A Marmor, 'The Rule of Law and Its Limits' (2004) 23(1) *Law and Philosophy* 1.
[5] J Waldron, 'The Rule of Law' in Edward N Zalta (ed), *The Stanford Encyclopedia of Philosophy* (Summer 2020 Edition). Available at: https://plato.stanford.edu/archives/sum2020/entries/rule-of-law/.

writers agree as to its importance however, the rule of law remains an elusive concept, the full contents of which are devoid of universal agreement. The best that we can say is that people tend to adopt either thinner or thicker versions of it.

A 'thin' account of the rule of law will hold that laws ought to act as guidance[6] – the 'guidance principle'. A person should, before committing themselves to any course of action, be able to know the legal consequences that will follow.[7] Raz, for instance, describes this as the 'basic idea' of the rule of law.[8] What advocates of thicker accounts argue is that the rule of law makes further, more substantive demands, such as respect for fundamental human rights[9] and private property.[10] It is not that proponents of thinner accounts dispute the importance of what proponents of thicker accounts regard as intrinsic to the rule of law, such as the protection of human rights. It is rather that they regard them as separate ideals. Thicker versions thus consider not just the inner (procedural and formal) morality of laws, but also what laws *should* regulate. Laws to that end should limit the arbitrary exercise of power.[11]

The Demands of the Rule of Law

Any account of the rule of law will feature two essential components – that official action is authorised by law and that laws should have certain qualities in order to perform their functions. From the two components, various demands can be deduced, but the focus for present purposes is on 'accountability through law' – something which is, in fact, demanded by both components. Where the accounts will differ is in respect of the degree to which law should constrain the exercise of power and what functions law should perform.

The first essential component, known as the principle of legality, is described by Waldron as the most important demand of the rule of law.[12] It is used to refer to the dictate for 'official action in a democratic state to be positively authorized by law'.[13] The principle of legality not only demands that government action should be constrained by law, but also that there should be accountability through law where there are potential infractions by officials.[14] For this to be realised, there must be infrastructure in place. For instance, there must be a court system which is competent to issue remedies for infractions[15] and individuals must be able to access this court system.[16]

[6] J Tasioulas, 'The Rule of Law' in J Tasioulas (ed), *The Cambridge Companion to the Philosophy of Law* (Cambridge: Cambridge University Press, 2020) 121.

[7] *Black-Clawson International Ltd v Papierwerke Waldhof-Aschaffenberg AG* [1975] AC 591 (HL), 638 (Lord Diplock).

[8] J Raz, 'The Rule of Law and its Virtue' (1977) 93 *Law Quarterly Review* 195, 196.

[9] R Dworkin, *A Matter of Principle* (Cambridge, MA: Harvard University Press, 1985) 11–12.

[10] John Locke, *Two Treatises of Government* (1689), para 138.

[11] TRS Allan, *Law, Liberty, and Justice: The Legal Foundations of British Constitutionalism* (Oxford: Oxford University Press, 1994) 23.

[12] Waldron, 'The Rule of Law', above n 5. Although Waldron does not label it the 'principle of legality'.

[13] C Gearty, *Principles of Human Rights Adjudication*, (Oxford: Oxford University Press, 2004) 60.

[14] Waldron, above n 5.

[15] Raz, 'The Rule of Law and its Virtue' above n 8, 218.

[16] ibid 217.

The second essential component similarly makes demands as to the content of the legal rules and the machinery for enforcing the law. Thus, even in a minimalist, thin account of the rule of law, the guidance principle makes formal and procedural demands. As for formal demands, legal rules should adhere to standards of (reasonable)[17] clarity and accessibility.[18] From this, procedural demands follow, such as an accessible court system and an independent and competent judiciary so that laws are clarified, rights are upheld, and disputes settled.[19] Litigants 'can be guided by law only if the judges apply the law correctly'[20] and enforcement is not distorted. The guidance principle and the principle of legality both require accountability through law.

Any thick account of the rule of law builds on a basic account by regarding laws as performing a function or functions beyond simply guiding action. Thick accounts ultimately impose greater constraints on the intrusive demands of government power.[21] With respect to accountability through law, more stringent standards would be imposed on the exercise of government power than in a thin account, and there would be greater ease of access to authoritative legal adjudication.

Other authors in this book have adopted a different approach to the rule of law. For instance, Brassey understands the rule of law as part of a broader phenomenon of rules-based governance – if the rule of law stands for the proposition that it is good for government action to be constrained by law, then it follows that it is also good for government action to be constrained by rules per se.[22] This does not map easily on to the thin/thick distinction by virtue of the fact that law is not central to it – law might be a means of constraining governments, but there are others, and the analysis does not regard the differences between these as of the essence.[23] Lindsay meanwhile invokes a distinction between narrow-scope rule of law, which aligns with a thinner conception of the rule of law, and wide-scope rule of law, that governments should govern through law.[24] The latter, whilst using different terminology, maps on to thicker accounts of the rule of law dictating that governments predominantly govern through laws.[25] Lindsay's wide-scope rule of law manifests a thick principle of legality.

[17] Rules cannot provide absolute certainty: T Endicott, *Vagueness in Law* (Oxford: Oxford University Press, 2000) ch 9.

[18] See *The Sunday Times v UK* (1980) 2 EHRR 245.

[19] Waldron, above n 5.

[20] Raz, above n 8, 217.

[21] Of course, the thin account also constrains the power of government, thicker accounts are *more* constraining.

[22] A Brassey, 'The Kindness of Strangers; The bond and FX markets, the rule of law and fiscal credibility' in D de Cogan, A Brassey and M Hen-Smith (eds), *Tax, Public Finance and the Rule of Law* (Oxford: Hart, 2024).

[23] For Raz, it is good to be ruled by law because law promotes the interests of the governed – but it is not clear that rules generally which constrain governments reflect the interests of the governed. J Raz, 'The Law's Own Virtue' (2019) 39 *Oxford Journal of Legal Studies* 1, analysed in I Lindsay, 'The Law of Tax Avoidance and Two Aspects of the Rule of Law' in de Cogan, Brassey and Hen-Smith (eds), above n 22.

[24] Lindsay, 'The Law of Tax Avoidance and Two Aspects of the Rule of Law' above n 23.

[25] This would find its home with some continental understandings of the rule of law. See Gribnau's explanation of the *Rechsstaat* in H Gribnau, 'On the Rule of Law and Democracy: Policy Rules and Principles in Dutch Taxation' [2024] 2 *British Tax Review* 211.

Rough Standard Limitations and Material Deviations

How easy access to, and the standards imposed by, legal adjudication should be will thus be answered differently by the different versions of the rule of law. But in either case it is important to recognise that there are limits to realising the ideal of the rule of law. Some are inherent in the sense that the demands are not definitively articulated and so can be satisfied by a range of different but reasonable choices. These are what could be called 'rough standard limitations'. Other limits are a matter of principle in that it is sufficiently clear what choices *would not* meet the demands of the rule of law and where these choices are made then the rule of law *is* undermined. These are what we might call 'material deviations'.

This distinction draws on Marmor's work. He tells us that 'some values or ideals', such as the rule of law, do not call 'for anything like full or perfect implementation' because such values 'set only a rough standard whereby gross deviations from it would be wrong'.[26] Fuller's influential account of the rule of law for instance regards stability in the law as being central to the guidance principle.[27] But this is quintessentially 'a rough standard'. The most we can say being that material deviations from it[28] – when the law is changed too frequently or cannot be changed – 'constitute a deficiency'.[29] The *right* level of stability is left open, however. Accountability through law too is a rough standard.

Material deviations, whereby access to an adjudicator is overly inhibited, will count as undermining the rule of law, as held in *Unison*,[30] on account of the impact that fees had on the economics of bringing a bringing employment law dispute. Prior to the *Unison* decision, it would cost £1,200 to bring an unfair dismissal claim or £390 for a claim for unlawful deduction from wages for instance.[31] Given that many employment disputes concern modest sums,[32] those whose employment rights have been potentially breached are practically compelled to apply to the employment tribunal for redress.[33] The fact that many people did (or hypothetically would) regard the fees as unaffordable,[34] meant that there was a 'real risk' that people would 'effectively be prevented from having access to justice'.[35] But that does not mean that practical and necessary limitations driven by resource constraints *cannot* be entertained. As per Lord Reed in *Unison*, '[f]ees paid by litigants can, in principle, reasonably be considered to be a justifiable way of making resources available for the justice system and so securing access to justice'.[36] Properly calibrated so as not to effectively prevent access to the court system, fees are a rough standard limitation.

[26] Marmor, above n 4, 9.
[27] Lon Fuller, *The Morality of Law*, revised edn (New Haven CT: Yale University Press, 1969) 44–45.
[28] 'Material' is used in place of 'gross' here as the latter term can imply a sort of nastiness, whereas Marmor's point was simply that there are certain obvious deviations.
[29] Marmor, above n 4, 34.
[30] *Unison*, above n 1.
[31] ibid at [17] and [96].
[32] ibid at [20].
[33] ibid at [92].
[34] ibid at [91].
[35] ibid at [87] and [98].
[36] ibid at [86].

Though material deviations undermine the rule of law, it does not follow that they cannot be justified. A rule of law 'deficiency' may be necessary so that other important ideals can be partially realised. A deliberate lack of clarity in the law, for instance, undermines the guidance principle, but may be the function of compromises necessary in a pluralist, democratic society.[37] Thicker accounts focused on constraining the power of the government will be less willing than thinner accounts to accommodate other values or ideals, with concern for the rule of law operating as a sort of trump card.

Accountability Through Law

Before it is possible to interrogate how accountability through law is realised and from which evidence can be generated as to how the rule of law is reflected in, and expressed by, UK administrative tax law, it is first necessary to articulate what exactly 'accountability through law' entails in a tax administration context.

Turning first to 'accountability'. The term is often used as a 'buzzword'[38] or as a 'protean concept … [encapsulating] multiple contemporary anxieties'.[39] There appears nevertheless to be consensus that there are five critical questions around which any model of accountability should revolve:

(1) Who/to whom?
(2) About what?
(3) Through what process(es)?
(4) By what standards?
(5) With what effect?[40]

In the tax law context, these would be answered as follows:

(1) the account of performance is due from the tax authority (HMRC) to the public in general and to an affected taxpayer in particular,
(2) about the execution of the tax authority's legal tasks and exercise of its legal powers,
(3) through determinations (where needed) by independent adjudicators,
(4) by standards appropriate to the adjudicating forum, and
(5) with the legal authority to determine legal disputes between HMRC and taxpayers.

To be clear, it is not only judges at the tribunal and court level that perform an adjudication function. There are other actors who can make determinations on legal issues concerning the exercise of HMRC powers, such as the Parliamentary Ombudsman.[41] It is left open here whether this amounts to 'accountability through law', or whether

[37] Marmor, above n 4, 27.
[38] R Mulgan, *Holding Power to Account: Accountability in Modern Democracies* (Basingstoke: Palgrave MacMillan, 2003) 1.
[39] J Mashaw, 'Accountability and Institutional Design: Some Thoughts on the Grammar of Governance' in M Dowdle (ed), *Public Accountability: Designs, Dilemmas and Experiences* (Cambridge: Cambridge University Press, 2006) 115.
[40] ibid, 118.
[41] See further S Daly, 'Oversight of HMRC Soft Law: Lessons from the Ombudsman' (2016) 38(3) *Journal of Social Welfare and Family Law* 363.

it is simply 'accountability'. There is only space here to consider the role played by the tribunals and courts.

As for when taxpayers *could* be entitled to ask for a tribunal or court to make legal determinations on the exercise of HMRC's powers, there are five 'calling points' on the taxpayer's journey through the tax system (though not all taxpayers, to further abuse the metaphor, will end up calling at each station). These are:

(1) the exercise of HMRC's collection and management powers;
(2) the mandatory provision of information germane to the determination of a taxpayer's liability or entitlement (information powers);
(3) the verification of the liability or entitlement (assessment powers);
(4) the collection or return of monies due (collection and refund powers); and
(5) the resolution of legal disputes about the quantum of the monies due.

Accountability Through Appeals

Taxpayers have rights of appeal at all these calling points, just not in respect of *every* potential infraction. Registering as a taxpayer activates HMRC's collection and management powers, but taxpayers can appeal against their registration as a taxpayer for VAT purposes.[42] Taxpayers can appeal information notices.[43] They can challenge HMRC's assessment powers – whether that is questioning the validity of an enquiry for instance[44] or asking a tribunal to force HMRC to close an enquiry.[45] Where HMRC seeks to collect taxes due, a taxpayer can apply for a postponement notice to delay collection until there has been a tribunal determination.[46] A taxpayer can challenge a penalty issued (or its quantum).[47] Importantly, a taxpayer can appeal virtually any assessment that HMRC makes in respect of the quantum of taxes due.[48] These appeal rights are an important means of holding HMRC accountable for the exercise of its coercive powers.

The Impediments

There are four barriers, however, that impact access to the tribunals and courts. First, whilst there may be no fees for an appeal to the First-tier Tribunal (FtT) and thereafter to the Upper Tribunal (UT), that is not the case with subsequent appeals to the Court of Appeal (CA) and Supreme Court (SC). For instance, where permission to appeal has been refused by the UT, the fee for applying to the CA is £569.[49] A fee for applying to

[42] VATA 1994, s 83(1)(a).
[43] FA 2008, Sch 36, para 29.
[44] *Tinkler v HMRC* [2021] UKSC 39.
[45] TMA 1970, s 28A(4), s 28B(5), FA 1998, Sch 18, para 33(1).
[46] TMA 1970, s 55(3)(b).
[47] ibid, s 100B.
[48] For instance, TMA 1970, s 31; FA 1998, Sch 18, para 30(3), VATA 1994, s 83.
[49] HM Courts & Tribunals Service, *Court of Appeal (Civil) fees (Form 200)* (30 September 2021). Available at: www.gov.uk/government/publications/court-of-appeal-civil-fees-form-200.

the SC, where permission has been refused by the CA, is £1,000.[50] Proceeding with the appeal will incur a fee of £1,292 in the CA and £1,600 in the SC.

Secondly, the scope of what may be appealed becomes more and more limited as the litigation continues until a taxpayer reaches the SC. Whilst an appeal to the FtT is essentially *de novo*, meaning that both facts and law can be disputed, appeals from the FtT are generally made to the UT on points of law.[51] Appeals from the UT to the CA lie on points of law raising an 'important point of principle or practice' or there is some other 'compelling reason' meaning that an appeal should be heard.[52] Appeals from the CA to the SC lie only on points of law of 'general public importance'.[53]

Thirdly, '[l]egal representation [in the UK] can result in considerable cost'.[54] HMRC has the resources to afford expert legal counsel and has a team of solicitors in its department that can prepare for litigation, whereas taxpayers (aside from the wealthy and larger businesses) will be less well equipped. Unrepresented, non-legally trained taxpayers will inevitably struggle with articulating their case before a tribunal.[55] Of course, judges will do their best to understand the taxpayer's case in its best light and somewhat neutralise the inequality of legal resources, but it would be naïve to think that this is sufficient to overcome the imbalance created by one party having trained legal advocates. In short, where taxpayers need but are unable to afford legal advice and representation, they are at a distinct disadvantage in their attempts to hold HMRC accountable.[56]

A fourth barrier is the costs-shifting rule, applicable in any appeal beyond the FtT,[57] which provides that the losing party will generally be liable for costs.[58] In terms of magnitude, fees may act as a deterrent, but negative cost consequences will have a far more significant effect – 'court fees pale into insignificance when compared with the fees charged by legal representatives for litigation services',[59] the 'fear' of the 'devastating consequences' of 'having to pay the costs of the other side … must inhibit the taking of the case to court'.[60] Of course, the cost-shifting rule goes both ways. Should HMRC lose on appeal, it will be liable for costs. However, due to its large budget and the fact that it is backed by the Treasury, HMRC is not sensitive to cost in the same way as most taxpayers.

[50] The Supreme Court Fees Order 2009, Sch 2.

[51] TCEA 2007, s 11(1).

[52] CPR Rule 52.7.

[53] Supreme Court Practice Directions, para 3.3.3. Given that the SC deals with matters of significant public interest, one would think that the fees would be lower to account for the fact that the public at large should benefit from the litigation.

[54] *European Commission v United Kingdom of Great Britain and Northern Ireland* [2013] EUECJ C-530/11, Opinion of AG Kokott delivered on 12 September 2013, [1].

[55] M Blackwell *The Tax Tribunals: The Next 10 Years (Report for the Tax Law Review Committee)*, (London: Institute for Fiscal Studies, 2021), para 1.12. Available at: https://ifs.org.uk/publications/15554.

[56] This chapter does not consider the more general question as to whether the high costs of litigation in the UK offend the rule of law.

[57] The Tribunal Procedure (First-tier Tribunal) (Tax Chamber) Rules 2009 (SI 2009/273 (L 1)), r 10.

[58] For instance, CPR Rule 44.2(2); HM Courts and Tribunals Service, *Appealing to the Upper Tribunal (Tax and Chancery Chamber)* (February 2020), p. 12. Available at: www.gov.uk/government/publications/upper-tribunal-appeals-tax-and-chancery-additional-guidance-t399 (on the Upper Tribunal (Tax and Chancery Chamber)).

[59] A Zuckerman, 'The Law's Disgrace', *UK Constitutional Law Blog* (27 Feb 2017). Available at: https://ukconstitutionallaw.org/2017/02/27/adrian-zuckerman-the-laws-disgrace/.

[60] *R (Corner House Research) v Secretary of State for Trade & Industry* [2005] EWCA Civ 192 [31].

There are, it should be said, various ways in which a taxpayer can limit their exposure to costs.[61] A protective costs order, if granted, will limit the costs payable by the unsuccessful party.[62] Or a taxpayer can hope to rely on HMRC exercising its discretion not to seek to recover costs, known as the 'Rees' practice, where there would be financial hardship for the taxpayer and the point at issue is one of significant interest to taxpayers as a whole.[63] But these protections are provided as a deviation from the general 'costs-shifting' principle and ultimately relies on the discretion of the judge, or HMRC (subject to judicial review,[64] which is laden with problems that the chapter will later identify) whether any are granted.

Analysis of the Impediments

These four factors cumulatively limit a taxpayer's ability to hold HMRC to account for the exercise of its coercive powers even in those instances where legislation provides a right of appeal. They present a nuanced picture of the rule of law as it is expressed in the tax appeals system, showcasing both rough standard limitations and material deviations.

Access to the FtT, where an appeal right is granted, is relatively unimpeded. There are no tribunal fees, the dispute is determined *de novo* and the tribunal does not generally operate as a cost-shifting jurisdiction. To that end, a taxpayer can represent themselves in any bona fide dispute where there is an appeal right without fear of consequences beyond, at worst, doing what HMRC had already requested the taxpayer to do (pay moneys determined to be due or provide certain information for instance). In short, the tribunal can exercise a good degree of control over HMRC actions. The only real impediment is a function of inequality of litigation resources. As such, the taxpayer more or less gets a free 'bite of the cherry'. After the first instance appeal, there are increasing barriers which often deter further appeals.

The first two barriers thereafter, fees and scope of appeal, reflect Marmor's idea that only a rough standard of accessibility is demanded by the ideal of the rule of law. The rule of law demands resources. Provided there is ease of accessibility to independent adjudication, as there is with the FtT, placing restrictions on resource-intensive appeals which narrow, but do not unreasonably limit, access does not result in a material deviation from the rule of law. Fees are imposed because it is costly to run a judicial system, hence why a portion of the costs are assumed by the litigants. But unlike in the case of fees for employment disputes (at issue in *Unison*), which operated as a material deviation from the rough standard, fees for tax cases only kick in at the CA level.

[61] A taxpayer may have insurance also.

[62] A Zuckerman, *Zuckerman on Civil Procedure: Principles of Practice* 4th edn (London: Sweet and Maxwell, 2021) para 28.305 explains that these orders derive from common law, as distinct from cost capping orders for instance which are permitted by CPR 3.19. These limit the costs that a successful party can recover from another.

[63] *Drummond v HMRC* [2016] UKUT 221 (TCC), [13] (Judge Sinfield).

[64] *HMRC v TGH (Commercial)* Limited [2016] UKUT 519 (TCC), [18] (Judge Sinfield).

Meanwhile, it might be said that there are good policy reasons also for delimiting the scope of appeal, but the author's view is that the preservation of scarce judicial resources principally drives this barrier (though even if the author is wrong, then this would merely need to be characterised as a material deviation justifiable by reference to policy). There are several counterpoints that one could take to this view. First, it could be said that preventing matters from being relitigated *de novo* is also a function of expertise. The First-tier judges will have the skills, and have had the opportunity, to make determinations based on witness evidence and information. Secondly, the reasons which the tribunal expresses for the various determinations will be unable to provide a complete account of the impressions which led to the determinations, so it would be improper for a later tribunal to overturn the determinations if it disagrees with the first instance tribunal's decision-making, when such original reasons would present only a partial picture.[65] Thirdly, it might be said that delimiting the role of appellate judges, and ultimately stopping cases at the SC level, is an expression of the principle of finality. There is value in the conclusion of litigation. Judges and the litigating parties can move on with their lives. Meanwhile, the rule of law requires authoritative resolutions of disputes[66] – *res judicata* – as there needs to be an independent body which is entrusted with the power to objectively determine legal issues.

These points are all well taken, but they only come into play *because* resources are limited. Expertise must be rationed. Would it be feasible to have higher orders of judges continuing to determine cases *de novo*? No, that would be impossible to operationalise for all disputes as it would require resources that are simply not available (there are only so many hours in the day and so many people that can act as judges). Choices based on scarce resources must be made and the decision in the case of disputes has been to manage those scarce resources through narrowing the scope of appeal.

With regard to the third barrier, costs, the lack of legal aid in tax cases can be understood as the sort of principled trade-off that Marmor envisages with the ideal of the rule of law – a justifiable material deviation. It is reasonable to argue that those of limited means who are unrepresented are denuded of the ability to access the tribunals. To that end, Tasioulas, for instance, has highlighted that even in respect of the thin account of the rule of law,[67] legal aid should be made available to those who need, but cannot afford to pay for, legal advice. In the UK, however, legal aid is not available for ordinary tax appeals[68] so those less-well-off taxpayers that *need* assistance must rely on the overstretched services of a few tax charities, such as the Low Incomes Tax Reform Group, and tax clinics or solicitors and barristers who are willing to take on a case *pro bono* or on a conditional fee agreement. The failure to guarantee legal representation in tax cases for those who need, but are unable to afford, representation is a deliberate policy choice, with government instead favouring other policies, which, it is argued, is a material deviation from the demands the rule of law makes in respect of accountability.

[65] *Piglowska v Piglowski* [1999] 3 All ER 632, 643 (Lord Hoffmann).
[66] Raz, above n 8, 217.
[67] Tasioulas, above n 6, 122.
[68] Legal Aid Agency, *Work Out Who Qualifies for Criminal Legal Aid* (20 January 2020). Available at: www.gov.uk/guidance/work-out-who-qualifies-for-criminal-legal-aid.

The fourth barrier, the costs-shifting rule, is another example of a material deviation. It can be rationalised on the basis that it would be unfair for parties to litigation to continue to be out of pocket whilst resisting or pursuing claims where the court has found in their favour.[69] The various means by which litigants can limit their exposure to these costs meanwhile seek to mitigate some of the harshness of the general costs-shifting rule, though these orders pale into insignificance when contrasted with the mandatory rules which operate in other jurisdictions to limit exposure to costs (through capping the legal fees which can be reclaimed).[70] What we see here in both instances are deliberate policy choices. Where no mitigation of the cost is permitted, we see the policy of ensuring fairness between the parties limiting legal accountability. Access to an independent adjudicator makes way for another consideration which is given more weight.

Accountability Through Judicial Review

Judicial review is a mechanism available at all the tax journey calling points as a means of checking the propriety of HMRC's decisions, actions or inactions,[71] but there are certain critical instances where HMRC can exercise its powers in the knowledge that there is *no* right of appeal provided by statute. With no appeal right available, the tribunals and courts can only hold HMRC to account through judicial review.

This section will first analyse the impediments that taxpayers face when seeking judicial review generally before looking at the specific exercise of HMRC's collection and management powers.

The Impediments

When dealing with judicial review, the taxpayer will face similar hurdles to those encountered on appeal. First, the taxpayer will face fees, but, unlike appeals, there are fees for first instance adjudication. Proceedings must be commenced in the High Court,[72] where the cost of commencing judicial review proceedings (now £154), of requesting a reconsideration a judicial review application at a hearing (£385) and of pursuing the claim if permission is granted (now £770)[73] add up to over £1,000. Litigants may apply to the Court to have their judicial review case heard by the UT,[74] but the Court must be satisfied that transferring the case would be 'just and convenient'.[75] The extent to which some Court fees can be avoided depends upon when, in the litigation, the case is transferred to the UT. Any subsequent appeals (to the CA and SC) are subject to the same fees regime already discussed. Secondly, as with appeals, the scope of what can

[69] Zuckerman, *Zuckerman on Civil Procedure*, above n 62 at [28.46].
[70] ibid at [28.396].
[71] CPR rule 54.1.
[72] SCA 1981, s 31.
[73] See Ministry of Justice, *EX50A: May 2023* (17 May 2023) 4.
[74] SCA 1981, s 31A.
[75] ibid, s 31A(3); TCEA 2007, s 19(1).

be appealed narrows – appeals lie to the CA on an 'important point of principle or practice' or some other 'compelling reason'[76] and to the SC on points of law of 'general public importance'.[77] Thirdly, like appeals, there is no legal aid available. Fourthly, the cost-shifting rule applies, but unlike appeals, it applies also from first instance reviews.[78]

Fifthly, judicial reviews are not an opportunity to litigate a dispute *de novo*. Indeed, complying with judicial review standards is far less demanding than complying with the standards used to hold HMRC to account on appeal. These standards check whether HMRC's action was, for instance, reasonable, proportionate and procedurally fair. They do not check whether HMRC acted *correctly*, but rather whether it acted *improperly* or *unreasonably*. Consider the doctrine of legitimate expectations, which broadly seeks to ensure that public authorities are held to their representations. There are very few litigated cases in which taxpayers in the UK have successfully invoked the doctrine against HMRC,[79] which is partly due to what Lord Diplock famously labelled HMRC's 'wide managerial discretion' in the seminal case of *IRC v National Federation of Self-Employed and Small Businesses Ltd (Fleet Street Casuals)*:[80]

> [HMRC has] a wide managerial discretion as to the best means of obtaining for the national exchequer from the taxes committed to their charge, the highest net return that is practicable having regard to the staff available to them and the cost of collection.[81]

Holding HMRC to undertakings which reduce rather than increase the immediate tax take would prima facie run contrary to this wide discretion, thus it is lawful for HMRC to resile from such an undertaking where the body has realised that the representation is based on an erroneous interpretation of the law.[82] This same 'wide managerial discretion' is the reason why the tax settlement between Goldman Sachs and HMRC, the subject of litigation in *UK Uncut v HMRC*,[83] was not considered unlawful even though the settlement included the non-collection of interest which HMRC internally struggled to justify[84] (as it was probably wrong).

Finally, an impediment to challenging the lawfulness of HMRC decisions, but one only faced by third parties, is *locus standi*.[85] Section 31(3) of the Senior Courts Act 1981 provides that 'the court shall not grant leave to make such an application unless it considers that the applicant has a *sufficient interest* in the matter to which the application relates' (emphasis added). *Locus standi* rules prevent courts from being overwhelmed by litigious citizens and protect the privacy of those whose affairs might have to be disclosed if judicial review proceedings took place. However, this hurdle is not insurmountable –

[76] CPR Rule 52.7.

[77] Supreme Court Practice Directions, para 3.3.3.

[78] SCA 1981, s 51 and CPR 44.2; Judiciary for England and Wales, 'The Administrative Court Judicial Review Guide 2018' (July 2018) para 23.1.2; CPR Rule 44.2(2); TCEA 2007, s 29; The Tribunal Procedure (Upper Tribunal) Rules 2008 (SI 2008/2698 (L 15)), r 10(3)(a).

[79] This excludes the cases HMRC settled of course.

[80] [1982] AC 617.

[81] ibid, 626.

[82] *R (Hely-Hutchinson) v HMRC* [2017] EWCA Civ 1075.

[83] *UK Uncut Legal Action Ltd v HM Revenue and Customs* [2013] EWHC 1283 (Admin).

[84] ibid at [17].

[85] For instance, *R (David Edwards) v The Environment Agency, Secretary of State & Rugby Ltd* [2004] EWHC 736 (Admin).

there is a trend in tax cases that public-spirited taxpayers are allowed to bring challenges even where they have no direct interest in a case.[86] The most generous relaxation of the rules occurred in the case of *UK Uncut v HMRC*,[87] where a challenge brought by a protest group to the lawfulness of a Goldman Sachs/HMRC settlement was allowed to proceed to a full hearing.[88] Nicol J explained that other taxpayers may have 'sufficient interest' to challenge HMRC's decision 'because an over-generous approach to one taxpayer may correspondingly increase the burden on all other taxpayers'.[89] However, the case may well represent a high watermark and standing may be limited in the future to instances where public-spirited taxpayers and advocacy groups bring cases 'in their fields of interest'.[90]

Analysis of the Impediments

Unlike appeal then, there is no free 'bite of the cherry'. These impediments limit the ability of judges to hold HMRC to account in respect of the propriety of its actions. Again, Marmor's distinction between rough standard limitations and material deviations from the rule of law is germane. The issues of fees and the scope of appeal, as already discussed, are examples of the former. Though, in respect of fees it should be said that these may drift into a material deviation if it can be shown that legitimate complaints are prevented due to the economics of pursuing litigation, as in *Unison*. Whether that is the case will depend upon whether there is litigation for modest sums, there is a practical necessity to bring a judicial review claim, and the fees would be regarded by taxpayers as unaffordable. The *locus standi* rules and their application too could be understood as a rough standard limitation – attempting to balance the need to ensure sufficient access to address improprieties whilst on the other hand managing scarce judicial resources. Even though there has been a general trend of permitting third parties to challenge HMRC by way of judicial review, it is always open to a judge to strictly apply the rules to deny standing to advocacy groups outside their express fields of interest. At the same time, the *locus standi* rules also manifest other considerations – the interest of a third party in seeing that HMRC has applied the rules correctly must be balanced against the protection of the interests of individual taxpayers, for instance in not having their affairs disclosed in an open court.

Costs and cost-shifting, as already discussed, are examples of material deviations. The standards that apply on judicial review are also an instance of material deviation, limiting the role of judges deliberately due to the importance of the separation of powers. It is not for judges to micromanage how the executive should carry out its

[86] For instance, *Fleet Street Casuals*, above n 80, and *R v Attorney General, ex parte ICI* [1987] 1 CMLR 72.

[87] *UK Uncut Legal Action Ltd*, above n 83.

[88] See D de Cogan, '*UK Uncut Legal Action v HMRC*: Legal Inaction and a Return to Fleet Street' [2013] *British Tax Review* 552, 555 fn 26.

[89] *UK Uncut Legal Action Ltd*, above n 83 [41]. It might be interesting to note that this same argument was *not* accepted in *Fleet Street Casuals*, above n 80, 632–33 (Lord Wilberforce).

[90] *R (The Good Law Project and The Runnymede Trust) v The Prime Minister and Anor* [2022] EWHC 298 (Admin), [21].

functions (as designated by the legislature). As a result, the standards limit the judiciary to a residual role.[91]

Finally, it should be noted that these impediments compound – a taxpayer is less likely to risk a costs order if the law is geared so heavily in HMRC's favour.

Impediments Specifically: Collection and Management Powers

Moving to specific examples, the exercise of HMRC's collection and management powers falls to be litigated by way of judicial review.[92] Section 5 of the Commissioners for Revenue and Customs Act (CRCA) 2005 embodies HMRC's collection and management powers, also sometimes referred to as HMRC's care and management powers (owing to the wording in the legislative provisions which gave effect to it)[93] or as the aforementioned 'managerial discretion'. The provision renders HMRC responsible for the collection and management of taxes and credits and thus enables it to enter into settlements for less tax than is fully due, to issue concessions to taxpayers[94] and to engage in compliance enhancing initiatives such as providing informal rulings and general guidance,[95] cooperative compliance programmes, nudging and maintaining hotlines. Conversely, HMRC decisions *not* to issue guidance, *not* to give a taxpayer the benefit of relying on guidance or concessions, and *not* to target certain taxpayers or allocate resources so that certain investigations can be sustained also fall within the collection and management powers.

In addition to the general impediments, holding HMRC to account for the exercise of these powers is hindered by the fact that the opportunity for the tribunal or court to intervene will not arise where there is lack of interest in pursuing litigation. This will occur in several cases. *One*, where a taxpayer has directly benefited from HMRC favouritism (they are unlikely to litigate the matter). *Two*, in general cases of favouritism which do not arouse anger amongst the public, as with some extra-statutory concessions. A concession in relation to miners' free coal and cash in lieu thereof (which should have been taxable benefit in kind)[96] went unchallenged by third parties from its inception (in at least World War II)[97] until 2003.[98] *Three*, where there is no knowledge of potential impropriety. A taxpayer will be unaware of an unpublished policy from which they might benefit or that they are being treated differently from similarly placed taxpayers,

[91] D de Cogan, 'Judicial Review in the Tax Field: Not a Spent Force' (2023) 28(2) *Judicial Review* 104.

[92] Though see S Daly, 'Public Law in the Tax Tribunals and the Case for Reform' [2018] *British Tax Review* 94.

[93] Inland Revenue Regulation Act 1890, s 13(1).

[94] *R (Wilkinson) v HMRC* [2005] UKHL 30, [21]. Other jurisdictions take different approaches to these issues. See, for instance, T Cramwinckel, 'Provision of Information by the (Dutch) Tax Authorities in the Context of the Rule of Law: A Multidisciplinary Analysis of Legitimate Expectations' in de Cogan, Brassey and Hen-Smith (eds), above n 22.

[95] *R (Davies) v HMRC; R (Gaines-Cooper) v HMRC* [2011] UKSC 47.

[96] HMRC, *EIM00530 – Employment income: benefits in kind taxable as earnings: meaning of money's worth* (24 April 2023). Available at: www.gov.uk/hmrc-internal-manuals/employment-income-manual/eim00530.

[97] Inland Revenue, *A List of Extra Statutory Wartime Concessions given in the Administration of Inland Revenue Duties* (October 1944) Cmnd 6559.

[98] Income Tax (Earnings and Pensions) Act 2003, s 306.

whilst a third party can only bring a tribunal or court's attention to alleged favouritism where it knows of the potential impropriety.

Analysis of the Collection and Management Powers' Impediments

The lack of interest is a function of material deviations driven by policy choices (regardless of whether these are conscious or not). In other words, there are initiatives or changes available to policymakers which can encourage greater use of the courts to hold HMRC to account, for instance, in respect of not challenging the non-collection of taxes due. A partial solution to that problem can be found in Finland where the Finnish Tax Recipients' Legal Services Unit is independent of the tax collection units within the Finnish Tax Administration and challenges favourable tax rulings.[99] As for general favouritism through published guidance, a partial solution can be found in Australia: rulings issued to the public at large may go through an expert 'advice and guidance' panel to ensure that there are no inaccuracies.[100] Meanwhile, the duty of confidentiality in the UK[101] operates such that details about settlements and rulings are not published, even in an anonymised form. The only way that third parties can know is if the information is leaked as with the *UK Uncut* case. This emanated out of leaks to national newspapers and evidence from an HMRC whistleblower.[102] The situation is to be contrasted with jurisdictions such as Australia which maintains a register for anonymised private rulings,[103] or Luxembourg where summaries of rulings are published in an anonymised form.[104] In jurisdictions like Norway, personal tax returns are publicly available.[105]

Collection Notice Powers

This final part considers HMRC's collection notice powers. These are worth considering in isolation from the examples studied previously because, although decisions pursuant to the exercise of these powers can (ostensibly) only be challenged by way of judicial review, their exercise *also* impacts the ability of a taxpayer to proceed with an appeal.

[99] See further S Daly, 'The OMC, Intelligent Accountability and the Monitoring of National Tax Authorities' (2022) 85(5) *Modern Law Review* 1109, 1131.

[100] S Daly, *Tax Authority Advice and the Public* (Oxford: Hart, 2020) ch 7.

[101] CRCA 2005, ss 18–20. This probably does not prevent publication of anonymised rulings and settlements.

[102] de Cogan, '*UK Uncut Legal Action*', above n 88, 554.

[103] Australian Tax Office, *Publishing of Private Rulings* (7 May 2018). Available at: www.ato.gov.au/General/ATO-advice-and-guidance/ATO-advice-products-(rulings)/Private-rulings/Publishing-of-private-rulings/.

[104] Règlement grand-ducal du 23 décembre 2014 relatif à la procédure applicable aux décisions anticipées rendues en matière d'impôts directs et instituant la Commission des décisions anticipées;.

[105] Norwegian Tax Administration, *Search the Tax Lists*. Available at: www.skatteetaten.no/en/forms/search-the-tax-lists/.

Impediments

The default rule in respect of both direct taxes and indirect taxes is captured by the Latin phrase *solve et repete* (pay now and protest later).[106] Taxpayers must pay the taxes purported by HMRC to be due before then disputing whether the amount is indeed due and, should the taxpayer be correct, obtaining a refund from HMRC. In the case of direct taxes though, the taxpayer can apply for a postponement order[107] such that the monies will not need to be paid where there is an appeal. Postponement will be granted provided there are reasonable grounds for believing that the taxpayer has been overcharged.[108] HMRC, however, can override the postponement provisions through exercising its collection notice powers, specifically by issuing an Accelerated Payment Notice (APN) (or Partner Payment Notice where the taxpayer is a partner in a partnership)[109] and/or a Follower Notice (FN).[110] Critically, no appeal right exists in relation to the decision to issue either.[111]

An FN can be given to a taxpayer where, inter alia, there is an ongoing dispute with HMRC but HMRC is of the opinion that there is a judicial ruling which is relevant to the chosen arrangements.[112] In essence, FNs are designed to tackle the phenomenon whereby tax avoidance schemes which fail in the courts are tweaked or were minimally different and entered into by other taxpayers who avoid having to pay the disputed tax until the appeal has been determined.[113] If HMRC issues an FN, the taxpayer is *required* to amend their tax return in line with HMRC's suggestions. If the taxpayer refuses to do so, they can be subject to a penalty of up to 30% of the value of the tax advantage[114] (which the FtT can increase to 50%).[115]

An APN can be issued where, inter alia, there is an ongoing dispute and an FN has been issued or the arrangements are Disclosure of Tax Avoidance Schemes (DOTAS) notifiable or a General Anti-Abuse Rule (GAAR) counteraction notice has been issued.[116] APNs are, essentially, issued in respect of what HMRC regards as tax avoidance schemes. Once an APN has been issued to the taxpayer, the money becomes payable within 90 days.[117] Failure to pay the disputed tax can result in a penalty of 5% of the amount of disputed tax when the 90-day payment period ends. If still unpaid five

[106] TMA 1970, s 55(2); VATA Act 1994, s 84(3A) and (3B).
[107] TMA 1970, s 55(3).
[108] ibid, s 55(6).
[109] The PPN rules are equivalent to the APN rules (FA 2014, Sch 32). For ease of reading, the chapter will refer only to APNs.
[110] TMA 1970, s 55(8C)–(8E).
[111] Right to make representations: FA 2014, ss 207 and 222; appeal rights for failure comply with an FN (FA 2014, ss 214) and against APN penalties (*Exclusive Promotions Ltd and Mark Fox v HMRC* [2022] UKFTT 00103 (TC)).
[112] FA 2014, s 204.
[113] HMRC, *Follower notices and accelerated payments* (7 March 2022) para 1.1. Available at: www.gov.uk/government/publications/follower-notices-and-accelerated-payments/follower-notices-and-accelerated-payments.
[114] FA 2014, ss 208 and 209.
[115] ibid, s 209(1A) and s 208A.
[116] ibid, s 219.
[117] Plus any time added on by virtue of representations.

months from the date of the first penalty, a further 5% penalty can apply and another 5% penalty can be imposed six months after that.

Both FNs and APNs de facto hinder access to the courts and tribunals. First, there is a cashflow issue as these notices are issued in respect of taxes other than VAT (and similar taxes where the taxes are remitted on a taxpayer's behalf).[118] HMRC know that taxpayers may struggle to raise the funds to pay the disputed amounts (and any further penalties) within the limited time frame. Secondly, the odds are stacked further in HMRC's favour through the operation of penalties which means that a taxpayer is pressured to amend their tax return (under threat of a 50% penalty) and then to pay the tax promptly (under threat of further penalties) in the case of an FN. Taxpayers therefore are pressured to settle rather than continue appealing through the tribunals and courts.

Analysis of the Collection Notice Powers' Impediments

Solve et repete is not necessarily an affront to access to the tribunals and courts[119] and could be classed as a rough standard limitation. Taxpayers can dispute the amount due, but they must still pay upfront. With taxes like VAT this might seem unproblematic given that the taxpayer should be capable of paying the disputed amount (as the taxpayer will have received the monies from customers). Postponement applications for direct taxes mitigate cashflow issues meanwhile.

Solve et repete, however, is a material deviation which *de facto* hinders access to the courts and tribunals, such as where an FN and/or APN are issued. The collection notice powers are essentially coercive settlement powers. A settlement offer from HMRC which does not require the taxpayer to immediately pay their taxes upfront, or face significant penalties, will obviously be attractive. That the tax rules permit such exercise of 'draconian' coercive collection powers significantly impacts a taxpayer's practical ability to access the tribunals and courts.[120]

Blackwell, in his excellent analysis of the *Haworth* case,[121] counters that 'any assessment of the seriousness of the hindrance [faced by those receiving an FN] should be seen in the context of other legislation which similarly deters litigation'.[122] Those subject to criminal charges will be granted a more lenient punishment for an early guilty plea for instance, and those subject to on-the-spot charges will have their fine reduced if they do not dispute the sanction.[123] Indeed, one can probably come up with countless other examples in the UK where public officials are granted coercive settlement powers. That these exist does not mean that the rule of law is not undermined. Their existence could instead point towards the proposition that the rule of law *is* undermined regularly

[118] FA 2014, s 210.

[119] J Kokott, P Pistone and R Miller, 'Public International Law and Tax Law: Taxpayers' Rights. The International Law Association's Project on International Tax Law – Phase 1' (2021) 52 *Georgetown Journal of International Law* 381, 401.

[120] *R (Haworth) v Revenue and Customs* [2019] EWCA Civ 747, [66] (Gross LJ).

[121] *R (Haworth) v HMRC* [2021] UKSC 25.

[122] M Blackwell, 'Unreasonably Limiting Recourse to the Courts? *R (on the application of Haworth) v HMRC*' (2022) 85(6) *Modern Law Review* 1562, 1570–71.

[123] ibid, 1571.

if they present a real risk that people are effectively prevented from having access to justice.[124] That would certainly be in line with a reading of Lord Reed's judgment in *Unison*, where he highlights that access to the courts is important so that businesses and individuals know that they can seek legal enforcement of their rights and obligations. The ability to settle disputes, it follows, is a good thing only to the extent that both sides know that there is an independent and fair adjudication option available should settlement fail: '[o]therwise, the party in the stronger bargaining position will always prevail'.[125] Coercive settlement powers (which effectively prevent accountability through law) tilt the negotiation scales further in favour of a public authority which will generally be in a stronger bargaining position.

The exercise of the collection notice powers is a material deviation, but it is capable of justification. Collection notice powers deter taxpayers from becoming involved in tax avoidance schemes, thus depressing mass-marketed avoidance schemes. It is not a quirk of the legislation that taxpayers caught by the notices are denuded of their ability to access the courts – it is a deliberate policy choice to deter and punish what government regards as undesirable.

Conclusion

This chapter examined how the rule of law is reflected in, and expressed by, UK administrative tax law, by looking at one of its demands, accountability through law. To do so, the thin/thick rule of law distinction has been situated within Marmor's rough standard/material deviation distinction. Whilst rough standard limitations are compatible with the rule of law, material deviations represent a rule of law deficiency. They are not, however, incapable of justification, as where a trade-off is necessary to accommodate other important values (like the separation of powers) or important policy goals (such as ensuring fairness between parties to litigation or deterring undesirable activity), but thick accounts would be less willing than thin accounts to accept such justifications.

When applied to UK administrative tax law, we find that both rough standard limitations and material deviations are ever-present. In the case of appeals, fees and the narrowing scope of appeal are understood as rough standard limitations, whilst the lack of legal aid and the cost-shifting rule are material deviations. As fees, the scope of appeal and the cost-shifting rule do not impede first instance appeals, strong accountability through law is provided at this level, though the lack of legal aid in tax disputes is a material deviation. Accountability through law weakens as litigation proceeds beyond the FtT. Where no appeal rights exist, taxpayers must proceed by way of judicial review wherein they face far more significant obstacles. In addition to the impediments faced on appeal, taxpayers must overcome further material deviations: the court must be convinced that the more HMRC-friendly standards imposed in judicial review have been transgressed for instance. In the case of challenging the exercise of collection and

[124] *Unison*, above n 1 [87]. See also H Hodgson, 'Asymmetrical Access to Information, Expert Systems and the Rule of Law in the Tax Transfer System' in de Cogan, Brassey and Hen-Smith (eds), above n 22.
[125] *Unison*, above n 1 [72].

management powers, the UK has adopted policies which hinder legal accountability. Finally, for HMRC to issue the collection notices is to exercise coercive settlement powers which de facto hinder access to the courts and tribunals.

What have we learnt about the rule of law? First, that resource constraints must inform the ideal of the rule of law. Resources are required for it to be realised whether that is simply to maintain a functioning legal system (in a thin account) or to maintain and enforce rules to protect human rights and private property (in a thicker account). A balance then must be struck in the case of accountability through law between granting access to independent adjudicators and securing the scarce resources necessary to provide such access. Moving to the content and contours of the rule of law in the UK we see, secondly, that only in the case of first instance appeals is there fidelity to a thicker rule of law account, though even then it accepts the lack of legal aid. Thirdly, we see that judicial review is a weak accountability mechanism which accommodates many material deviations and thus aligns only with a very thin rule of law account.

3

Tax Avoidance and Two Aspects of the Rule of Law

IRA LINDSAY

Abstract

Tax avoidance disputes present a conflict between preventing tax schemes that frustrate public policy and the rule of law. When considering the connection between taxation and the rule of law, it is helpful to distinguish between two aspects of the rule of law. The narrow-scope rule of law concerns whether disputes are decided according to legal norms that are general, prospective and impartial. The wide-scope rule of law concerns whether the government rules through law or through some extra-legal method and whether the government respects existing legal entitlements. Although closely connected, the two aspects of the rule of law are distinct: a violation of the rule of law in one sense does not necessarily have significant implications for the aspect of the rule of law. Tax disputes implicate both aspects of the rule of law. Tax adjudication violates narrow-scope rule of law when it ignores established law, appeals to legal norms that are not known in advance or renders judgments on grounds of personal partiality. Taxation violates wide-scope rule of law when used to expropriate politically unfavoured parties, confer benefits on politically favoured parties, or regularly shift tax burdens in arbitrary and unpredictable ways. This understanding of the rule of law does not yield any straightforward argument in favour of more formal methodologies of statutory interpretation or against anti-abuse rules. If the applicable legal norms are known in advance, it is not a violation of the narrow-scope rule of law to decide cases according to principles rather than rules or economic substance rather than legal form. Less formal, more purposive forms of adjudication tend to rely more on sound judgment by judges. In a legal system with a skilled and impartial judiciary, anti-abuse rules are not inherently threatening to the rule of law. They are less desirable in polities with wide-scope rule-of-law deficits. When tax disputes are highly politicised and the impartiality of the tax authorities and judiciary is open to question, it may be preferable to adopt more formal methods of adjudication that rely less on abstract reasoning about tax policy and that are easier to monitor for signs of bias. Tax law methodology should be calibrated to political context. Approaches that might be best suited for politically stable polities with highly skilled impartial judiciaries might be ill-suited for other contexts.

Introduction

Adjudication of tax disputes presents a conflict between the state's interest in preventing tax avoidance schemes that frustrate tax policy and taxpayers' interest in being able to rely on tax statutes. This implicates values of distributive justice and economic efficiency on the one hand and the rule of law on the other. The extent to which courts can curtail tax avoidance schemes using anti-abuse rules, anti-abuse doctrines and purposive interpretation without infringing upon the rule of law is a question of both theoretical importance in drawing the boundaries of the rule of law and practical importance in resolving tax disputes.

This chapter takes a new perspective on what is well-travelled territory. It does so by distinguishing between two types of rule-of-law considerations and using the relationship between them to consider the interplay between the law of tax avoidance and the rule of law. Evaluating compliance with the rule of law is complicated by the multifaceted nature of the concept and by the tendency of different authors to appeal to differing conceptions of the rule of law. This is caused not only by conceptual disagreement about the concept, but also by disagreements about broader political and moral values that underpin the proper function and aims of the legal system.[1]

To disentangle the different kind of considerations that are sometimes discussed under the heading of the rule of law, it is helpful to distinguish between two senses of the term. One sense of the rule of law, which I will call narrow-scope rule of law, concerns whether disputes are decided according to legal norms that are general, prospective and impartial. For the most part, narrow-scope rule of law is a question of whether the government follows the existing legal rules. It is especially concerned with the conduct of adjudicative bodies of government, although it has implications for other parts of government as well. The other, which I will call wide-scope rule of law, concerns whether a society is governed through law or through some other means. The wide-scope rule of law is implicated by whether political authorities respect existing legal entitlements rather than conferring benefits and burdens on an ad hoc basis. Wide-scope rule of law is a matter of whether the government rules through law or governs through some extra-legal method. Whereas narrow-scope rule of law focused mainly on legal adjudication and on the formal properties of law and law-making, the wide-scope rule of law concerned with the substantive role of law in politics and society. Analysis of the rule of law in legal theory are mostly, although not exclusively, concerned with the narrow-scope rule of law. Discussion of the rule of law in the social sciences and by international organisations such as the World Bank and the United Nations is mostly, although not exclusively, concerned with the wide-scope rule of law. Although distinct, the two senses of the rule of law are closely connected. A violation of the rule of law in one sense will very often undermine the rule of law in the other. Resolving legal disputes in ways that are not in accord with pre-existing, publicly accessible legal norms tend to undermine a law-based political order. And a lawless political order will, over time, tend to corrupt a precise and well-functioning legal system.

[1] See generally J Waldron, 'The Rule of Law' in EN Zalta and U Nodelman (eds) *The Stanford Encyclopaedia of Philosophy* (Fall 2023 Edition). Available at: https://plato.stanford.edu/archives/fall2023/entries/rule-of-law/.

Tax disputes implicate both narrow-scope and wide-scope rule of law. Tax adjudication violates narrow-scope rule of law when it ignores established law, appeals to legal norms that are not knowable in advance or renders judgments on grounds of personal partiality rather than legal entitlement. Tax disputes implicate wide-scope rule of law concerns when taxation is used to expropriate politically unfavoured parties or confer benefits on politically favoured parties. Violation of narrow-scope rule of law principles is one way of infringing wide-scope rule of law principle, but not the only way. Public policy that undermines settled expectations based on existing legal entitlements may threaten wide-scope rule of law even if adjudication scrupulously follows the new legal norms. Likewise, a violation of narrow scope rule-of-law may not impinge greatly on the wide-scope rule of law if it only involves isolated instances of unfairness to individual taxpayers and has no systemic implications.

Narrow scope and wide scope rule of law considerations are both relevant to interpretation of tax statutes. In what follows, I will consider statutory anti-abuse rules, judicially created anti-abuse doctrines and purposive interpretation of tax statutes. Purposive interpretation on the one hand and specific anti-abuse rules and doctrines on the other raise different methodological issues. However, because general anti-abuse rules often apply when the purpose of a transaction is tax avoidance and when the results of the transaction are not in accordance with the purposes of the relevant tax statute, purposive interpretation and anti-abuse rules have a complementary and interdependent relationship in this context.[2] I will argue that anti-avoidance doctrines and interpretive methodologies for tax statutes must be evaluated in light of both narrow-scope rule of law considerations and wide-scope rule of law considerations, and that the relationship between the two is dynamic. Legal norms that allow revenue authorities and judges a great deal of scope to combat abusive tax schemes may not infringe upon the narrow-scope rule of law if they are carefully drafted and faithfully applied but may be inadvisable in contexts where the wide-scope rule of law is fragile. The first section will explain the narrow scope rule of law and its implications for tax avoidance disputes. The second section will introduce the wide scope rule of law and differentiate it from the narrow scope rule of law. The third section argues that the advisability of anti-abuse rules depends in part on whether the political and legal systems of a polity show strong commitment to the rule of law. The final section concludes.

Narrow-Scope Rule of Law: Following the Rules

The narrow-scope rule of law is the primary focus of most work on the rule of law in legal theory. This is natural since it is the aspect of the rule of law that is most closely connected to the operation of the legal system. Although Lon Fuller's and Joseph Raz's multifaceted analyses of the rule of law have implications for both aspects of the rule of law, the narrow-sense conception is foregrounded.[3] For this reason, it makes sense

[2] V Thuronyi, K Brooks and B Kolozs, *Comparative Tax Law* (Alphen aan den Rijn: Kluwer Law International 2016) 158–59.

[3] J Raz, 'The Rule of Law and its Virtue' in *The Authority of Law* (Oxford: Oxford University Press, 1979) 214, 226; L Fuller, *The Morality of Law* 2nd edn (New Haven CT: Yale University Press, 1969) 156–57.

to briefly consider the theories of each theorist with the caveat that the focus will be on points of commonality rather than on the important differences between the two. In *The Morality of Law*, Fuller identifies eight necessary attributes of law: generality, publicity, prospectivity, intelligibility, consistency, practicability, stability, and congruence.[4] A system of rules that entirely fails to exhibit any one of these features is not a system of law, according to Fuller, but at most is a failed attempt to create law. For the analysis here, we need not decide whether these are necessary attributes of law or merely features of a legal system conducive to the rule of law. The point is that insofar as rules fall short in one of these ways, this is a rule of law shortcoming.

Joseph Raz provides a non-exclusive list of principles of the rule of law. His principles include attributes of legal norms such as that the law should be 'prospective, open, and clear', 'relatively stable' and that the making of laws 'should be guided by open, stable, clear, and general rules'. However, they also include attributes of legal institutions and procedures such as an independent judiciary, 'open and fair hearings', absence of bias in adjudication, judicial review of conformity with the law, accessible courts, and impartial exercise of prosecutorial discretion.[5] As the focus of this analysis will be on substantive tax law rather than tax procedure, it makes sense to focus on the first category of Raz's principles which also happen to be those with the greatest overlap with Fuller's.[6] Both Fuller and Raz agree that the rule of law requires that laws be clear and publicly accessible in advance to those expected to comply with them.[7] They also agree that great instability in the rules in force at any given time is a threat to the rule of law and that laws should, in some minimal sense, be general.

Because the generality criterion will be especially important to questions concerning tax avoidance, it is worth exploring in slightly more detail to avoid potential misunderstandings. Both Fuller and Raz suggest that the generality criterion should be read narrowly to require that legal norms have formal significance across the legal system but not as putting substantial constraints on the substance of the law. Fuller notes that generality does not rule out laws naming particular individuals, although such laws might violate 'external' considerations of fairness that are not part of the 'law's internal morality'.[8] Raz emphasises that the requirement that laws be general in nature does not bring with it any sort of anti-discrimination norm and that substantively objectionable discrimination may be compatible for the rule of law.[9] The generality criterion on Fuller's and Raz's understanding therefore should not be seen as a barrier to targeted anti-abuse rules or as significantly limiting the form that general anti-abuse rules can take.

Both Raz in his earlier work and Fuller suggest that a common attribute of most aspects of the rule of law is that they are required for the law to be action guiding.[10] Citizens cannot follow law that is secret, contradictory, incomprehensible, retrospective, or requires actions that are impossible. It is difficult for citizens to follow or officials

[4] Fuller, *The Morality of Law* ibid, 39.
[5] Raz, 'The Rule of Law and its Virtue' above n 3, 214–18.
[6] For analysis of the relationship of the rule of law to tax administration, see Daly, Chapter 2 in this volume.
[7] For detailed analysis of the prospectivity requirement, see Gillis, Chapter 4 in this volume.
[8] Fuller above, n 3, 47.
[9] Raz above n 3, 215–16.
[10] ibid, 214, 226; Fuller, above n 3, 156–57.

to enforce laws that change too frequently or are not sufficiently general in character. Incongruency between the law as enacted and the law as applied frustrates attempts to comply with the law and subjects people to inconsistent standards. Raz's procedural aspects of the rule of law can be seen as supporting the action guiding function of law by making it more likely that the substance of the law will be applied consistently and accurately.

In more recent work, Raz expressed reservations about his earlier formulation and in particular about the contention that the action guiding nature of law provides sufficient scope for explaining the conceptual unity and moral significance of the rule of law.[11] He proposed that the formal principles of the rule of law should instead be seen as aimed at preventing arbitrary government, which 'is the use of power that is indifferent to the proper reasons for which power should be used'.[12] The proper end of government is the promotion of the interests of the governed, as opposed to, for example, the private interests of the rulers.[13] Conformity to the rule of law requires action 'with manifest intention to serve the interests of the governed, as expressed by the law'.[14] This is consistent with well-intentioned incompetence or honest mistakes about the interests of the governed. Therefore, the rule of law does not require that government actually advance the interests of the governed but merely that it acts in a way that aims to do so.[15] And although Raz's new account is somewhat thicker than his old account, it sharply differentiates the rule of law from other virtues of a legal system such as democratic legitimacy, human rights, or substantive equality before the law.[16] It is not clear that it makes a difference for the topic of tax avoidance which of Raz's two formulations of the rule of law one selects. A tax judgment that violates the rule of law typically undermines both higher level interests protected by the rule of law. It does not provide sufficient guidance to taxpayers about how they can comply with the law and is arbitrary from the perspective of the conception of the public interest implicit in the tax statute. The second formulation, perhaps, frames the issue with greater clarity since the law of tax avoidance seems to involve a tension between two ways in which a tax decision may be arbitrary: a tax may be arbitrary in the sense of going beyond what is authorised by statute or arbitrary in the sense of contradicting the policy implicit in the tax statute.

Raz's conception of the rule of law (and to a lesser extent Fuller's) is thin in the sense that it seeks to avoid incorporating substantive values such as freedom, democracy, equality, or human rights in the concept of the rule of law.[17] Some readers will doubtless find this thin conception of the rule of law unsatisfying. Other approaches to the rule of law imbue the concept with substantive values such as freedom, equality, or human rights.[18] I believe that this is undesirable for several reasons. First, it does not serve conceptual clarity to combine what are analytical distinct values in a single concept.

[11] J Raz, 'The Law's Own Virtue' (2019) 39 OJLS 1, 5.
[12] ibid, 5.
[13] ibid, 7.
[14] ibid, 7–8.
[15] ibid, 14.
[16] ibid, 8–10.
[17] T Bingham, *The Rule of Law* (London: Allen Lane, 2010) 67.
[18] ibid. FA Hayek, *The Constitution of Liberty* (Chicago: The University of Chicago Press, 1960).

This kind of unclarity encourages arguments that seem to rely upon the rule of law but, upon closer inspection, actually turn on a different substantive value that could be analytically separated from the rule of law and is only connected to it by the particular thick conception of the rule of law adopted. Second, thick conceptions of the rule of law encourage unproductive arguments between partisans of different substantive values over which substantive values should be included in the definition of the rule of law. It is far better to argue over substantive values directly (eg the relative priority of freedom and equality, the value of private property, etc) rather than conducting this debate in a covert form. Third, the more substantive political values incorporated into its definition, the more difficult it is to understand what is uniquely important about the rule of law or secure agreement on its normative significance. This is especially unfortunate since it is sometimes possible to achieve argument on rule of law values between people with deep substantive disagreements on the merits of free market capitalism, the nature of democracy, the meaning of equality and other 'thick' rule of law values. Finally, it is somewhat doubtful that a thicker concept of the rule of law would change many of the conclusions below. The basic conflict between legal certainty for taxpayers and alignment with the substantive aims of tax legislation can be drawn without a thicker conception of the rule of law. Why use a complex concept when a simple one will do?

Even working with a thin conception of the rule of law, the connection between the rule of law and other values is controversial. Raz emphasises the degree to which aspects of the rule of law are necessary for the law to be efficacious. If the function of the law is to guide behaviour, then the law fails to perform its function if it is not capable of providing guidance.[19] It is a contingent matter whether, all things considered, this is a good thing: a wicked government that acts more efficaciously is not, thereby, a good government but is only more effectively wicked. Of course, a more efficacious legal system may be desirable for all sorts of instrumental reasons since it tends to make life more predictable for citizens and to encourage trust in government and perhaps social trust more generally. If the function of the legal system is to advance the interests of the governed by creating and applying law, then the legal system fails to perform its function if it does not aim to promote the interests of the governed as expressed by the law.[20] This is a failure of law, qua law, and usually, but not always a bad thing in itself. But since the law sometimes does not, in fact, serve the public interest, it is a contingent matter whether complying with it is a good thing. Fuller takes a different view, arguing that the law has an internal morality such that violation of the rule of law is not merely instrumentally bad but intrinsically so. This difference is connected to a long-running debate between positivists such as Raz who believe that the content of the law has no necessary connection to morality and depends instead on social facts and anti-positivists such as Fuller who believe that the content of the law depends on moral value as well as on social facts,[21] although both positivists and anti-positivists might embrace a great range of theories of the rule of law. For our present purposes, there is no need to resolve such debates as the sorts of procedural fairness interests implicated by interpretation of tax

[19] Raz, above n 3, 226.

[20] Raz, 'The Law's Own Virtue' above n 11, 7–8.

[21] L Green and T Adams, 'Legal Positivism' (*The Stanford Encyclopaedia of Philosophy*, 17 December 2019). Available at: https://plato.stanford.edu/entries/legal-positivism/ (last accessed 22 November 2023).

statutes will likely have instrumental moral significance, at least in minimally just states, even if they do not have intrinsic moral significance.

Several things follow from this analysis of the narrow-scope rule of law. First, compliance with the narrow-scope rule of law is a graded property, one that comes in degrees.[22] Some violations of the rule of law are more serious than others either because a violation infringes against more attributes of the rule of law or because it infringes on a given set of attributes more severely. The rule of law has both intrinsic value in its protection of procedural fairness and instrumental value in the improved effectiveness of government and trust in government. The latter values are sensitive to the degree to which government pursues desirable ends. Second, perfect conformity with the rule of law is neither possible nor desirable. No set of legal norms can provide guidance for all possible circumstances without any trace of vagueness or ambiguity and, even if this were possible, it would be inferior to a system in which certain questions were left open for resolution by those better informed about future circumstances. Third, the rule of law must be balanced against other values.[23] There is no assurance that it will not conflict with other important objectives. When it does, the relevant considerations must be weighed to determine which value will give way. Fourth, because the rule of law has multiple aspects, these sometimes come into conflict with one another.

The internal conflict between different aspects of the rule of law can be found in the law of tax avoidance. For example, there is tension between clarity and stability in tax law. On the one hand, anti-abuse doctrines and general anti-abuse rules introduce potential uncertainty in the law as they require two levels of analysis rather than one. It is often somewhat uncertain whether they will apply to particular transactions. In this sense they reduce the predictability of law relative to a more formalistic mode of interpretation that considers statutory provisions in isolation. On the other hand, if courts uphold transactions that subvert statutory purposes this encourages frequent legislative changes in the law to close perceived loopholes. This decreases legal stability relative to a system in which courts use a set of relatively stable anti-abuse principles to prevent results that subvert statutory purposes. Reasonable minds may differ as to the relative priority of stability and clarity in tax law. It is likely that the best approach will consider both virtues and reflect a compromise between the two.

This tension has a particular bite because clarity in tax law might be less valuable than in other areas of law. For most areas of law, it is preferable if those subject to the law change their behaviour to conform to it. We usually prefer that citizens uphold contracts, avoid torts, respect the property rights of others, comply with environmental, financial, public health and traffic regulations and avoid perpetrating crimes. The position of tax law is more complicated. Ex post certainty is desirable because this provides taxpayers with certainty about how much they must pay the government. Ex ante certainty is not necessarily advantageous from the perspective of the public good. For taxes aimed primarily at raising revenue, it is typically undesirable for taxpayers to change their behaviour in response to the law since this creates economic inefficiencies and reduces tax revenue. Some economists have even argued that imposition of taxes

[22] Raz, above n 3, 222.
[23] ibid, 228–29.

at random rates known only at the close of the tax year would be most efficient since they would raise more revenue with less deadweight loss.[24] This means that the value of legal certainty is more limited and depends, in part, on whether greater certainty encourages or discourages behaviour that is undertaken for tax reasons. As a result, it is difficult to say whether greater knowledge of tax laws aimed at raising revenue improves welfare and if so when.[25] For Pigouvian taxes, by contrast, it is desirable that taxpayers are aware of the tax and change their behaviour in response to it.[26] Minimising externalities requires taxpayers to take notice of the law whereas collection of tax revenue is most effective when taxpayers do not. Because most taxes aim primarily to raise revenue rather than changing taxpayer behaviour, clarity may be something of a mixed blessing: serving the rule of law by giving citizens notice of their legal obligations but making the law less efficacious by reducing tax revenue.

A second internal tension in tax law involves conflict between clarity and generality as legal virtues. Clarity is better served by formal principles of statutory interpretation that prioritise plain meaning and bright line interpretive rules even at the expense of policy coherence. However, doing so will make the most salient high-level norms in the tax law less general as outcomes depend more heavily on the particular circumstances of each taxpayer and less on the overarching principles (eg as more taxpayers avoid tax the effective tax rate deviates from the statutory tax rate more often). Generality, therefore, provides a reason to favour application of anti-abuse doctrines that can be used to bring outcomes for individual taxpayers in line with the general norms underlying tax statutes. It is difficult to say how significant this aspect of the generality is for the rule of law. As noted above, Fuller and Raz favour a narrow reading of generality on which a legal provision that affects only a few taxpayers is, in some sense, general if all taxpayers are formally subject to it. However, it is obviously possible to draft laws in such a way that they are formally general, but foreseeably impact only a few taxpayers. In extreme cases, this might be thought to undermine the rule of law, for example when legislators decide to target personally identifiable politically disfavoured parties. On balance, it seems that anti-abuse rules only contribute modestly to the generality of law in the sense that is important to the narrow scope rule of law. The most egregious instances of political favouritism are not likely to run afoul of anti-abuse rules since they are clearly intended by the legislature. The connection between anti-abuse rules and the politicisation of the tax system raises questions that go beyond the theories found in Raz and Fuller and will be addressed below in connection with the wide-scope rule of law.

The narrow-scope rule of law has implications for both the substantive and procedural tax law. It requires that the law be publicly accessible, prospective, clear and internally consistent. There are two central concerns with anti-abuse rules from the perspective of the rule of law. One is that a rule may not be sufficiently clear to provide guidance to taxpayers who wish to understand their legal obligations before receiving

[24] J Stiglitz, 'Utilitarianism and Horizontal Equity: The Case of Random Taxation' (1982) 18 *Journal of Public Economics* 1.

[25] D Weisbach, 'Is Knowledge of the Tax Law Socially Desirable?' (2013) 15 *American Law and Economics Review* 187, 210.

[26] ibid, 188.

instruction from the tax authorities or a ruling from a court. A second concern is that an anti-abuse rule may be applied inconsistently across taxpayers or in a way that is biased in favour of the tax authorities so that the rule as a practical matter grants discretion to the tax authorities unfettered by any judicial oversight. The analysis in this section will focus on the former concern. The issue of systemic bias will be considered below in the context of wide-scope rule of law.

A sufficiently vague or open-ended anti-abuse rule might flout the rule of law by providing insufficient guidance for taxpayers, tax authorities and courts. For example, a rule that states 'A taxpayer shall pay an amount of tax that is fair' without any further specification of how to understand fairness in this context would raise serious rule of law concerns as it appears nearly impossible to understand a taxpayer's obligations before they are pronounced upon by a court. Likewise, a rule that transactions may be recharacterised if they appear to be structured by consulting relevant tax law to achieve a particular result would probably fall into the same category as it would appear on its face to apply to virtually all transactions involving sophisticated taxpayers. This would amount to granting tax authorities and courts discretion to characterise transactions at will without any requirement of consistency, adherence to principle or coherence with stable norms.

Although anti-abuse rules potentially conflict with the narrow-scope rule of law, it should not be difficult to design general anti-abuse rules that do not do so. The key is to establish some background norm against which transactions can be found to be abusive that provides sufficient guidance for taxpayers and revenue officials. This animates the anti-abuse rule by providing a justiciable standard for identifying abusive transactions. Such a norm can be established by inferring the underlying purposes of a statutory scheme or by reference to some general set of background norms, such as anti-abuse doctrines, recognised in case law. Without such background norms, anti-abuse rules risk degenerating into a free-flowing permission for tax authorities and judges to recharacterise transactions for any reason it wishes or to impose tax against disfavoured taxpayers at will. However, if the tax statute in question has intelligible purposes that can be used to identify abusive transactions, then the application of a general anti-abuse rule ('GAAR') to transactions that fall within its scope is not a breach of the rule of law. Of course, some statutes may not have sufficiently clear charging provisions to allow interpreters to determine which transactions are abusive. In such cases, there may be no way to find that a transaction should not receive the treatment that the best reading of each section of the statute would suggest. Finding such a transaction to be abusive would be a breach of the rule of law not because anti-abuse rules violate the rule of law but because the *application* of the anti-abuse rule to these facts violates the rule of law. This kind of legal mistake is possible in applying any kind of legal rule: there is no substitute for sound legal judgment. Opponents of GAAR might contend that it strikes the balance between reliance on plain meaning and purposive interpretation unwisely or that it gives too much power to the Revenue rather than taxpayers. But these are best understood either as disagreements about legal method or about the relative importance of values internal to the narrow-scope rule of law rather than an argument that GAARs are categorically antithetical to the rule of law.

Overlaying a statutory scheme with a set of principles used to determine how it is applied to facts makes the law more complicated. But this does not in itself create a conflict with the rule of law. The law should put citizens on notice of the rules that they must follow and provide enough guidance so that citizens and officials can usually tell whether these norms have been violated. This does not require that the legal norms take the form of bright line rules rather than abstract principles.[27] Properly enacted prospective legal norms may comply with the rule of law even if they require judgment to apply the abstract norms to a specific fact pattern. Not infrequently, the law sets down a standard that requires the adjudicator to determine how highly abstract principles apply given the concrete facts of the situation at hand. This might involve deciding whether a defendant's conduct has been 'reasonable', 'dishonest', 'unconscionable', 'reckless' or any one of the many other thickly descriptive terms that appear in the law.[28] Or it might involve applying terms such as 'distortion of competition' that require a particular form of policy analysis.[29] Although bright line rules typically yield greater certainty, this is not always so and in complex areas of law such as tax it is not possible to eliminate all uncertainties. Moreover, preference for rules over standards may lead to more complex statutes with more scope for internal contradictions or unclarities as drafters try to provide a rule for every possible contingency.[30] A strongly principle-based approach to tax statutes might find the resources to disallow transactions to seem to flout the purposes of a statute even without a statutory anti-abuse rule.[31] There are reasonable disputes to be had about the relative merits of rules and principles as legal norms.[32] But almost any perspective would allow that adjudication in light of principles is sometimes superior to use of bright-line rules even if reasonable minds might differ on how often such situations arise.

One might object that even if use of thickly descriptive terms is apt in areas of law such as criminal law or tort law that partially track ordinary moral judgments about human conduct, it is out of place in law that determine citizen's property entitlements where certainty and stability have special priority. But the law uses principles or standards in these cases as well. Consider the prohibition on agreements that 'have as their object or effect the prevention, restriction or distortion of competition'[33] or the role of unconscionability in proprietary estoppel.[34] The former threatens businesses with enormous fines for what would otherwise be ordinary, perfectly legal, commercial activity while the latter transfers property rights based on morally infused judgments about a party's conduct. Unfettered discretion to determine what behaviour is anti-competitive or conscionable might leave judges with excessive discretion in ways that would make

[27] F Schauer, 'Rules and the Rule of Law' (1991) 14 *Harvard Journal of Law & Public Policy* 645, 648–57.

[28] B Williams, *Ethics and the Limits of Philosophy* (Cambridge MA: Harvard University Press, 1985) 140–45.

[29] Competition Act 1998, s 2.

[30] David Weisbach attributes an argument to Stanley Surrey that the replacement of rules by standards allows for statutes that are simpler. D Weisbach, 'Formalism in the Tax Law' (1999) 66 *University of Chicago Law Review* 860, 861, citing S Surrey, 'Complexity and the Internal Revenue Code: The Problem of the Management of Tax Detail' (1969) 34 *Law & Contemporary Problems* 673, 707 n 31.

[31] E Simpson, 'The *Ramsay* Principle: A Curious Incident of Judicial Reticence?' (2004) 4 *British Tax Review* 358.

[32] R Dworkin, *Law's Empire* (Cambridge MA, Harvard University Press, 1986); M Berman, 'How Practices Make Principles, and How Principles Make Rules' (University of Pennsylvania Carey Law School, 2022) All Faculty Scholarship 2765. Available at: https://scholarship.law.upenn.edu/faculty_scholarship/2765; A Scalia, 'The Rule of Law as a Law of Rules' (1989) 56 *University of Chicago Law Review* 1175.

[33] Competition Act 1998, s 2(1)(b).

[34] *Taylors Fashions v Liverpool Victoria Trustees Ltd* [1982] 1 QB 133.

it difficult to comply with the law. However, in practice, the meanings of these terms are filled in by legal precedents (and in the case of competition law regulatory guidance) that provides exemplars of the prohibited types of actions, giving substances to what otherwise might be objectionably vague standards. The use of standards or principles to construe statutory provisions may slightly shift the balance of power away from legislatures and toward judges or toward administrative agencies. This may be desirable as a means to fine-tune statutory rules in light of new circumstances and of background normative commitments or undesirable as a matter of democratic legitimacy. In any case, the rule of law does not require that legal norms are created only by legislatures, unless the legal system in question has a constitutional rule of legislative supremacy that makes the legislature the only source of law.

To apply the distinction between constrained and unconstrained anti-abuse rules to specific legislation, consider the UK's recently enacted GAAR, which contains passages that arguably fall on either side of this distinction.[35] This is a particularly fraught example given the UK's historically formalistic approach to tax statues and that one motive for the enactment of the GAAR was the purported inadequacy of UK court's more recent turn to purposive interpretation of tax statutes in combatting tax avoidance schemes.[36] The GAAR's states that weather a taxpayer's position is abusive should be considered in light of 'the principles and policy underlying the tax provisions' and whether the transaction involves 'contrived and abnormal steps'.[37] The former provides a normative baseline against which a transaction might be considered abusive[38] while the latter implicates a body of pre-existing case law that provides guidance regarding what types of actions might constitute 'contrived and abnormal steps'.[39] In these respects, the GAAR provides a workable standard for identifying abusive transactions, albeit one that requires thoughtful interpretation of statutory schemes and a precise understanding of the true nature of the transaction and a strong grasp of how the economics of a particular transaction interacts with the policy aims of a statute. Similar considerations apply to doctrines used to police tax avoidance schemes such as the step transaction doctrine and the economic substance doctrine, which both provide rules, albeit highly abstract ones, that can separate permissible from impermissible claims.[40] Less reassuring is the GAAR's admonition to consider 'whether the arrangements are intended to exploit any shortcoming in the tax provisions'.[41] If this is construed as meaning something like 'whether the arrangement is intended to subvert the purpose of the statute by exploitation of technical mistakes in drafting', then this is probably harmless. However, since this would arguably be duplicative of the first criterion, one fears that something more is intended here. If the reference to 'shortcomings' is meant to invite revenue

[35] Finance Act 2013, ss 206–215.

[36] See A Brassey, 'Tax, GAAR and the Rule of Law' (PhD thesis, University of Cambridge, 2017) 32–38.

[37] Finance Act 2013, s 207(2).

[38] It is also in accord with the dominant trend in recent case law. See, eg, *Collector of Stamp Revenue v Arrowtown* [2003] 6 ITLR 454, cited approvingly in *Barclays Mercantile Business Finance Ltd v Mawson* [2004] UKHL 51.

[39] *WT Ramsey Ltd v IRC* [1982] AC 300; *IRC v Burmah Oil Co Ltd* [1982] STC 30; *Furniss v Dawson* [1984] AC 474.

[40] *Knetsch v United States*, 364 US 361 (1960); *McDonalds Restaurants of Illinois v Commissioner*, 688 F2d 520 (7th Cir 1982); *Hitch v Stone* [2001] EWCA Civ 63.

[41] Finance Act 2013, s 207(2)(c).

officials and judges to make judgments about shortcomings in tax statutes unmoored from any limiting principles provided by statute or case law, this undermines the rule of law by creating unfettered discretion to impose taxes. The problem is not so much that normative language such as 'shortcomings' is inappropriate as that it is difficult to see how case law could provide sufficient guidance to narrow the meaning of 'shortcomings' given that tax avoidance cases will often require analysis of new combinations of statutory provisions that do not closely match any 'shortcoming' identified in previous cases. Outside of generic technical mistakes such as scrivener's errors, the reasons that a particular provision is a shortcoming may be particular to the facts of a specific transaction or to the statutory provisions involved.

Wide-Scope Rule of Law: A Law Governed Order

Whereas the narrow-scope rule of law is concerned with whether laws have the right form and are applied properly by the legal system, the wide-scope rule of law is concerned with whether a political system is ordered through law or by some other means. The former considers whether the legal system is bound by rules, the latter considers the role of law and the legal system in the polity. In a polity characterised by the wide-scope rule of law, law constrains the actions of the state, regulates the relations between citizens and determines the allocation of benefits and burdens of cooperation between citizens. Ruling through law can be contrasted with personal commands of a king or dictator, with the decisions of some collective body as in a one-party system, and with customary social norms operating outside the context of a full legal system with secondary rules.[42] The wide-scope rule of law is thus a matter not only of following the rules, but also of the role of legal rule following in government and society. Law, in the sense of a set of norms that are general, impersonal, prospective, and stable, is only one way to govern. It happens to be extremely convenient for societies with complex economies and, for this reason, it is tempting for those brought up in such societies to regard legal governance as natural or inevitable. But this perspective should not be allowed to obscure the nature of law as a cultural artifact that performs functions that might be carried out – albeit not always very well – by other means.

Although some authors use to term 'rule by law' to describe authoritarian law-bound governments,[43] it is helpful here to use the term in a morally neutral way to describe states that govern through law whether they are relatively free, relatively unfree, or somewhere in between. Under the wide-scope rule of law, governmental decisions are made according to a pre-existing body of rules that have been enacted by following the correct procedures for creating law in the given legal system. Even in a domain as seemingly law bound as taxation, there is scope for determining tax payments by direct negotiation between the taxpayer and the revenue authorities. Such negotiations take

[42] On the nature of secondary rules, see HLA Hart, T*he Concept of Law* (Oxford: Oxford University Press, 1961) 78–79.

[43] B Tamanaha, *On the Rule of Law: History, Politics, Theory* (Cambridge: Cambridge University Press, 2004).

place against the background of legal norms but the negotiations themselves may be more constrained or less constrained by law depending on the nature of the legal rules and the political culture within which they operate.

The distinction between the narrow-scope rule of law and the wide-scope rule of law is orthogonal to the distinction discussed previously between thin and thick conceptions of the rule of law. In keeping with the thin conception of the rule of law defended previously, the analysis here will treat the wide-scope rule of law as consistent with democracy, substantive equality and a market economy, but as neither requiring nor entailing any of these.[44] In this, usage will depart from Hayek whose conception of the rule of law is close to what I call the wide-scope rule of law, but who posits a close connection between the rule of law and the protection of freedom, both political and economic.[45] It is, of course, possible, perhaps even likely, that as an empirical matter the wide-scope rule of law is more likely in polities that are democratic, have a free market economic system or embrace some conception of substantive equality, but analytical clarity is not well served by building controversial empirical claims into normative concepts.

The relationship between the narrow-scope rule of law and the wide-scope rule of law is complex. A legal system that meets a certain minimum standard in terms of the narrow-scope rule of law is required for the wide-scope rule of law. A society cannot be ordered by law unless it has a legal system that meets certain minimal conditions for the narrow-scope rule of law. Although having laws and legal institutions that conform to the rule of law is a necessary condition for having a law-governed society, it is not sufficient. There are several ways in which a polity with a functional legal system might fail to exemplify the wide-scope rule of law. It is possible to have a system of government with a good deal of law and some legal institutions in which government, or at least the type of high-stakes decisions that determine the character of a polity, are not made according to law. Such a system might have a more or less important place for law, but the key decisions are made on political grounds. This disconnect can arise in a variety of ways. One way is that the rule of law might exist only for a small elite with the masses being ruled by some combination of customary social norms and brute force. This state of affairs is often found in societies, such as many of those in medieval and early modern Europe, which feature multiple legal systems with partially overlapping jurisdictions that govern relations between particular estates or social groups.[46] Such a society might evolve into a law-governed social order as the rule of law is progressively extended from the elite to the rest of society[47] but, of course, many legal systems of this kind fail to evolve in this way. A second way in which the narrow scope rule of law may come apart from the wide scope rule of law is where a reasonably well-functioning legal system exists alongside a political system the operates outside the legal system with few

[44] With respect to the relationship between free markets and the rule of law, the terms of debate have perhaps not entirely caught up to political realities. In much of the developed world, defenders of the social welfare state are, in some senses, conservatives seeking to preserve the status quo whereas libertarian critics are reformers. This means that concern for the wide-scope rule of law does not necessarily have a right-wing valence: the established order includes not only entitlements to private property but also to public benefits.

[45] Hayek, above n 18, 309–10.

[46] See H Berman, *Law and Revolution: The Formation of the Western Legal Tradition* (Cambridge, MA: Harvard University Press, 1983).

[47] D North, J Wallis and B Weingast, *Violence and Social Orders* (Cambridge: Cambridge University Press, 2009) 154–58.

legal constraints. Various one-party dictatorships, for example some of the Warsaw Pact countries during the Cold War, might fit this description. These might be contrasted with one-party dictatorships, such as the People's Republic of China during the cultural revolution, which lack rule of law in either the narrow or the wide sense. Finally, the narrow-scope rule of law can come apart from the wide-scope rule of law if laws are systematically ignored or if judicial rulings are systematically disregarded. It is possible for a legal system to be internally in good working order in the sense that courts issue rulings in accordance with the law but for these to have limited influence on social, economic or political matters.

Although the two senses of the rule of law are distinct, they are mutually reinforcing. A legal system that complies with the narrow-scope rule of law is necessary for a polity that is ordered by the wide-scope rule of law. And a polity with a strong rule-of-law culture creates demand for legal institutions that apply the law fairly and impartially. This kind of virtuous cycle is mirrored by a cycle in which deficits in each sense of the rule of law reinforce each other. A legal system that does not comply with the narrow scope rule of law will tend to undermine the wide scope rule of law since well-functioning legal institutions are necessary for a polity to be organised through law. Likewise, a society which is lawless will tend to undermine the narrow-scope rule of law by corrupting legal institutions. It will also cause distrust, even when this is only partially justified, because citizens who have little positive experience with impartial application of the laws by the government will not expect this of judges, prosecutors, and other legal officials.

The wide-scope rule of law has a different relationship to specific legal provisions than the narrow-scope rule of law. As discussed above in the context of Raz's theory, the narrow-scope rule of law protects the interests of individuals subject to the legal system from arbitrary government action and allows law to perform its function of guiding action. By contrast, the wide-scope rule of law is largely concerned with the systemic effects of law rather than with individual acts of rule following and the virtues of rule-based governance and social order structured by law. Because it is concerned with the role of law in the polity as a whole, the wide-scope rule of law does not typically imply limits on the formal properties of laws beyond those already implied by the narrow-scope rule of law. However, it introduces a range of additional normative considerations that go beyond the narrow-scope rule of law including whether particular laws are conducive to a law-governed social order and which laws are suitable given the extent to which rule of law principles pervade government and society. A law may be consistent with the narrow-scope rule of law, yet tends to undermine government by law. Alternatively, a legal rule might be well-adapted for contexts with impartial judiciaries, law-abiding citizens and rule-following government officials but deeply inappropriate for polities with none of these.

Taxation and Trust: The Political Context of the Legal System

The suitability of general anti-abuse rules depends on political context including the degree to which the wide-scope rule of law is observed. Because collecting taxes requires application of the law by a wide range of officials and quasi-voluntary compliance with the law by large numbers of citizens, the wide-scope rule of law is of great importance for taxation.[48] Trust by taxpayers in the state is important for the efficient collection of taxes.[49] Brute force always remains a fallback option, but this is expensive and only partially effective since jailed or exiled taxpayers may not yield much revenue. The amount of coercion required to collect revenue is inversely related to tax morale, which is the willingness of taxpayers to comply with the law for reasons other than threat of punishment.[50] Taxpayers who perceive the tax system as fair and legitimate, the tax authorities to be following the law and the courts to be impartial when hearing disputes between taxpayers and the state are more likely to pay their taxes with less resistance.[51] This is not only because taxpayers are more likely to believe that their own tax assessment is in accordance with the law, but also because taxpayers are more likely to believe that others will pay their fair share. Distrust from taxpayers has the inverse result: less willingness to comply with tax law, more coercion necessary for collecting taxes and scepticism that others will pay their fair share.

Although hardly the only factor in trust in government, whether political authorities follow the law and resolve conflicts according to the law plays a significant role in whether citizens trust political authorities and comply with the law.[52] In societies with a weak rule of law culture, taxpayers are unlikely to trust revenue authorities or courts and are likely to expect that their fellow citizens will not comply with tax laws except under threat of punishment.[53] This undermines tax morale.[54] To some extent, this distrust is justified since polities with wide-scope rule of law deficits have less effective political and legal institutions. However, even when courts and revenue officials apply the law impartially and fairly, they are apt to be regarded with suspicion since taxpayers will approach new encounters with the legal system in light of their previous experiences with officials who often do not follow the law.

When trust in tax officials and courts is low, it is better to adopt rules that reduce official discretion and are easier for taxpayers to monitor, partially because this prevents abuse of discretion, and partially because making it easier for taxpayers to tell that officials are following the law builds trust in government[55] As a general matter, formalistic methods of statutory interpretation make it easier to monitor the compliance of officials with the law than do purposive interpretation, anti-abuse doctrines and anti-abuse rules. They also serve the limit the discretion of those who apply the rules.[56] Purposive

[48] M Levi, *Of Rule and Revenue* (Berkeley CA: University of California Press, 1988) 52–57.

[49] B Torgler, 'Tax Morale, Rule-Governed Behaviour and Trust' (2003) 14 *Constitutional Political Economy* 119, 119.

[50] E Luttmer and M Singhal, 'Tax Morale' (2014) 28 *Journal of Economic Perspectives* 149, 151–54.

[51] Torgler, above n 49, 134; B Torgler, 'Tax Morale in Asian Countries' (2004) 15 *Journal of Asian Economics* 237; B Torgler, 'Tax Morale in Latin America' (2005) 122 *Public Choice* 133; B Torgler, 'Tax Morale and Direct Democracy' (2005) 21 *European Journal of Political Economy* 525.

[52] T Tyler, 'Does the American Public Accept the Rule of Law? The Findings of Psychological Research on Deference to Authority' (2007) 56 *DePaul Law Review* 661, 661.

[53] MFM Martinangeli, M Povitkina, S Jagers and B Rothstein, 'Institutional Quality Causes Generalised Trust: Experimental Evidence on Trusting under the Shadow of Doubt' (Forthcoming 2024) *68 American Journal of Political Science*, https://doi.org/10.1111/ajps.12780; F Herreros, 'The State and Trust' (2023) 26 *Annual Review of Political Science* 117, 124.

[54] Luttmer and Singhal, above n 50, 157.

[55] Tyler, above n 52, 693–94.

[56] F Schauer, 'Formalism' (1988) 97 *Yale Law Journal* 509, 540–44.

interpretation and the application of anti-abuse rules require considering how particular statutory provisions interact with the policy aims of statutes and the background principles of statutory interpretation. In a tax context, this requires a considerable degree of sophistication about the economics of taxation as well as legal skill. Applying anti-abuse rules and doctrines is considerably more demanding than decoding particular statutory provisions (itself often a difficult task in long and technical tax statutes) since the former requires the latter but the latter does not require the former. Anti-abuse rules additionally run the risk of being used as cover for tax authorities making demands that go beyond any reasonable interpretation of the statute and involve unequal treatment of similarly situated taxpayers. The failure mode of anti-abuse rule as free-floating permission to recharacterize transactions is more likely in polities with a weak culture of wide-scope rule of law.

Matters are different where adherence to the wide-scope rule of law creates greater trust between taxpayers and the state. In this context taxpayers are more likely to trust courts and (to a lesser extent) revenue officials to use complex tools such as anti-abuse rules and purposive interpretation fairly and in a way that reflects a good-faith attempt to get the law right even when they do not agree with their judgments about how to apply the law. In a high-trust context, anti-abuse rules can potentially boost tax morale by increasing taxpayers' confidence that other taxpayers will make reasonable contributions and that the tax system as a whole reflects a coherent policy aimed at apportioning contributions fairly among taxpayers. A polity with a well-developed rule of law culture may therefore be able to realise any benefits that anti-abuse rules yield in reducing tax avoidance without diminishing tax morale. Anti-abuse rules, at least when well drafted, are apt for polities characterised by the rule of law in both the narrow scope and wide scope sense.[57]

Conclusion

The case of tax avoidance illustrates how the complex internal structure of the rule of law requires trade-offs between different aspects of the rule of law and how the proper approach to tax avoidance law may depend on the political context of a particular legal

[57] If this analysis is correct, the history of UK tax avoidance jurisprudence is peculiar. The UK is widely considered to have an admirable tradition of judicial independence, political stability and adherence to the rule of law. It exploits this reputation by serving as a forum of choice for resolving commercial disputes. Yet despite this, its twentieth law of tax avoidance embraces a formalism that implies distrust of the judiciary and the elevation of certainty for individual taxpayers over fair allocation of tax burdens. An admittedly speculative explanation for this phenomenon is that UK tax avoidance jurisprudence developed in the early to mid-twentieth century against the background of political conflict over progressive taxation (see, eg *IRC v Duke of Westminster* [1936] AC 1). This might have made judges more sympathetic to taxpayers engaged in efforts to minimise their tax obligations and pushed UK tax avoidance jurisprudence in a formalist direction in a key formative period. In any case, the pendulum has now swung far enough in the other direction that the UK might no longer be an outlier in the law of tax avoidance relative to similar jurisdictions (see, eg *Barclays Mercantile Business Finance Ltd v Mawson (Inspector of Taxes)* [2004] UKHL 51). Alternatively, this phenomenon may reflect a more general preference in the UK legal system for formalistic modes of interpretation and rule-bound decision making. See generally P Atiyah and R Summers, *Form and Substance in Anglo-American Law: A Comparative Study of Legal Reasoning, Legal Theory, and Legal Institutions* (Oxford: Oxford University Press, 1987).

system. Legal norms that leave taxpayers chronically uncertain of their legal obligations are a threat to the narrow-scope rule of law. Nevertheless, this insight does not yield a straightforward argument in favour of more formal methodologies of statutory interpretation or against anti-abuse doctrines. As long as the applicable legal norms are known in advance, it is not a violation of the rule of law to decide cases based on principles rather than rules or on economic substance rather than legal form. Less formal, more purposive, forms of adjudication tend to rely more on complex reasoning and sound judgment by judges. However, in a legal system with a skilled and impartial judiciary, they are not inherently threatening to the rule of law.

Purposivist methods of statutory interpretation and anti-abuse doctrines are less desirable in polities with deficits in the wide-scope rule of law. When the judiciary is highly politicised and tax disputes are connected to broader political conflict it is better to adopt more formal methods of adjudication that rely less on abstract reasoning about tax policy by judges and that are easier to monitor for signs of bias. Tax law methodology, therefore, should be calibrated to political and cultural context.[58] Approaches that might best for politically stable polities with highly skilled impartial judiciaries might be ill-suited for other contexts.

[58] Elsewhere, I have made a similar argument regarding the choice between methods of statutory interpretation. See I Lindsay, 'Convention, Social Trust, and Legal Interpretation' in K Vallier and M Weber eds, *Social Trust* (New York: Routledge, 2021).

4

Two Conceptions of the Rule of Law's Prospectivity Requirement in Taxation

RORY GILLIS

Abstract

Amidst growing concerns over income inequality and public sector finances, governments across the developed world have re-embraced 'retrospective taxes', taxes that have an effective date preceding their enactment date. Among other examples, governments have introduced retrospective excess profits taxes in Canada, Italy, Greece, Luxembourg, the Netherlands and Spain, and retrospective remedial taxes on long-established tax planning arrangements in the UK. Taxes of this sort are routinely condemned by tax scholars and lawyers for breaching Fuller and Raz's prospectivity requirement, which provides that laws should only apply on a going-forward basis. This claim, however, obscures an important difference between Fuller and Raz's conceptions of prospectivity in taxation. Fuller endorses a 'compliance conception' in which retrospective taxes on past transactions are permissible so long as taxpayers are provided with a future payment window to comply with their new obligation. Raz, in contrast, endorses a much-less permissive 'reliance conception' in which taxes on past transactions are problematic, even with a future payment window, because they disrupt reliance interests in pre-existing law.

This chapter compares and weighs possible justifications for the compliance and reliance conceptions of prospectivity. Its central claim is that it is surprisingly difficult to construct a satisfying rule-of-law rationale for the reliance conception, even though the reliance conception is implicitly adopted in most accounts of the rule of law in taxation. One implication is that the widespread condemnation of many retrospective tax laws requires reassessment. Another is that more attention should be paid to developing the compliance conception or other plausible alternatives.

Introduction

Over the past five years, governments across the developed world have expressed renewed interest in 'retrospective taxes', taxes that have an effective date preceding their enactment date.[1] This resurgence partially results from the implications of the pandemic, including windfall private-sector profits and stressed public-sector finances. Canada[2] and Italy,[3] for instance, have introduced retrospective windfall taxes on banks; Greece,[4] Luxembourg,[5] and the Netherlands[6] have proposed or introduced retrospective windfall taxes on energy and electricity producers; and the European Commission has recommended that all of its members implement windfall energy profits taxes, which are difficult to implement without a retrospective component.[7] The resurgence also results from growing concerns about tax avoidance. Most notoriously, the UK government implemented a controversial 'loan charge' in 2019 that imposed a retrospective tax on an aggressive tax planning scheme that dated back to 1999.[8] At least ten suicides have been attributed to the tax.[9] And more recently, the Labour Party in the UK has proposed a retrospective tax on private school fees in order to remedy a tax plan that enables taxpayers to avoid consumption tax by pre-paying 12 years of school fees at once.[10]

Retrospective taxes of this sort are subject to voluminous literature in law. The most common view is that retrospective taxes breach Fuller and Raz's prospectivity requirement, which provides that laws should only apply on a going-forward basis. Loomer, for example, argues that retrospective tax laws 'grossly violate the minimum requirements of the rule of law'[11] because it is 'impossible for subjects to comply with or rely upon laws which are unannounced and retroactive'.[12] Prebble et al. similarly argue that retrospective tax laws 'will never be desirable' because 'retrospectivity erodes the law's ability to guide people's actions'.[13] And Sampford, who attaches less weight to the prospectivity

[1] For simplicity, this article uses the term 'retrospective' to describe any tax that has an effective date preceding its enactment date. Some scholars, in contrast, use the term 'retroactive'. Others draw a distinction between 'retroactive' laws and 'retrospective' laws. See, eg EA Driedger, 'Statutes: Retroactive Retrospective Reflections' (1958) 56 *Canadian Bar Review* 268.

[2] Fall Economic Statement Implementation Act, 2022, SC 2022, c 19, Part VI.2.

[3] EY Global, 'Italy Announces Proposed One-Time Windfall Tax for Banks', 7 August 2023. Available at: www.ey.com/en_gl/tax-alerts/italy-announces-proposed-one-time-windfall-tax-for-banks. The Italian tax applies in 2023, the year it was introduced, but is tied to the value of banks' assets in 2022.

[4] Reuters, 'Windfall Tax Mechanisms on Energy Companies across Europe', 8 December 2022. Available at: www.reuters.com/business/energy/windfall-tax-mechanisms-energy-companies-across-europe-2022-12-08/.

[5] 'Luxembourg Proposes Windfall Tax on Surplus Revenue from Electricity Production', RegFollower, 21 March 2023. Available at: https://regfollower.com/luxembourg-proposes-windfall-tax-on-surplus-revenue-from-electricity-production/.

[6] Reuters, 'Netherlands to Raise $3.2 Billion with Windfall Tax on Fossil Fuel Companies', 1 November 2022. Available at: www.reuters.com/article/idUSL1N31X1HN/#:~:text=Companies%20with%20activities%20in%20the,%2D2021%2C%20the%20ministry%20said.

[7] European Council, 'Council Formally Adopts Emergency Measures to Reduce Energy Prices', 6 October 2022. Available at: www.consilium.europa.eu/en/press/press-releases/2022/10/06/council-formally-adopts-emergency-measures-to-reduce-energy-prices/.

[8] Finance (No 2) Act 2017, Sch 11.

[9] C Gifford, 'HMRC tax crackdown linked to ten suicides is "next Horizon scandal"', *The Telegraph*, 18 Jan 2024. Available at: www.telegraph.co.uk/money/tax/hmrc-tax-crackdown-linked-to-ten-suicides-next-horizon/.

[10] P Wood, 'Labour to Close Private School Loopholes for Avoiding VAT on Fees', iNews, 5 Jan 2024. Available at: https://inews.co.uk/news/labour-crack-down-private-schools-loopholes-avoid-vat-2840549.

[11] G Loomer, 'Taxing Out of Time: Parliamentary Supremacy and Retroactive Tax Legislation' [2006] 1 *British Tax Review* 64, 90.

[12] ibid, 72.

[13] J Prebble, R Prebble and C Vidler Smith, 'Retrospective Legislation: Reliance, the Public Interest, Principles of Interpretation and the Special Case of Anti-Avoidance Legislation' (2006) 22 *New Zealand University Law Review* 307, 334.

requirement than others, still argues 'that greater degrees of retrospectivity are justifiable in inverse proportion to the reasonableness of reliance on existing law'.[14] Some scholars argue that this rule of law concern can be outweighed in specific circumstances by other considerations, such as social welfare, fiscal necessity, or various conceptions of justice.[15] But even then, they argue that the taxes remain inconsistent with the prospectivity requirement, and more broadly, the rule of law.

These scholarly views are nuanced and reflect powerful intuitions about fairness. They rest, however, on a surprisingly fragmented intellectual foundation. At least with respect tax law, Fuller and Raz have conflicting views of the prospectivity requirement. In *The Morality of Law*, Fuller writes that retrospective changes to tax rates and bases comply with the prospectivity requirement, so long as the deadline for paying the new amount lies in the future.[16] Retrospective taxes of this type are permissible because they merely impose future liability on the 'basis of events occurring in the past', whereas retrospective taxes without a future payment window 'order[] a man to pay taxes yesterday'.[17] Fuller does not articulate a precise rationale for this view, but the most obvious explanation is that laws imposing past duties, such as a past duty to pay taxes, are problematic because actors cannot retrospectively change their behaviour to comply with the duty. I will call this view the *compliance conception* of prospectivity because it insists that taxpayers have an opportunity to comply with their duties under the law. On this view, most retrospective taxes, such as windfall taxes on past profits[18] and remedial taxes on otherwise permissible tax-avoidance schemes[19] are compatible with the prospectivity requirement because they typically provide taxpayers with a window to fulfil their new obligations.

In contrast, Raz suggests that most or all retrospective tax laws are inconsistent with the prospectivity requirement because they 'shatter [] … the appearance of stability and certainty which encourages people to rely and plan on the basis of the existing law'.[20] Raz argues that these reliance interests are particularly important in taxation because 'knowledge of at least the general outlines and sometimes even of details of tax law and company law are often important for business plans which will bear fruit only years later'. On this view, retrospective laws imposing new obligations on the basis of past actions are problematic because actors cannot retrospectively change their actions to avoid the obligation. I will call Raz's view the *reliance conception* of prospectivity because it insists that taxpayers should be able to rely on the law as it stood at the time they acted.

The choice between these competing conceptions has at least two implications for modern debates on retrospective tax laws. First, the common claim that retrospective tax laws are necessarily inconsistent with the rule of law requires qualification. When the Canadian Bar Association, for instance, recently condemned new 'taxes on transactions that have already taken place … as a breach of the rule of law', it explained that

[14] C Sampford, *Retrospectivity and the Rule of Law* (New York: Oxford University Press, 2006) 91.
[15] See, eg Prebble et al, above n 13.
[16] L Fuller, *The Morality of Law* (New Haven CT: Yale University Press, 1964) 59–60.
[17] ibid.
[18] See, eg Fall Economic Statement Implementation Act, 2022, SC 2022, c 19, Part VI.2.
[19] See, eg Finance (No 2) Act 2017, Sch 11.
[20] J Raz, *The Authority of Law: Essays on Law and Morality* (New York: Oxford University Press, 1979) 222.

the problem with these laws was that taxpayers could not 'foresee the consequences of their conduct in order that [they] be given fair notice of what to avoid'.[21] This view implicitly adopts the reliance conception of prospectivity without noting that retrospective tax laws of this type may be permissible under Fuller's compliance conception. The compliance conception is commonly overlooked in tax debates because scholars and practitioners focus on Fuller's more general writings on prospectivity, rather than his specific application to taxation.

Second, either the compliance or reliance conception must be justified. Justification is obviously important if, as Weinrib and others argue, a law loses its authoritative force if it fails to comply with the rule of law.[22] But it is also important even if rule of law considerations can be outweighed by social welfare considerations, such that the policy acceptability of retrospective laws typically turns on social welfare. The claim that a law is inconsistent with the rule of law has significant normative and expressive force, even if the rule of law is just one factor that governments should ultimately consider.

In this chapter, I compare and weigh possible justifications for compliance and reliance conceptions of prospectivity. While there are many other theories of both prospectivity and the rule of law,[23] these two conceptions are of special significance to tax scholars. Most tax scholarship on prospectivity – especially condemnations of retrospective tax laws – cites Fuller and Raz rather than other authors. And Fuller and Raz's accounts of prospectivity expressly address taxation, whereas many other accounts are primarily concerned with criminal law or other expressly regulatory fields.

This chapter advances three claims. The first is that both conceptions of prospectivity entail some uncomfortable consequences. The compliance conception fails to condemn certain retrospective tax laws that almost certainly impair the autonomy and dignity of individuals. The reliance conception has the opposite problem in that it condemns certain retrospective laws that do not meaningfully affect autonomy or dignity.

The second claim is that it is not obvious that the reliance conception should be preferred, even though many modern treatments of retrospectivity implicitly adopt it. While the compliance conception permits forms of retrospectivity that are almost certainly unfair, its rationale is coherent and fits comfortably within the family of 'thin' rule of law theories that condemn some, but not all, injustices.[24] The reliance conception's rationale, in contrast, sets an impossibly high standard that most modern laws, even prospective laws, fail to meet. In this respect, the reliance conception is incompatible with modern governance.

[21] Canadian Bar Association, 'Taxes Should Not Be Retroactive', 18 August 2023. Available at: https://www.cba.org/Our-Work/cbainfluence/Submissions/2023/August/Taxes-should-not-be-retroactive#:~:text=%E2%80%9CRetroactive%20tax%20legislation%20seeks%20to,law%2C%E2%80%9D%20the%20Section%20says.

[22] EJ Weinrib, *Reciprocal Freedom: Private Law and Public Right* (New York: Oxford University Press, 2022) 185.

[23] See, eg A Ripstein, 'The Rule of Law and Time's Arrow' in LM Austin and D Klimchuk (eds), *Private Law and the Rule of Law* (Oxford: Oxford University Press, 2014) 306, 308; J Finnis, *Natural Law & Natural Rights*, 2nd edn (Oxford: Oxford University Press, 2011) 270–81; TRS Allen, *Constitutional Justice: A Liberal Theory of the Rule of Law* (Oxford: Oxford University Press, 2003) 61–88.

[24] For review of 'thin' versus 'thick' theories of the rule of law, see Lindsay, Chapter 3 in this volume; and Daly, Chapter 2 in this volume.

The third claim is that the broad condemnation of retrospective laws that is common in tax scholarship requires either re-assessment or new justification. It is surprisingly difficult to generate a satisfying rule-of-law rationale for sweeping condemnations of retrospective tax laws.

To set out these claims, this chapter has three parts. Parts I and II set out the rationales and limitations of the compliance and reliance conceptions. Part III advances a comparative argument for preferring the compliance conception and considers the implications for a number of contemporary debates on retrospectivity, including windfall profits taxes, remedial taxes, reversals in judicial tax precedent, and restorative legislation that retrospectively fixes the manner and/or form of tax laws.

The Compliance Conception

It is possible to construct a rationale for the compliance conception that consists of a general and a specific claim. The general claim is that the rule of law's formal requirements condemns laws that impose 'impossible duties' – duties that necessarily cannot be fulfilled by the people to which they apply. The specific claim is that the prospectivity requirement condemns a specific instance of impossibility – laws that impose past obligations. This section sets out the general and specific claims, shows how they combine to create a reasonably administrable conception of prospectivity, and then considers the implications of a seemingly problematic retrospective law that the compliance conception fails to condemn.

The General Claim

The general claim that the rule of law condemns laws imposing impossible duties consists of two premises and two inferences. The premises are (1) that the formal requirements identify at least some of the necessary conditions for a rule to function as law; and (2) laws are rules that regulate conduct through the imposition of duties (prohibitions and obligations). If these premises are correct, we can infer that rules imposing 'impossible' duties fail to function as 'law' in two respects: (1) they are ineffective at regulating conduct, since individuals cannot intentionally conform their conduct to the law; and (2) they fail to impose a true 'duty', since there cannot be a duty to do something that is impossible.

Each of these premises and inferences are contestable, but for the purposes of this chapter, it is sufficient to note that they are reasonable claims. The premise that the formal requirements set out at least some of the minimum requirements of law is foundational to many theories of the rule of law. Oakeshott, for example, argues that the formal requirements are 'conditions which distinguish a legal order' from a non-legal order.[25] Weinrib similarly claims that 'prescriptions' that fail the formal requirements

[25] M Oakeshott, 'The Rule of Law' in M Oakeshott, *On History and Other Essays* (Oxford: Basil Blackwell, 1983) 119, 140.

'cannot function as authoritative norms'.[26] While Oakeshott and Weinrib might contest some of the thicker theories which argue that 'law' must also satisfy many other values that lie outside of the formal requirements, our premise sidesteps this debate with the modest qualification that the formal requirements identify *at least some of* the necessary conditions for a rule to function as law.

Similarly, the premise that the law's function is to regulate conduct through the imposition of duties finds broad support in legal scholarship. For example, Zipursky, in applying Fuller's eight 'desiderata', or formal requirements, to tort law, notes that 'the idea at the root of Fuller's brilliant argument is that real law is a kind of governance that works by treating subjects as capable of altering their conduct because they grasp that there is a rule with which they are expected to comply'.[27] Green similarly claims that there cannot be law without duties since all legal rules either impose duties or can be understood only in 'reference to' other legal rules that impose duties.[28] While it might be objected that legal rules sometimes serve an expressive, rather than regulatory, function,[29] it is fair to question whether a jurisdiction with laws that are entirely expressive (with no regulatory component or rules of conduct) actually has 'law'.

The inference that laws imposing impossible duties are ineffective at regulating behaviour is, with some qualification, similarly reasonable. Assuming that compliance is binary (an individual complies with a law or not), a law that imposes impossible duties cannot change conduct in the intended way.[30] For this reason, Fuller includes 'laws requiring the impossible' as one of the eight ways in which a rule can fail to be 'law'.[31] In his account, impossible duties have a 'brutal pointlessness'.[32]

The remaining inference – that impossible duties are not true duties – also stands on arguable grounds. On an intuitive level, there is an inherent unfairness in saying that someone failed to comply with a duty that was impossible to satisfy. The challenge is precisely identifying the basis for this intuition. Joseph Raz relies on the concept of obedience. In his account of the rule of law, he argues that 'the law must be capable of being obeyed,' and that a person 'obeys the law only if part of his reason for conforming is his knowledge of the law'.[33] Applying this concept, actors can only obey the law if 'they can find out what it is and act on it'.[34] Weinrib similarly argues that the 'practical impossibility … of complying with the state's prescriptions precludes the obedience due to them as law', but grounds this argument in the notion of Kantian freedom, which is 'disrespect[ed]' by the imposition of duties that are 'impossible to fulfil'.[35] Both of these conceptions suggest that duties can only exist if the duty-bearer has a degree of agency

[26] Weinrib, above n 22, 185.
[27] BC Zipursky, 'The Inner Morality of Private Law' (2013) 58:1 *American Journal of Jurisprudence* 27, 35.
[28] L Green, 'The Forces of Law: Duty, Coercion, and Power' (2016) 29(2) *Ratio Juris* 164, 166–67.
[29] ES Anderson and RH Pildes, 'Expressive Theories of Law: A General Restatement' (2000) 148 *University of Pennsylvania Law Review* 1503.
[30] For claims that retrospective law is ineffective at changing behaviour, see Fuller, above n 16, 53; Weinrib, above n 22, 185; Prebble, Prebble and Smith, above n 13, 310.
[31] Fuller, above n 16, 39, 70.
[32] ibid. 71. See also Weinrib, above n 22, 185.
[33] Raz, above n 20, 213–14.
[34] ibid. 214.
[35] Weinrib, above n 22, 185.

in choosing whether or not to fulfil the duty. Regardless of the precise articulation, it is fair to question whether duties that cannot be fulfilled are true duties.

In combination, these premises and inferences create a coherent claim that the formal requirements protect compliance interests. The primary objection relates to scope. Almost all laws raise compliance issues of a sort. Some individuals, for example, will be unable to satisfy prospective tax liabilities because of inability to pay, either because they have earned too little or spent too much, just as some individuals will fail to comply with criminal prohibitions due to factors partially within their control (choice) and partially without (genetically or environmentally influenced behaviours). If the protection of compliance interests condemns all or much of tax and criminal law, there is likely a problem with the general claim.

This objection has merit, but it is possible to distinguish between laws that impose impossible duties and laws that raise the more typical compliance issues that are commonly seen in tax and criminal law. The distinction relates to degree and type. With respect to degree, laws imposing duties that are necessarily impossible for *any* individual to intentionally fulfil fall at a different point on the probability spectrum than laws that raise typical compliance issues. It is possible for the rule of law to condemn laws that extinguish compliance interests without condemning laws that have more modest effects on the probability of compliance. The precise location of the dividing line is, of course, challenging to identify, but the line nevertheless serves as a limiting factor.

With respect to type, there is a difference between duties that are impossible to perform because there is no temporal window in which to perform them and duties that are impossible to perform because of some factor connected to an individual's choices (or to the blurry line between determinism and choice). For example, it may be impossible for a taxpayer to pay an income tax debt today because they overspent yesterday, but the decision to overspend yesterday is plausibly related to choice. To the extent that the decision to overspend was not a free choice, either because of environmental or genetic factors, the duty to pay the income tax debt may raise rule of law concerns. But the degree of agency that should be ascribed to people is a broader question that permeates all aspects of law's regulatory function, not just the prospectivity requirement.

In both respects (degree and type), the rule of law can offer protection to compliance interests without condemning all laws that raise any degree of compliance problems.

The Specific Claim

The specific claim is that the prospectivity requirement condemns laws that impose past duties because past duties are impossible duties. Most obviously, individuals cannot go back in time to change their actions to comply with duties imposed retrospectively. And even if their past actions fulfil their duty by chance, their compliance with the law was not 'knowing' or intentional. In this respect, the law imposing the duty fails to influence behaviour or impose a 'true' duty.

There are two related objections. The first is that individuals might anticipatorily comply with retrospective duties. The problem here is that the mechanics of anticipatory compliance are challenging. Individuals can anticipatorily comply only if they (1) anticipate that future laws might have retrospective application; (2) anticipate the duties that the future retrospective laws might impose; and (3) comply, in advance, with the yet-to-be-imposed duties. The first condition is arguably satisfied in jurisdictions that have a long history of imposing retrospective laws. The second and third, however, are more problematic. In most cases, there are simply too many potential duties for actors to foresee all of them. Even if all potential duties can be foreseen with clarity, compliance may not be possible. For example, satisfying a near-infinite number of potential duties would require a near-infinite amount of time and energy; some of the potential duties may conflict, such as simultaneous requirements to perform and not perform the same action; and the conditions necessary for the fulfilment of the duty may not yet exist. On this last point, consider taxpayers, who, anticipating the future imposition of a retrospective capital gains tax, seek to prepay the tax to the government. The government's administrative apparatus may not accept the payment or may simply treat it as a donation and refuse to credit the amount against future tax debts.

The second objection is that it is possible to conceive of laws that impose retrospective duties that are not necessarily impossible duties. For example, a government may announce on Monday that it will enact a capital gains tax on Wednesday that retrospectively requires payment on Tuesday (the day before enactment). Taxpayers here have advance notice of their payment obligation. An arguable real-world example occurs when governments retrospectively re-enact tax laws that have been previously nullified by the courts due to manner and form violations.[36] These cases are challenging for the compliance conception because (1) taxpayers had prior notice of their obligation (through the now nullified tax law) and (2) may have already paid their liability (in response to the now-nullified law).

Difficult analytical work is needed to determine whether either of these examples, despite imposing retrospective duties, satisfy the compliance conception. If they do, the compliance conception has a modest problem with 'fit': the specific claim's condemnation of *all* laws imposing retrospective duties does not follow from the general claim. Significantly, however, if duties of this type do exist, they are relatively infrequent. In contrast, the reliance conception has a much more pronounced problem with fit, which will be discussed in Part II of this chapter.

Administration

The administration of the compliance conception is relatively straightforward in most cases. Two brief examples illustrate this. In Example 1, a government enacts a new law on 1 January 2023 that retrospectively imposes a 40% tax on all capital gains earned in 2020. The law provides that taxpayers have until 31 December 2023 to pay. In Example 2, the government enacts a nearly identical law on 1 January 2023, with the sole difference that taxpayers are required to have paid their new obligation by the now-past date of 31 December 2020. Taxpayers who failed to anticipatorily pay the new liability have breached their obligation to pay their taxes on time and are potentially liable for interest and penalty payments.

[36] See the discussion of *Eurig Estate (Re)* [1998] 2 SCR 565 below.

The compliance conception holds that the law in Example 2 breaches the prospectivity requirement because it imposes an impossible duty: individuals in 2023 cannot possibly change their past actions to comply with the obligation to pay the capital gains tax in 2020. In contrast, the law in Example 1 satisfies the compliance conception because individuals in 2023 have a full year to pay the new tax. In general, a law will satisfy the compliance conception if the duty it imposes is to be fulfilled at a date following the law's enactment.

Epistemically difficult cases can potentially arise, but they do not implicate the prospectivity requirement itself. For example, a new tax law that sets a payment deadline of five minutes after enactment may not provide taxpayers with enough time to actually learn of and fulfil their obligation. In this respect, the law, while imposing a prospective duty, raises the same problems as a law that imposes a retrospective duty. In cases like this, the general claim supporting the compliance conception – laws cannot impose impossible duties – calls for an epistemically challenging definition of sufficient notice. However, the specific claim supporting the compliance conception – that the prospectivity requirement condemns laws that impose past obligations – is not implicated because the law technically applies prospectively.

Limitations

The chief limitation of the compliance conception is that it fails to condemn retrospective laws that interfere with meaningful reliance interests. A brief non-tax example can illustrate. Consider an 18-year-old who performs two years of community service work solely because it will provide her with an exemption from a two-year term of military service. The government then retrospectively eliminates the community service exemption one day after she finishes her term. She is now required to complete two years of military service. The 18-year-old can reasonably claim that, but for the community service exemption, she would have chosen to spend the previous two years doing something more personally meaningful or, alternatively, would have completed the military service instead of the community service, so that she would be free to spend the next two years doing something more personally meaningful. In this respect, the retrospective law has disrupted her reliance interests in existing law and, in turn, offended her autonomy and arguably her dignity. She has made a choice (to perform community service) that relates to a meaningful interest (how she spends two years of her time) in reliance on a pre-existing law that has been retrospectively repealed.

The compliance conception cannot condemn this example because the obligation that is imposed by the retrospective law – to complete two years of military service – lies in the future. This uncomfortable implication is not necessarily a fatal problem. There is a robust scholarly debate over how 'thin' or 'thick' the rule of law is. Unless the rule of law is so 'thick' that it encompasses all that is required by fairness, the objection that a particular conception permits some instances of unfairness is not in itself determinative. Nevertheless, the compliance conception would be easier to wholeheartedly embrace if it condemned certain obvious instances of unfairness.

The Reliance Conception

Raz's reliance conception of prospectivity is based on the claim that harms to reliance interests 'offend dignity in expressing disrespect for people's autonomy'.[37] When fully articulated, it has three components: (1) the rule of law's formal requirements, including the prospectivity requirement, collectively condemn laws that offend autonomy and dignity; (2) laws that disrupt reliance interests offend autonomy and dignity; and (3) retrospective laws, including retrospective tax laws, disrupt reliance interests. Notably, this conception is broad enough that it probably can also condemn laws that harm compliance interests, since the imposition of impossible duties is probably inconsistent with autonomy and dignity. In this respect, the reliance conception is much broader than the compliance conception in that it condemns retrospective laws that impose either past obligations *or* future obligations.

In this Part, I critique the reliance conception's three-part rationale. The first claim – that autonomy and dignity are central to the rule of law – is sufficiently complex that it is not possible to examine here, beyond noting that a number of scholars argue that autonomy and dignity are, and should be, central to public law[38] and private law.[39] The second and third claims, however, are problematic for two reasons. First, if the second claim – the disruption of reliance interests offends autonomy and dignity, and in turn, the rule of law – is true, most laws, including necessary and uncontroversial *prospective* laws, offend the rule of law. Since this implication is unpalatable, the second claim is either mistaken or of no normative significance. Second, when the second claim is substantially qualified to address these unpalatable implications, it can no longer justify the third claim that retrospective laws necessarily contravene the rule of law. This Part concludes by briefly critiquing two alternative justifications for the reliance conception.

Unpalatable Implications

The first objection has three parts: (1) most laws, including prospective laws, disrupt reliance interests; (2) if the rule of law condemns most prospective laws, the rule of law is incompatible with law's regulatory function; and (3) since this implication is unpalatable, the second claim that laws contravene the rule of law if they disrupt reliance interests is either mistaken or of no normative significance.

First, a variant of an example that has been developed, for other purposes, in the law and economics literature can illustrate how most laws, even prospective laws, harm reliance interests.[40] In Example A, the government enacts a law on 1 January 2023 that

[37] Raz, above n 20, 222.

[38] J Weinrib, *Dimensions of Dignity: The Theory of and Practice of Modern Constitutional Law* (New York: Cambridge University Press, 2016).

[39] Weinrib, above n 22.

[40] See M Graetz, 'Legal Transitions: The Case of Retroactivity in Income Tax Revision' (1977) 126 *University of Pennsylvania Law Review* 47, 57–58; Louis Kaplow, 'An Economic Analysis of Legal Transitions' (1986) 99 *Harvard Law Review* 509, 515–19.

retrospectively imposes a 40 per cent tax on all capital gains earned in 2022 and sets a future payment deadline of 31 December 2023. In Example B, the government enacts a law on 1 January 2023 that imposes a 40 per cent tax on all capital gains earned in 2023 and sets a future payment deadline of 31 December 2024. In Example C, the government enacts a law on 1 January 2023 that imposes a 40 per cent tax on all capital gains earned in 2025 and sets a future payment deadline of 31 December 2026.

Only the law in Example A is retrospective, but all three laws disrupt reliance interests. In Example A, some taxpayers will have previously invested in capital assets in reliance on the pre-existing tax exemption for capital gains. In Example B, taxpayers have no advance notice of the imposition of a capital gains tax, which means that they cannot sell their capital assets before the tax comes into effect. In Example C, taxpayers have an opportunity to sell their capital assets before the capital gains tax comes into effect, but the impending capital gains tax will almost certainly decrease the price that they receive for their capital assets. If the taxpayers in Example A can claim that they would not have purchased capital assets but for the pre-existing tax exemption, so too can the taxpayers in Examples B and C.

If we accept the claim that the disruption of reliance interests offends autonomy and dignity, and in turn, the rule of law, then most laws with prospective application will contravene the rule of law, even laws that are relatively uncontroversial. Consider the following examples in which a seemingly reasonable policy change undermines the reliance interests of actors: (1) new subsidies for the purchase of electric vehicles harm the reliance interests of automakers who have invested in the production of carbon-emitting vehicles in reliance on a neutral competitive landscape; (2) a change in a central bank's inflation target from 2% to 5% harms the interests of the many actors who have made decisions in reliance on a low-interest-rate environment, such as investors who have purchased non-inflation protected bonds or retirees who have purchased non-inflation protected annuities; (3) changes to zoning rules to permit ten-storey buildings in a residential neighbourhood of single-storey bungalows harm the interests of sun-loving gardeners who have purchased properties in the neighbourhood because of the low building heights; and (4) the introduction of special assessments, land value capture taxes, or increased property taxes to pay for existing infrastructure harms the reliance interests of property owners who purchased property with the benefits of the existing infrastructure capitalised into the purchase price. Some of these legal changes, of course, may be challenged on other grounds, such as planning law or competition law, but if they are impermissible on reliance grounds there is little room for legislative action.

Second, this implication is incompatible with law's regulatory function and, more broadly, modern governance. Legal changes like the changes in the examples above are necessary so that law can respond to new problems or changed circumstances. The reliance rationale means that it is impossible or nearly impossible for governments to satisfy the rule of law unless they forgo legal change. This implication is particularly problematic if law, and its regulatory function, serve (or should serve) the broader purpose of protecting autonomy and dignity, as some scholars argue. For instance, changes to zoning rules might advance autonomy and dignity by creating housing for the homeless, but the rule of law would condemn this change, also on the grounds of human dignity, for disrupting the reliance interests of gardeners.

Third and finally, these unpalatable implications present a dilemma for the claim that laws contravene the rule of law if they disrupt reliance interests: either the claim is mistaken, or it is of no normative significance. On the latter point, the claim that retrospective tax laws breach the rule of law has little force if disrupting reliance interests is a necessary and unavoidable part of governance.

One response to this line of argument is that the rule of law is just an ideal or an aspiration that should guide government behaviour. Both Raz and Fuller claim that compliance with the formal requirements is (1) a matter of degree[41] and (2) not always desirable because the formal requirements can be outweighed by other considerations, such as efficiency, distributive justice, and political feasibility.[42] On this view, the impossibility of always protecting reliance interests is not necessarily a problem.

This response raises a question about the purpose of the formal requirements. If the purpose is to set out a series of factors that governments should consider when enacting laws, Raz and Fuller's view seems to naturally follow. If, in contrast, the purpose is to set out a series of precise conditions that rules must satisfy to be 'law', then the view does not. Unfortunately, the choice between these two views is so foundational that it cannot be resolved, or even properly canvassed, in this essay. Nevertheless, it is possible to note that the response is quite limiting for debates on retrospectivity in taxation. If the rule of law sets out an impossible aspiration, it cannot be used to condemn *all* laws that fail to satisfy the aspiration. At a minimum, condemnation needs to be reserved for a smaller subset of laws, as discussed further below.

A Qualified Reliance Rationale

An alternative response to the objection above is to develop a limiting principle. For example, the rule of law might only condemn laws that substantially disrupt reliance interests; substantially offend autonomy and dignity; or offend autonomy and dignity to the minimum extent necessary. The challenge with this approach is that each of these limiting principles is unlikely to track the retrospectivity/prospectivity distinction. Other things equal, a retrospective law is likely to have a greater impact on reliance interests than a prospective one, but many other factors will influence the harm to reliance interests. For example, a prospective law imposing a large capital gains tax increase as of today is likely to have a much greater effect on reliance interests than a retrospective tax increase of $1. A qualified reliance rationale is unlikely to justify a blanket prospectivity requirement.

This problem is particularly evident in taxation. Many retrospective tax statutes change the legal form of transactions in ways that either do not affect reliance interests or do not meaningfully affect autonomy and dignity. Consider a variation on the famous case of *IRC v Duke of Westminster*.[43] The duke decides to hire a large number of personal servants regardless of cost. Since he prefers to reduce his taxes when he can,

[41] Raz, above n 20, 211 (although, with respect to prospectivity, Raz claims that a 'law is either retrospective or not', at 215); Fuller, above n 16, 41.

[42] Raz, above n 20, 228–29; Fuller, ibid 53–54.

[43] *IRC v Duke of Westminster* [1936] AC 1.

he pays his new servants through tax-deductible gifts under deeds of covenant rather than through non-deductible salaries. After the servants have worked for three months, the UK Parliament retrospectively changes the law to deny the deduction for gifts made under deed of covenant. The duke and all the other taxpayers in the same position are given one year to pay their new tax liability.

From a rule-of-law perspective, the duke cannot say that he relied on the deductibility of the gifts in deciding to hire the servants, since the example posits that he would have made the hires regardless of tax treatment. The duke can only argue that he relied on the existing tax law in choosing the *legal form* of the hires. But the duke surely does not have a meaningful dignity or autonomy interest in legal form itself. Apart from the tax consequences, it is immaterial to him whether his employees are paid through salary or gift. Since a substantial portion of tax planning focuses on the legal form of actions, rather than the actions themselves, many retrospective tax laws do not affect autonomy and dignity interests. Whenever a taxpayer decides to withdraw money from a corporation, transfer money between corporations, or fund a corporation, she must choose between a variety of options with different legal characterisations. While a retrospective tax law might change the legal characterisation of the option they have chosen, it does not frustrate their intention of withdrawing money, transferring money or funding the corporation.

Alternative Rationales

There are two related rationales for the condemnation of laws that impose future obligations based on past actions. Both rationales are related to reliance and arguably identify rule-of-law problems, but, like the reliance rationale, neither can justify the blanket condemnation of retrospective laws.

The first alternative, which Raz raises, is that the imposition of future obligations on the basis of past actions is, in some cases, a form of 'entrapment' that amounts to an abuse of power.[44] Imagine a government announces a 'sales tax holiday' for the month of January to stimulate the economy. Consumers rush out to make unplanned purchases to take advantage. In February, the government announces that purchases made in January are retrospectively subject to sales tax at twice the normal rate. If the imposition of the retrospective tax increase was planned all along, the sales tax holiday was an act of deception.

There is merit to this rationale, but it is also subject to a qualification. Laws that deliberately entrap taxpayers are, in practice, only a small subset of the broader category of laws that impose future obligations on the basis of past actions. Moreover, entrapment is especially unlikely in taxation, since a government can always raise equivalent additional revenues without entrapping taxpayers. In our example, for instance, the government could retrospectively double the sales tax rate without first deceptively inducing increased expenditures. Alternatively, the government could impose a prospective head tax on all individuals, regardless of past action. The presence of viable alternatives reduces the likelihood of deliberate entrapment in taxation.

[44] Raz, above n 20, 222.

The second rationale is that the failure to protect reliance interests interferes with compliance interests. This argument can take two forms, both of which address reliance on the conditions giving rise to tax liability. The first, and less persuasive, form is that laws that retrospectively change the conditions giving rise to tax liability are incompatible with the prospectivity requirement because actors cannot retrospectively change their actions to 'comply' with the conditions. The problem with this argument, as noted briefly in Part I of this chapter, is that the conditions giving rise to obligations are not in themselves duties. More broadly, a central principle of modern tax policy is that the conditions giving rise to tax liability should maintain 'neutrality' by *not* changing behaviour. In this respect, the conditions giving rise to tax liability have the opposite purpose of legal duties.[45]

The second, more persuasive form of this argument is that retrospective changes to the conditions giving rise to tax liability impair actors' capacity to pay their tax obligations. When the conditions giving rise to a tax obligation are stable, actors can anticipate their tax liability and start saving to pay their tax bill. An individual who sells a capital asset in a jurisdiction with a pre-existing capital gains tax, for example, knows that he should save a portion of the proceeds to pay his tax. In contrast, when the capital gains tax is enacted after the date of sale, the individual may already have consumed or dispersed the proceeds and be unable to pay his tax liability.

The main limitation with this argument is that it is highly contingent. Some individuals will have insufficient funds on hand because of the retrospective change, but others will not; and of those with insufficient funds on hand, some will not be able to earn or access additional funds in time, but others will. In this respect, the argument differs from the compliance conception, which condemns the imposition of past obligations because they are *necessarily* ineffective and *necessarily* impossible to fulfil.

In sum, the reliance rationale and its alternatives struggle to justify the condemnation of all retrospective tax laws. Either the reliance rationale is unqualified, in which case it has unpalatable implications; or it is qualified, in which case it cannot generate the blanket prohibition on retrospectivity that is so commonly proposed.

Implications for Contemporary Debates

The previous Parts reveal that powerful intuitions lie behind the compliance and reliance conceptions, but that both arguably have problems with scope: the compliance conception is quite narrow and the reliance conception is quite broad. If we are to choose one or the other, the compliance conception's weakness – failure to condemn certain unfair laws – is probably more palatable. It is at least consistent with 'thin' approaches to the rule of law that set out minimum requirements for legality. In contrast, the reliance conception's incompatibility with modern governance is probably fatal regardless of whether a thin or thick theory is preferred, since the rule of law must not make governance by law impossible.

This Part considers the implications of the compliance conception for retrospective tax statutes and judicial decisions. In general, the compliance conception is less

[45] 'Sin' taxes on harmful goods or services are the exception.

friendly to taxpayers than the reliance conception, but more friendly than current judicial doctrines. Case law in Canada,[46] the United States,[47] and the United Kingdom[48] currently permits retrospective tax laws of any sort, even laws that impose past obligations, although there is often an interpretive presumption against retrospectivity.

Two preliminary qualifications are necessary. First, applying the compliance conception sometimes requires engaging in challenging theoretical debates, such as whether the law is 'made' or 'discovered'. In these instances, it is not possible to do more than note that the compliance conception requires very different analysis than the reliance conception.

The second, and more challenging qualification, is that there are possible alternatives to both the compliance and reliance conceptions. One alternative is to find a middle conception of prospectivity that protects compliance interests and some, but not all, reliance interests. For example, if Raz is correct that the rule of law seeks to protect autonomy and dignity, then retrospective laws imposing past or future obligations contravene the rule of law if they violate autonomy or dignity. A dignity conception of prospectivity almost certainly condemns laws imposing past obligations and some laws imposing future obligations, such as the military service example set out above. But it probably permits a retrospective law denying the Duke of Westminster the benefits of his clever tax plan.

A dignity approach requires difficult analytical work that is beyond the scope of this chapter. Among other issues, it can be challenging to determine whether a particular retrospective tax law affects autonomy and dignity, both for conceptual reasons (eg can the loss of money affect dignity?) and empirical reasons (if yes, how much?). These problems are particularly acute when the taxpayer is a legal fiction like a corporation or a trust. A dignity approach also raises the question of 'whose dignity matters'? Retrospective taxes on corporations, for instance, affect the corporate actor, then the shareholders who own the corporation, and maybe even the corporation's employees and business partners. Each of these actors may be affected in different ways.

Significantly, however, the adoption of a dignity approach would not disturb the general conclusion that sweeping condemnations of retrospective tax laws are problematic. A dignity approach requires case-by-case assessment of each retrospective tax law to determine the specific interests affected by the law and the degree of impact. This approach is very different than the condemnations of retrospectivity that are common in tax law.

Retrospective Statutes

Statutes that retrospectively change tax law can be divided into at least four categories: (1) statutes that change tax objectives or policies; (2) remedial statutes that close tax loopholes to preserve existing tax objectives or policies; (3) restorative statutes that

[46] *Air Canada v British Columbia* [1989] 1 SCR 1161, 1192.

[47] *United States v Carlton* 512 US 26 (1994).

[48] *Phillips v Eyre* (1870) 6 QBD 1, 23; see also, E Fletcher, 'Retrospective Fiscal Legislation' (1959) 6 *British Tax Review* 412.

address deficiencies with the manner and/or form of tax laws; and (4) tax statutes that are retrospective to their date of introduction in the legislature. Since each of these categories raises distinct questions, this Part addresses them separately.

Statutes that Change Tax Objectives or Policies

Governments sometimes retrospectively amend or introduce tax legislation to raise additional revenue. Since the purpose is not punitive, these statutes almost always have a future payment window. One example is windfall profits taxes in which governments seek, after the fact, to increase tax rates on the extraordinary gains that result from extreme, unanticipated events. For instance, the Canadian government recently enacted a windfall profits tax on Canadian banks, known as the 'Canada Recovery Dividend'.[49] Introduced and enacted in 2022, the tax imposed a retrospective 15% tax on each bank's average profits above $1 billion in 2020 and 2021,[50] but permitted banks to pay the tax in five equal instalments between 2022 and 2026.[51] A historical example is the United Kingdom's wartime profits tax in 1915.[52] The tax retrospectively taxed profits from 1914, but gave businesses two months to pay the tax after it was assessed.[53]

Other examples of retrospective taxes with prospective payment periods occur in normal times. For example, the UK's Finance Act 1974, retrospectively increased the surtax rate for certain individuals in the 1972–73 tax period in order to raise additional revenue.[54] The Act satisfied the compliance conception by setting prospective deadlines – 1 July 1974 and 1 January 1975 – for payment of the new liabilities.[55] Similarly, the US Congress retrospectively raised income tax rates in 1918 and 1926 because legislators were unable to reach agreement before the end of the previous tax year. The retrospective legislation included prospective payment windows.[56]

Windfall taxes of this sort are compatible with the compliance conception because they provide taxpayers with an opportunity to comply with their new obligation. In general, the compliance conception provides governments with substantial freedom of action. They can implement almost any retrospective tax policy change, so long as they extend the payment deadline into the future.

Remedial Statutes that Close Tax Loopholes

Governments often retrospectively change tax laws to close loopholes that enterprising taxpayers have discovered. These statutes differ from statutes that change tax objectives or policies in that their intention is to restore an objective or policy that has been disrupted by taxpayers. The compliance conception permits these statutes, but only if they create a prospective obligation to pay the initially avoided tax.

[49] Fall Economic Statement Implementation Act, 2022, SC 2022, c 19, Part VI.2.
[50] ibid, s 191.5(2).
[51] ibid, s 191.5(9).
[52] Finance (No 2) Act 1915, c 89, s 38.
[53] ibid, s 45(1).
[54] Finance Act 1974, c 30 (UK).
[55] ibid, s 8.
[56] *Revenue Act of 1926*, 44 Stat 9 (US); *Revenue Act of 1918*, 40 Stat 1057.

An example is the UK's 2019 'loan charge'.[57] The loan charge was a retrospective tax imposed on employees who had avoided income tax through a plan in which their salaries were paid into employee benefit trusts, which then 'loaned' the amounts to the employees on the implicit understanding that the loans would never be repaid.[58] The 2019 loan charge retrospectively levied a one-time prospective tax on taxpayers who had benefited from one of the 250 variations of the scheme between 1999 and 2019.[59] The loan charge was criticised for breaching the rule of law's prospectivity requirement[60] and was ultimately the subject of an All-Party Parliamentary Group inquiry.[61] Under the compliance conception, however, the loan charge is compatible with the prospectivity requirement because taxpayers were provided with a prospective window to pay.

An example of a law that may run afoul of the compliance conception is a retrospective amendment made by the Canadian Government in 1994 to its General Anti-Avoidance Rule (GAAR).[62] Following a series of judicial decisions in which taxpayers avoided the GAAR's application, the Canadian Parliament amended the GAAR, retrospective to 1988, to restore what it claimed was the GAAR's appropriate scope. Since the effect of the changes was to retrospectively impose an obligation to pay taxes where previously there had been none, the changes breach the compliance conception.

Retrospective Statutes Amending Manner and Form

Retrospective tax laws can be used to re-enact statutes that have been found invalid due to defects with their manner and form. For example, in 1998 the Supreme Court of Canada struck down Ontario's probate tax on estates as an unconstitutional nullity because the tax was implemented by regulation rather than legislation.[63] The Ontario Government responded by enacting retrospective legislation that re-imposed the tax as of the regulation's initial effective date.[64] The result was that taxpayer's were not refunded their previous probate tax payments.

On face, the compliance conception condemns this statute because it imposes a retrospective obligation to pay tax in a situation where there was previously no legally binding obligation. The complication, however, is that taxpayers had a previous opportunity to comply with this new statutory obligation, since the obligation under the invalid regulation was identical. So long as taxpayers believed the regulation was valid, the substitution of the statute for the regulation had no bearing on their capacity to discharge the obligation.

This case is difficult to resolve. The justification for the compliance conception is that laws imposing retrospective obligations are problematic because they (1) are ineffective at changing behaviour and (2) impose duties that are impossible to fulfil. In this case, both problems apply to the statute, since the statute could not possibly have affected

[57] Finance (No 2) Act 2017, Sch 11.
[58] M Blackwell, 'The April 2019 Loan Charge' [2019] 3 *British Tax Review* 240, 242–44.
[59] ibid, 244–46.
[60] ibid, 246–49, 257.
[61] All-Party Parliamentary Group, *Loan Charge Inquiry: April 2019: Final Report* (2019).
[62] Budget Implementation Act, 2004, No 2, SC 2005, s 52 (Can).
[63] *Eurig Estate (Re)* [1998] 2 SCR 565.
[64] Estate Administration Tax Act 1998, SO 1998, c 34, Sch.

taxpayer behaviour or been the object of intentional compliance. But the two problems do not apply to the underlying obligation (to pay the tax), since taxpayers had an (incorrect) belief that the obligation previously existed. Statutes that retrospectively restore constitutionality are challenging because they separate the form of the law (the statute) from the obligation it purports to create.[65]

Statutes Effective as of their Date of Introduction

A common practice in Commonwealth countries is to make tax statutes effective as of their date of introduction in the House of Commons.[66] The rationale is that the often-lengthy parliamentary process would otherwise give taxpayers time to re-arrange their affairs to avoid the forthcoming tax.[67] This practice often escapes contentious debates because at least some authorities define 'retrospective' to mean that a statute's effective date precedes its date of *introduction* in the legislature, rather than its date of enactment.[68] The practice, however, raises similar issues as the other forms of retrospectivity canvassed in this article and therefore deserves brief comment.

Under the compliance conception, the practice is unproblematic, since any obligation to pay lies in the future. The application of the reliance conception is more complex. The conception's rationale – the protection of reliance interests – suggests that this practice is permissible, since taxpayers can change their behaviour to avoid the new tax as of the effective date. If, however, the reliance conception is a blanket condemnation of any form of retrospectivity, as tax scholarship sometimes suggests, then the practice is impermissible. In this respect, the reliance conception once again has a problem with 'fit': it condemns laws that fail to interfere with meaningful reliance interests.

Retrospective Court Rulings

Courts occasionally overrule or alter precedents in a way that retrospectively increases liability for taxpayers. For example, in 2022, the Canadian Supreme Court held that taxpayers could not use equitable remedies, such as recission, to undo transactions that had resulted in unanticipated tax liability.[69] The Supreme Court's decision overturned a number of lower court decisions affirming the right to use equitable remedies. In so doing, the decision raised the possibility that taxpayers who had recently avoided tax

[65] In this respect, retrospective statutes amending manner and form are similar to the Gettier problem in philosophy, which asks whether a person has 'knowledge' if they believe X to be true for justifiable reasons, but X turns out to be true for other reasons. This problem has spurred great controversy in epistemology. EL Gettier, 'Is Justified True Belief Knowledge' (1963) 23(6) *Analysis* 121.

[66] M Bosc and A Gagnon, *House of Commons Procedure and Practice*, 3rd edn (Ottawa: Éditions Yvon Blais, 2017), ch 18.

[67] V Thuronyi, ed, *Tax Law Design and Drafting*, vol 1 (Washington, DC: IMF, 1996) ch 2, 12.

[68] A Seely, 'Retrospective Taxation', House of Commons Briefing Paper No 4369, 27 Aug 2020, 3.

[69] *Canada (Attorney General) v Collins Family Trust*, 2022 SCC 26. The law differs in the UK. See *Pitt v Holt* [2013] UKSC 26; R Gillis, 'The Limits of Legal Substance: Tax Avoidance and Equitable Remedies after *Collins Family Trust*' (2022) 66(3) *Canadian Business Law Journal* 323, 326–27.

liability using equitable remedies would be subject to re-assessment, payment of tax, and compounded interest for previous years' tax returns.

On a straightforward application of the compliance conception, the Supreme Court's decision, and other judicial decisions overturning taxpayer-friendly precedents, breach the compliance conception because they retrospectively impose a tax obligation that did not previously exist. Zipursky, for example, argues that the common law of torts 'flouts' the prospectivity requirement because many landmark decisions, such as *Donoghue v Stevenson*, retrospectively create duties that did not exist at the time the parties acted.[70] The Canadian Supreme Court has similarly refused to apply any conception of the prospectivity requirement outside of criminal law because judicial changes to the common have historically applied retrospectively.[71]

This view, however, is disputed. Weinrib argues that the judicial evolution of tort law complies with the prospectivity requirement. When courts 'announce a new norm that retrospectively imposes an obligation, that obligation arises not out of a legal vacuum, but out of the intimations of legal material antecedently available to and binding on the parties'.[72] In these cases, the court simply 'makes definitive what ought to and could have been done earlier on the basis of the law as it existed earlier'.[73] By analogy, judicial decisions that retrospectively impose tax liability by overturning precedents do not create new tax liability, but merely reveal the liability that has always existed. This approach is reminiscent of the declaratory theory of the common law, which posits that "judge-made law' is actually pre-existing law that judges discover and not something that they create'.[74] As Zamulinski notes, this debate about whether court decisions make or discover law is an enduring one in legal scholarship. Whether the compliance conception condemns retrospective court rulings ultimately turns on its resolution.[75]

Conclusion

The reliance conception of prospectivity is commonly endorsed by tax scholars and lawyers, either expressly or by implication. This chapter argues that the reliance conception's rationale encounters a number of challenges related to scope. One alternative, which has historically hidden in plain sight, is Fuller's compliance conception. The compliance conception is grounded in a coherent account of the rule of law and articulates important intuitions about impossible duties. Its apparent weakness – the failure to condemn certain instances of retrospectivity that appear to impair dignity and autonomy – is arguably less significant than the reliance conception's excessive breadth.

[70] Zipursky, above n 27, 32–33.
[71] *British Columbia v Imperial Tobacco Canada Ltd*, 2005 SCC 49.
[72] Weinrib, above n 22, 205.
[73] ibid.
[74] B Zamulinski, 'Rehabilitating the Declaratory Theory of the Common Law' (2014) *Journal of Law & Courts*, 171–72.
[75] ibid.

This comparative analysis does not necessarily mean that the compliance conception is the only viable or 'best' conception of the prospectivity requirement. As noted in the final Part of this chapter, there are alternatives to both the compliance and reliance conceptions. At a minimum, however, the reliance conception's deficiencies mean that sweeping rule-of-law condemnations of retrospective tax laws require either new justification or reassessment.

5

General Information and Legitimate Expectations in the Context of the Rule of Law: A Multidisciplinary Analysis

TIRZA CRAMWINCKEL

Abstract

This chapter addresses taxpayer communication and issues of legitimate expectations. The Dutch Tax and Customs Administration (DTCA) provides general information to citizens about tax laws, which requires a 'translation process' from tax law to comprehensible information.[1] The DTCA provides general information to citizens about tax laws, which requires a 'translation process' from tax law to comprehensible information. This can lead to miscommunication, because of a trade-off between legal correctness and comprehensibility. The legal protection of taxpayers is based on the doctrine of legitimate expectations. It is argued that the current legal framework for the legal protection regarding the DTCA's duty to inform needs to be re-evaluated to better reflect the citizen's perspective. Communication theories offer inspiring viewpoints for the legal perspective below.

Introduction

In the tax literature it is widely acknowledged that tax authorities have the duty to inform taxpayers about tax laws to help them in their tax matters.[2] In the Netherlands, the tax

[1] The chapter is based on my dissertation, TA Cramwinckel, *Voorlichting door de Belastingdienst in rechtsstatelijke context. Een juridisch en communicatiewetenschappelijk onderzoek naar gewekt vertrouwen [Provision of information by the Dutch Tax and Customs Administration in the context of the rule of law. A legal and communication science study into legitimate expectations]* (Leiden University 2022), to which I refer for more background and references.

[2] Inter alia: RH Happe, *Drie beginselen van fiscale rechtsbescherming [Three principles of tax legal protection (Dissertation Leiden University]* (Deventer, Kluwer, 1996); K Gangl et al, 'How Can I Help You? Perceived Service Orientation of Tax Authorities and Tax Compliance' (2013) 69 *Finanz Archiv/Public Finance Analysis* 487–510; JD Blank and L Osofsky, 'Simplexity: Plain Language and the Tax Law' (2017) 66 *Emory Law Journal 189–264.*

authorities (Dutch Tax and Customs Administration: 'DTCA') do indeed extensively provide general information to the public about the interpretation and application of tax laws to guide taxpayers in their legal rights and obligations, for example in the form of information on their website (www.belastingdienst.nl), by a special telephone line (*Belastingtelefoon*) and in explanations accompanying (digital) tax return forms. In this chapter 'General Information' (in Dutch: *voorlichting*) is defined as information that, unlike an individual tax ruling for instance, is not tailored to the specific circumstances of a particular taxpayer but contains general guidance about the interpretation, implementation or application of tax rules, institutionally embedded within the duty of the DTCA.[3] The aim of such information is to provide clarification, instruction and explanation to taxpayers about tax matters in general terms, for example to help taxpayers fill in their tax returns. In the Dutch legal framework, General Information is perceived as intended to be helpful to taxpayers but in principle, it has no legal status like the tax law itself.

The Problem

In fulfilling its duty to implement and enforce tax laws, the DTCA is faced with the task of 'translating' often complex tax laws into comprehensible and accessible information.[4] By necessity, the DTCA must bridge the gap between 'legal reality' on the one hand and the 'taxpayer's reality' on the other hand. Especially with respect to non-sophisticated taxpayers, such as citizens with relatively little tax knowledge, this translation process requires that tax laws, written in technical language, be presented in an understandable non-technical way. Shortcomings, such as inaccuracies, incompleteness or lack of clarity, may arise in the 'translation process'. This makes General Information a high-risk type of communication.

Problems may arise, for instance, when a taxpayer uses General Information to prepare his or her tax return, this Information proves to be incorrect after the fact, the tax inspector applies the law (instead of that Information) when imposing the tax assessment, and the citizen receives a tax assessment that is higher than expected. This raises the question whether the taxpayer should be able to rely on the Information.

The duty of the tax authorities itself to provide General Information raises fundamental questions in the context of the rule of law, such as: What is the relationship between the democratically legitimised tax law and the 'translation' by the tax authorities as a law enforcement agency? What is the legal protection for taxpayers that rely on the Information provided by the tax authorities instead of the tax law itself? These types of questions instantly reveal that, with respect to the definition of the rule of law, this chapter is based on a relatively thick and wide-scope conception (see further *Legal Basis in the Principles of the Rule of Law*).

[3] General Information seems to share some features with the concept of *guidance* in terms of explanation and information. Key characteristics of General Information are its lack of status (in principle not legally binding), communication style (more comprehensible) and target audience (taxpayers).

[4] See also TA Cramwinckel, 'Lost in Translation? A Multidisciplinary Approach on Legal Issues in Tax Communication', (2016) 74 *The Clarity Journal* 13–17.

What has been overlooked in Dutch academic literature so far is the legal embedding of the DTCA's task to provide General Information, including a critical analysis of the legal consequences.[5] This topic is scientifically, practically and socially of great importance, since most citizens do not read tax laws, but use the more comprehensible information (a 'translation' of the tax law) provided by the tax authorities.[6]

Although this chapter is embedded in and focuses on Dutch tax law, the underlying issue may come into play when tax authorities communicate in more comprehensible language than the underlying source text (the law), leading to questions about the trade-off between *legal correctness* and *comprehensibility*, the need for weighing (sometimes conflicting) interests, and legal protection for taxpayers. Literature indeed shows a cross-jurisdictional relevance, although the specific legal approach depends on the relevant legal system.[7]

Research Question

This chapter explores the tension between the legal perspective and the citizen's perspective with respect to General Information. The aim is to re-evaluate the current Dutch legal approach regarding the doctrine of the principle of legitimate expectations with respect to General Information, with due regard for both the legal perspective and the citizen's perspective. This requires a careful analysis of relevant viewpoints and interests. The research question is:

> Should the application of the principle of legitimate expectations in the provision of General Information by the DTCA to citizens be re-evaluated, and if so, how?

To answer the normative question, an assessment framework is needed. This will be determined based on the underlying values, assumptions and principles of the current legal framework. Moreover, the citizen's perspective will be included in the re-evaluation. This perspective is especially relevant given the intensified legal awareness for the interests of citizens in the context of the wider debate about the relationship between the government and citizens in the Netherlands. To interpret the citizen's perspective, insights from the discipline of language and communication science are used. This approach is particularly suitable, because the provision of General Information is (a form of) communication.

[5] However, Happe, above n 2, provides an extensive Dutch study with respect to the principle of legitimate expectations. International literature, inter alia: A Monroe, 'Hidden in Plain Sight: IRS Publications and a New Path to Tax Reform', vol 1 21 (2017) *Florida Tax Review*' 81–147; Blank and Osofsky above n 2; E Cauble, 'Detrimental Reliance on IRS Guidance', 3 (2015) *Wisconsin Law Review* 421–74; S Daly, *Tax Authority Advice and the Public* (London: Bloomsbury Publishing, 2020).

[6] Office of Tax Simplification, *Guidance for Taxpayers: A Vision for the Future* (October 2018) 8: Very few taxpayers will ever wish to read tax legislation; guidance is the only way in which taxpayers can know and understand what the law means for them in practice', 13; Monroe above n 5, 83: 'Very few taxpayers turn directly to the Internal Revenue Code to determine their federal income tax liability. Instead, taxpayers rely on intermediaries-legal experts, tax return preparers, commercial software, and the IRS-to navigate their annual filing obligations.'; Blank and Osofsky above n 2, 235; JLM Gribnau, 'Belastingen en de burger. Over het burgerperspectief in het belastingrecht' [*Taxes and Citizens. Regarding the Citizen's Perspective in Tax Law*], *Tijdschrift Formeel Belastingrecht* 2018/42, 26.

[7] See also Blank and Osofsky above n 2; Monroe above n 5.

The *legal perspective* is defined as the approach taking Dutch tax law as its starting point. The *citizen's perspective* is defined as the approach taking taxpayers as its starting point, being citizens in their capacity of language users. With respect to the citizen's perspective it should be noted that there are different kinds of taxpayers, from sophisticated to non-sophisticated, varying in terms of recourses, capabilities, knowledge, interests and skills. The focus is on non-sophistic taxpayers, meaning average individuals, with an average, relatively limited, knowledge of (tax) law ('citizens'), since they are a prominent and specific target audience of General Information provided by the DTCA. Moreover, sophisticated taxpayers may have better tools and recourses to mitigate risks in relation to their communication with the tax authorities.

This chapter addresses the legal perspective, the citizens perspective and a confrontation of both perspectives, and closes with final remarks.

The Legal Perspective: The Legal Framework for the DTCA's Duty to Provide General Information

What is the legal framework for the DTCA's duty to provide General Information? Although the (Dutch) legal literature on taxation agrees on the *existence* of that duty and the Dutch Supreme Court explicitly refers to the DTCA's 'duty to inform'[8] (*voorlichtende taak*), hardly any theory is available on what that duty entails and what information is expected to provide from a legal perspective. Why and, on what grounds and with what level of discretion is the DTCA expected to inform citizens? What are the quality requirements for the provision of information? These questions will be addressed below.

The 'Why': Legal Basis for the DTCA's Duty to Inform in the Rule of Law

Three related arguments should primarily be identified as to why the DTCA provides General Information to the public.

Three Arguments: Fundamental, Practical and Policy

The first argument is of a *fundamental* nature: in short, the DTCA should provide General Information because of its institutional position (the executive power in the constitutional system of separation of powers and checks and balances[9]). The second argument is of a *practical* nature: General Information is practically useful and necessary in the practice of taxation, both for taxpayers and the DTCA. The third argument

[8] The Dutch Supreme Court of 26 September 1979, ECLI:NL:HR:1979:AM4918: '... that the Dutch tax authorities perform their duty to inform ...'.

[9] JLM Gribnau, 'Netherlands', in AP Dourado (ed), *Separation of Powers in Tax Law* (Amsterdam, IBFD/EATLP, 2010) 145–75.

is of a *policy* nature: it proves to be efficient and effective for the DTCA's implementing tasks (see *DTCA's Communication Strategy*).

Legal Basis in the Principles of the Rule of Law

These three arguments are based on various written and unwritten legal rules, each derived from rule-of-law principles. According to authoritative literature[10] in the Dutch legal debate, which entails a substantive and thick conception[11] of the rule of law, the main principles for the rule of law consist of:

(i) the principle of legal certainty (clarity on legal position);
(ii) the principle of equality (equal treatment of equal cases);
(iii) the principle of democracy (democratic procedures); and
(iv) the principle of the service-minded government (the idea of 'government for the people' not citizens serving the interests of the government).

In this substantive[12] conception of the rule of law, it can be argued that the underlying principles do generate a duty for the DTCA to communicate with taxpayers. From this angle, the main driver and fundamental legal basis for the DTCA's duty to inform stems from the principle of *legal certainty*. As tax legislation has become too complex for most citizens and most citizens do not read and understand (complex) tax laws. General Information fills – and *should* fill – the gap where the tax law itself fails to ensure legal certainty in the context of the rule of law. General Information is a sort of compensation strategy where the law itself fails to provide legal certainty.

General Information furthermore stimulates equality (principle of *equality*), supports transparency (principle of *democracy*) and shows a willingness to help and a service-minded approach of the DTCA (principle of *the service-minded government*). General Information therefore serves several related functions in the context of the rule of law: to enhance their information position, to improve their legal certainty, to stimulate taxpayer's compliance and to show a service-minded attitude towards citizens.

Level of Discretion of the DTCA

The DTCA's duty to inform is not codified in Dutch law, but is acknowledged by the Dutch Supreme Court[13] and the Dutch Government.[14] Within its powers as a law

[10] M Scheltema, De rechtsstaat' (*The Rule of Law*), in JW Engels et al (ed), *De rechtsstaat herdacht [The Rule of Law Rethought]* (WEJ Tjeenk Willink: Zwolle, 1989) 15; for a theoretical underpinning of this substantive conception of the rule of law, based on Dworkin's idea of equal concern and respect, see JLM Gribnau, '*On the Rule of Law and Democracy: Policy Rules and Principles in Dutch Taxation*' (2024) 2 *British Tax Review* 211–38.

[11] Reference is made to the definition of the rule of law in Daly, Chapter 2 in this volume (who contrasts 'thin' and 'thick' conceptions of the rule of law) and Lindsay, Chapter 3 in this volume (who contrasts a narrow scope and a wide scope rule of law).

[12] See also Gribnau, above n 10.

[13] Inter alia, the ruling of the Dutch Supreme Court of 26 September 1979, ECLI:NL:HR:1979:AM4918.

[14] Strategy of the DTCA as set out in the explanatory memorandum of the state budget (Parliamentary papers II, 2023–2024, 36 410 IX, 2, 78): 'Through its strategy, the DTCA aims to influence the behavior of citizens and businesses in such way that they structurally comply on their own initiative with (tax) rules (compliance); that is, without (coercive and costly) actions on the part of the DTCA. This should safeguard the continuity of tax revenues. The DTCA strives to act in accordance with the principles of proper administration

enforcement agency, the DTCA has a certain amount of discretion in fulfilling its duty to inform, whereby it is bound by the law and general legal principles, including the general principles of proper administration (see *Legal framework of the Dutch Doctrine Regarding the Protection of Legitimate Expectations*).

Quality Requirements

The DTCA's duty to inform turns out to be not merely a 'service' to citizens – contrary to what is generally brought forward in Dutch case law.[15] In fact, it is embedded in the rule of law principles (see *Legal Basis in the Principles of the Rule of Law*). General Information must meet certain quality requirements to fulfil its functions, such as legal correctness and comprehensibility. But these requirements are, to some extent, at odds with each other. This is a balancing act, meaning that General Information may contain imperfections (eg inaccuracies, omissions and ambiguities) because of eliminating legal complexity in favour of comprehensibility.

The balancing act can be adequately illustrated by the concept of 'simplexity', introduced by Blank and Osofsky,[16] a contraction of *simplicity* and *complexity*. It exposes that communication types such as General Information presents a matter in a relatively understandable and comprehensible way, while at the same time the underlying matter itself is not simplified. The underlying complexity moves to the background, as a result of the trade-off between legal correctness and comprehensibility. Simplexity, which is indeed manifest in General Information, raises normative questions about the legal status of such information, the trade-off, the influential position of the tax authorities in making this trade-off and the allocation of risks between taxpayers and the DTCA.

The way for Dutch tax law to safeguard legal protection in the context of General Information should be assessed within the legal framework as identified in this section.

DTCA'S Communication Strategy

Let's shift to a more practical angle. How does the DTCA itself interpret its duty to provide General Information in terms of policy?[17] To answer this question, primary

and, wherever possible, tries to act proactively and in time rather than being reactive. Within this context, the DTCA, wherever possible, puts citizens and businesses at the centre, taking into account their personal situation. All this means that the DTCA, where possible in cooperation with public and private parties: (–) gives citizens and businesses adequate treatment (proper, timely, proportionate); (–) *effectively informs citizens and businesses about their rights and obligations*; (–) *strives to make it as easy as possible for citizens and companies to comply with (tax) obligations*; and (–) takes appropriate corrective action in case of non-compliance.'

[15] Dutch Supreme Court judgment of 9 March 1988, ECLI:NL:HR:1988:ZC3780: 'In the case of statements which are not to be construed as a promise or statement but in which *only general information is given to facilitate the completion of a tax return* ….'

[16] Blank and Osofsky, above n 2.

[17] A service-based approach in international tax literature: Gangl, above n 2, and Blank and Osofsky, above n 2.

sources (ie. communication policy documents of the DTCA) and secondary sources (such as scholarly literature and research reports) are analysed. It is striking that the DTCA as a government organisation developed a well-considered vision of comprehensible communication with citizens already in the 1980s ('Communication Policy').

Developments in the DTCA's Communication Policy

The DTCA is remarkably productive and transparent about its Communication Policy.[18] Nowadays, it is 'a matter of course' for the DTCA to be service-orientated and helpful, provide a great deal of information, assume trustworthiness of taxpayers, and take corrective action only where necessary. But taxpayers were not always approached in this way. Initially, the DTCA presented itself as an authoritative authority and communication with citizens was barely a topic of interest.

A solid analysis of the Communication Policy over the past decades shows that the interpretation of the duty to inform has changed greatly since the 1980s.[19] From that time onward, communication became a key instrument in the implementation strategy of the DTCA, which, as a law enforcement agency aimed to promote *compliance*.

The orientation of communication as an instrument enhancing compliance is illustrated strikingly by the wording in the DTCA 2011–2015 Communication Policy Plan:

> Mission and vision
>
> The DTCA wishes to promote that citizens and businesses fulfill their obligations and exercise their rights. An important condition for this is that people are aware of their rights and obligations. According to the Government Communication Principles the DTCA is obliged to inform people of those rights and obligations. But communicating involves more than providing people with information. It can contribute in many ways to compliance.
>
> When we communicate, we always start from the question: how do we communicate in such a way that we promote the desired behaviour? To do that well, we make use of knowledge of how behaviour works. We do not look at what people should do, but at what they actually do, and why they do it.[20]

The DTCA's Communication Policy conveys that it serves the interests of both parties: adequate communication enables taxpayers to excise their rights and fulfil their obligations (citizen's interests), *and* it enables the DTCA to perform its duty to impose and collect taxes more efficiently (DTCA's own interest).

In conclusion, the policy angle on taxpayer communication clearly shows that the implementation of the DTCA's duty to inform is based on a well-considered policy strategy that has changed significantly since the 1980s. This raises the question whether the ambitions of DTCA's duty to inform are sufficiently considered in the current legal framework.

[18] The communication policy of the DTCA is published in *ia* communication policy plans, reports, policy memoranda and policy audits studies.

[19] Cramwinckel, above n 1, ch 3.

[20] Belastingdienst Beleidsplan Communicatie [*DTCA's Communication Policy Plan*] 2011–2015, 10–11.

Legal Framework of the Dutch Doctrine Regarding the Protection of Legitimate Expectations

What is the current legal position in Dutch tax law on the doctrine regarding the protection of expectations raised by General Information, and should it be re-evaluated? To answer this question a critical analysis of Dutch Supreme Court case law since the 1970s is to be made.[21]

Doctrine: General Principles of Proper Administration

In the Dutch legal framework, the protection of taxpayers with respect to expectations raised by acts of the DTCA is assessed by the doctrine of the general principles of proper administration (*algemene beginselen van behoorlijk bestuur*) and more in particular, the principle of legitimate expectations (*vertrouwensbeginsel*).[22]

The general principles of proper administration provide binding standards for the DTCA to act in a proper and fair manner. The doctrine regarding the general principles has been developed by the Dutch Supreme Court over the last decades. Since 1978 the Court accepted that, under specific circumstances, certain principles, including the principle of legitimate expectations, do have *contra legem* effect.[23] Within the Dutch legal system, this means that the strict application of the law is set aside by the acts of the DTCA in order to protect the taxpayer, often resulting in a more favourable tax treatment of the taxpayer than based on the strict application of the tax law.[24]

It should be noted that in the Dutch system, the principle of legitimate expectations with respect to the taxpayer's substantive tax position may result in (only) two options: (i) upholding the expectation in full (the taxpayer's expectations of his tax treatment are fully honoured) or (ii) disappointing in full (the taxpayer's expectations are violated and his tax treatment is different than expected based on his expectations). This binary 'all or nothing' distinction when it comes to substantive tax treatment is peculiar to the Dutch approach. It does not offer much remedial creativity when it comes to substantive tax treatment.

Balancing between Principles

If the DTCA does not act in accordance with expectations that were raised by the taxpayer based on General Information, the question is whether the expectations should

[21] For the UK see *Gaines Cooper* [2010] UKSC 47.

[22] See JLM Gribnau, 'Horizontal Monitoring: Some Procedural Tax Law Issues and Their Broader Meaning' in R Russo (ed), *Tax Assurance* (Deventer: Kluwer, 2015) [8.3.1]: 'The law does indeed leave the tax administration room for an informal cooperative compliance strategy.'

[23] The Dutch Supreme Court decision of 12 April 1978, ECLI:NL:PHR:1978:AX3264. The *contra legem* effect evidences Dworkin's idea of equal concern and respect which in this situation prevails over the principle of equality (equal treatment), see Gribnau, above n 10.

[24] It should be noted that legitimate expectations also can be raised regarding, for example, procedural tax matters, such as if the DTCA gives the taxpayer the expectation that they will not undertake an audit or that

be legally protected. In such a case, in the Dutch approach, tension arises between, on the one hand, the *principle of legitimate expectations* and, on the other hand, the *principle of legality* (which ensures that the law is applied).[25]

In its case law since 1978, the Dutch Supreme Court has provided legal rules on how to weight these principles for categories with specific type of acts and statements of the DTCA that may raise expectations among taxpayers, such as *policy rules* ('*beleidsregels*'), *commitments* and *position statements* ('*toezeggingen*' and '*standpuntbepalingen*') and *general information* ('*algemene voorlichting*' and '*inlichtingen*'). For each of these categories, the Dutch Supreme Court formulated a legal rule that prescribes under which specific circumstances legitimate expectations should be honoured.

For example, for the category of *commitments* the legal rule states that if the tax inspector made a commitment to a taxpayer, the taxpayer's expectations based on this commitment are protected if, in short:[26]

(i) the taxpayer has provided the information that is correct and relevant to the commitment; and
(ii) the commitment is not so clearly contrary to the correct application of the law that the taxpayer could not reasonably rely on it.

If both conditions are met, the principle of legitimate expectations takes priority over the principle of legality, meaning that the DTCA is legally bound to its commitment and the taxpayer may rely on the DTCA's commitment, even if was a *contra legem* commitment. The legal rule regarding the category of commitments thus comprises the basic position of the protection of expectations ('yes, provided that').

Protection of Legitimate Expectations Regarding the Category of General Information

With respect to expectations raised by General Information, the legal rule of the Dutch Supreme Court is based on the principle that expectations are *not* honoured, *unless* certain conditions are met ('no, unless'). Save in exceptional cases, a strict application of the law takes precedence based on case law of the Dutch Supreme Court from 1979 (the 'current legal position').[27] This main rule means that, in principle, the risk of incorrect information must be borne by the taxpayer, unless the taxpayer meets both of the following conditions:[28]

(i) the lack of knowledge requirement (*niet-kenbaarheidsvereiste*); and
(ii) the disposition requirement (*dispositievereiste*).

The lack of knowledge requirement (i) implies that the information provided was not so clearly contrary to a correct application of the law that the taxpayer could

an extension of a certain time limit is granted. Again, in principle, in the Dutch approach, the legal effect of the principle of legitimate expectations is binary.

[25] A Dutch systematic study on the general principles of proper administration. See Happe, above n 2.

[26] ECLI:NL:HR:1979:AM4918; Dutch Supreme Court decision of 19 June 2020, ECLI:NL:HR:2020:1069.

[27] ECLI:NL:HR:1979:AM4918; more recently see the Dutch Supreme Court judgment of 5 November 2021, ECLI:NL:HR:2021:1654.

[28] ECLI:NL:HR:1979:AM4918; recently ECLI:NL:HR:2021:1654.

and should in all reasonableness have been aware that the information provided was incorrect.

With respect to the disposition requirement (ii) for decades this requirement implied that the taxpayer, relying on the incorrect or incomplete information, has performed or omitted an act that results in a situation in which the taxpayer not only has to pay the tax legally due, but also, the taxpayer suffers damages.[29] It is apparent from Dutch case law that taxpayers in a great many cases do not meet the disposition requirement.[30]

Recently, after 40 years of established case law, the Dutch Supreme Court mitigated the disposition requirement to a certain extent.[31] The current interpretation of the disposition requirement implies that the taxpayer, relying on the incorrect information, has performed or omitted an act that results in a situation in which a higher amount is levied from the taxpayer than he believed to be due based on that information.

Under this new interpretation, a higher amount of taxes than expected may qualify. But the condition still entails a high threshold by requiring that the taxpayer must have acted based on the information, for instance by making an investment, cancelling an insurance or buying a car. However, this implies acting or omitting an act, *besides* acts that relate to the performance of tax obligations (such as filing a form based on information provided, or following instructions based on the DTCA's explanatory notes).

Arguments Supporting the Current Legal Position

The main argument of the Dutch Supreme Court for its legal rule 'no, unless' was motivated in the 1970s by the taxpayers' interest in allowing the DTCA to carry out its duty to inform unimpeded.[32] The underlying viewpoint of the Dutch Supreme Court seems to be that the DTCA should not be too readily bound by erroneous information. The law should not be set aside easily if 'only' General Information is provided, since the feature of this information is that it is not tailored to the situation of the specific taxpayer at hand. In addition, from a legal point of view, *contra legem* application of the principle of legitimate expectations should be applied with restraint.

The Dutch Supreme Court recently affirmed the current principle and main rule.[33] However, the argument of 'effective legal protection' has resulted in the mitigation of (ii) the disposition requirement (see section *Legal Framework of the Dutch Doctrine Regarding the Protection of Legitimate Expectations*). But this does not afford better legal protection to citizens who have done nothing other than to follow the information (and have not suffered any additional disadvantage due to actions or omissions based on the information). Still, the current legal framework thus provides relatively little legal protection to taxpayers who have derived expectations from General Information.

[29] ECLI:NL:HR:1979:AM4918; Based on the Dutch Supreme Court judgment of 29 January 2021, ECLI:NL:HR:2021:142.
[30] Cramwinckel above n 1, [4.3.4.1].
[31] ECLI:NL:HR:2021:1654.
[32] ECLI:NL:HR:1979:AM4918.
[33] ECLI:NL:HR:2021:1654.

By Way of Illustration: Case Law Study

How often do taxpayers successfully invoke the principle of legitimate expectations with respect to expectations raised by General Information? A systematic study into published Dutch case law[34] for the 1979–2020 period provides illustrative numbers. This case law study – containing of in total 131 relevant results – shows that in most cases taxpayers did not have legally protected expectations in the case of expectations raised by General Information.[35] In approximately 95 per cent of the decisions, the principle of legitimate expectations was invoked unsuccessfully. Taxpayers therefore successfully invoked the principle of legitimate expectations in only 5 per cent of the cases.

Critical Analysis of the Arguments Supporting the Current Legal Rule

Following a detailed analysis of the case law, the current legal approach appears to be based on presumptions that no longer apply in full. The most striking findings in this respect are, summarised, that information is not *just* information; not to the DTCA, nor to taxpayers, nor in light of the legal and policy functions of the provision of information. The current approach thus places a disproportionate amount of risk on taxpayers.

Furthermore, the distinction made by the Dutch Supreme Court between communicative acts within the DTCA's duty to inform and within the DTCA's other duties turns out to be a theoretical one. It results in legally constructed distinctions between categories of communicative acts and their respective legal rules regarding the protection of expectations, that turns out to be problematic in case law.

The conclusion of the analysis of this Part of the chapter is that the application of the principle of legitimate expectations is inconsistent, does not offer remedial flexibility, does not meet the legal framework for the DTCA's duty to inform and lags behind developments in law and society. A re-evaluation is needed, which should also involve the citizen's perspective.

The Citizen's Perspective

The 'citizen's perspective' has garnered a great deal more attention in Dutch legal discourse.[36] This development underlines the importance of assessing the legal soundness of the current legal approach also from this angle.

While taxpayers (citizens) in general will expect that the DTCA acts in line with its own communication, Dutch tax case law has showed that General Information by the

[34] See www.rechtspraak.nl. In the Netherlands, in general far from all (tax) case law is published.

[35] See Annex I of Cramwinckel above n 1.

[36] Partly as a result of the Dutch childcare benefits scandal, in which citizens were 'crushed' by the legal system and the tax authorities due to the very strict implementation of repayment rules of childcare benefits. This scandal led to a great deal of attention from institutions such as the Dutch Parliament, legislature and judiciary. See, eg the Dutch Parliamentary Questioning Committee Childcare Benefits Report 'Unprecedented Injustice' (*Ongekend Onrecht*) of 17 December 2020.

DTCA is mostly considered to be merely non-binding communication. The approaches to the reliability of General Information thus diverge. How do citizens perceive communication by the DTCA and what do they expect in terms of commitment?

To answer this question an approach is needed that provides insight into communication between the DTCA and citizens. An interpretation of the citizen's perspective through language and communication science provides these insights. The purpose is to lay the groundwork for the citizen's perspective. This enhances the development of a re-evaluated legal position that better reflects (also) the perspective of the citizen, and thus the reality covered by the law.

The Citizen's Perspective on the Expectations to be Derived from DTCA'S Information

What is the citizen's perspective on the expectations to be derived from General Information? In this chapter, the perspective of citizens is given a communicative interpretation, which is particularly suitable, because the provision of information is (a form of) communication.

Research Method for the Citizen's Perspective

The citizen's perspective is to be operationalised using insights from various subdisciplines of language and communication science, such as linguistics (language as object of study), text science (text as object of study), pragmatics (focused on language use), discourse studies (focused on the quality and effectiveness of language use) and psycholinguistics (focused on psychological effects of communication). A *functional* approach to the citizen's perspective is used. The purpose of this perspective in relation to the central research question is to understand the citizen's perspective regarding the expectations that are derived from General Information. The multidisciplinary approach in this study aims to obtain a more accurate legal approach to legal protection.

Communication Framework and Quality Requirements for Government Information

The most important insight from communication theory is that communication of the government, including the DTCA, is embedded in an *institutional context*. According to theoretical insights of Renkema, institutions (such as the institution of taxation) involve power relations and asymmetry.

> In the interaction between government and citizens (…) one of the most prevailing characteristics is asymmetry.[37]

[37] J Renkema and C Schubert, *Introduction to Discourse Studies* (Amsterdam/Philadelphia: John Benjamins Publishing Company, 2018) [14.5].

This asymmetry is manifest in terms of expertise, being a more (or less) sophisticated communicative partner and impact.

As Bax aptly discusses, General Information in this context is not 'just information' with respect to the speech act of providing information (in Dutch: *voorlichten*):

> According to common definitions, the purpose of providing information – unlike advertising – is to increase knowledge (e.g. of consumers): informing is about providing accurate information. As such, information falls under representative speech acts. Yet the purpose of providing information is not adequately and fully characterised in this way. If I inform someone that France is not currently a kingdom, that my brother is a physiotherapist or that a bee dance is a subtle communication medium, I may have conveyed correct information, but it goes against intuition to say, that I have entered the field of the provision of information. This is partly related to the fact that information practices are usually embedded in some institutional framework (a government agency, a business organisation). But more important in this context is the fact that the provision of information pursues underlying goals. The government provides information about the harmful effects of cigarette smoking, so that the smoking citizen, given this increased knowledge, changes his behaviour (i.e. quits smoking altogether or decides to smoke a pipe or cigar). Through the transmission of factual information (…) the sender seeks to influence the behaviour of the receiver (…). The initial function of the provision of information undeniably serves that underlying function.[38]

General Information is information *from the authorities*, embedded in the institutional context of taxation. It is *targeted* and *goal-orientated* information, not just providing factual information but also seeking to influence taxpayers' behaviour (see *Legal Basis in the Principles of the Rule of Law* and section *DTCA's communication strategy*).

Furthermore, the theory of the Dutch scholars Janssen and Steehouder from the 1980s provides interesting perspectives on the type of interventions that need to be applied in transforming ('translating') a law into a comprehensible informative text for the public.[39] They distinguish four steps, including (1) the adaptation of the perspective of the user instead of the law, (2) the selection process of information, (3) the restructuring process of information, and (4) the wording of the information. These aspects show that providing General Information requires more of the DTCA than merely using comprehensible words. This makes the position of the 'translator' influential.

Communication Creates Expectations, Obligations and Responsibilities

Communicative theory explains that the specific communicative context of providing information to taxpayers has effect in terms of expectations, obligations and responsibilities in the communication with citizens. Specifically relevant here is the

[38] MHM Bax, *Een spiegel van de geest. Over taal, communicatie en cognitie* [*A Mirror of the Mind. On Language, Communication and Cognition*] (Groningen: Martinus Nijhoff Uitgevers, 1995) 84.

[39] Inter alia, MF Steehouder amd CJM Jansen, *Taalverkeersproblemen tussen overheid en burger. Een onderzoek naar verbeteringsmogelijkheden van voorlichtingsteksten en formulieren* [Communication problems between government and citizens. A study on improvement possibilities of information texts and forms] (Den Haag, Sdu Uitgevers, 1989) 16.

theoretical framework of Grice, the founder of influential language philosophy.[40] Grice's *Cooperative Principle* says: 'Make your conversational contribution such as it is required, at the stage at which it occurs, by the accepted purpose or direction of the talk exchange in which you are engaged.'[41] It makes clear that communicative partners *cooperate* to communicate successfully. This principle explains why taxpayers, as a basic assumption, will expect that General Information of the DTCA enables them to fulfil their tax responsibilities in a correct way. It also shows that not taking responsibility for communicative utterances (for instance, if the DTCA was not bound by its General Information) breaches this basic principle of cooperation. Furthermore, Grice's *Maxims of Conversation* explain that taxpayers expect that the information is correct (*Maxim of Quality*), sufficient (*Maxim of Quantity*), relevant (*Maxim of Relevance*) and understandable (*Maxim of Manner*).

The work of the psycholinguist Clark on language use makes clear that communication is a form of acting together (*joint action*) that creates *commitment* between communicative partners. This can be easily illustrated by the fact that a person who breaks a promise will be called to account for it. Someone who asks a cup of coffee but leaves without drinking it will be looked at with a raised eyebrow. A person who asks a question but then does not want to hear the answer will evoke a puzzled or even angry reaction. A person who walks away in the middle of a conversation or denies his words may expect to be called to account for it socially.

Applied to the context of the provision of General Information to taxpayers by the DTCA, Clark's theory shows that joint actions in taxation by means of communication to enhance compliance creates some sort of *commitment* between the DTCA and taxpayers as communicative partners.[42] This commitment cannot be breached easily, given what is at stake in acting together for a common purpose, such as taxation. Because the way language users communicate is guided by the universal communication principles, they are also relevant to tax authorities-taxpayer communication to gain a better understanding of the issues with the current legal position from a different angle.

Miscommunication

Communicative theories also provide a better understanding of *miscommunication* between communicative partners. As Sperber and Wilson have explained, communication is not based on 'a failsafe algorithm' but merely on 'a less-than-perfect heuristic'.[43] That makes the risk of miscommunication realistic. Miscommunication can occur, for example, if the taxpayer does not have a correct understanding of the information provided, if the DTCA does not provide a correct interpretation of the underlying law, if both parties do their best effort but legal nuances got 'lost in translation' as a result of simplexity, or more in general if taxpayers perceive information as 'the law' while the

[40] HP Grice, *Logic and Conversation (William James Lectures, delivered at Harvard University in 1967)*, (Cambridge MA: Harvard University Press, 1975).

[41] Grice, above n 40, 45.

[42] HH Clark, *Using Language* (Cambridge, Cambridge University Press, 1996); HH Clark, 'Social Actions, Social Commitments', in N J Enfield and SC Levinson (eds), *Roots of Human Sociality, Culture, Cognition and Interaction* (London: Routledge, 2006), ch 4.

[43] D Sperber and D Wilson, *Relevance. Communication and Cognition* (Oxford: Blackwell 1986) 45.

DTCA only intended to provide non-binding information about the law. What is accurate to solve miscommunication, depends on the circumstances, but in terms of communication there is much remedial flexibility (see sub section *An assessment framework*).

Expectations to be Derived from Communication of the Tax Authorities

Another important theoretical insight is that citizens will perceive government information with the assumption that it is *in conformity with* the law. This law conformity is what language users (citizens) expect, and reasonably *may expect*.[44]

For citizens, information about the law, as a translation of the law, functions as if it were the law itself. Of course, this is not the legal reality, but it does however better reflect the approach of citizens. As shown here, from the perspective of the citizens, they see their communicative relation with the DTCA, and not with the legislator, who is moved to the background.

The communicative approach demonstrates that the DTCA's provision of General Information *inherently* creates communicative expectations. Primarily because of the DTCA's *authority* and *capacity*, by the *institutional context* and by the *communicative purpose* of the provision of information. This leads to normative assumptions regarding the accuracy and reliability of the information provided to taxpayers.

From a communicative perspective, the provision of information is to be seen as a 'translation' of laws and regulations that functions in a new communicative context.[45] Contrary to the legal perspective, in which the law remains dominant, from a communicative perspective the information provided is an autonomous text.

The communicative approach sheds new light on key aspects of the expectations derived from the information provided. Communication comes with responsibilities and obligations – both for citizens and the DTCA. Communicative commitment between partners cannot be breached easily, at the risk of risking – ultimately – acting together at all.

To conclude, the fundamental insight is that the provision of General Information is a form of communication between the DTCA and citizens and that this should be included in re-evaluating the legal perspective on protecting legitimate expectations.

The Legal Perspective Taking into Account the Citizen's Perspective

In this part of the chapter, the lines from the legal perspective and the citizen's perspective are considered together. The objective is to re-evaluate the legal framework with due

[44] C Jansen and M Steehouder, 'How Research Can Lead to Better Government Forms', in D Janssen and R Neutelings (ed), *Reading and Writing Public Documents* (Amsterdam/Philadelphia: John Benjamins Publishing Company, 2001) 13; Cramwinckel, above n 1 [5.4.3, 5.4.5].

[45] J Hulst and L Lentz, 'Public Documents in a Multilingual Context', in D Janssen and R Neutelings ibid, ch 5, 87–88: 'a translation is seen as an autonomous document that functions in a new communicative environment, and not as a derivation of the (…) original text'.

regard for the legal perspective and the citizen's perspective. It is, however, not about 'merging' both perspectives into a single perspective, but about enhancing the legal approach.

Confronting the Legal Perspective with the Citizen's Perspective

The focus shifts towards the question how the legal perspective relates to the citizen's perspective when it comes to the protection of expectations raised by General Information. The starting point is the interim conclusion from above that the legal soundness of the current legal position ('no, unless') falls short. Below it is examined whether, and to what extent, the legal perspective conflicts with the citizens' perspective.

In terms of methodology, the legal perspective is functionally compared with the citizens perspective, with the aim of determining the added value of this perspective for the envisaged re-evaluation of the principle of legitimate expectations.

Clash of Perspectives

The key conflict between the legal perspective and the citizen's perspective can be illustrated by the following visuals.

Figure 1 Legal Perspective

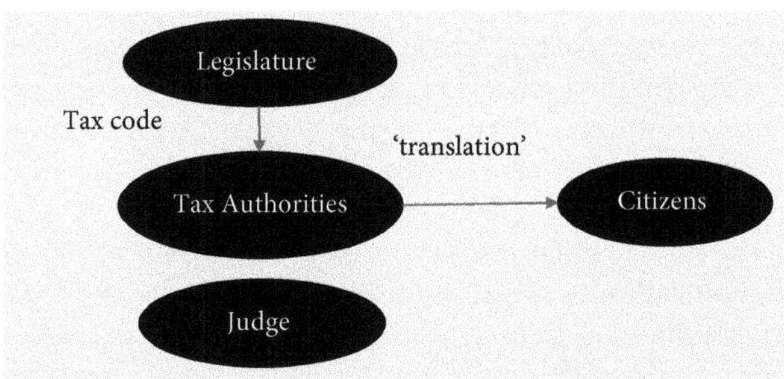

Figure 2 Citizen's Perspective

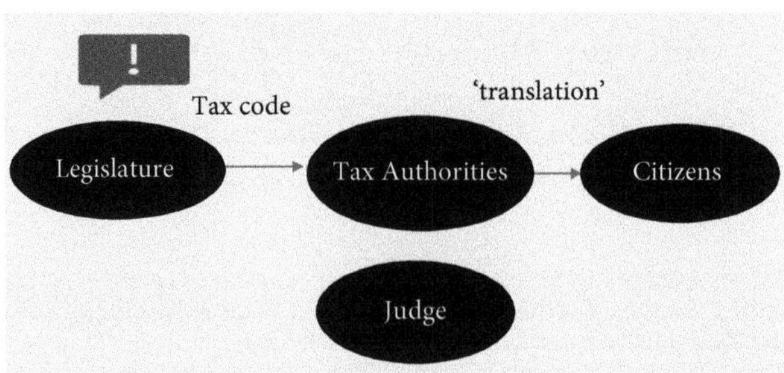

While the legal perspective explains why primacy lies with the law, given the democratically legitimised legislature, the citizen's perspective shows that the taxpayer has a communicative relationship with the DTCA. The DTCA explain the tax law; as if the DTA is the legislature. The legislature disappears from this picture: for the citizen, the information provided is 'the law'. Of course, this is not the legal reality, but it explains that taxpayers may perceive it differently.

Further Analysis of Conflicting Perspectives

Conflicts between the two perspectives essentially occur because, in short, the citizens and the DTCA:

(a) use different source texts (the information provided and the law, respectively);
(b) see different starting points for commitment to communication (through the act of communication or only after meeting certain legal criteria); and
(c) their views on the status of the text differ (a comprehensible representation of the law or an autonomous text functioning in a new context).

The Added Value of the Confrontation of Perspectives

The confrontation of perspectives shows that the current legal rule regarding the protection of expectations based on General Information ('no, unless') is 'uncooperative' from a communicative perspective. This is not only contrary to the citizen's perspective and the DTCA's compliance strategy but is also at odds with the objective and purport of the principle of legitimate expectations. Moreover, from both perspectives, the current allocation of risk poses a great amount of risk to taxpayers, resulting in a disbalance between the interests of law enforcement and legal protection.

Furthermore, the confrontation shows that the weighing of interests required by law is not visible in the communicative approach from the citizen's perspective. At the same time, the confrontation also shows that the support for the main rule 'no, unless' is supported by legal arguments that are as such insufficiently persuasive in the citizen's world. The importance of the 'unimpeded duty to inform' turns out to be insufficiently convincing to taxpayers to justify such a significant deviation from the citizen's perspective. Ignoring this may alienate citizens from the law.

Back to the 'Why': Why should the Citizen's Perspective be Relevant to the Legal Perspective?

Why bother about the citizen's perspective? Indeed, it could be argued that the two perspectives mirror different worlds, with different outcomes. However, the law serves the society with its citizens, not the other way around. If the gap between the two worlds becomes too large, the law alienates itself from the world to which it should relate.[46] That may be harmful to the legitimacy of and the trust in the government and to the effectivity of DTCA's implementation strategy. These words may sound vague, but a case study based on Dutch case law illustrates that these effects actually manifest themselves in certain ways.[47] Despite the fact that the Netherlands is a relatively high-trust society, trust in the DTCA and the government is currently under pressure.[48]

A re-evaluation of the application of the principle of legitimate expectations turns out to be inevitable, both from the legal perspective and the citizen's perspective. The most important reasons to do so follow from the previous parts of the chapter, in sum: (i) the main legal rule 'no, unless' is incorrect in light of the legal framework for the DTCA's duty to inform; (ii) the legal characterisation of General Information as 'only' informational is not adequate; and (iii) there is a lack of balance between on the one hand the goals and ambitions of the DTCA's duty to inform and on the other hand the legal protection against information arising from this task.

Re-Evaluation Proposal

The focus shifts to improving the current Dutch doctrine regarding the principle of legitimate expectations with respect to General Information by the DTCA. What is the best way to re-evaluate the application of the principle of legitimate expectations?

Assessment Framework for Designing a Better Legal Position

The search for a better solution obviously involves a dilemma, where – given the approach in the Dutch legal system – two (or more) interests point in different directions, as the interest of honouring legitimate expectations may interfere with the interest of a strict application of the law.

In terms of research methodology, a standard is needed to determine how to weigh these interests in a proper – and even improved – legal manner. In short, the way in which Dutch tax law should deal with the protection of expectations derived from General Information provided by the DTCA, should meet the criteria of the rule of law (*Legal Basis in the Principles of the Rule of Law*). These existing criteria should be completed by taking into account the citizen's perspective. This leads to the proposal of 'the assessment framework of the rule of law that observes the citizen's perspective'.

The citizen's perspective is not a principle, but it provides a viewing direction in the interpretation and testing of rule of law principles. In other words, it 'colours' the contemporary interpretation of the rule of law principles. The assumption is that the law observes the citizen's perspective if the application of legitimate expectations can be

[46] See Adviescommissie praktische rechtsbescherming in belastingzaken [*Advisory Committee Practical Legal Protection in Tax Cases*], MBA van Hout et al, *Burgers beter beschermd* [*Citizens Better Protected*] 2021, 3.

[47] See Cramwinckel above n 1, [6.2].

[48] According to the DTCA's 2022 Annual Plan, 6, in general, confidence in the DTCA is at its lowest level since the DTCA has measured the trust of taxpayers.

explained to and understood by citizens. Of course, this is not the same as saying that citizens should always get their way.

Proposal for Re-evaluation

Essentially, the proposed re-evaluation for the application of legitimate expectations is that a change of course and method is needed, in which the main rule 'no, unless' is replaced by an assessment framework.

The proposal can be summarised by the following basic principles:

- **New legal position**
  The principle of legitimate expectations should be applied with less restraint, providing a more comprehensive legal protection, observing the citizen's perspective to a broader extent, and providing a better balance between legal equality and legal certainty. The basic legal assumption should be that citizens must be able to rely on information from the DTCA.
- **New assessment framework**
  To determine whether the principle of legitimate expectations should apply, replace the main rule 'no, unless' with a balancing framework, taking into account the circumstances of the case.

An Assessment Framework

The assessment framework provides a model for the assessment of the principle of legitimate expectations regarding taxpayers' expectations raised by General Information. Essentially, the assessment framework consists of two steps:

Step 1: Reasonable expectations
Are the taxpayers' expectations that are raised by the General Information reasonable in the case at hand, given the relevant circumstances?

Step 2: Legal effect
What is the legal effect of reasonable expectations in the case at hand?

With respect to Step 1, it should be noted that it includes an assessment of the relevant wording, the context and the circumstances of the case. In principle, legitimate expectations must be protected if they are *reasonable* in the given circumstances.

With respect to Step 2, it should be noted that under the current Dutch approach of the doctrine of the principle of legitimate expectations the legal effect is limited to a binary 'all or nothing' approach. There is no remedial flexibility when it comes to substantive tax consequences of legitimate expectations (see *Doctrine: General Principles of Proper Administration*).

However, the communication analysis offers inspiration for a more sophisticated approach in terms of remedial creativity. That is particularly relevant in cases in which expectations are raised while the information provided is not clearly incorrect but is incomplete or unclear. In other words, especially in the grey area where it is unclear who is to 'blame' for miscommunication between the DTA and the taxpayer. Miscommunication thus turns out to be not a matter of 'all or nothing'.[49] To illustrate this, in some situations correcting a misunderstanding will require a communicative partner to keep his word and to uphold the expectation in full ('all'). In another case, where the communicative commitment is relatively weaker, a misunderstanding may also be resolved by both parties making some concessions ('a little'). In yet another case, for example if the communication partners do not have an ongoing relationship, all that is needed is a statement that there was a misunderstanding ('nothing'). In yet another case, for example if the interests are limited, sincere apologies may be sufficient ('alternative').

The communicative angle offers to the Dutch tax approach a wider and more tailored range of remedies. More flexibility better represents the citizen's perspective and offers a better reflection of the specific communication that has taken place between the taxpayer and the DTCA. The range of remedies may include, among other things, alternative financial consequences such as compensation in the form of tax interest, litigation costs, court fees or fines. Furthermore, alternative remedies can be considered such as flexibility in payment arrangements or personal assistance with tax questions. Remedial creativity could also be found in a more 'proportional' rather than 'binary' outcome of the principle of legitimate expectations (for example by means of a discount on the tax to be paid or a partial reduction of the tax assessment), noted that this would require a change regarding the current Dutch approach. However, from a legal perspective, more flexibility could impact legal certainty but, on the other hand, it may reflect better the citizen's perspective.

All things considered, it is clear that the added value of the communication angle on the 'input side' (what expectations are raised in communication between the DTCA and taxpayers) also provides added value on the 'output side' (what remedies are possible). This enriches the legal perspective.

Does the Proposal Lead to Improvement?

If the re-evaluation proposal is tested against the normative standard (see *Assessment Framework for Designing a Better Legal Position*) it follows that the proposal represents a 'good solution': it meets the relevant rule-of-law criteria. Further, it shows an improvement over the current application of the principle of legitimate expectations, as the proposal strengthens the value of *legal certainty*, while it does not impair the value of, in particular, *legal equality* in the context of the rule of law.

Counter-thinking: Main Objections to the Proposal

Subsequently, the most important objections to the proposal need to be discussed ('counter-thinking'[50]). The main concern of providing more legal protection relates to

[49] See Cramwinckel, above n 1 [6.5, 7.4.3.2].
[50] Cramwinckel, above n 1 [7.6] for an extensive overview.

unforeseeable financial consequences for the government in the case of a risk allocation shift, the fear of a more restrained implementation of the DTCA's duty to inform and the risk of a decreased willingness to communicate. These arguments should be taken seriously, but they do not lead to the conclusion that the current legal position should be upheld. The proposed re-evaluation better aligns the application of the principle of legitimate expectations in the provision of information within the legal framework. Moreover, it leads to a better balance between law enforcement and legal protection, it meets the preconditions of the legal system and better reflects the citizen's perspective.

Final Remarks

The main conclusion of the analysis is that the provision of General Information by the DTCA is a form of communication and – following from communication theory – this has consequences in terms of responsibilities, expectations and commitment. The current legal approach does not take this sufficiently into account, while there is room to do so in a legally adequate manner – *more* than is currently the case.

From a tax scholarly viewpoint, this analysis adds value to existing knowledge with respect to the DTCA's communication, since hardly any theoretical framework about the DTCA's duty to inform was available. Further, the research findings expose a conflict between the legal perspective and the citizen's perspective, and then contributes a solution to minimise that conflict and reduce it as much as possible.

The main added value of the research findings is that they reveal that, when dealing with a legal issue that in fact affects all citizens, it is not enough to approach the problem purely from a legal perspective. When the citizen's perspective is involved in the analysis of the legitimate expectations derived from General Information, this sheds a different light on the issue, in particular with respect to remedial creativity regarding the principle of legitimate expectations.

The most important take away is that General Information in the context of the rule of law is much more important for both the DTCA, for taxpayers and for taxation than has been acknowledged in tax law to date. This requires adequate legal protection.

6

Is GAAR in Breach of Rule of Law? Balancing Fairness and Flexibility

SURANJALI TANDON AND CHETAN RAO*

Abstract

General anti-avoidance rules (GAAR) are legislated to deal with instances of unacceptable tax avoidance. Lack of definition of unacceptable avoidance and the resulting executive discretion introduce uncertainty. This is seen to be in conflict with the principles of rule of law. However, such conflict may not exist where there are specific design features that act as checks on discretionary application of the law. This chapter looks at the design of GAARs, particularly in the Indian context, to demonstrate that a GAAR cannot be simply said to be in breach of rule of law because of its wide application. The process of invoking GAAR, with clear guidelines, independent review processes and the possibility to challenge the decision before Courts and advance rulings to safeguard against the future application of GAAR are all design features that vitiate concerns regarding the conflict with rule of law. The chapter puts forth a framework for thinking about rule of law in relation to GAAR and then evaluates the anti-avoidance rule based on the features.

Introduction

General Anti-Avoidance Rules (GAAR) play a crucial role in promoting fairness within the tax system. However, at times, concerns have been raised regarding their broad interpretation and discretionary application, which some argue are incompatible with the principles of the rule of law. This chapter delves into the various frameworks for rule of law and identifies potential sources of incompatibility between GAAR and these frameworks. However, these concerns about uncertainty in application need to be weighed against the evolving landscape of tax avoidance. As tax avoidance strategies become increasingly complex, and the application of tax laws adapts accordingly,

* Views expressed in this chapter are personal views of the authors and do not reflect the views of their respective organisations.

it's essential to evaluate GAAR within this context. This chapter analyses the cases of the UK and India, which adopted GAAR relatively late after extensive consultations, to demonstrate the continued need for such rules. Despite the existence of numerous specific anti-avoidance measures, GAAR was enacted to address remaining gaps in tax legislation. The chapter then goes on to examine design features of GAARs, highlighting how these rules can be crafted to promote fairness and transparency within the legal system. By incorporating specific design elements, GAARs can effectively address concerns about the rule of law while ensuring they remain adaptable to evolving social norms. The chapter's findings suggest that well-designed GAARs, with minimal discretionary application, can find a strong balance between addressing tax avoidance and upholding the principles of the rule of law.

Rule of Law in the Context of GAAR

Between tax planning and tax evasion there are a spectrum of activities that qualify as tax avoidance.[1] Tax avoidance is not illegal conduct but violates the spirit of the law, where the latter is a function of social norms and often such norms measure the distance between the letter and spirit of the law.[2] It is difficult to precisely define what constitutes tax avoidance and for this reason general anti-avoidance rules have become more prevalent. The anti-avoidance rules require determination of 'scheme' that results in a taxpayer receiving a tax benefit and also determination of substance of scheme, ie if the sole or dominant or the main purpose of the scheme[3] is to obtain that tax benefit. A fine line separates unacceptable forms of tax avoidance and other commercial transactions. It can be a challenge to strike the balance in law such that it does not prevent commercial transactions that legitimately take advantage of opportunities made available.[4] The main concern with GAARs is that determining the intent behind grants discretion to the executive and the courts concerns about their compatibility with the rule of law. AV Dicey's first principle is that 'no man is punishable or can lawfully be made to suffer in body or goods except for a distinct breach of law established in the ordinary legal manner before ordinary legal courts of the land'.[5] Since rule of law is the pre-eminent guiding principle of executive restraint,[6] there is a tension between the application of GAAR and fulfilling the principles of rule of law. It is important to define, then, what constitutes the rule of law to evaluate the functioning of GAAR.

Legal scholars including Lon Fuller, Joseph Raz, John Finnis and Neil MacCormick have written extensively on rule of law.[7] The framework provided by Fuller, though with

[1] AN Brassey, 'Tax, GAAR and the Rule of Law' (PhD Thesis, Faculty of Law, University of Cambridge 2017).

[2] MT Gordon and S Garcia, 'The Letter Versus the Spirit of the Law' (Thesis, University of Michigan 2014).

[3] Legislatures grapple with the appropriate threshold for triggering anti-avoidance rules in tax law. Three main approaches are on the table: sole purpose, main purpose, and dominant purpose.

[4] C Waerzeggers and C Hillier, 2016, 'Introducing a general anti-avoidance rule (GAAR) – Ensuring that a GAAR achieves its purpose', Tax Law IMF Technical Note 2016/1, IMF Legal Department.

[5] AV Dicey, *Introduction to the Study of the Law of the Constitution*, 8th edn (London: Liberty Fund Publishing, 1885, reprint 2001), 110.

[6] See Brassey, above n 1, 126.

[7] A Marmor, 'The Rule of Law and its Limits' (2003) USC Public Policy Research Paper Np. 03-16, 6. Available at: https://ssrn.com/abstract=424613.

its own limitations, is one possible way of defining the rule of law. For the sake of brevity, there are eight principles of legality as per Fuller – generality of law, promulgation, retroactive laws should constitute an exception and not rule, clarity in laws, no contradiction in laws, laws should not require the impossible, constancy of laws through time and congruence between official action and declared rule. GAAR is shown to violate three of Fuller's principles – clarity, retroactivity and congruence between official action and declared rule.[8] Greater emphasis is also placed on relative certainty to ensure maintenance rule of law.[9]

Yet, it may be argued that merely the breach of aforementioned criteria by itself is not necessarily a defect of GAAR. This would have to be counterbalanced with an evaluation if the transaction in question is violative of justice. That is, reference should be made to substantive justice rather than formal justice.[10] This shift in perspective is particularly important as the moral acceptability of tax avoidance has come under increasing scrutiny. The OECD/G20 Base Erosion and Profit Shifting (BEPS) project, with its focus on preventing double non-taxation and its recent advancements like the Inclusive Framework's Pillar Two with Global Minimum Tax rules (GloBE) and Subject-to-Tax Rules (STTR), exemplifies growing intolerance for tax avoidance practices. In fact, even in the domestic context a tax avoidance scheme used by a taxpayer consciously puts other taxpayers at a relative disadvantage.[11]

A law is often evaluated against principle of legitimate expectations, which is applied asymmetrically on taxpayers and administrators.[12] Both procedural and substantive rights can be protected through the doctrine of legitimate expectations.[13] The doctrine requires a careful balance to be struck between certainty and fairness for the individual on the one hand, and flexibility and public interest on the other.[14] One consideration to be taken into account is the possible effect of a rigorous enforcement of legitimate expectation, which might include dampening the authorities' appetite for producing policies or other documentation.[15] GAAR is meant to regulate 'area of behaviour the legislator wished to bring under control but did not succeed in doing so'.[16] In its absence, the judiciary relies on a number of doctrines for this – substance over form doctrine, sham transaction doctrine, step transaction doctrine, economic substance doctrine and business purpose doctrine,[17] often reaching a conclusion at conflict with precedents. So, even if GAAR's case-by-case application or 'vagueness' is seen as a violation of rule

[8] S Apostolou, 'General Anti-Avoidance Rules and the Rule of Law' (Bachelor Thesis, Faculty of Law, Lund University 2016) 22.

[9] R Hamowy (ed), *The Collected Works of FA Hayek – Volume XVII, The Constitution of Liberty* 2011; see also J Rawls, (1999). *A Theory of Justice: Revised Edition.* (Cambridge MA: Harvard University Press).

[10] J Freedman, 'Defining Taxpayer Responsibility: In Support of a General Anti-Avoidance Principle' (2004) BTR 332, 347.

[11] Lord Templeman, *Tax and the Taxpayer* (2001) 117 LQR 575, 575.

[12] S Tandon, 'Issues and Challenges with Applying Investment Agreements to Tax Matters in the Context of India's Experience' (2023) 31(1) *Asia Pacific Law Review.* See also: J McCarthy, 'Why Do So Few People Pay Income Tax in India?' *npr* (22 March 2017).

[13] L Woolf, J Jowell and AL Sueur, *De Smith's Judicial Review* (London: Sweet & Maxwell, 6th edn, 2009) 609.

[14] P Craig, *Administrative Law* 6th edn (London: Sweet & Maxwell, 2008) ch 22. See also: House of Commons Information Office, *Statutory Instruments*, Factsheet L7 Legislative Series (May 2008).

[15] Craig, ibid.

[16] See Apostolou, above n 8, 11.

[17] ibid, 14.

of law, it must be compared with uncertainty imposed by the taxpayer's intent and the limits imposed by the Courts on the regulation of avoidance.

Prebble and Prebble (2010) argue that all legislation is vague to some extent. As per Hart, all laws admit 'core' situations where the law will definitely apply and then there are 'penumbra' where it is less certain that it will apply.[18] Therefore Pebble and Pebble (2010) argue that the fact that the GAAR is unclear in some situations is subjecting the rule to a higher standard[19] because GAARs have a higher number of penumbras. This raises the question: Should the existence of these penumbras automatically lead to critiques of GAARs being incompatible with the rule of law?

Tax certainty is certainly an aspirational virtue. At the G20 Summit in Hangzhou, China in September 2016, the OECD and the IMF were tasked to work on issues of tax certainty. The outcome of this work was a joint OECD/IMF report published in March 2017.[20] In the report, general anti-avoidance rules (GAAR), applicable in some countries, were thought to be effective in reducing aggressive tax planning by changing taxpayer behaviour, even though they were also perceived as increasing tax uncertainty as GAAR is necessarily less rules-based and more discretionary in its application. For this reason, care should be taken with the choice of an anti-avoidance instrument, its drafting and its implementation. A point that this chapter seeks to develop.

Certainty is important to both the taxpayer and administrator that laws are effective when they are certain. However, the GAAR is more effective where there is a higher degree of vagueness.[21] GAAR is 'carefully designed to be balanced and to target only the most egregiously artificial and abusive tax avoidance arrangements on a just and reasonable basis'.[22] That is, the legislation is meant to overcome existing shortcomings of the statute through its broad applicability. This characteristic, combined with taxpayer's intent to avoid taxesand fundamental problems with tax law, makes certainty an 'inappropriate value to strive for'[23] in the context of a GAAR.

It must also be acknowledged that rule of law in criminal law does not hold the same value as in tax law; in the case of GAAR, the advantage of certainty is outweighed by the limitations.[24]

It is not necessary for a law to set out every circumstance in detail; in fact, it is possible to argue that GAAR meets the criteria set forth for the fulfilment of rule of law.

[18] HLA Hart, 'Positivism and the Separation of Law and Morals' (1958) 71 *Harvard Law Review* 593; reprinted in *Essays in Jurisprudence and Philosophy* (Oxford: Oxford University Press, 1983) 49, 63.

[19] R Prebble and J Prebble, 'Does the Use of General Anti-Avoidance Rules to Combat Tax Avoidance Breach Principles of the Rule of Law?' (2010) 55 *Saint Louis University Law Journal*, Sanford E Sarasohn Memorial Conference on Critical Issues in International and Comparative Taxation, 2010, Victoria University of Wellington Legal Research Paper No. 8/2012. Available at: https://ssrn.com/abstract=1523043, 29.

[20] IMF and OECD, '*IMF/OECD Report for the G20 Finance Ministers*' (March 2017). Available at: www.imf.org/external/np/g20/pdf/2017/031817.pdf.

[21] Freedman, above n 10, 347.

[22] L Moxham and J Stefanelli, 'Safeguarding the Rule of Law, Democracy and Fundamental Rights: A Monitoring Model for the European Union' (Bingham Centre for the Rule of Law, 15 November 2013). Available at: https://binghamcentre.biicl.org/publications/safeguarding-the-rule-of-law-democracy-and-fundamental-rights-a-monitoring-model-for-the-european-union?cookiesset=1&ts=1720774803.

[23] Freedman, above n 10, 347.

[24] See Prebble and Prebble above n 20, 43.

For example, Stefanelli and Moxham (2013), while evaluating GAAR in the UK, argue that GAAR is a mechanism set down in primary legislation – it has been created by Parliament. They compare the legislation with the Human Rights Act which provides for the 'reading down' of other UK statutes that breach Convention rights. Thus the 'effect which the GAAR can have on tax law has been approved by Parliament – seen in this way, it is perfectly in keeping with the rule of law'.

Therefore, a more practical approach to assessing the GAAR is if its design can balance the concerns of breach of rule of law while addressing social norms of fairness in taxation. This chapter looks at specific legal and administrative design features that act as institutional backstops that can counteract the limitations of a broadly defined GAAR.[25] Prior to discussing design issues, the next section dwells on the rationale behind introduction for GAAR which explains why its broad applicability and vagueness must be viewed in the light of intractability of tax avoidance.

Need and Emergence of GAAR

While there can be some tension between GAAR and the strict application of the rule of law, experience has shown its value in addressing tax avoidance. The growing complexity of tax avoidance schemes and the limitations of specific anti-avoidance rules (SAARs) led to the introduction of GAAR. This empowers tax authorities to address abusive arrangements that exploit loopholes or undermine the intended spirit of tax laws, even if they technically comply with existing regulations. In this regard two of the relatively later adopters of GAAR – the UK and India – help illustrate the intractability of avoidance and the adoption of the rule.

Lessons from the UK

For as long as taxes have existed there has been a propensity to avoid their payment. Experts have documented early instances of such practices. In 1920, the Royal Commission on Income Tax in the UK reported the case of William Vestey, an owner of a cold storage business and beneficiary of the war, who domiciled in Argentina to avoid taxes and blatantly admitted to it.[26] Churchill was often reported to have retired from writing merely to ensure the payments after his 'cessations' would be treated as non-taxable capital receipts.[27] Offshoring too flourished in the UK to jurisdictions such as the Channel Islands and was also prevalent in the 1920s.[28] Yet apprehensions

[25] JN Stefanelli and L Moxham (eds), 'Do Our Tax Systems Meet Rule of Law Standards?' (2014) Bingham Centre Working Paper 2014/06. Available at: www.biicl.org/documents/315_tax_booklet_-_final.pdf.

[26] J Hollis and C McKenna, '*Union Cold Storage and the Birth of Multinational Tax Planning*, 1897–1922', (cs): *The Global History of Capitalism*, Case Study No 9. (University of Oxford, January 2019) 23. Available at: https://globalcapitalism.history.ox.ac.uk/files/ case09unioncoldstoragev2pdf.

[27] D Lough, *No More Champagne: Churchill and his Money* (London: Picador, 2015), 128–9.

[28] P Scott, 'A Fiscal Constitutional Crisis: Tax Avoidance and Evasion in Inter-war Britain' (2022) 137(584) *The English Historical Review* 170–97.

of uncertainty with application of anti-avoidance rule often stalled its introduction. Judicial practices, lack of successful examples of GAAR implementation, rule of law concerns as well as need for stronger tax legislation were all ways to push back such amendments.[29] Therefore the UK adopted an approach of introducing amendments to deal with specific kinds of tax planning arrangements once they have been revealed.[30] Although the effect that such legislation had was akin to 'squeezing the balloon in one area only to see a new bulge emerge in another'.[31] The debate on the introduction of GAAR re-emerged in 1999 in the UK. The tax avoidance was supposedly getting worse at the time not so much because of the revenue authority's lack of power to close schemes but more so from the case by case challenge necessary to close these schemes.[32] The Labour Government in 2004 Budget did not announce a GAAR but introduced legislation to curb specific anti-avoidance schemes alongside disclosure requirements for those marketing these schemes.[33] The scope of the regime was widened in 2005 to include all income tax, corporate tax and capital gains tax. The scope was further expanded to National Insurance contributions (2007), inheritance tax on trusts (2011). 607 schemes were reported in 2005–06 and declined to less than 10 by 2014.[34] The disclosure of tax avoidance schemes did make a difference by ensuring closure of marketed schemes[35] but there remained challenges with non-reporting and that the schemes could not be dealt with in their infancy as legislation would take time.[36] Even with the targeted anti-avoidance rules, these are aimed at specific arrangements and often it is observed that these do not mitigate uncertainty or complexity.[37] Yet, in the Finance Bill 2009, the GAAR was cast aside under the pretext of uncertainty and concerns were reiterated in 2010.

At the policy level, it is important to consider which among two is an uncertainty to bear with – one arising from specific rules enacted to counter avoidance or the expansive cover of a general rule. There are different kinds of SAARs that exist both in domestic law (limitation of deduction of interest or related party expense, transfer of losses and unexplained increase in income and assets) and in treaties (limitation of benefits rule, PE in third jurisdictions and saving clause). Yet SAARs are effective only until they fit the description of arrangement to which they must apply.[38]

[29] J Freedman, 'GAAR: Challenging Assumptions' (*Tax Journal*, 27 September 2010). Available at: www.taxjournal.com/articles/gaar-challenging-assumptions.

[30] A Seely (2020), *Tax Avoidance: a General Anti-Avoidance Rule-Background history (1997–2010)*, House of Commons Library Briefing Paper No 2956, 3.

[31] Dave Hartnett, then Director General at HM Revenue & Customs in a speech in 2005: *Address to CIOT as part of 75th anniversary celebrations* (19 July 2005). See also: MP Devereux, J Freedman and J Vella (2012), '*Tax Avoidance*' Oxford University Centre for Business Taxation. Available at: https://papers.ssrn.com/sol3/papers.cfm?abstract_id=3754562.

[32] 'UK looks at tougher regime on tax avoidance', *Financial Times* 10 March 2004.

[33] HC Deb 17 March 2004, col 32.

[34] HMRC, *Disclosure Statistics (for 1.8.2004 to 30.9.2014)*, October 2014.

[35] '*Regulatory Impact Assessment: Tackling Tax Avoidance – Disclosure Requirements*' (April 2004) [10].

[36] G Aaronson, '*GAAR Study: A Study to Consider Whether a General Anti-Avoidance Rule Should be Introduced into the UK Tax System*' (HM Treasury 11 November 2011) [3.1] (GAAR Study).

[37] University of Dundee 'Does the General Anti-Abuse Rule (GAAR) improve upon pre-existing methods of tackling Tax Avoidance?' 2018.

[38] J Vargas, 'Specific Anti Avoidance Rules: Domestic and International', (2022) *Manual: Manual for the Control of International Tax Planning.*

The Ramsay approach although at first did act as a deterrent, but subsequent decisions reduced the doctrine to a rule of statutory interpretation and led to uncertainty.[39]

In 2011, the Aaronson Committee recommended a narrowly focussed GAAR that would somehow meet the goals of simplification of the tax law, reduce uncertainty and at the same time would deter tax avoidance.[40] The Mirrlees Review in 2011 by the IFS argued that the solution lay elsewhere, ie in improving the design of tax systems than the GAAR. This view was also supported by the 1997 committee, so the GAAR would not interfere too much with the commercial affairs of a business.[41] Aaronson Committee's recommendation on GAAR was implemented through the Finance Bill 2013[42] to cover abusive tax arrangements. At this time, the estimated legacy stock of avoidance cases was 65,000 (2013), of which 85% predated 2010.[43] Therefore, the UK GAAR was legislated to overcome the lack of success in dealing with tax avoidance.

Lessons from India

In the Indian context, the GAAR evolved after several rounds of discussions on its implementation. The early discussions began as India drafted its Direct Taxes Code (DTC) which was a long-standing project to simplify the Income Tax Act 1961. Revised Discussion paper of Direct Taxes Code in 2010 suggested that the GAAR be introduced but as against the usual application of section 90(2) of the Income Tax Act where a taxpayer could choose between a preferential treatment between the ITA and the tax treaties, it was proposed the DTAA would not have preferential treatment over GAAR in the Act.[44] The Discussion Paper of the DTC Bill concluded that the anti-avoidance measure would be more useful than specific legislative amendments to deal with anti-avoidance. India has often introduced specific anti-avoidance rules,[45] for example, expenses or payments that are not deductible in certain circumstances involving related parties[46] and deemed dividend.[47] As mentioned earlier these covered a range of

[39] J Freedman, '*United Kingdom*' in M Lang, J Owens, P Pistone, A Rust, J Schuch and C Staringer (eds) *GAARs – A Key Element of Tax Systems in the Post-BEPS Tax World.*

[40] HM Treasury 'Independent Study on General Anti-Avoidance Rule Published', *GOV.UK* 21 November 2011.

[41] 'A General Anti-Avoidance Rule for Direct Taxes: A Response to the Inland Revenue's Consultative Document' (1999) *Tax Law Review Committee.*

[42] HM Revenue & Customs 'HMRC's GAAR Guidance approved by the Advisory Panel with effect from 15 April 2013'. Available at: https://assets.publishing.service.gov.uk/government/uploads/system/uploads/attachment_data/file/396179/gaar-part-abc.pdf.

[43] Antony Seely (2021), '*Tax Avoidance and Tax Evasion*'. House of Commons Library.

[44] The 'double reasonableness test' requires HMRC (the UK tax authority) to demonstrate that the arrangements in question are not only unreasonable for achieving a legitimate commercial outcome, but also that no reasonable person could consider them a reasonable course of action in light of the relevant tax provisions. This two-pronged approach offers taxpayers a level of protection against overly broad interpretations of tax avoidance rules.

[45] Income Tax Department of India, *Direct Tax Code Revised Discussion Paper*, June 2010, 32.

[46] Income Tax Act 1961 *(India)*, s 40A(2).

[47] ibid at 2(22)(e).

transactions or situations and there remained a gap in terms of what is defined as tax avoidance. In the absence of a general statutory provision dealing with tax avoidance, the judiciary could only play a limited role in dealing with all issues of tax avoidance, not dealt with by the specific anti-avoidance rules. In fact, the 2012 final expert committee report mentioned that the introduction of legislative amendments to deal with specific instances of tax avoidance was not sufficient.

The Direct Tax Code Bill introduced in 2009 made a strong case for the introduction of GAAR. It was observed that liberalisation of the Indian economy led to '*increasingly sophisticated forms of tax avoidance ... The problem has been further compounded by tax avoidance arrangements spread across several tax jurisdictions. This has led to erosion of the tax base*'.[48] Therefore it was thought to be necessary and desirable to introduce a general anti-avoidance rule.

There was also difficulty with judicial pronouncements, that historically concluded at variance and frustrated the Revenue's attempts. The doctrine that a person is entitled to make any lawful arrangement of his affairs that he sees fit to reduce liability to tax – known as the Westminster principle – applied in many cases. This did not allow the court to look through a transaction to identify the underlying substance. This principle was followed in India in a number of judicial rulings. The Privy Council in the case of *Bank of Chettinad Ltd v CIT*[49] made reference to the decision of the House of Lords in the *Duke of Westminster* case and rejected the argument of the tax department that, in revenue cases, the substance of the matter may be regarded as distinguished from the strict legal position.[50] Similar views were taken by the Supreme Court of India in the cases *of CIT v Motors & General Stores (P) Ltd* (1967)[51] *and CIT v BM Kharwar* (1969).[52] In *BM Kharwar*, the Supreme Court observed that

> the taxing authority is entitled and is indeed bound to determine the true legal relation resulting from a transaction. If the parties have chosen to conceal by a device the legal relation, it is open to the taxing authorities to unravel the device and to determine the true character of the relationship. But the legal effect of a transaction cannot be displaced by probing into the substance of the transaction.

Though the *Westminster* principle was applied by the judiciary consistently for decades, the debate between morality and legality while assessing matters of tax avoidance took a dramatic turn in the early 1980s in the UK. The issues in the cases of *WT Ramsay Ltd v Commissioner of the Inland Revenue* (1982)[53] and *Commissioner of the Inland Revenue v Burmah Oil Co Ltd* (1982)[54] related to a pre-arranged scheme by the taxpayers to create an allowable capital loss for tax purposes. Effectively this case gave more weight to substance over form by holding that where there is a series of transactions which are pre-ordained and into which there are inserted steps that have no commercial purpose

[48] Department of Revenue, Ministry of Finance, *The Direct Taxes Code Bill, 2010: Forty Ninth Report* March 2012.

[49] *Bank of Chettinad Ltd v The Commissioner of Income Tax* (1940) 8 ITR 522.

[50] *Inland Revenue Commissioners v Duke of Westminster* [1936] AC 1; 19 TC 490.

[51] *Commissioner of Income Tax, Hyderabad v M/S. Motor and General Stores (P) Ltd* (1967) 66 ITR 692.

[52] *Commissioner of Income Tax v BM Kharwar* (1969) 72 ITR 603.

[53] *Ramsay (WT) Ltd v Commissioners of Inland Revenue* (1981) 54 TC 101.

[54] *Inland Revenue Commissioners v Burmah Oil Co Ltd* (1981) 54 TC 200.

apart from tax avoidance, then the whole scheme has to be considered as such. This came to be known as the *Ramsay* principle.

In India, the *Ramsay* principle was analysed by the Supreme Court in the landmark ruling in the case *of McDowell & Co Ltd v Commercial Tax Officer* (1985).[55] The taxpayer was a licensed manufacturer of Indian liquor and the issue before the Supreme Court was whether sales tax authorities could include the excise duty which was not charged by the taxpayer but instead paid directly to the excise authorities by the buyers of the liquor, in the taxpayer's turnover to determine the amount of sales tax payable. The Supreme Court held against the taxpayer and observed that

> colourable devices cannot be part of tax planning and it is wrong to encourage or entertain the belief that it is honourable to avoid the payment of tax by resorting to dubious methods. It is the obligation of every citizen to pay the taxes honestly without resorting to subterfuge.

Reliance was placed on the English jurisprudence on the subject and, in his separate concurring judgment, Justice Chinnappa Reddy further observed:

> Thus, the ghost of Westminster (in the words of Lord Roskill) has been exorcized in England. Should it be allowed to rear its head in India? …

In the matter the judge questioned why the *principle of Westminster* that had been given a decent burial in its country of origin continued to be invoked. This was despite the shift in the judicial attitude towards tax avoidance – from the 'smile, cynical or even affectionate though it might have been at one time, has now frozen into a deep frown'.[56]

It was suggested that it

> is neither fair nor desirable to expect the Legislature to intervene and take care of every device and scheme to avoid taxation. It is up to the Court to take stock to determine the nature of the new and sophisticated legal devices to avoid tax and consider whether the situation created by the devices could be related to the existing legislation with the aid of 'emerging' techniques of interpretation was done in Ramsay, Burma Oil and Dawson, to expose the devices for what they really are and to refuse to give judicial benediction.

Therefore, the contentious issue of how far the courts could go to pierce the corporate veil needed to be resolved. The validity of the *Westminster* principle, despite the Supreme Court's ruling in *McDowell*, was upheld in the landmark case of *Union of India v Azadi Bachao Andolan* (2003).[57] In this case, the Supreme Court upheld the validity of the Central Board of Direct Taxes' Circular No 789, dated 13 April 2000, which, in the context of the India Mauritius treaty, clarified that a certificate of residence issued by the Mauritian authorities would constitute a sufficient evidence for accepting the residential status of a Mauritian entity. The respondents relied on the decision in *McDowell* to urge that the act of incorporation of a company in Mauritius by foreign institutional investors was a 'sham' and 'a device' used to obtain the benefits of the India Mauritius treaty and that such arrangements should not be recognised by the Court.

The Supreme Court held that the decision in *McDowell* cannot be read as laying down that every attempt at tax planning was illegitimate and must be ignored, or that

[55] *Mc Dowell & Company Limited v The Commercial Tax Officer* (1985) 154 ITR 148.
[56] See *Mc Dowell*, ibid at [55].
[57] *Union of India and Anr v Azadi Bachao Andolan & Anr* (2003) 263 ITR 706.

every transaction or arrangement which is perfectly permissible under law but has the effect of reducing the tax burden of the taxpayer must be looked upon with disfavour. Contrary to the pronouncement in *McDowell*, the Court's view was that '*... the principle in Duke of Westminster's case is very much alive and kicking in the country of its birth*'. Then again the Supreme Court in the *Vodafone* ruling acknowledged that '*Tax avoidance is a problem faced by almost all countries following civil and common law systems. ...*'[58] and many countries took legislative measures to scrutinise transactions. It was the Court's view that '*Lack of proper regulatory laws, leads to uncertainty and passing inconsistent orders by Courts, Tribunals and other forums, putting Revenue and taxpayers at bay*'.[59] Therefore, the Courts could not agree about whether they should look at substance over form. The difficulty with applying an anti-avoidance rule through judicial pronouncements can be even more difficult.

Not only was there limited legal recourse but the growing concerns of equity also led to support for GAAR.

> 24.1 Tax avoidance, like tax evasion, seriously undermines the achievements of the public finance objective of collecting revenues in an efficient, equitable and effective manner. Sectors that provide a greater opportunity for tax avoidance tend to cause distortions in the allocation of resources. Since the better-off sections are more endowed to resort to such practices, tax avoidance also leads to cross-subsidization of the rich.[60]

The Direct Taxes Code (DTC) Bill was presented before Parliament in 2010 and was referred to an expert committee for review.[61] The Standing Committee was appointed to analyse and recommend on the Code. The process of implementation was further delayed, and continued to be revised until 2013. What was instrumental in pushing the early adoption of the GAAR was the *Vodafone International Holdings BV v Union of India* (2012)[62] where the Revenue contended that the decision in *Azadi Bachao Andolan* should be overruled insofar as it departed from the decision in *McDowell.*

In the light of the growing pressures, the GAAR provisions were finally proposed in the Finance Bill, 2012. While introducing these provisions, the finance minister stated that GAAR was introduced 'in order to counter aggressive tax avoidance schemes, while ensuring that it is used only in appropriate cases, by enabling a review by a GAAR panel'.[63]

The Bill was enacted and the GAAR provisions were incorporated in the Income Tax Act, 1961. They were proposed to be applicable from AY 2014–15. However, in view of the concerns raised by stakeholders, primarily on account of discretionary powers of the authority, an expert Committee on GAAR was constituted under the chairmanship of Dr Parthasarathi Shome (Shome Committee) to consult the stakeholders and finalise the GAAR guidelines. The Shome Committee noted 'The GAAR provisions codify (this) 'substance' over 'form' basis of the tax law. It is, therefore, necessary and desirable

[58] *Vodafone International Holdings v Union of India & Anr* (2012) 1 SCR 573 [54].
[59] ibid at [55].
[60] *Vodafone*, n 60 above at 46.
[61] ibid at 34 and 46.
[62] *Vodafone International Holdings BV v Union of India* (2012) 341 ITR 1.
[63] India Budget, *Union Budget Speech 2012* [154].

to introduce a general anti-avoidance rule which will serve as a deterrent against such practices.'

Many of the suggestions of the Shome Committee were accepted and the new provisions were inserted through the Finance Act 2013. The applicability of GAAR was deferred to AY 2016–17, then further deferred to AY 2018–19. The GAAR provisions finally became applicable in India from the financial year 2017–18. Although GAARs, there are specific anti-avoidance measures that continue to be introduced.

GAARs are politically difficult to implement since taxpayers are apprehensive of the implications about the certainty of future commercial transactions. The experiences of India and the UK, both of which adopted the GAAR much later than countries such as Australia and Canada, show that specific anti-avoidance legislation, disclosures as well as judicial pronouncements, can be insufficient in tackling avoidance. Although GAARs are viewed with scepticism due to the uncertainty in application, there is uncertainty and complexity even in their absence. As shown in India, there was less consistency in the application of the 'substance over form' principle by the judiciary and the introduction of GAAR has not lessened the use of Targeted anti avoidance rules (TAARs) in the UK and SAARs in India.

It is possible that legislation design, along with administrative processes, can help bring about certainty. For example, the panel system for GAAR, prevalent in the UK and India can provide additional checks of the tax administration through reference. Freedman argues that it may not be appropriate to evaluate the GAAR solely on uncertainty, and this may be more an issue of design and process of application.[64] Therefore, it may be important to look at the design features of GAAR. The next section evaluates some of these design features of tax law and administration which can ensure that the law is compatible with rule of law.

Design Features of GAAR

Legislators often walk the tightrope of balancing certainty with simplicity in tax law. It is hard to design a law that covers all scenarios. In fact, more detail in tax legislation can, on the contrary, increase opportunities for tax avoidance.[65] The point of the rule is to ensure that the arrangements are consistent with the intent of the legislature, as conveyed in the tax legislation.[66] Therefore, there is some rationale for a general anti-avoidance rule that acts as a catch all legislation. Although the proper operation of GAAR requires a well-defined legislation based on clearly defined principle,[67] the

[64] Above, n 22, 354–56.

[65] D McBarnet and C Whelan, *The Elusive Spirit of the Law: Formalism and the Struggle for Legal Control* (1991) 54(6) *Modern Law Review* 848.

[66] RS Avi-Yonah and A Pichhadze, 'GAARs and the Nexus between Statutory Interpretation and Legislative Drafting: Lessons for the U.S from Canada' (2015) *Econ Law* 1.

[67] J Freedman, 'Designing a General Anti-Abuse Rule: Striking a Balance' (2014) *Asia-Pacific Tax Bulletin* 167, Oxford Legal Studies Research Paper No 53/2014. Available at: https://papers.ssrn.com/sol3/papers.cfm?abstract_id=2488541.

successful design of a GAAR includes sound drafting and administrative capacity.[68] The successful application of anti-avoidance rules ultimately depends on: (i) the design and drafting of the particular anti-avoidance rule, which is often less rules-based and therefore more discretionary in its application; and (ii) the capacity of the tax authority to appropriately apply such an anti-avoidance rule in a measured, even-handed and predictable way. Both aspects are critical to achieving greater tax certainty.[69]

There are four models of GAAR.[70] The first identifies transactions with the purpose or effect of tax benefits, regardless of economic substance. The second, the 'substance over form' rule, allows tax authorities to reassess transactions to reflect their true economic nature. The third is a judicial GAAR based on the 'abuse of law' doctrine. Finally, the fourth category is the statutory GAAR. The section focuses on, and attempts to identify, features that would address the vagueness and discretion in application of GAAR and examines the main criticisms of the rule.

Definition of Purpose, Abuse and Avoidance

It is reasonable to expect that a simplified model of a GAAR will be set in the context of a country, including constitutional limitations, political and administrative structures and its fiscal policies.[71] Irrespective, there are three important elements of the construct – the definition of the tax avoidance scheme that is entered into, if the person has obtained a tax benefit from the scheme, and the sole or dominant purpose of the scheme was to obtain a tax benefit.[72] The UN practical portfolio[73] also provides guidance on the underlying principles for the development of a GAAR. Sometimes these principles may require tax policy officials to balance competing interests. That is, the GAAR should apply as widely as possible to all incomes and expenses, domestic and cross-border transactions, individuals and corporations and all kinds of arrangements. Although it is difficult, GAAR should distinguish between abusive tax avoidance transactions and legitimate commercial transactions. GAARs in different countries incorporate this distinction by using words such as abusive, artificial, impermissible, illegitimate, and unacceptable.[74] But it is critical for this definitional clarity that the purpose test should be simple. There are different ways in which the purpose test is designed. For example, the Australian GAAR has eight factors/circumstances[75] that are considered jointly in forming a view of the purpose.[76] However, the Canadian GAAR

[68] Above, n 4.

[69] Above, n 21.

[70] R Krever, 'General Report: GAARs' in *GAARs – A Key Element of Tax Systems in the Post-BEPS World* (IBFD) 1, 3.

[71] Above, n 4.

[72] Above, n 4 at 10.

[73] B Arnold, 'Protecting the Tax Base of Developing Countries through the use of General Anti-avoidance Rules' (2019) United Nations Practical Portfolio.

[74] Above n 73 at 90.

[75] Income Tax Act *(Australia)*, s 177D(2)(f).

[76] M Stewart, 'Australia's GAAR Turns 40: In its Prime or Mid-Life Crisis?' (2021) 52(4) *Victoria University of Wellington Law Review.*

does not consider a transaction as one for 'avoidance' where it is undertaken for a bona fide commercial purpose, other than to obtain tax benefit.[77] In the case of the UK, the double reasonableness test is applied, where the GAAR applies to 'tax arrangements' that are 'abusive'. Where the former is one in which obtaining tax benefit is one of the main purposes, this is followed by a test of whether the arrangement is abusive. In India, GAAR applies to impermissible avoidance arrangements whose main purpose, in part or step, is to obtain a tax benefit. Therefore, a statutory GAAR can be designed to apply broadly with a check of criteria as in the case of the UK or it can be restricted to establishing 'main' or 'dominant' purpose in the case of India and Hong Kong. A related feature that can have a strong bearing on the application of GAAR is judicial interpretation. In Canada, GAAR was invoked in 1,300 instances in its years of operation and the Revenue lost only 24 cases.[78] Even though cases have been referred to the judiciary in multiple cases, it has been found to work well. However, its narrow focus has not allowed the courts to apply GAAR even where tax avoidance was one of the purposes.[79] (*Swirsky*,[80] *Loblaw*[81]). Others argue that the Supreme Court in Canada has not previously provided clear guidance on whether a transaction is abusive.[82] Therefore, a broadly applicable GAAR can be effective in addressing tax avoidance, even though it may bring with it some degree of uncertainty. The contemporaneous design of checks as additional objective tests or administrative processes can be useful in counteracting discretion.

Panel and Rulings

A transaction or arrangement may be designed for avoidance, but there is also a need for technical experts to determine whether it is avoidance based on facts. GAAR panels can play a crucial role in ensuring that GAAR is applied consistently and fairly. These independent or semi-independent bodies operate separately from the tax authority involved in a dispute with a taxpayer. Primarily, GAAR panels act as advisors, offering the tax administration expert insights on applying the GAAR in specific situations. They also function centrally, reviewing all relevant GAAR application cases. This centralised approach fosters consistent and uniform application; this is particularly important due to the subjective nature of applying GAAR to various scenarios. Additionally, publishing the panel's decisions helps taxpayers to understand situations where the GAAR might

[77] '2023 Canadian Federal Budget: General anti-avoidance rule' (*Norton Rose Fulbright*, March 2023). Available at: www.nortonrosefulbright.com/en/knowledge/publications/8979c10e/2023-canadian-federal-budget-general-anti-avoidance-rule.

[78] Pooja Mihailovich and Joanne Vandale, 'Concern Grows Over Canada's Mission to Update Tax Avoidance Rule' (*Bloomberg Tax*, 15 February 2023). Available at: https://news.bloombergtax.com/tax-insights-and-commentary/concern-grows-over-canadas-mission-to-update-tax-avoidance-rule.

[79] Government of Canada, *Modernizing and Strengthening the General Anti-Avoidance Rule*' Consultation Paper 2022.

[80] *Swirsky v The Queen* (2013) TCC 73, affirmed 2014 FCA 36.

[81] *Loblaw Financial Holdings Inc. v The Queen* (2021) SCC 51.

[82] BJ Arnold, 'Policy Forum: Confusion Worse Confounded – The Supreme Court's GAAR Decisions' (2006) 54(1) *Can. Tax J.* 167.

be triggered, providing valuable guidance. Ultimately, GAAR panels play a vital role in safeguarding taxpayers from the inappropriate application of the GAAR.

Several countries have adopted a panel system but with varying authority in determination of avoidance. In Australia the GAAR panel is composed of external experts that includes business and professional people in a position to provide expert advice and senior tax officers. The panel is purely consultative[83] and is designed to provide advice to decision makers.[84] However, it does afford those affected by the application of the GAAR with the right to be heard.[85] The Australian GAAR panel can invite oral as well as written concise submissions but does not investigate facts. The right to a hearing is not afforded under Canadian GAAR but written submissions may be filed.[86]

In India, the GAAR panel comprises one sitting High Court judge, a scholar or academic and one member of the Revenue not ranking below Chief Commissioner of Income Tax. The assessing officer determines whether GAAR will apply to a transaction and will refer the same to the Commissioner Income Tax (CIT). If the CIT is satisfied that the GAAR is applicable, will make a reference to the panel for its approval.

Unlike in India, the UK's GAAR panel does not have any tax official member although the Chair is appointed by the tax authorities.[87] The panel discusses the distinction between abusive and non-abusive tax mitigation.[88] All cases are put to the panel if they are to proceed and the panel provides an opinion on whether entering into or carrying out a tax arrangement is a reasonable course of action.[89] In cases where the HMRC's decision is challenged before the Court, the latter must take into consideration the panel's opinion and guidance. Therefore, GAAR panels have varying jurisdiction across countries. While a panel can investigate and decide matters in India, it is merely consultative in Australia. Further, the decision of the panel in India is binding on the Revenue and the taxpayer[90] whereas in the UK it is not.[91] Moreover, there is potential to appeal against the decision. The issue remains as to whether the panel is truly independent, especially where instances of GAAR being invoked are predominantly upheld. For example, from 1 July 2007 to 30 June 2011, the Australian Panel applied GAAR in 64% of cases.[92] As of 31 March 2011, the Canadian Committee had applied GAAR in 73% of cases since GAAR was first introduced in Canada.[93] On the other hand, in the UK, the panel has issued around twelve decisions and only in one case did it conclude that the relevant arrangements were not abusive.[94] However, it is likely that HMRC may initially

[83] Justice GT Pagone at the Australian GAAR Panel (GAAR Conference, London) 10 February 2012.

[84] 'General Anti-Avoidance Rules Panel' Australian Taxation Office, Australian Government. Available at: www.ato.gov.au/about-ato/ato-advice-and-guidance/in-detail/private-rulings/general-anti-avoidance-rules-panel.

[85] *Annetts v McCann* (1990) 170 CLR 596; *Ainsworth v Criminal Justice Commission* (1992) 175 CLR 564.

[86] A Korde, *GAAR – Are Safeguards Adequate?* Bombay Chartered Accountants' Journal, June 2012.

[87] HM Revenue & Customs, '*General Anti-Abuse Rule (GAAR) Advisory Panel: Terms of Reference*', June 2018. Available at: https://assets.publishing.service.gov.uk/government/uploads/system/uploads/attachment_data/file/723704/GAAR_Advisory_Panel_-_Terms_of_Reference__2018_.pdf.

[88] Above, n 67.

[89] Finance Act 2013, s 209 (Sch 42) *(United Kingdom).*

[90] CBDT Circular No 7 of 2017, 27 January 2017.

[91] 'How HMRC uses the GAAR Advisory Panel's opinions on tax avoidance'. HM Revenue and Customs. Available at: www.gov.uk/guidance/tax-avoidance-enablers-gaar-advisory-panel-opinions-on-tax-avoidance.

[92] Above n 86.

[93] ibid.

[94] 'Tax Avoidance: general anti-abuse rule guidance-latest version' (2014) HM Revenue and Customs. Available at: www.gov.uk/government/publications/tax-avoidance-general-anti-abuse-rules.

have referred only 'safe' cases to the panel that it knew it would win.[95] It is not known if there are cases where the panel has recommended that the arrangement is reasonable and HMRC has not published the opinion.[96]

However, implementing GAAR panels requires careful consideration. Resource limitations might be a concern, particularly when the anticipated number of GAAR applications is low. Jurisdictions must also evaluate if a panel aligns with their existing legal and administrative framework.

Advance Rulings are another way to ensure that GAAR is not frequently triggered and to introduce more certainty around the application of tax law. In India, the erstwhile Authority of Advance Ruling (AAR) could issue a ruling on whether there is an impermissible avoidance arrangement (IIA); where the AAR found there is no IIA, GAAR could not be triggered.[97] In the UK the large businesses can reach out to the large taxpayers' unit, and rulings are not available as an option. While evaluating the GAAR on its compatibility with rule of law it is essential to examine if such design features exist to ensure that there is a backstop.

Other than executive discretion, there is also uncertainty where a GAAR applies alongside an expanding set of specific anti avoidance rules and tax treaties. Clarity in the application of tax law and treaties can help further tackle uncertainty.

Interactions between SAAR and GAAR

In all jurisdictions SAAR coexists with GAAR.[98] In the UK, for example, there were 300 Targeted Anti-Avoidance Rules (TAARs) before the introduction of GAAR with their own definition of what constitutes purpose.[99] It was thought that the introduction of the GAAR would help cut down some of the TAARs.[100] Yet, TAARs continue to be employed in the UK. The introduction of SAARs even where GAARs exist is because while SAAR covers specific transactions, GAARs apply more generally. Fundamentally, the two are argued to have different goals and modus operandi.[101] While GAAR substitutes hypothetical transactions in place of an arrangement to recompute tax liability, a SAAR accepts the legitimacy of the transaction for tax purposes but negates the tax benefit.[102] For this reason, the two are thought to be compatible. Yet, there is a possibility that the two could be applied simultaneously, but this decision would rest ultimately with the tax authorities and courts.[103] Tax certainty hinges on the selection of appropriate anti-avoidance measures.[104] General Anti-Avoidance Rules, while effective in

[95] J Freedman, 'The UK General Anti-Avoidance Rule: Transplants and Lessons' (2019) *Bulletin for International Taxation* 73.

[96] Above, n 95.

[97] 'Clarifications on Implementation of GAAR Provisions under the Income Tax Act, 1961' (27 January 2017) *Ministry of Finance, Government of India* F.no 500/43/2016-FT&TR-IV.

[98] M Lang, J Owens, P Pistone, A Rust, J Schuch and C Staringer (eds) *GAARs – A Key Element of Tax Systems in the Post-BEPS Tax World*, 2016.

[99] Above, n 40.

[100] ibid.

[101] Above, n 98.

[102] ibid.

[103] ibid at 93.

[104] Above, n 21.

deterring aggressive tax planning (through their very existence), can create uncertainty due to their discretionary nature. Conversely, SAARs are generally less ambiguous but might incentivise the creation of complex structures to circumvent them.

Consider the legal policy choice for addressing debt bias in tax systems. A GAAR shouldn't hinder legitimate financing decisions (debt vs equity) when the chosen instrument offers genuine non-tax benefits (legal, commercial, accounting). In such cases, a specific integrity provision or SAAR (eg interest deduction limitations like those in BEPS Action 4) would be a more suitable tool. However, a GAAR could still play a residual role in striking down blatantly artificial arrangements designed to exploit loopholes in the SAAR.[105]

The European Commission, for example, noted that the SAARs are often inadequate for arresting the growth of aggressive tax planning structures. The adoption of a common GAAR would avoid the complexity of SAARs,[106] especially where the European Court of Justice's principle of abuse of law has been subject to change over time.[107] This is also relevant when looking at the interactions between a SAAR and a GAAR. As mentioned, if there is both a SAAR and GAAR, this would preclude the application of the latter where a transaction covered by the former has not led to the invocation of the GAAR. There are order preferences that can limit the uncertainty. In the UK, for example, GAAR overrides other anti-avoidance rules, although GAAR and SAAR may apply since arrangements can be challenged under multiple provisions.[108] Further, GAAR will apply where an arrangement is 'blatantly abusive'.[109] In India, GAAR and SAAR apply based on facts and circumstances.[110] In a recent case, *Ayodhya Rami Reddy Alla v PCIT*,[111] the Telangana High Court dealt with the issue of an overlap and ruled that GAAR would apply to an arrangement that is impermissible tax law even though a SAAR was applicable. The purpose of legislating GAAR is precisely to overcome the gaps in tax law, that are on account of inability to cover all avoidance transactions or arrangements. Therefore, the applicability of GAAR to situations where a SAAR may also apply creates uncertainty for the taxpayers; however, it would not apply unless an abuse of tax law has been established in the said arrangement. The option of advance rulings and reference to panel should also help address some of the concerns.

GAAR and Tax Treaties

GAARs are introduced in domestic law and coexist with tax treaties. The important aspect is whether the domestic GAAR would apply before treaties or otherwise.

[105] ibid.

[106] 'Commission Recommendation of 06 December 2012 on aggressive tax planning' (2012) *Official Journal of the European Union*, 3.

[107] *Toolkit for the Design and Effective Implementation of Domestic and International General Anti-Avoidance Rules*, The Inter-American Center of Tax Administrations (CIAT), 2022, 21.

[108] HM Revenue and Customs, 'General Anti-abuse Rule (GAAR) Guidance (Approved by the GAAR Advisory Panel with effect from 28 March 2018)' [B.7.2].

[109] Above, n 108 at [B 6.2].

[110] Above, n 97.

[111] *Ayodhya Rami Reddy Alla V PCIT* TS-398-HC-2024(TEL) (2024).

Moreover, increasingly tax treaties carry a principal purpose test (PPT). A GAAR may differ from that in a treaty in its scope. There are ways to resolve the conflict between applicability of domestic and tax treaty GAAR based on their scope and coverage. The first approach is to not apply domestic GAAR where there is a tax treaty GAAR in the context of cross-border transactions. The second approach is where the domestic GAAR has a similar or broader scope and a tax treaty makes no mention of this, then domestic GAAR may be applied. The third approach is that applying domestic GAAR in tax treaty situations may entail double taxation and defeat the object and purpose of the treaty.[112] There is no clear-cut answer, so it depends on the factual and legal matrix within which the rules are to be applied. The applicability of domestic GAAR may be determined by interpretation of treaty GAAR and abuse of treaty doctrine.[113]

As of November 2023, 102 countries had signed the Multilateral Instrument (MLI)[114] which has come into effect in 85 countries.[115] While preserving the right of bilateral tax treaties to eliminate double taxation, the MLI also provides a way to deal with low tax rates or treaty abuse. While there are many opt-ins and opt-outs, the agreed minimum standard within the treaties are the Articles pertaining to anti-abuse (Articles 6 and 7) and dispute resolution (Article 14). It is possible that, while dealing with treaty abuse, countries may choose to adopt a principal purpose test (PPT), a PPT with simplified or detailed Limitation of Benefit (LOB) or a detailed LOB clause to cover each of the tax agreements. Of the approximate 3,000 treaties, it is expected that the PPT will apply to 1,944.[116] As per the author's previous estimates, in 2017 large number of submissions by signatories or, to be precise 83.57% of the treaties, had opted for a PPT, in either of the combinations.[117] As per the language of the PPT its application would

> be a benefit under the Covered Tax Agreement shall not be granted in respect of an item of income or capital if it is reasonable to conclude, having regard to all relevant facts and circumstances, that obtaining that benefit was one of the principal purposes of any arrangement or transaction that resulted directly or indirectly in that benefit, unless it is established that granting that benefit in these circumstances would be in accordance with the object and purpose of the relevant provisions of the Covered Tax Agreement.[118]

Therefore, the tax administration can determine if the treaty benefit is not in accordance with the object of the treaty and deny any benefit where it is established that obtaining that benefit is one of the principal purposes.

In India, the GAAR takes a narrow approach whereas PPT adopts an intermediate approach. At the same time, GAAR allows the Revenue a wider reach. It has been

[112] E Furuseth, *GAARs in the Tax Treaty (Chapter 18: Part IV: The Relevance of a GAAR/SAAR in the Tax Treaty)* (2018) in *The Interpretation of Tax Treaties in Relation to Domestic GAARs.*

[113] Above, n 112.

[114] OECD Database: *BEPS MLI Matching Database.* Available at: www.oecd.org/en/data/tools/beps-mli-matching-database.html.

[115] Above, n 114.

[116] ibid.

[117] S Tandon, 'The Multilateral Legal Instrument: A Developing Country Perspective' (2018) *NIPFP Working Paper No 220.*

[118] MLI, art 7(1). Available at: www.oecd.org/content/dam/oecd/en/topics/policy-sub-issues/beps-mli/multilateral-convention-to-im.at:plement-tax-treaty-related-measures-to-prevent-beps.pdf.

clarified that GAAR and the PPT will apply, depending on the transaction. GAAR would need to be tested on a standalone basis and can be invoked even where the SAAR or LoB conditions are satisfied. There may be situations where the tax authority may choose to apply the PPT instead of the GAAR.

Principles of Equity, Justice in Tax and Rule of Law: Concluding Remarks

To be consistent with rule of law 'the law of taxation, including its discretionary elements, should be clear; capable of guiding taxpayers; stable; fairly enforced; non-retrospective; capable of implementation; and open to adjudication before an independent tribunal'.[119] However, the 'rule of law values do not express every characteristic that is desirable in a tax system'.[120] It may be argued that the rule of law may have to be balanced with other considerations such as efficient administration or distribution of burdens in accordance with ability to pay.[121] It may be reasonable to introduce discretion while remaining sensitive to taxpayers' concerns through participatory procedures, judicial review, and appeals system.[122]

The increasing complexity of financial transactions necessitates a legal framework that can adapt. This has led to the development of General Anti-Avoidance Rules (GAAR) alongside existing Specific Anti-Avoidance Rules (SAARs). GAARs address arrangements that exploit loopholes or undermine the spirit of the tax law, even if they technically comply with specific rules. While SAARs remain important, GAARs fill a crucial gap in ensuring a fairer tax system.

However, for GAARs to be effective, they require thoughtful implementation. Clear guidelines and independent review processes are essential to ensure consistent and principled application. Some countries have established GAAR panels with diverse expertise precisely to address these concerns and promote objective decision-making.

This focus on transparency and fairness in tax administration extends beyond national borders. The international tax landscape is constantly evolving, with initiatives such as the BEPS project (Base Erosion and Profit Shifting) introducing new standards like the Principal Purpose Test (PPT) in tax treaties. By engaging in a continuous dialogue with international tax and investment law developments, we can leverage this collective knowledge to refine national GAAR frameworks and anti-avoidance rules in general. This collaborative approach fosters a more robust and equitable tax environment for all stakeholders.

The principles of equity, justice, and the rule of law are fundamental to a well-functioning tax system. GAAR, when implemented with clear guidelines and strong legal safeguards, can actually contribute to a more just and predictable tax environment.

[119] D de Cogan, *Tax, Discretion and the Rule of Law* in C Evans, J Freedman and RE Krever (eds) *The Delicate Balance: Tax, Discretion and the Rule of Law* (Amsterdam: IBFD 2011).

[120] Above, n 119.

[121] ibid.

[122] ibid.

By establishing clear design features for anti-avoidance rules, including the application of the proportionality principle, we can minimise conflicts arising from discretionary interpretations and uphold the rule of law.

In conclusion, GAAR, coupled with a commitment to transparency and international collaboration, presents a valuable opportunity to create a fairer and more efficient tax system for the future.

7

'Erosion' of the Rule of Law in a Taxation Context: Reflections on Recent New Zealand Experiences

ADRIAN SAWYER

Abstract

The rule of law is a fundamental principle upon which law-making and governing are founded and is the cornerstone of a civilised society. At its heart, is the notion that the power of the Executive is exercised according to an independent judicial system, with that power being restricted by the law that has been enacted by the Legislature (enhanced when this is a democratically elected body which is answerable to the public). The rule of law is fundamental to the development and administration of a nation's tax laws, to prevent taxpayers being subject to arbitrary action by the government. This chapter uses a case study approach to explore the 'erosion' of the rule of law in a taxation context in New Zealand, particularly in the lead up to, during, and post the COVID-19 pandemic. Taking a 'thick' perspective, the evaluation sheds light on the risks that may arise to the operation of the rule of law in times when a government 'sets aside' or shortcuts long-established practices in developing and implementing tax policy and legislation. These actions also facilitate a decline in trust by the general populace in the government, their ability to understand and apply the law to their situations (along with associated levels of tax compliance), as well as their expectations that the rule of law applies to all.

Introduction

What is meant by the 'rule of law'? In the context of a democracy, Spiller[1] defines it as 'the doctrine that all are equal before the law and that acts of officials in carrying out government orders are cognisable in the ordinary courts'. Alongside the rule of law is the fundamental principle of the separation of powers between the Legislature,

[1] P Spiller, *New Zealand Law Dictionary* 10th edn (Wellington, NZ: LexisNexis, 2022).

Executive and Judiciary. Without such separation, there remains a risk that the fundamental tenants of a democracy will become blurred and breakdown. Concurrently there is a risk that the rights of the jurisdiction's residents and citizens will be infringed when these rights are not able to be recognised as law and any limitations on these rights will not be reasonable and justifiable for those that live in a free and democratic society. Once the rule of law breaks down or is not seen to be binding on all (especially the Executive), mutual trust and cooperation will erode significantly, and it will be exceedingly difficult to regain.

From a theoretical perspective of the rule of law, there is a spectrum, with two dominant perspectives being, first the classic 'thin vs thick' debate as to whether the rule of law deals primarily with matters of procedure (such as, publicity, non-retrospectivity) or whether to a greater or lesser extent it should encompass substantive matters such as the protection of human rights and wider accountability.[2] The second perspective views the rule of law as a protective mechanism for individuals (such as protecting personal autonomy in a 'thin' account, or human rights in a 'thick' account) or a way of organising society that benefits the collective and which is closely analogous to rules-based good governance.[3] The analysis in this chapter principally focuses on the 'thick' end of the spectrum, embracing substantive matters including human rights.

In a New Zealand context, the Ministry of Justice states on its website:

> The rule of law also forms a significant part of the New Zealand constitution. The principles of the rule of law are not easily defined but encompass *ideas* such as:
>
> - the powers exercised by parliamentarians and officials are based on legal authority; …
> - the law should have safeguards against the abuse of wide discretionary powers.[4]

Focusing on the rule of law in the context of taxation, Leibler (2022) observes: '[E]xtreme potential consequences should never be far from our minds as a backdrop for policy development and administering the tax system.'[5]

The focus of this chapter closely aligns to the two quotation extracts set out above. In this regard, the chapter takes an exploratory case-study approach focusing on one jurisdiction, New Zealand, with which the author is familiar. In adopting a sole case study-approach, the design and analysis considerations are of significant importance, along with the description of events or the scenario(s) under review.[6] The need for a case study frequently arises out of the desire to understand complex social phenomena which, in this situation, is the erosion of the rule of law within the ambit of taxation policy in New Zealand. The case-study approach enables the researcher to investigate

[2] For an excellent analysis of the need for wider accountability through the rule of law, see Daly, Chapter 2 in this volume, who explores the state of the rule of law in the UK taking a 'thick' account in a tax administration context.

[3] Writing in the context of the law of tax avoidance, two major perspectives of the rule of law (the narrow and wide scopes, or the 'thin' versus 'thick' perspectives) are comprehensively explored in Lindsay, Chapter 3 in this volume.

[4] See www.justice.govt.nz/about/learn-about-the-justice-system/how-the-justice-system-works/the-basis-for-all-law.

[5] M Leibler AC, 'Tax and the Rule of Law,' *Annual Tax Lecture*, Melbourne Law School, (23 March 2022), 1.

[6] RK Yin, *Case Study Research and Applications: Design and Methods* 6th edn (Thousand Oaks, CA: Sage Publications, 2017).

and review, in a holistic and meaningful way, the various characteristics of real-life events. However, while the chapter contains a single-country case study, it has wider ramifications for other jurisdictions that apply the rule of law as separation of powers and provide fundamental protections for taxpayers' rights, such as the United Kingdom. Researchers in these jurisdictions may compare experiences and lessons between their jurisdiction and New Zealand with respect to how the respective jurisdictions have applied the rule of law within a tax context. The focus in this chapter is on two of the three bodies that exercise significant powers, namely the Executive and the Legislature; it does not directly consider the role of the Judiciary. In some respects, this is an arbitrary decision to exclude the Judiciary from the analysis. The author's reasoning is two-fold. The first is a capacity constraint, reflecting the challenges of the word length available. The second reflects the reality in New Zealand that the Judiciary have been reluctant to intervene in situations involving the scope and roles of the Executive and Legislature unless there is evidence of a failure to adhere to legislation or regulation. The principal focus of this chapter is tax policy development and taxpayers' rights which, unfortunately in the author's view, are not underpinned by legislative or regulatory instruments.

The remainder of this chapter is set out as follows. The next section discusses the general concept of the rule of law and how it applies to taxation (drawing principally upon New Zealand debate). This is followed by the core of this chapter, namely a review of the evidence suggesting a significant erosion of the rule of law in New Zealand (with a focus on taxation) from a 'thick 'perspective. The chapter concludes with discussion and observations.

Rule of Law – General Propositions and Application in a Taxation Context

General Propositions

When it comes to what is meant by the rule of law in a New Zealand context, the Legislation Design and Advisory Committee (LDAC), in its 2021 guidelines,[7] states (taking a 'thin' perspective):

> **The rule of law**: The full scope of the rule of law is the subject of debate, but at its core are the following principles:
>
> - **Everyone is subject to the law, including the government** – People and institutions that wield power must do so within legal limits, and be accountable for their actions; everybody is equal before the law and is subject to it. …
> - **The law should be clear, and clearly enforceable** – The law should be publicly accessible and able to be easily understood by all to whom it applies. Rights and obligations need to be matched with enforcement mechanisms (civil or criminal) and remedies so that people and/or the State can enforce it.

[7] Legislation Design and Advisory Committee, *Legislation Guidelines 2021 edition* (NZ Government, 2021), Chapter 4, part 1. Available at: www.ldac.org.nz/guidelines/legislation-guidelines-2021-edition/constitutional-issues-and-recognising-rights-2/chapter-4/.

- **There should be an independent, impartial judiciary** – Certain decisions must be made by judges who are independent of the government. Judges interpret legislation and develop the common law. They decide disputes between individuals and between individuals and the Government. Courts are the only institutions that should impose criminal convictions or sentence people to imprisonment.

Lord Bingham, taking a 'thick' perspective, enunciates eight principles that desirably should underpin the rule of law, of which two are especially relevant to this chapter:[8]

> 2. Ministers and public officials at all levels must exercise the powers conferred on them in good faith, fairly, for the purposes for which the powers were conferred, without exceeding the limits of such powers and not unreasonably.
> 3. The law must afford adequate protection of fundamental human rights.

Writing extrajudicially in a New Zealand context, Justice Susan Glazebrook from the New Zealand Supreme Court comments (from a 'thin' perspective) on the rule of law in a taxation context and concludes her address with the following statement:[9]

> Taxation obligations permeate almost every facet of society. *The central importance of tax collection to the functioning of government, means that it raises rule of law issues.* This paper has touched on some of these and has also dealt with some litigation issues. It is often said that taxes are one of the two certainties in life (the other being death). The important issues that taxation law and procedure present are not likely to disappear soon.

Also writing in a New Zealand context, Sage suggests (from a 'thick' perspective) that:[10]

> New Zealand is committed to democratic rule. … When Parliament's intention is made clear, whatever has been enacted in the legislature, the courts in New Zealand have no power to neither invalidate nor decide otherwise. *Elected representatives, after assessing and securing the public interest of the majority of voters, produce legislation that is passed through parliament, but the will of the majority should not be allowed to prevail when fundamental rights are being breached.* There must be consent, creating political obligation, which is binding upon the citizens to obey the laws.

Sage also argues that:[11]

> In addition, the rule of law exists as a system of control on government behaviour and authority, constraining government behaviour by law (government according to the law) and the respect for the law; this is often contrasted with the rule of a despotic, which is regarded as the opposite of the rule of law.

This level of control is one that has been severely weakened in New Zealand in recent times through the Executive's complete control of the Legislature. In terms of the fundamental tenant of the separation of powers, the LDAC also states:[12]

> **Separation of powers** – Each branch of Government (executive, legislature, and judiciary) must perform only those functions associated with that branch and not intrude into,

[8] T Bingham, *The Rule of Law* (London: Allen Lane, 2010). For an earlier discussion of these principles, see T Bingham, 'The Rule of Law' (2007) 66(1) *The Cambridge Law Journal*, 67–85 (emphasis added).

[9] Justice S Glazebrook, 'Tax and the Courts', *Address to the Chartered Accountants Australia and New Zealand Tax Conference*, (Auckland, 19 November 2015), at 25 (emphasis added).

[10] I Sage, *Democracy, Constitutionalism and the Rule of Law: Beholden to Constituent Power* (Victoria University of Wellington Faculty of Law Paper, 2014), at 8 (emphasis added).

[11] Above n 10, 23 (emphasis added).

[12] Above n 7, ch 4, part 1.

> or assume the functions of, another branch. … While the executive and legislative branches share a common membership in New Zealand (Ministers must be members of Parliament), there is still a functional separation between the two branches that means the Legislature can hold the Executive to account.

Application in a Taxation Context

Focusing on the issues raised in the previous subsection of this chapter, and from a revenue perspective, it is clear that only the New Zealand Parliament (the Legislature) can authorise the raising of money by way of new or increased taxes, and not the Executive. The LDAC states in this regard:[13]

> **Legislation needs to clearly authorise the raising, spending, and borrowing of money.**
>
> Government agencies can only spend those funds that Parliament specifically grants them each year. Agencies that run over budget must seek approval from Parliament for more funds. Only Parliament can authorise the borrowing of money by the Government, and *only Parliament has the power to authorise the raising of money by way of new or increased taxes.* …

Thus, there can be no taxation by Executive decree. Writing in 2011, Griffiths assesses how revenue authority discretion operates within the rule of law in New Zealand. She observes that the Tax Administration Act 1994 has improved the quality of tax administration but also conferred wide discretion on the Commissioner of Inland Revenue (Commissioner) and Inland Revenue more broadly.

Griffiths[14] argues that there is an essential role for the courts to maintain this delicate balance in the context of New Zealand's constitutional norms, and that it is imperative that we avoid being complacent in this regard. More recently Griffiths and Hartshorn observe with respect to the New Zealand constitution that:[15]

> In New Zealand, this intersection of law, convention and a strong sense of institutional morality has produced an ever-emerging and shifting constitutional makeup, one which can be changed and developed comparatively easily *but which also gives Parliament more power than those in other Westminster systems.*

Thus, while the authors in that paper suggest that this gives the New Zealand Parliament more power than those in other Westminster systems, this power can be thwarted when the Executive effectively controls the Legislature. Later Griffiths and Hartshorn acknowledge the value of New Zealand having flexibility and less legal precision than most other jurisdictions, although this introduces additional risks. In relation to taxation and the constitution, the authors observe (incorporating a thick perspective):[16]

> It is worth pausing to reflect upon how those administrative aspects of the Commissioner's role interact with the notion that the Commissioner cannot misapply the law and that it is

[13] ibid, ch 4, part 8 (emphasis added).

[14] S Griffiths, 'Revenue Authority Discretions and the Rule of Law in New Zealand', in C Evans, J Freedman and R Krever (eds), *The Delicate Balance: Tax, Discretion and the Rule of Law* (Amsterdam: IBFD, 2011), 149–72.

[15] S Griffiths and J Hartshorn, 'Fragile and Strong: The Oxymoron of Tax Administration and Constitutionality in New Zealand' (2023) *Review of International & European Economic Law* 198–215, at 199–200 (emphasis added).

[16] ibid, 206 (emphasis added).

> the Courts who have the final word on the meaning of a statutory provision. These ideas are crucial in the history of taxation – *they allow for a traceable link from a tax liability directly to Parliament, the representative body through which the people exert their democratic rights.* Parliamentary sovereignty is arguably the most fundamental principle in New Zealand's constitutional landscape. *However, taxation draws out circumstances whereby these very fundamental constitutional principles are eroded in favour other goals which are not strictly 'legal', such as efficiency and the 'integrity of the tax system'.*

Griffiths and Hartshorn then explore this point further in the context of taxpayers' rights and the Generic Tax Policy Process (GTPP) in NZ, two areas close to the heart of the current author.[17] They observe that there have been occasions when both subject matters have come under pressure such as when the integrity of the tax system is seen as being paramount and that legislative action requires urgency and thereby bypassing the GTPP. They conclude their work with the following important observation:[18]

> An approach that espouses trust, values adaptability and prioritises the 'carrot' over the 'stick', so to speak, permeates across the organs of Government in New Zealand. In this sense, the levying of tax and the administration of the tax system in New Zealand does not operate in a constitutional vacuum. It does not exist in its own bubble, but is very much an expression of that general constitutional culture.

Thus, while New Zealand does not have a formal constitution, which is unlike the situation most jurisdictions, it does have a number of constitutional-type documents, such as the Treaty of Waitangi and the New Zealand Bill of Rights Act (NZBORA). The latter is of particular relevance to this chapter, and its 'thick' perspective of the rule of law, in that it applies to the three branches of the government and to '… any person or body in the performance of any public function, power, or duty conferred or imposed on that person or body by or pursuant to law' (NZBORA, s 3(b)). It also provides in s 5 that '… the rights and freedoms contained in this Bill of Rights may be subject only to such reasonable limits prescribed by law as can be demonstrably justified in a free and democratic society'. Interpretations that are consistent with the NZBORA are to be preferred (s 6) and the Attorney-General must report to Parliament on any provisions in a bill that are inconsistent with the NZBORA requiring a formal response from the relevant minister (ss 6–7B). Also, of relevance to this chapter is the right to freedom of movement (s 18), an issue that arose during the COVID-19 lockdowns.

One important observation is that the NZBORA does not specifically protect rights to property and, as such, it should not be a surprise that actions to utilise the NZBORA to resist actions by the Inland Revenue and the Commissioner to collect or assess tax

[17] For further discussion on the GTPP, see P Vial, 'The Generic Tax Policy Process: A "Jewel in Our Policy Formation Crown"?' (2012) 25(2) *New Zealand Universities Law Review* 318–46. For contributions from the current author, see: A Sawyer, 'Reviewing Tax Policy Development in New Zealand: Lessons from a Delicate Balancing of "Law and Politics"' (2013) 28(2) *Australian Tax Forum* 401–25; A Sawyer, 'Tax Policy Without Consultation: Is New Zealand on a "Slippery Slope"?', (2022) 37(4) *Australian Tax Forum*, 481–513; and A Sawyer, 'Navigating Challenging Times: A New Zealand Perspective', (2023), 29(4) *New Zealand Journal of Taxation Law and Policy*, 341–65. In the context of taxpayers' rights, the current author has commented in relation to increased use of technology and wider powers for the Commissioner of Inland Revenue: A Sawyer, 'Enhancing Taxpayers' Rights in New Zealand – An Opportunity Missed?', (2020) 18(2) *e-Journal of Tax Research*, 441–65; and A Sawyer, 'Expanding the Commissioner's Core Powers – Should New Zealanders be Concerned?', (2021) 75(4) *Bulletin for International Taxation*, 162–73.

[18] Griffiths and Hartshorn, 'Fragile and Strong' n 15, at 212 (emphasis added).

have nearly always failed when taken to the courts.[19] Thus, apart from restrictions of movement that may affect one's ability to work and earn income, there is minimal application of the NZBORA to taxation matters, assuming there is no discrimination applied that would come within the scope of the human rights that are protected through the NZBORA.

The chapter now turns to focus on how the rule of law has been eroding during the last few years in New Zealand, particularly within the sphere of taxation.

Erosion of the Rule of Law in New Zealand – Recent Evidence

Erosion of the Rule of Law – The Early Signs

In the context of this chapter, the focus is on how the New Zealand Government (specifically the Executive branch) has operated with respect to adhering to the rule of law in making statements purporting to have legislative force, the setting aside of constitutional conventions through exercising Executive power, and the degree of clarity of application of tax legislative materials. Specifically, it focuses on how the Executive has been making statements about changes in the law and determining their application without the prior authorisation of the New Zealand Parliament.

Furthermore, subsequent authorisation and clarification of details has been made retrospectively by statute enacted by the New Zealand Parliament, frequently by taking urgency and avoiding the select committee process through introducing supplementary order papers (SOPs). A SOP is used to make policy and legislative changes after a bill has had its first reading and reported back from the select committee (usually the Cabinet would have discussed it – the inner group within the Executive). The intention is that these SOPs contain minor technical improvements or urgent changes that are not contentious and require a prompt legislative response. They are not supposed to be utilised for 'major' policy changes or those that should go through the entire policy process, including the GTPP, thereby affording an opportunity for public consultation (which forms part of the author's 'thick' perspective of the operation of the rule of law).

Another aspect is the balance between certainty, which can be provided by legislation, and discretion that may be afforded through delegated powers, such as via the Governor General through an Order in Council or to a public official, such as the Commissioner. In this regard Kalderimis et al argue (from a thin perspective) that:[20]

> The democratic legitimacy of regulation derives from its formulation by, or consistent with the delegated authority granted and supervised by, a duly elected representative body. Plainly, in a democratic state, the democratic legitimacy of the exercise of state power against its citizens is

[19] A recent exception when a taxpayer was successful in their claim under the NZBORA was in the case of *Parore v The Attorney-General* [2023] NZHC 1010. The plaintiff was awarded close to $NZ71,000 damages for legal costs plus $NZ5,000 for emotional harm. In a subsequent decision, the plaintiff was awarded costs of around $NZ41,000 plus disbursements of $NZ10,900; *Parore v The Attorney-General* [2023] NZHC 1241. It is understood that the Attorney-General has appealed these decisions to the Court of Appeal. The analysis is set out as at 31 March 2024.

[20] D Kalderimis C Nixon and T Smith, *Certainty and Discretion in New Zealand Regulation*, in Regulatory Reform Toolkit, Victoria University of Wellington Regulatory Reform Project, Chapter 4, online resource

of particular importance. *However, due to New Zealand's autochthonous constitutional structure, democratic accountability cannot be seen as an overriding criterion in regulatory design, nor the only basis by which to assess the constitutional legitimacy of regulation.*

Ladyman contends that tax law design needs to reflect key public law principles, which should be acknowledged by the New Zealand Parliament particularly when it delegates it powers to the Commissioner. Ladyman also observes (from a thin perspective) that:[21]

> Parliament's control over the power to tax is a manifestation of its supremacy over the Executive. …
>
> If the Executive disregards or overrules the legislation, this is seen as offensive to the rule of law. Under the separation of powers, Parliament's role is to impose tax while the Commissioner's role is administrative. Undermining the separation of powers by the delegation of legislative power may put the rule of law and parliamentary supremacy in jeopardy. This may further contribute to the roles of the branches of government becoming blurred, as some have said has occurred in recent years.

Ladyman acknowledges the importance of discretion for the Commissioner in administering tax laws although there must be limits and guidance as to how the discretion is exercised. Ladyman further comments on the discretion as provided in sections 6 and 6A of the Tax Administration Act 1994 (TAA 1994). These powers were extended a few years ago to enable the Commissioner to remedy legislative anomalies by recommending regulations, making determinations or undertaking administrative actions.[22]

Isaacs also explores the implications of sections 6 and 6A of the TAA 1994 (suggesting how they need to be amended), along with the obligations imposed on taxpayers under s 15B of the TAA 1994 and calls for a charter of taxpayers' rights. She concludes that greater clarity is needed, noting:[23]

> Perhaps it is time for the development of a taxpayer charter of rights and responsibilities. It is certainly time for adjustments to ss 6 and 6A to ensure the Tax Administration Act makes dollars as well as sense.

Hartshorn investigates the tensions between the balancing of substantive tax law, administration and public law in New Zealand. Like Ladyman, he suggests how ss 6 and 6A of the TAA 1994 should be reworded and calls for a separate Tax Ombudsman to be put in place in NZ.[24] Hartshorn observes:[25]

> *The somewhat dichotomous objectives of independence and rule of law ideas on the one hand and the ruthless necessity of the pillar of efficiency in tax on the other have been dealt with*

(2023), (emphasis added). Available at: www.regulatorytoolkit.ac.nz/resources/pdfs/book-3/certainity-and-discretion-final.pdf.

[21] A Ladyman, 'A Public Law Perspective on Tax Law: The Proposed Power to Remedy Legislative Anomalies' (2018) 15(2) *New Zealand Journal of Public and International Law* 67–100 (emphasis added).

[22] See Taxation (Annual Rates for 2018–19, Modernising Tax Administration, and Remedial Matters) Act 2019. While further discussion on this development is beyond the scope of this chapter, it is further evidence of the erosion of the rule of law in New Zealand from a 'thick' perspective.

[23] A Isaacs, *Making dollars, not sense: The Tax Administration Act's requirement for impartial partiality*, University of Otago Bachelor of Laws (Hons) Dissertation (2018), 56.

[24] TAA 1994, ss 6 and 6A provide in s 6 for the Responsibility of Ministers and officials to protect the integrity of the tax system; and in s 6A for the Commissioner's duty of care and management.

[25] J Hartshorn, *The Sound of 'One Hand Clapping'? The construction of meaning, the push of deference and the pull of unity in New Zealand tax law*, University of Otago Bachelor of Laws (Hons) Dissertation (2020),

> *in other jurisdictions by an extra-judicial, independent supervisory voice.* Both Australia and Canada have a specialist Taxation Ombudsman as an external yet specialist mechanism to supervise the revenue authority, and Australia also has an Inspector General of Taxation who acts as an independent adviser to the Australian Government on tax administration matters, with a particular focus on systemic problems. …
>
> *It is a form of public law middle ground that balances principles of good administration and efficiency with those more traditional unifying ideas around the rule of law, and accountability. Crucially, such a model acts as an efficient and purpose-built external and independent check on the power of the revenue authority.*

Looking Further Back – The Absence of an Upper House

It is important to take a step backwards to provide further context on how the authority of the Legislature in New Zealand was weakened over 70 years ago. In New Zealand the Legislature (House of Representatives) is considered to have the supreme law-making power; when the Executive dominates the Legislature (as is the case at present), the distinction becomes blurred. In practice the Executive controls the Legislature in New Zealand through use of the parliamentary whip system.[26] New Zealand also has a single House of Representatives so there is no upper house review or oversight, unlike countries such as Australia and the United Kingdom. The growing dominance of the Executive over the Legislature raises the issue of how effective the Legislature can be when scrutinising draft legislation proposed by the Executive. The answer, in a New Zealand context, is the worrying conclusion that this is minimal at best, especially with the growing use of SOPs, ministerial decrees and the frequent moving of Parliament to sit under urgency.

Would some form of upper house or senate be an effective control? New Zealand's former upper house (the Legislative Council), which was based on the United Kingdom's House of Lords' model, was abolished on 1 January 1951. Abolition followed the tabling of a bill on 18 August 1950 by the Clerk of the Legislative Council of New Zealand, referred to as the Legislative Council Abolition Bill 1950, to the House of Representatives, without amendment. The bill, having passed both houses, was forwarded to the Governor-General for assent. Almost a century after its inception, the New Zealand Legislative Council ceased to be, with the upper house 'assigned to a growing pile of constitutional debris'.[27] In his comprehensive treatise on the Upper House, Jackson observes that the abolition of the New Zealand Legislative Council provides a rare example of an upper house being abolished by a conservative government.[28]

60–61 (emphasis added). The failure by the Tax Working Group in 2019 to recommend the establishment of a Tax Ombudsman, and the New Zealand government's rejection of any recommendations to move towards restoring the balance for taxpayers, is explored by Sawyer (2020), above n 15.

[26] Parliamentary party whips in New Zealand are MPs who, amongst other matters, make sure their party's MPs are present in Parliament when they are needed to vote.

[27] K Jackson, *The New Zealand Legislative Council: A Study of the Establishment, Failure and Abolition of an Upper House* (Toronto: University of Toronto Press, 1972), Introduction. Jackson provides an excellent review of the Legislative Council's establishment, appointments, role, and the causes and consequences of its abolition.

[28] K Jackson, 'The Abolition of The New Zealand Upper House of Parliament', in Lawrence D Longley (ed), *Two into One: The Politics and Processes of National Legislative Cameral Change*, (London: Routledge, 1991), ch 2.

Sir Geoffrey Palmer[29] also comments on why the Legislative Council failed and was abolished (a principal reason being that its membership was not elected), and on attempts to create an elected Senate in both 1914 and, more recently, in 1992 that accompanied the proposed Mixed Member Proportional (MMP) electoral system.[30] Palmer concludes his analysis as follows:[31]

> From this record, there can be salvaged some second chamber functions that can, and should be, included in the single Chamber we have. *The key issue involves scrutiny of legislation – the prime point that proponents of a second chamber point to and which historically remains the major justification for a second chamber. As to further checks and balances, they are probably best designed by means other than a second chamber.*
>
> The Legislative Council saga tells how difficult it was to alter our underlying constitutional structure which was first set out in legislation in 1852. Designing a functional upper house that would meet the test of both functionality and public acceptability could not be achieved. That suggests it is probably because it is impossible in the New Zealand political culture to find a place for one. *It is, therefore, fascinating to revisit the debates between 1947 and 1993 and assess what elements of New Zealand's constitutional arrangements have changed and how much they remain the same.*

Aroney makes a compelling case for reintroducing an upper house in NZ, concluding:[32]

> So, to bring my remarks to a close, my respectful conclusion is that a better path to contemplate – for Queensland at least and perhaps also for New Zealand – is more thorough-going reform: *the re-establishment of a second chamber or upper house of parliament, democratically elected on a proportionate basis, combined with a lower house based on single-member electorates, under a system of non-compulsory preferential voting.* … But, as I have said, there are profound problems associated with the concentration of power that this entails in a unicameral system; and so *I think that the power of the lower house needs to be counter-balanced by a second chamber, democratically elected and equal in power, except in relation to money bills and votes of no confidence.*

An interesting point worthy of further analysis is whether the recent practices would have continued if New Zealand had retained its former Upper House or replaced it with one which was more relevant and effective. Extensive discussion on this point is beyond

[29] Sir G Palmer, 'The Constitutional Significance of the Abolition of the Legislative Council in 1950', (2017) 14(2) *New Zealand Journal of Public and International Law* 123–47. Sir Geoffrey is a foremost constitutional law expert and former Prime Minister of New Zealand.

[30] Briefly, MMP is known as an 'additional member' voting system used to elect representatives. MMP is a form of proportional representation in that the overall total of party members in the elected body is intended to mirror the overall proportion of votes received. Thus, if a party were to get 40% of the party votes, it should have 40% of the seats in Parliament. In New Zealand, MMP includes a set of members elected by geographic constituency (currently 60 seats out of the total of 120, comprising 5 Māori seats and 55 general electorate seats) who are deducted from the party totals to maintain overall proportionality. Thus, the additional party seats are compensatory in that they 'top up' the electorate seat results to maintain overall proportionality. There are minimum thresholds which, in New Zealand, means that a party must gain at least 5% of the party vote to gain seats, unless an electorate seat is secured in which case there is no minimum threshold and party seats are provided to top up.

[31] Palmer, 'The Constitutional Significance of the Abolition of the Legislative Council in 1950' n 29, 148 (emphasis added).

[32] N Aroney, 'Tale of Two Houses: Does MMP mean New Zealand Doesn't Need an Upper House? *Maxim Institute Guest Paper* (June 2011), 10 (emphasis added).

the scope of this chapter, although the author would contend that some form of upper house would certainly slow down the process of enacting legislation.

Notwithstanding the logic in these arguments, with the current New Zealand Government's thirst for power and reluctance to allow even the formal processes to prevail (such as with the use of SOPs and taking of urgency), there would appear to be no realistic hope of a move away from the current direction. Thus, it would appear that there is almost no chance that some form of upper house could be reintroduced to provide scrutiny over the House of Representatives and the Executive. While the MMP system has provided a reasonable degree of scrutiny and balance when there have been minority or coalition governments, this has failed when a single party controls the Legislature, as occurred in October 2020 following the General Election. This situation was made worse by the controls imposed during the COVID-19 pandemic with lockdowns and limited ability Parliament's limited ability to scrutinise the actions of the New Zealand Government. The chapter now focuses more closely on the erosion of the rule of law in a tax context with the periods of lockdowns during the COVID-19 pandemic.

The Impact of the COVID-19 Pandemic on the Rule of Law

What emerged in NZ during the COVID-19 pandemic was the first single-party majority government in the history of MMP elections following the 2020 General Election. It is with this unprecedented event that the return to the pre-MMP days has been witnessed in New Zealand, with a rapid erosion of the rule of law from a 'thick' perspective, especially in a tax context, with frequent taking of urgency in an Executive-controlled Parliament, the almost complete absence of consultation through the GTPP, and Executive procurements of major law changes, frequently contrary to advice from public officials.

The events commencing in the early 2020s is somewhat of a deja vu moment for New Zealand. In discussing the legislative process in New Zealand in the late 1970s (before the MMP system was introduced for the 1996 general election and subsequent elections), McGee states:[33]

> The New Zealand Parliament was said in 1979 to make the fastest law in the west. Not only was Parliament seen as passing too many laws, but it also was observed that it was passing them too quickly in an 'end of session rush' at the behest of the Government of the day. *This meant that often legislation – both more and less important – was introduced hastily and not considered thoroughly before it was passed. This has been described as a poor process constitutionally.* Under MMP there are more constitutional and political constraints on legislating than prevailed in the late 1970s. *Minority Governments are the norm, and they require the Government to secure the backing of one or more other parties for each bill; parties that undertake to support the Government on confidence and supply matters tend to reserve the right to distinguish their positions on legislative proposals. Moreover, it is in a Government's interest to consult and compromise with other parliamentary parties if it is to progress its legislative agenda*

[33] D McGee, *Parliamentary Practice in New Zealand* 4th edn (Auckland: Oratia Books, edited by M Harris and D Wilson 2017), ch 26 'The Legislative Process', 394-452, (emphasis added).

> *smoothly and with minimal opposition*. House procedure has been changed to compensate the Government for the greater political difficulty of progressing a legislative programme under MMP.

In terms of examples of how the rule of law has not been followed in a NZ context in the last few years, Sawyer provides examples of this approach and the associated implications for the balance of power and trust using the Slippery Slope Framework (SSF). The SSF was developed by Kirchler et al in 2008,[34] and Sawyer extends it to the tax policy arena.[35] Sawyer's work extends the SSF by:[36]

> … explor[ing] this concept further in terms of the *power and trust relationship in the context of high-level tax policy development*, where the public (especially those that engage in consultation on tax policy) are equated to 'taxpayers', and the government (potentially but not necessarily including the major public sector bodies – Inland Revenue and the New Zealand Treasury) that develops the tax policy represents the 'tax authority'.

Sawyer concludes his analysis pessimistically, stating:[37]

> It would appear that New Zealand is heading down on a slippery slope with respect to its tax policy development. This is reflected in the movement away from high levels of trust, with the government asserting its power, being rooted in its unprecedented position in the last twenty-five years of being able to control the Legislature. That said, the people of New Zealand gave the Labour Party the mandate on election night in October 2020, and in that regard, is the Labour government merely making full use of the position it was provided with by the electors? Is there a need for those interested in tax policy to reflect that at the end of the day politics will always win over policy?

A further contribution in the context of COVID-19 is a recent article by Sawyer.[38] In that article he traverses the approach taken by the New Zealand Executive and Inland Revenue with respect to legislative and regulatory initiatives just prior to and during the period of the COVID-19 pandemic in NZ. In addition to demonstrating how this period reflects an erosion of trust and a rise in the power of the Executive over the Legislature (given that the Executive dominates the Legislature this should not come as a great surprise), he concludes:[39]

> *The current government likes to remind the world that it strives to be an example of best practice in what it does (it promised to be the most open and transparent government New Zealand yet), but with tax policy it has sunk to levels below most jurisdictions*. This extends to the level of cutting out a core function of the parliamentary process to scrutinise its proposals, namely the select committee (FEC), through introducing major proposals by way of a SOP.

Thus, since the full impact of the COVID-19 pandemic was felt from March 2020 with the first of many lockdowns in New Zealand, the Labour (-led) Government has developed an appetite for ministers in particular making statements purporting to be

[34] E Kirchler, E Hoelzl and I Wahl, 'Enforced Versus Voluntary Tax Compliance: The Slippery Slope Framework' (2008) 29 *Journal of Economic Psychology* 210–25.
[35] Sawyer (2022), above n 17, 491.
[36] ibid, 495 (emphasis added).
[37] ibid, 512 (emphasis added).
[38] ibid.
[39] ibid, 362 (emphasis added).

law and binding on New Zealand residents/citizens without the prior determination by Parliament as the Legislature. This ranges from an illegal declaration of the first lockdown[40] to statements about significant changes to the tax system made by ministerial announcement prior to the tabling of legislation, and a growing appetite for enacting legislation within a matter of days without any form of public consultation on the premise of the need for urgency. Concurrently, the well-established process for developing and implementing tax policy, the GTPP, has been put to one side, contrary to what had become 'constitutional' convention. Furthermore, it has become clear that, after the release of confidential documents, ministers have ignored the advice of their key officials (Treasury and Inland Revenue in particular), again contrary to constitutional convention. Transparency and consultation, hallmarks of an open and democratic government, have been steadily eroding.[41]

While the COVID-19 period of lockdowns is over, the erosion of the GTPP and the Executive's dominance of the Legislature, including the use of SOPs, remained until a new coalition government was formed after the October 2023 General Election. Thus, until late 2023, without the 'excuse' of the COVID-19 period, the Executive retained its grip over the Legislature, ensuring that the rule of law continues to be eroded, especially with respect to tax policy in New Zealand. Even with the new coalition government there is little sign, as at early 2024 (with respect to tax policy changes continuing to be undertaken under urgency[42]), of a return to the pre-2020 General Election period where the Executive 'respected' the role of the Legislature by enabling sufficient time for the scrutiny of draft legislation. Even more importantly, there is, as yet, no sign of a return to full use of the GTPP to provide for transparency and consultation over both tax policy and draft legislation by the public and other interested persons/organisations.

Alongside this analysis is the Royal Commission of Inquiry into the NZ COVID-19 response (the Inquiry) that commenced in February 2023 and is due to report in mid-2024.[43] The principal purpose of this Royal Commission of Inquiry is to strengthen New Zealand's preparedness for, and response to, any future pandemic by identifying those lessons learned from New Zealand's response to COVID-19 that should be applied in preparation for any future pandemic. While this inquiry is premised principally from a health setting, it was hoped that it may be extended to the fiscal stimulus and tax reforms initiated during the period. However, numerous matters are specifically

[40] See further *Borrowdale v Director General of Health and others* [2020] NZHC 2090. See also, D Knight, 'New Zealand: Legal Response to COVID-19' in *Oxford Constitutional Law* (Oxford: Oxford University Press, 2021).

[41] See further Sawyer (2022), above n 17.

[42] For example, the Tax Principles Reporting Act 2023 was hurriedly enacted during the middle part of 2023, and was abolished under urgency by the new coalition government just prior to the break for Christmas and New Year in 2023–24; see further, A Sawyer, 'A Taxation Principles Reporting Act for New Zealand – What May the Future Hold?' (2024) No 2 *British Tax Review* 262–83.

[43] The full title is: Royal Commission of Inquiry into Lessons Learned from Aotearoa New Zealand's Response to COVID-19 that Should be Applied in Preparation for a Future Pandemic. A Royal Commission of Inquiry in New Zealand is one established under the Inquiries Act 2013. In the case of a public inquiry, the Governor-General may, by Order in Council, establish a public inquiry for the purpose of inquiring into, and reporting on, any matter of public importance (Inquiries Act 2013, s 6(2)). A Royal Commission is one established under the Letters Patent Constituting the Office of the Governor-General of New Zealand 1983.

excluded from the terms of reference, including any adaptation of parliamentary processes during the COVID-19 pandemic.

Thus, it is not anticipated that changes to how Parliament operated, the taking of urgency, the setting aside of the usual consultation process, including bypassing the Finance and Expenditure Committee (FEC) of Parliament and use of SOPs, will be examined during this Commission of Inquiry, unless there is a change to its terms of reference.[44] Only time will tell if the Inquiry touches upon these areas where it feels it is necessary to do so to achieve its purpose.

Discussion and Observations

What can we take away from this discussion? The rule of law is a critical component for democracy to flourish, ensuring the effective maintenance of the separation of powers. In a taxation context within the 'thick' perspective, this can be read as ensuring that taxpayers' rights are respected, and that the Legislature is well-informed when enacting legislation (assuming it has the chance to do so), which includes having the opportunity to consult with the wider public (desirably on both the policy and the draft legislation).

So how does New Zealand come up against this standard? Traditionally, New Zealand has been seen as having elements of best practice in terms of its development of tax policy and resulting legislation, especially since the introduction of the GTPP in the mid-1990s. This has been achieved against the backdrop of an absence of an upper house since 1951, with the operation of a unicameral single House of Representatives with a First Past the Post (FPP) system until 1996, after which the MMP system commenced. Until the 2020 General Election under MMP, all governments were formed by coalition, frequently as a minority government. Thus, within the parliamentary process, a significant degree of scrutiny was able to be maintained by the Legislature over the Executive, as the Executive required wider consensus across the Legislature to have its policies and resulting legislation enacted. With the advent of a single party government in 2020, this scrutiny was lost, with a government thirsty for power operating with ministerial decrees announcing policy changes without following due process, the rampant exercise of urgency in Parliament (given that the Executive controlled the New Zealand Parliament), and an overall erosion of taxpayers' and wider human rights through the policy and legislative developments put in place during the COVID-19 (lockdowns) period. Thus, the rule of law, from a thick perspective at least, has been under serious threat.

As New Zealand emerges from the COVID-19 period, what has changed? In the author's view, nothing significantly tangible has changed both in terms of the way in which the New Zealand Government operated, at least until the 2023 General Election, given the Executive retained full control over Parliament until that point. Theoretically,

[44] In early February 2024, the coalition government, through the Royal Commission, opened a facility for public consultations. Available at: https://haveyoursay.covid19lessons.royalcommission.nz/. The new coalition government is also consulting on whether the terms of reference for the Royal Commission should be expanded: see www.voxy.co.nz/politics/brooke-van-velden-govt-consults-on-expanding-covid-19-inquiry-terms-of-reference/8535/.

at least, with the October 2023 General Election resulting in the formation of a coalition government in late 2023, the Executive no longer controls the Legislature in the same manner. However, with the new government, the GTPP remains yet to be (fully) restored although, as Sawyer observes,[45] the Inland Revenue has striven to make it work, at least in terms of officials' issues papers being subject to consultation.

Erosion of the rule of law from a 'thick' perspective is a serious state of affairs for a democracy and creates the risk that the associated loss of trust through excessive use of power in regard to the democratic operation of the state will take many years to be restored.[46] What recent events have shown is that New Zealand cannot afford to rely upon constitutional conventions, Cabinet directives, and an understanding of how the three branches of government should operate. Rather, New Zealand requires more concrete constitutional enactments similar to what are in place for most other democracies.

Specifically, what is needed in New Zealand is a combination of greater constitutional protections, including the development of an upper house to scrutinise the House of Representatives, more entrenched legislation to protect the independence of the Executive and Legislature, the enactment of an entrenched statute to enforce the use of the GTPP, with minimal opportunities for it to be put to one side for issues such as (perceived) urgency. Overall, greater accountability of the Executive is also needed to both the Legislature and to the public with respect to the Executive's actions. Advice from expert public officials should be heeded unless justified reasons for departure are provided and these are put to the scrutiny of Parliament (including to the FEC, which has its own independent tax expert for providing advice).[47] Furthermore, as the author has argued elsewhere,[48] what is really needed with respect to developing tax policy is for an independent body to the NZ government to be established as a Crown entity, removing much of the 'politics' out of developing principled tax policy. Even the much-vaunted Taxation Principles Reporting Act, which was enacted with effect from 29 August 2023, will have no influence as it was repealed by the new government on 22 December 2023.[49]

[45] Sawyer (2022), above n 17.

[46] One example of the ramifications of this decline in trust is the annual Transparency International Corruption Index where, in 2023, New Zealand slipped from second equal (87/100) to third place (85/100); see further, www.transparency.org/en/cpi/2023/index/nzl?utm_source=newsletter&utm_medium=email&utm_campaign=capital-letter-newsletter.

[47] The Finance and Expenditure Committee (FEC) has its own specialist tax advisor who has been appointed to advise the FEC on a bill-by-bill basis since 1992, in accordance with the relevant protocol; see Hon Margaret Wilson, (Speaker of the House of Representatives, New Zealand), Protocol for the provision of independent specialist assistance to select committees, J5A (2007). Available at: www.parliament.nz/resource/en-nz/48DBHOH_PAP15218_1/a020737cc00a82bf54b3c519fbe1141cae0e07cc. In terms of the expectations of officials providing advice to select committee, see State Services Commission (NZ), *Officials and Select Committee – Guidelines* (2007). Available at: www.publicservice.govt.nz/assets/Uploads/officials-selectcommittees-guidelines07.pdf.

[48] A Sawyer, *The Effectiveness of Tax Reviews in New Zealand: An Evaluation and Proposal for Reform*, (Centre for Commercial and Corporate Law Inc: University of Canterbury Christchurch, 2020). For a contrasting perspective, see J Snape, *The Political Economy of Corporation Tax: Theory Values and Law Reform* (Oxford: Hart, 2011).

[49] For further discussion of the short history of the Taxation Principles Reporting Act, see Sawyer (2024), above n 42.

What of the Royal Commission into the COVID-19 response? The author holds out little hope that this will provide any recommendations to support the points raised in this chapter as it does not currently have within its ambit (its terms of reference) the power to investigate the adaptations of the parliamentary processes during the COVID-19 pandemic. This may change as a result of the new government's review. Furthermore, taxation is unlikely to form a major part as the focus is on the health response. If the new coalition government follows up on the terms of the coalition agreements, then the scope of the terms of refence may be extended to encompass the concerns over the parliamentary processes and may be even to how this influenced tax policy development. However, the New Zealand story needs to be kept in perspective; there are many jurisdictions, including those that operate under a democracy, where the rule of law (from a thick perspective) is experiencing greater challenges. That said, when a jurisdiction that is highly regarded globally for its approach to the rule of law loses its position as a role model and experiences significant threats and undermining of the rule of law, this is a matter of concern.

PART II

Contextualised Theories

8

A Political Perspective on the Rule of Law and Taxpayers' Rights: A Bourdieusian Analysis of the Chilean Experience

RODRIGO ORMEÑO-PÉREZ AND LYNNE OATS*

Abstract

Contrary to common belief, the rule of law is not confined to the legal domain, but it is intimately intertwined with politics. Agents with various political leanings acting in different political regimes hold varied conceptions of the rule of law, which in turn impact differently on the definition of taxpayers' rights to be protected. This chapter examines the interaction between politics, the rule of law and the resulting taxpayers' rights through the theoretical lens of the French social scientist Pierre Bourdieu in the Chilean context, an empirical site that is going through a substantial political transformation and has an increasing interest in taxpayers' rights.

Introduction

In a world governed by laws, the rule of law is 'important to life in peaceful, free, and prosperous societies'.[1] The rule of law is a contested concept,[2] indeed some commentators have argued that it is meaningless despite its international relevance.[3] Bingham states that the core of the concept could be defined, although not comprehensively, as 'all persons and authorities within the state, whether public or private, should

* We are grateful to Alberto Cuevas-Ozimica, Tax Partner at KPMG and lecturer at the University of Chile, for helpful comments on an earlier draft.

[1] T Carothers, 'The Rule of Law Revival' (1998) 77 *Foreign Affairs* 95.

[2] There are different definitions within legal scholarship. See R Daniels and M Trebilcock, 'The Political Economy of Rule of Law Reform in Developing Countries' (2004) 26(1) *Michigan Journal of International Law* 99. See also J Waldron, 'The Rule of Law as an Essentially Contested Concept' (2021) *New York University Public Law and Legal Theory Research Paper Series*, Working Paper No 21-15.

[3] T Bingham. *The Rule of Law* (London: Penguin, 2011).

be bound by and entitled to the benefit of laws publicly made, taking effect (generally) in the future and publicly administered in the courts'.[4] While often depicted as belonging to law, the rule of law resonates well beyond the legal field[5] including politics.[6] The rule of law has been politicised in certain contexts impeding its modification and functioning.[7] This political dimension points to the malleability of the rule of law, such that different political regimes or state organisations with opposing views of the rule of law could still claim adherence to this principle.[8]

In the tax domain, the rule of law implies that taxes 'can be levied only if a statute lawfully enacted so provides',[9] with a focus on the process by which the law is brought into being. It also requires that tax administrations have suitable institutional arrangements to ensure compliance while respecting taxpayer rights.[10] Although the creation of tax liabilities by discretion of authorities may be rare, there is an increasing interest in protecting taxpayers' rights to prevent abuse that violates the rule of law. The interrelationship between taxation and politics is undeniable, if sometimes underappreciated.[11] As with other tax laws, those concerned with taxpayers' rights are result of political battles between various politicians, bureaucrats, consultants and other agents, who try to impose their own beliefs on their content;[12],[13] ie, which rights to protect, and what State mechanisms are needed for their implementation,[14] which includes courts, Constitutional Courts, and Ombudspersons.[15] Political encounters occur at the intersection of 'power and conflict'.[16] Differing political interests will lead to conflict, wherein those that command greater power will become victors. Securing positions in different branches of the State at different times is a reflection of either authoritarianism – in which majority is imposed by force and opponents silenced- or the democratic game of elections. The changes in the constellation of political agents over time may entail changing views on the rule of law and the resulting taxpayers' rights to be protected.

Our ambition in this chapter is twofold. Firstly, to counter the perception that the rule of law is primarily an issue for legal scholarship, we bring to the fore its political dimension by tracing the changing dominant political views over time, including the transition from authoritarianism to democracy and its consolidation,

[4] ibid, 8.

[5] For an illustration in economics, see D Kaufmann, A Kraay and P Zoido-Lobatón, 'Governance matters' (1999) *Policy Research Working Paper 2196*, World Bank.

[6] T Carothers, above n 1; Daniels and Trebilcock, above n 2; K Hoff and J Stiglitz 'After the big bang? Obstacles to the emergence to the Rule of Law in Post-Communist societies' (1998) Working Paper No 9282.

[7] Daniels and Trebilcock, above n 2.

[8] N Cheesman 'Thin Rule of Law or Un-rule of Law in Myanmar?' (2009) 82(4) *Pacific Affairs* 597.

[9] F Vanistendael, 'Legal Framework for Taxation' in V Thuronyi (ed) *Tax Law Design and Drafting*, Volume 1 (Washington, DC: International Monetary Fund, 1996) 1.

[10] Daniels and Trebilcock, above n 2.

[11] B Spies-Butcher and G Bryant 'The History and Future of the Tax State: Possibilities for a New Fiscal Politics Beyond Neoliberalism' (2024) *Critical Perspectives on Accounting*, 98, 1.

[12] V Thuronyi 'Drafting Tax Legislation' in Thuronyi (ed), *Tax Law Design and Drafting* above n 9.

[13] R Ormeño-Pérez and L Oats, 'The Making of Problematic Tax Rules: A Bourdieusian View' (2024) 99 *Critical Perspectives on Accounting*, 1.

[14] R Ormeño-Pérez and L Oats, 'Implementing Problematic Tax Regulation: Hysteresis and Bureaucratic Revolutionaries Within Tax Administrations' (2023) 55(3) *The British Accounting Review* 1.

[15] R Gordon, 'Law of Tax Administration and Procedure' in Thuronyi (ed) above n 9.

[16] ME Warren, 'What is Political?' (1999) 11(2) *Journal of Theoretical Politics* 207, 208.

and the concomitant shifts in the protection of *taxpayers' rights*. Secondly, we illustrate the usefulness of drawing upon social theory as a *lens*[17] through which make further sense of these shifts. Specifically, we draw upon the social theory of practice developed by the French theorist Pierre Bourdieu,[18] whose conceptual 'toolbox' has been instrumental in legal scholarship to explore, for example, elite lawyers,[19] international commercial arbitration,[20] legal education,[21] corporate crime,[22] legal translation,[23] legal consciousness,[24] and public enquiries.[25] His work has also informed critical tax scholarship in the explanation of, for example, tax policy design,[26] drafting of tax rules,[27] the implementation of (problematic) tax rules by tax administrations,[28] legitimisation of tax planning by multinational enterprises,[29] the relationship between taxpayers and tax authorities,[30] and, tax transfer pricing professionals' practices.[31] In this chapter, we mobilise part of Bourdieu's contributions to political sociology[32] through the concepts of *doxa* and *illusio*, in tandem with other constructs in the areas of the rule of law and taxpayers' rights in the Chilean setting.[33]

[17] We draw upon a broad definition of theory in social sciences as an articulated set of concepts through which findings could be interpreted, ie, as a *lens* through which we will look through our findings. See A Bryman, *Social Research Methods* 3rd edn (Oxford: Oxford University Press, 2008), and D Silverman, *Interpreting Qualitative Data: Methods for Analysing Talk, Text and Interaction* (London: Sage Publications, 1993).

[18] P Bourdieu, *The Logic of Practice* (Cambridge: Polity Press, 1990).

[19] Y Dezalay and B Garth, '"Lords of the Dance" as Double Agents: Elite Actors in and Around the Legal Field' (2016) 3 *Journal of Professions and Organization* 188.

[20] Y Dezalay and B Garth, 'Merchants of Law as Moral Entrepreneurs' (1995) *29*(1) *Law & Society Review* 27.

[21] LA Jewel, 'Bourdieu and American Legal Education: How Law Schools Reproduce Social Stratification and Class Hierarchy' (2008) 56 *Buffalo Law Review* 1155.

[22] S Bittle and J Frauley, 'The Profits of Recogniton: A Praxeological Approach to Corporate Crime' (2018) 26 *Critical Criminology* 611.

[23] CA Vidal-Claramonte, 'Re-presenting the "Real" Pierre Bourdieu and Legal Translation' (2005) 11(2) *The Translator* 259.

[24] M Garcia-Villegas, 'Symbolic Power Without Symbolic Violence' (2003) 55 *Florida Law Review* 157.

[25] R Mullender, 'Politeia's Place in our Practical Life: Pierre Bourdieu on the Modern State' (2018) 68(4) *The University of Toronto Law Journal* 694.

[26] BR Wilkinson and AM Hageman 'The Role of Political Elites in Income Tax System Design and Tax Fairness' (2023) 55(3) *The British Accounting Review* 1; D Kraal, 'Paul Keating, Tax Alchemist? A Study Proposing the Interpretive Tools of Pierre Bourdieu' (2014) 8(1) *Journal of the Australasian Tax Teachers Association* 77; A Mumford 'Inheritance Taxation, Notions of Legitimacy and Bourdieu' in G Erreygers and J Cunliffe (eds), *Inherited Wealth, Justice and Equality* (London: Routledge, 2012).

[27] Ormeño-Pérez and Oats, above n 13.

[28] ibid.

[29] M Anesa, N Gillespie, AP Spee and K Sadiq, 'The Legitimation of Corporate Tax Minimization' (2019) 75 *Accounting, Organizations and Society* 17.

[30] L Gracia and L Oats, 'Boundary Work and Tax Regulation: A Bourdieusian View' (2012) 37(5) *Accounting, Organizations and Society* 304.

[31] H Rogers and L Oats, 'Transfer Pricing: Changing Views in Changing Times' (2022) 46(1) *Accounting Forum* 83.

[32] DL Swartz. *Symbolic Power, Politics and Intellectuals: The Political Sociology of Pierre Bourdieu* (Chicago, IL: University of Chicago Press, 2013).

[33] This responds to calls to increase interdisciplinary research in tax law. See L Parada 'Conclusions: The Future of Research in Tax' in L Parada (ed) *A Research Agenda for Tax Law* (Cheltenham: Edward Elgar Publishing, 2022).

The Chilean context is an interesting case study for several reasons. Firstly, despite a troubled history, including the military coup of 1973 which ushered in a period of violent dictatorship under Pinochet followed by a difficult transition to democracy in the early 1990s, Chile stands out in Latin America in terms of overall support for the rule of law. Secondly, despite being held up as a stronghold of neoliberalism heavily influenced by the 'Chicago boys',[34] the recent picture is much more complex and obscures an ongoing tension between socialist and right-wing leanings in policy making. Thirdly, despite geographical proximity to countries burdened by violent uprisings, social protest in post-authoritarian, democratic Chile has been more muted, and arguably more effective in prompting change, including moves towards increased protection of taxpayers' rights. Fourthly, despite constitutional reforms in neighbouring countries in the 1990s, Chilean citizens only voted in 2020 in favour of a Constitutional Assembly, initiating a moderate and rule bound process to replace the authoritarian Constitution inherited from Pinochet's regime (later reformed in 2005), although two attempts at reform were rejected by citizens in September 2022 and December 2023. Fifthly, despite increasing internationalisation, including accession to the OECD in 2010, the Chilean tax system remains skewed in its heavy reliance on VAT and in terms of direct taxes, accommodation of high-net-worth individuals and large businesses. And last, but not least Chile, as an empirical tax domain, has been largely ignored.[35]

To meet our two ambitions, we have structured this chapter in the following fashion. In the following section, we provide a brief overview of contemporary political history of Chile to set the scene in which the rule of law and taxpayers' rights are examined. This is followed by a description of the key Bourdieusian concepts to interpret our material. After this, we interpret our material of the rule of law and defence of taxpayers' rights through a Bourdieusian lens. The final section offers some reflections on the value of a Bourdieusian framework for better understanding tax law, politics and the State.

Contemporary Political History of Chile

The legal, political and social order has been framed in the Political Constitution of the country,[36,37] being the first one dated in 1833 followed by significant modifications in 1925. Citizens and state officials are recognised for their high respect and adherence to constitutional rules and procedures, which made the country stand out in the region for its high democratic stability and civility since it gained independence from

[34] LH Oppenheim, *Politics in Chile: Socialism, Authoritarianism, and Market Democracy* 3rd edn (Boulder CO: Westview Press, 2007).

[35] Some exceptions include: M Bergman, *Tax Evasion and the Rule of Law in Latin America: The Political Culture of Cheating and Compliance in Argentina and Chile* (Harrington: Penn State Press, 2010).

[36] EC Snyder, 'The Dirty Legal War: Human Rights and the Rule of Law in Chile 1973–1995' (1995) 2 *Tulsa Journal of Comparative & International Law*, 253, 255.

[37] The first Political Constitution was issued in 1833 followed by a new one in 1925.

the Spanish rule.[38] In this scenario, political debate was always circumscribed by the boundaries of law.

Adhering to the democratic rules of the game at the time, the election of 1970 gave a thin victory to Salvador Allende, who became the first democratically elected Marxist president aiming to transform the political, social and economic realms in pursuance of a socialist state.[39,40] These transformations entailed abuse of loopholes in law, state seizure of private property, intervention of companies, etc., which were frowned upon by several actors including the judiciary. Judges argued that Allende 'openly flouted legal procedures and abused executive authority in his drive to build socialism'.[41] Eventually, this broke the legal order of Chile and, business elites promoted a coup with the assistance of US corporations, the CIA, and the US Secretary of State Henry Kissinger.[42]

Allende was overthrown in 1973 by a military coup led by the *Junta* made up of the head of the army (Augusto Pinochet), navy, air force and the police. Just after days of the coup, the junta started to exercise government by the issuance of decrees.[43] The first decree stated that the junta took over the country to restore democracy and the *rule of law*, which had been abused under Allende's government, and that Pinochet was the head of the junta granting him executive powers.[44] After side-lining other members of the junta, Pinochet took over the military government around 1975, leading to the replacement of the socialist project by the pure neoliberal project, which came entrenched in the 1980 Political Constitution.

Using Pinochet's own constitutional rules and institutions, political opponents beat Pinochet in a referendum to return to democracy in 1988, triggering a transition to civilian rule in 1989–1990.[45] The end of the dictatorship was defined in a referendum in 1988 with effect from March 1990. The presidential elections of 1989 gave the victory to the opposition, the *Concertación*, made up of centre-left wing political parties which governed steadily between 1990-2010, under the 1980 Constitution. Concertación actors organised towards thickening the *rule of law* and leaving behind the dictatorial past, embracing democracy and overcoming ideological discrepancies.[46] In 2005, there was a constitutional reform repealing some authoritarian enclaves of Pinochet's Constitution to make it more democratic.

This was followed by a series of social movements highlighting Chile's structural inequalities and calling into question the core of the neoliberal model.[47] An attempt to reform the Constitution occurred under the second government of the centre-left-wing

[38] Snyder, above n 36.
[39] ibid.
[40] L Hilbink, 'Constitutional Rewrite in Chile: Moving Toward a Social and Democratic Rule of Law?' (2021) 13 *Hague Journal on the Rule of Law*, 223.
[41] Snyder, above n 36, 258.
[42] D Harvey, *A Brief History of Neoliberalism* (Oxford: Oxford University Press, 2005).
[43] Snyder, above n 36.
[44] ibid.
[45] Hilbink, above n 40.
[46] Oppenheim, above n 34.
[47] T Undurraga, 'Neoliberalism in Argentina and Chile: Common Antecedents, Divergent Paths' (2015) 23 *Revista de Sociologia e Política* 11.

coalition's president Michelle Bachelet (2014–2018), but was unsuccessful due to a lack of political consensus.[48]

During the second government of the centre-right-wing coalition of president Sebastian Piñera (2018–2022) a social revolt disrupted the stability of the country in October 2019 after the increased of public transport prices ($30 CLP). These protests increased in scope extending to demands to change the 1980 Constitution, which was blamed for the significant inequality resulting from neoliberalism. In response, two constitution drafts were prepared and eventually rejected by citizens in the referendums of September 2022 and December 2023, respectively. As result, the 1980 Constitution, modified in 2005, still acts as the legal framework for the functioning of social, economic, and political life in Chile.

After this brief overview, we describe the key theoretical constructs that are instrumental in the interpretation of the rule of law and taxpayers' rights from a political perspective.

The Theoretical Lens of Pierre Bourdieu

The work of French sociologist Pierre Bourdieu (1930–2002) has been influential in various disciplines within the broad social sciences. His later work contributing to political sociology and the philosophy of democratic politics[49] and also to law, remains incomplete as a result of his untimely death. For the purposes of this chapter, we focus on some of his writings on the State, politics and tax law.

The master concepts of Bourdieusian theory of practice are field, capital and habitus,[50,51] whose intersection constitutes *practice*, ie, what agents do in societies. We conceptualise that the protection of taxpayers' rights (the formulation and implementation) is a *political practice* underpinned by power, the operation of which is frequently obscured by the technical dimension of tax laws.[52,53] Here, we mean that agents articulate their political interests and mobilise their power in the definition of the content of taxpayers' rights laws. The interplay between politics and law is constitutive of taxation as a practice.[54] This practice emerges because the relationship between tax administrations and taxpayers might be unequal, in the sense that the implementation (including interpretation) of tax statutes by the former may violate the latter's rights and be unfair. To understand why and how states enact this practice, we need to delve into these three master concepts. A field is a network or configuration of social relations occupied by different agents where they struggle/compete over

[48] CG Soto, MAM Meucci and R Sánchez-Urribarrí, (2021) 'Winds of Change: Comparing the Early Phases of Constitutional Redrafting in Chile and Venezuela' (2021) 13 *Hague Journal on the Rule of Law* 315.

[49] L Wacquant, 'Pointers on Pierre Bourdieu and Democratic Politics' (2004) 11(1) *Constellations* 3.

[50] P Bourdieu, *Outline of a Theory of Practice* (Cambridge: Cambridge University Press, 1977).

[51] P Bourdieu, *The Logic of Practice* (Cambridge: Polity Press, 1990).

[52] R Boden, S Killian, E Mulligan, and L Oats, 'Critical Perspectives on Taxation' (2010) 21(7) *Critical Perspectives on Accounting* 541.

[53] L Oats, *Taxation: A Fieldwork Research Handbook* (London: Routledge, 2012).

[54] Gracia and Oats, above n 30.

resources valued in the field.[55,56] Fields take various forms, such as the bureaucratic, political, juridical/ legal, economic, professional services, scholastic, philanthropic, artistic, etc. The tax field is a space where several of these converge.[57] Located within the tax field the State (bureaucratic), political and legal fields intervene in the protection of taxpayers' rights.

The State or bureaucratic field is the space where agents compete to rule through laws, regulation and administrative procedures.[58] Relevant bureaucratic agencies in taxpayers' rights protection include ministries of finance where tax policies are devised, constitutional courts, tax courts, and *Ombudspersons*, which are public entities created by the state to restrain itself from the exercise of unlimited coercive taxing power by tax administrations against taxpayers, mediating, eventually, between the two. The bureaucratic field may be permeated by the political field when political agents access positions in the bureaucracy either by authoritarian or political nomination upon meeting certain conditions. The political field is a social space where there is conflict regarding the definition and implementation of public policies.[59] This means that players in the political field seek to control the State,[60] and the public policies to be enacted as result. Parliaments, political parties,[61] political assemblies, businesses and professional associations acting as political agents, are relevant agents in the creation of and debates about taxpayers' rights protections. In the political field, these agents articulate their interests regarding the form and influence the State (bureaucratic field) should have (including revenue needs depending on their political leanings), the content of tax and taxpayers' rights laws, the institutional design securing the protection of those rights, among others. The political encounters leading to those definitions are not frictionless, as they are based on divergent political interests.[62] Due to the role of the rule of law in taxation, the result of these political encounters are captured in the content of enacted laws. This illustrates that the political field influences the functioning of the legal or juridical field,[63] and, in turn, the juridical field constantly (re)defines the State. Bourdieu sees the State as a 'fiction of jurists who contribute to producing the state by producing a theory of the state, a performative discourse on public things'.[64]

An important element of social fields is their *doxa*. Bourdieu describes fields as being 'games' which follow rules and wherein field actors 'concur in their belief (doxa) in the game and its stakes',[65] such that doxa becomes taken for granted, simply the way

[55] P Bourdieu and LJD Wacquant, *An Invitation to Reflexive Sociology* (Chicago, IL: University of Chicago Press, 1992).
[56] MR Madsen and Y Dezalay, 'The Power of the Legal Field: Pierre Bourdieu and the Law' in R Banakar and M Travers (eds), *An Introduction to Law and Social Theory* (Portland, OR: Hart Publishing, 2002) 189.
[57] Gracia and Oats, above n 30.
[58] Bourdieu and Wacquant, above n 55.
[59] Swartz, above n 32.
[60] ibid.
[61] P Bourdieu, *Language and Symbolic Power* (Cambridge, MA: Harvard University Press, 1991).
[62] Ormeño-Pérez and Oats, above n 13.
[63] Swartz, above n 32.
[64] P Bourdieu, 'From the King's House to the Reason of State: A Model of the Genesis of the Bureaucratic Field' in L Wacquant (ed), *Pierre Bourdieu and Democratic Politics* (Cambridge: Polity, 2005) 46.
[65] Bourdieu and Wacquant, above n 55, 98.

things are understood and practised within the field. The State has the power to structure the order of fields through its policies and thereby construct doxa. Neoliberalism, social democrat/welfare or Marxists states are manifestations of particular doxas. Normally, these macrostructures go unchallenged by actors; however, rebellions, upheavals and military coups can trigger the adoption of new doxas, which might be eventually legitimated by political accords and the promulgation of laws. As discussed below, doxas can be legitimated via political constitutions. There might be coherence between an emerging doxa and the institutional arrangements that guarantee the protection of taxpayers' rights.

The position that agents occupy in the bureaucratic, political and juridical fields is determined by the type of power, or capital, they command; which is the second construct in Bourdieusian theory. Capital takes the basic forms of economic (eg, wealth and financial resources), cultural (eg, knowledge, skills, know-how of the political and bureaucratic processes, juridical capital to interpret the law), social (networks including linkages to political parties known as political capital), and symbolic (eg, prestige, reputation, renown).[66] Those agents that command more of the capital valued within the field have the power to control the field more widely.

The third construct is habitus. In basic terms, habitus refers to the behaviour of agents in any field. The investment of players in a field game is referred to by Bourdieu as *illusio*, players 'taken in by the game, they oppose one another … to the extent that they concur in their belief (doxa) in the game and its stakes, they grant these a recognition that escapes questioning'.[67] The illusio 'represents and unreflexive commitment to reproducing and enforcing the rules of the game'.[68] Actors become 'enchanted' by the game and 'adhere blindly to the rules of the game and its underlying principles'.[69] The continued existence of the game relies upon agents believing in it and understanding the rewards attached to competing in the field's struggles.[70] The illusio is not concerned with the practices of the game, but rather the mechanism that generates unthinking commitment to reproducing the rules of the game.[71] At the risk of oversimplification, it could be argued that the illusio of agents with neoliberal leanings is that of developing and strengthening the functioning of markets, increasing profitability and investment by lowering tax rates, generally deregulating[72] and, to some extent, disarticulating and disempowering the state so as to bolster the success of the prevailing doxa.[73] Depending on the position in the tax field, these agents are able to create views of the social world, for example, by stigmatising the functioning

[66] P Bourdieu, 'The Forms of Capital' in JG Richardson (ed), *Handbook of Theory and Research for the Sociology of Education* (New York: Greenwood Press, 1986).

[67] Bourdieu and Wacquant, above n 55, 98.

[68] I Lupu and L Empson, (2015) 'Illusion and Overwork: Playing the Game in the Accounting Field' (2015) 28(8) *Accounting, Auditing & Accountability Journal* 1310.

[69] Lupu and Empson, above n 68, by reference to Bourdieu (1998).

[70] J Ibrahim, *Bourdieu and Social Movements: Ideological Struggles in the British Anti-capitalist Movement* (Basingstoke: Palgrave Macmillan, 2015).

[71] A Griffiths, 'Using Exploratory Factor Analysis and Bourdieu's Concept of the Illusio to Examine Inequality in an English School' (2018) 10(1) *Power and Education* 40.

[72] Harvey, above n 42.

[73] Ormeño-Pérez and Oats, above n 13.

of some areas of the state/public organisations as inefficient, discretionary, abusive or even corrupt (negative symbolic capital), pursuing policies that shift power back to the private sector.

In the following section, we interpret our material through the Bourdieusian lens.

A Bourdieusian Analysis of the Rule of Law and Taxpayers' Rights: Authoritarianism and Democracy, and the Rule of Law

At a theoretical level, the neoliberal state favours the protection of property rights, *the rule of law* and the strengthening of the institutions that allow the free functioning of the market and trade.[74] In simple terms, right-wing political and economic elites aspire to develop neoliberalism (doxa) with little interference of the state, which is mostly conceived so as to protect citizens' rights, including property rights.[75] Moreover, at the risk of overgeneralisation, neoliberal states have a preference for the exercise of government by executive order and judicial decisions, rather than democratic and parliamentary decision-making.[76] In the Chilean setting, these issues became palpable with the abolition of the Congress and conferral on the military junta of the executive, legislative and powers enshrined in the constitution in force.[77] In other words, coercion was the mechanism by which neoliberalism was consolidated in Chile, including violation of human rights, which provoked an 'enormous psychic shock to Chileans, who were used to the rule of law'.[78] This historical episode suggests that claims about commitment to the rule of law are politically motivated discourses. As noted earlier, the rule of law is a contested concept implying that different perspectives coexist. While advocates of the 'thin' version of the rule of law tend to conceive legislation as a guide to be obeyed with acceptance of its consequences; the advocates of the 'thick' version respond to greater demands of law such as protection of private property and human rights.[79] As a useful political concept (political capital) within the political field to gain legitimacy, this historical episode shows that even within the same 'thick' version different emphases appear. In particular, while the Pinochet coalition contended that Allende had broken the rule of law through the violation of private property and related rights,[80] it aimed at untramelled protection

[74] Harvey, above n 42.

[75] M Thom, *Tax Politics and Policy* (New York: Taylor & Francis, 2017).

[76] Harvey, above n 42. Indeed Davies (2014) describes neoliberalism as being 'the pursuit of the disenchantment of politics by economics'. It is also recognised that neoliberalism is more than just a movement towards the political right, but in various incarnations across space and time can be thought of as more of a general family of ideas (cited in Weakliem, 2020). D Weakliem, 'Politics, Ideology and the Economy' in M Zafirovski (ed), *A Modern Guide to Economic Sociology* (Cheltenham: Edward Elgar, 2020). See also B Dunn, 'Against Neoliberalism as a Concept' (2017) 41(3) *Capital and Class* 435.

[77] Oppenheim, above n 34.

[78] ibid, 103.

[79] See S Daly, Chapter 2 in this volume. Using the terms narrow-scope and wide-scope rule of law, Lindsay illustrates the 'thin' and 'thick' conceptions of the rule of law. See Lindsay, Chapter 3 in this volume.

[80] Allende is not known for a systematic abuse of human rights as Pinochet is.

of them[81] at the cost of political prosecution of political opponents and the resulting inexcusable violation of human rights,[82,83] while still contending adherence to the rule of law. Under some conceptions of the rule of law, this constitutes a contradiction in that the rule of law must guarantee the protection of citizens from the 'tyranny of government'.[84] Political claims of commitment to the rule of law under these democratic and authoritarian regimes may be explained by the lack of a fixed set of criteria to determine whether states acts 'fall under the rubric of the rule of law' or not.[85]

Pinochet's 1980 constitution, approved in the 1988 referendum, reorganised the functioning of the state;[86] deeply incorporated the military regime[87] departing from the Chilean democratic tradition;[88] and, embraced neoliberalism. In so doing, it vastly reduced the functions of the state.[89,90] In other words, neoliberal doxa was legalised becoming part of the rule of law. The neoliberal state centres on the rule of law and close interpretation of the constitution; conflict and opposition tend to be resolved through courts, i.e., solutions are found within the legal system.[91] The implicit principle of subsidiarity means that state intervention is justified only where the market is unable to participate, or has no interest in participating in social spending.[92] Thus, the state was precluded from directly providing social services leading to a 'policy of targeted social spending that displaces the universal provision of rights'.[93] Neoliberal doxa through the subsidiarity principle is visible in the functioning of various critical areas such as the private social security system, an under resourced public vis-à-vis a private healthcare system, and different quality standards between public and private education.

[81] Property rights are part of the natural rights. See Thom, above n 75.

[82] As noted by Ungar, police agents were active in political repression and abuses of civil and political rights. M Ungar, *Elusive Reform: Democracy and the Rule of Law in Latin America* (Boulder CO: Lynne Rienner, 2002).

[83] Harvey, above n 42. Claims that Chile was a model to other countries in the implementation of neoliberalism are challenged 'because of the global awareness of the Pinochet regime's abysmal human rights record, Chile has never enjoyed a "model" status'. T Fischer, 'The Influence of Neoliberals in Chile Before, During, and After Pinochet' in P Mirowski and D Plehwe (eds), *The Road from Mont Pèlerin: The Making of the Neoliberal Thought Collective* (Cambridge MA: Harvard University Press, 2009) 305.

[84] BZ Tamanaha, (1995). 'The Lessons of Law-and-Development Studies' (1995) 89(2) *American Journal of International Law* 470, 476.

[85] Daniels and Trebilcock, above n 2.

[86] Fischer observes that not only was the 1980 Constitution named after Hayek's book *The Constitution of Liberty*, but it was also heavily influenced by Hayek's thinking, and that Hayek 'went to some lengths to bestow legitimacy' on it. Fischer, above n 83, note 68.

[87] F Uggla, 'For a Few Senators More?' Negotiating Constitutional Changes During Chile's Transition to Democracy' (2005) 47(2) *Latin American Politics and Society* 51.

[88] Oppenheim, above n 34.

[89] S Borzutzky, 'From Chicago to Santiago: Neoliberalism and Social Security Privatization in Chile' (2005) 18(4) *Governance* 655.

[90] F Cumplido, 'Reforma constitucional en Chile' (2006) *Anuario de derecho constitucional Latinoamericano* 105.

[91] Oppenheim, above n 34.

[92] C Heiss, 'Revuelta social y el proceso constituyente en Chile' (2021) 2 *Revista de Ciencias Sociales Ambos Mundos* 69.

[93] V Orellana-Calderón, 'In Chile, the Post-Neoliberal Future is Now: In the laboratory of neoliberalism, Chileans are rejecting the commodification of humanity and widening the cracks that will tear the system down' (2020) 52(1) *NACLA Report on the Americas* 100.

With the restoration of democracy in 1990, the centre-left-wing coalition, the Concertación, adopted an even thicker conception of the rule of law, comprising the previously violated human rights and private property rights. This thicker conception of the rule of law encompasses an unrestricted respect for human rights through concrete actions such as the creation of two commissions to investigate and repair the violations of human rights during the dictatorship.[94] At the same time, the Concertación continued operating under the doxa of free market/open economy[95] and facing several constraints in the development of policies and laws as result of the impositions created by the 1980 Constitution, some of which them disappeared with the constitutional reform of 2005.

Although some citizens and organisations were disenchanted with the prevailing neoliberal doxa, having a different *illusio*, their power (set of capitals) was insufficient to challenge it organically. However, this changed in October 2019 when an increased in public transport prices ($30CLP) triggered a social upheaval that destabilised the political arena and shifted power to those with this different illusio. The protesters' demands revolved around inequality, the source of which was the 1980/2005 Constitution leading to calls for its replacement.[96,97,98] The proposed new, radical, constitution would represent a significant shift in *doxa* with greater involvement of the State and less reliance on the functioning of markets in areas considered to be of state interest, such as pensions, healthcare, education and others.[99] A political accord between most of the political parties agreed the new constitution would be drafted by a democratically elected assembly with significant representation of women and aboriginal people, so as to overcome the political crisis.[100] Left and centre-left wing candidates won the election, leaving the right-wing in minority to make accords in relation to the definition of the new constitution.[101] The winners intended to establish a social democratic doxa which entails a financial empowerment to build a larger State which, inevitably, would demand a higher tax effort from taxpayers which, in turn, may discourage production and the generation of profits.[102] In response to this threat, the assembly might have considered greater protection of taxpayers' rights in the constitution draft in pursuit of political legitimacy as shown below. These political victors' commitment to rebuild a stronger tax State (illusio) could explain this additional protection of taxpayers'

[94] The Rettig and Valech reports were the result of these investigations during three of the four Concertación governments.

[95] Oppenheim, above n 34.

[96] Heiss, above n 92.

[97] Chile is one of the most inequitable OECD countries after redistribution of taxes. See O Causa and M Hermansen, 'Income Redistribution Through Taxes and Transfers Across OECD Countries' (2019) Economics Department Working Papers No 1453.

[98] Hilbink, above n 40.

[99] For a discussion of financial access to healthcare as a human right in the context of the 1980 Constitution and proposed changes thereto, see E Arenas-Catalán, 'Chile's New Constitution: What Right to Health?' (2021) 13 *Hague Journal on the Rule of Law* 295.

[100] Heiss, above n 92.

[101] The centre-right, right and extreme-right acted concertedly obtained 37 seats while requiring 52 to block left-wing initatives. See Heiss, above n 92. Heiss comments that the 20% of seats obtained by the centre-right coalition in addition to the inexperience of independent candidates in legislative work, made difficult the negotiation and accords. C Heiss, 'El proceso constituyente en Chile' (2023) 305 *Nueva Sociedad* 126.

[102] Spies-Butcher and Bryant, above n 11.

rights contained in the constitutional draft. The proposed constitution was eventually rejected, however, in a referendum in September 2022 in the grounds of being considered 'too left' by voters, among other factors.[103] As dissatisfaction with the neoliberal state remained, prolonging the political instability of the country, in December 2022 members of parliament agreed to create a new constitutional assembly.

This time, however, the writing of the new constitution would be in the hands of appointed and elected members. Unlike the previous assembly, the centre-right and right- wing ideology held majority this time, concluding their work in October 2023. As expected, such process is imbued with political struggles over its final content.[104] This time, the constitution again defines Chile as a 'social and democratic state', ie, a modification to the neoliberal doxa to override the subsidiarity principle of the 1980/2005 constitution. This doxic shift would require higher tax revenues. In the view of Francisco Selamé, leading PwC tax and legal partner, a social democrat state is in essence a tax state, which requires balancing the higher burden with a greater protection of taxpayers' rights.[105] This draft was rejected in the referendum held in December 2023, this time for leaning 'too right'. The inability to reach accords to solve conflicts and the citizens' concerns shifting to other areas such as national security and migration were the main impediments.[106]

The reshaping of doxa as Chile moved from extreme socialism under Allende, to neoliberalism under Pinochet and then to social democracy reflects an increasing thickening of the rule of law, albeit imperfectly with the rejection of attempts to reformulate the constitution. In the following subsection, we discuss the relationship between doxa and taxpayers' rights.

Doxa and Taxpayers' Rights

As doxic shifts in the conception of the rule of law occurred, one question that arises is what was the impact on taxpayers' rights? The extent of protection of taxpayers' rights is a reflection of the prevailing doxa. While the State shifts from a neoliberal to a social democratic doxa, greater protection of taxpayers would be expected to be guaranteed. A modest level of protection is seen under the Pinochet 1980 constitution, later reformed in 2005, whereas greater protection is seen in the constitutional draft of 2022. In particular, the 2022 draft includes the novel notions of necessity, reasonability and transparency. We interpret that this greater protection of taxpayers' rights aligns with fiscal responsibility, and democratic rationality and legitimacy. Potentially higher tax burdens to finance the state without adequate levels of protection may face opposition

[103] Heiss, above n 101. See also D Landau and R Dixon 'Utopian Constitutionalism in Chile' (2024) 13(1) *Global Constitutionalism* 228.

[104] See www.duna.cl/programa/informacion-privilegiada/2023/10/18/francisco-selame-de-pwc-chile-frente-a-una-presion-fiscal-mas-alta-es-importante-balancear-con-garantias-de-los-contribuyentes/. Last accessed 31 October 2023. See Heiss, above n 101, about the four forces in the definition of the content of the proposal.

[105] ibid, 104.

[106] Heiss, above n 101. See also CE Gómez, 'Lo que deja el último referéndum constitucional chileno' (2024) 55 *Más Poder Local* 150.

in passing tax reforms. Surprisingly, the 2023 draft does not guarantee greater rights at the constitutional level despite the declaration of the adoption of a social democratic doxa. This variation shows that different political leanings have different impact on the level of protection of taxpayers' rights, in both authoritarian or democratic governments.

The 1980/2005 Constitution respected equality principles in the sharing of the tax burden and restricted the imposition of taxes that are disproportionate or hypothecated. The 2022 draft sought to embrace a system that would reduce inequalities and poverty, permitting taxes for purposes other than revenue collection while still precluding confiscatory and hypothecated taxes. The 2023 draft also precluded confiscatory taxes and also retroactivity, with the state compensating for discriminatory, disproportionate or retroactive taxes.

Following the rejection of both the 2022 and 2023 constitutional reforms, the protection of taxpayers' rights remain enshrined in the 1980/2005 constitution and in the tax code.

Citizens have the responsibility to contribute to finance State's operation. This responsibility is not explicitly contained in Pinochet's 1980 Political Constitution/2005 modifications; however, it can be inferred by linking the power to tax conferred on the State to fostering the common good. In the view of some legal scholars, this civic duty should be gathered in a new political constitution.[107]

Chapter III of Pinochet's 2005 Constitution is entitled 'Constitutional Rights and Duties' and enshrines a broad tax right for all individuals.[108] It reads:

> The equal distribution of taxes in proportion to income or in the progression or manner established by law, and the equal distribution of other public charges.
>
> In no case may the law establish manifestly disproportionate or unfair taxes.
>
> The taxes that are collected, whatever their nature, will enter the Nation's patrimony and may not be assigned to a specific destination.
>
> However, the law may authorize that certain taxes may be effected for the purposes of national defence. Likewise, it may authorize that those that tax activities or goods that have a clear regional or local identification can be applied, within the frameworks that the same law indicates, by the regional or communal authorities for the financing of development works.

From this, four principles are derived. Firstly, there is no tax without law (rule of law). As taxes are in constant tension with the defence of property rights,[109] this constitutes a democratic protection for taxpayers.[110] This is because tax laws transit through parliament, which broadly represents citizens' preferences, to finally become law,[111] rather than being a pure imposition from the executive branch in a strong presidential system

[107] Tramón (n.d.). ¿Qué dice la Constitución en materia de impuestos? Available at: https://nuestrosimpuestos.cl/que-dice-la-constitucion-en-materia-de-impuestos/. Last accessed 10 June 2023.

[108] Article 19 No 20, Political Constitution of the Republic of Chile. 2005.

[109] Thom, above n 75.

[110] Tramón, above n 107.

[111] R Ormeño-Pérez, *The Tax Policy Making Process in Practice: A Field Study in Chile* (2014) Unpublished PhD Thesis, University of Exeter Business School, UK. See also Ormeño-Pérez and Oats, above n 13.

like Chile.[112] Tax rule-makers make sure that all the elements of taxes, i.e., taxable event/transaction, tax rate, calculation, collection mechanisms, and taxpayers affected, are included in the enacted laws.[113] Secondly, authorities must not make arbitrary distinctions between taxpayers that are in equivalent positions. Thirdly, taxes cannot be confiscatory or prevent the development of certain legal economic activities. In the view of Chilean rule-makers, tax rates of 50% upwards are undoubtedly confiscatory.[114] Fourthly, there should be no specific destination for tax revenue. This reflects Chilean preference for not earmarking the use of tax revenues. Tax revenues thus enter the country's budget without a specific policy objective.[115]

Taxpayer confidentiality is protected by the Constitution, indeed personal tax data protection is stricter than that applicable in the rest of the legal system. There is a strong prohibition on disclosure by the tax authority – the Servicio de Impuestos Internos SII – covering sharing data with third parties whether internally sourced or secured from third parties.[116]

In addition to these broad taxpayers' rights contained at the constitutional level, Chile has included taxpayers' rights in the tax code, which are discussed below.

Taxpayers' Rights in the Tax Code

Framed by the prevailing rule of law and 1980/2005 Political Constitution in the old tax justice administration system, the SII had played a dual role: it was in charge of the normal duties of tax enforcement, while it was also in charge of dispute resolution, acting as first instance judge in tax matters. Despite the legitimacy given by the higher courts to this system, this duality was widely criticised in the tax community because of a SII's lack of independence, whose powers were seen by centre-right politicians as disproportionate in relation to taxpayers, leaving room for discretion.[117] After a long parliamentary discussion that lasted for years, independent Tax and Customs Courts were created and started their gradual operation between 2010 and 2013.

At the same time, the centre-right-wing coalition promoted a parliamentary initiative in 2005 to remedy the impartiality of the SII through greater protection of taxpayers' rights through a special law that included the right to be treated respectfully by tax officials, to be informed about the audits that concern them, to refrain from providing information previously submitted to the tax authority, to raise complaints

[112] O Sanchez, *Mobilizing Resources in Latin America: The Political Economy of Tax Reform in Chile and Argentina* (New York: Palgrave Macmillan, 2011).

[113] Ormeño-Pérez, above n 111.

[114] ibid.

[115] There have been instances, however, in which political accords establish the use of additional revenues brought by new reforms in critical areas such as education or pensions.

[116] M Navarro-Schappacas, A Magasich-Airola and R Jijena Leiva, 'Personal Data Protection: The New Paradigm of the Tax Secret or Tax Reserve in Chile' (2023) 13(1) *International Data Privacy*, 79.

[117] Ormeño-Pérez and Oats, above n 13.

and give suggestions about the tax authority's acts that concern them.[118] This is aligned with the neoliberal doxa that taxes are a cost to be minimised,[119] including compliance costs, and that the private sector should hold more power. This law was finally incorporated in the tax code in 2010. However, the increased number of audits in addition to the complexity of tax reporting requirements as result of subsequent tax reforms led taxpayers to experience the 'feeling of inequality and *defencelessness*'[120] despite existing rights. In response, the centre-right-wing governing coalition passed a bill to strengthen taxpayers' rights and, as a result, in 2020, the taxpayers' rights charter was modified and strengthened. The current taxpayers' rights revolve around receiving information from the SII (e.g., procedures and their rationale including related documentation, specific timeframe, etc.), protection of private information of taxpayers, reduction of tax compliance costs whenever possible, the availability of SII's interpretation (circulars) on its website for easier accessibility, a settlement procedure, among others.[121]

The 2020 reform also introduced a new institution, the Defensoría del Contribuyente, DEDECON, to defend rights of the most vulnerable taxpaying population, namely individuals and, small and medium enterprises (SMEs), to provide advice and guidance to them, and to mediate the relationship between them and the SII.[122] The DEDECON's highest authority is the national defender, which embodies the public service ethos as noted in a recent statement of the current national defender, 'my objective is to be the taxpayers' voice before the SII'.[123] The DEDECON[124] has four defined strategic objectives: the protection of taxpayers' rights; the protection of fairness through administrative representation (not legal representation powers); the promotion of tax education and taxpaying culture;[125] and, contributing to strengthening the tax system.

During the period March 2022-March 2023, however, the DEDECON only managed 320 tax services requests. Of these, 64 per cent were made by individual taxpayers and the remaining 36 per cent by incorporated entities.[126] There seems to be little awareness of taxpayers about their rights and the role of the DEDECON in their defence,[127] which may explain the low number of taxpayers' services requests.

[118] History of the law 20.420. See www.bcn.cl/historiadelaley/nc/historia-de-la-ley/4806/ Last accessed 28 April 2024.

[119] Anesaet al., above n 29.

[120] History of the law 21.210. See www.bcn.cl/historiadelaley/nc/historia-de-la-ley/7727/. Last accessed 28 April 2024.

[121] See Article 8 *bis*, Tax Code. Available at: www.bcn.cl/leychile/navegar/imprimir?idNorma=6374&idVersion=2022-06-30. Last accessed 31 October 2023.

[122] The creation of DEDECON follows international experience. For example, the bill mentions Mexico explicitly.

[123] S Valdenegro, Nuevo Defensor nacional del contribuyente: 'Mi objetivo es ser la voz de los contribuyentes frente al SII' (9 June 2023) Diario Financiero. Available at: Diario Financiero (pressreader.com). Last accessed 8 May 2024.

[124] See www.dedecon.cl.

[125] To do so, DEDECON has agreements with other public institutions to target various segments of micro, small and medium enterprises that do not command sufficient economic resources to hire a tax specialist to resolve their problems. Over 1,800 attendees have participated in these education events.

[126] DEDECON, Cuenta Pública: Informe de Gestión 2022–2023 (2023) 31.

[127] ibid, 125 65/66.

Conclusion

Our ambitions in this chapter are to illustrate the political dimension of the rule of law and its connection with taxpayers' rights, and to illustrate the usefulness of drawing upon Bourdieusian theory as a *lens* through which to analyse and further understand this political dimension.

Our analysis suggests that the rule of law is a politicised concept. Different regimes claim commitment to the rule of law while discrediting their opponents. This is visible in Pinochet's justification of the coup d'État to reestablish the rule of law broken during the socialist Allende's government in terms of property rights. In this case, we find that the rule of law was deployed as a discursive device to mask a violent regime yet was part of the doxa of the tax field as constituted at that time. Successive democratic governments have adopted even thicker approaches to the rule of law by strong respect of human rights. This suggests that there is a continuum, rather than a binary distinction between 'thin' or 'thick'.

It has taken a long time subsequently for the field configuration, and associated doxa, to shift to a thicker conception of the rule of law under which Chile has come into line with other countries in the provision of stronger protection for taxpayers in the Constitution and also in the institutional framework of the tax administration.

This chapter has also illustrated the Chilean experience of a subtle strengthening of the rule of law over successive political regimes, through a Bourdieusian lens. Bourdieusian constructs allow for an in-depth understanding of the broader operation of the tax field in the context of interactions with adjacent fields, in particular the political and juridical fields. In this way, this study supplements prior critical tax scholarly work. The following main conclusions emerge from our analysis.

Firstly, the chapter illustrates that the rule of law and defence of taxpayers' rights is not purely a matter of law, but it is also deeply imbued with politics. Different political regimes and ideologies aim to create and impose their doxa at national and tax field levels. At the national level, the imposition of neoliberalism by the dictatorship and the subsidiary state implied relatively less tax effort, and accordingly a modest level of taxpayers' right protection was guaranteed in the 1980 Political Constitution and its modifications of 2005. The developing institutional design of the time involved the tax authority holding and able to mobilise significant power in the tax field and juridical field by being first instance judge in tax disputes. After the restoration of democracy in 1990, several actors were vocal in reducing the power of the revenue authority, including tax professionals and professional politicians. This was achieved through the creation of specialist tax courts in 2010 which aimed at harmonising the national doxa with the functioning of the tax, bureaucratic and juridical fields. Importantly, this reallocated the juridical capital associated with the final interpretation of tax laws from the revenue authority to the tax courts, allowing the application of tax laws to be more equitable. This shift of power is a reflection of ruling politicians' illusio of consolidating a fair and efficient tax system.

The political constitution rejected in 2022 sought to build a new form of state, a social democratic state. In response to social protests and substantial discontent, the new state was to finance and guarantee social rights previously not provided under the existing neoliberal doxa. The new tax state would then require taxpayers to bear higher taxes to fund its operation. In alignment with this new doxa, drafters of the new constitution, with a left-wing majority, expanded on taxpayers' rights at the constitutional level. This contrasts with the political constitution rejected in December 2023. Despite the centre-right-wing holding a majority in the drafting assembly, the new social democratic state does not expand or guarantee additional taxpayers' rights at the constitutional level. This suggests that political leanings impact the protection of taxpayers' rights differently. While the centre-left-wing assembly aimed at securing taxpayers' right as a matter of legitimacy (fiscal and democratic responsibility), the centre-right-wing coalition legislated taxpayers' rights in the tax code in the search for coherence with the neoliberal doxa in which the private sector recovers power from the state.

Secondly, our analysis illustrates that centre-right-wing governments display a stronger illusio in building a more balanced power relationship between tax authorities and taxpayers. This is demonstrated in the laws enacted in 2010 and 2020 in which taxpayers' rights were explicitly included and systematised in the tax code. Eventually, this would lead to greater legitimacy and efficiency in the operation of the tax system. The extent to which the rule of law and protection of taxpayers' rights will be modified in response to further doxic shifts remains to be seen.

9

Virtue Ethics: Supplement to the Rule of Law in Taxation

JO BADISCO AND ELLY VAN DE VELDE*

Abstract

This chapter proposes that legal and technical tax provisions are inadequate for the purposes of creating a 'just' tax system. The chapter claims that ethical factors need to be addressed given their impact on taxpayers' attitudes and behaviour. The proposal is to encompass normative ethics in order to supplement the rule of law, encouraging the use of virtue ethics to evaluate appropriate conduct. The chapter firstly considers what is meant by virtue ethics before turning to explain how it might be used to strengthen the rule of law considering contextual factors. It finishes by exploring what it means to act virtuously in the realm of taxation.

Throughout the chapter the authors suggest that individuals use the virtues to morally evaluate rules and laws before slavishly implementing them. They argue that this will lead to better, fairer outcomes subject to the virtues, such as *phronesis* (practical wisdom), *sophrosyne* (temperance), *dikaiosyne* (justice) and *andreia* (courage) being deployed appropriately.

Introduction: From 'Just Taxation' to 'Ethical Taxation'

Tax law is a critical component of any functioning society, as it is necessary to fund public goods and services within a welfare state. However, individuals and corporations are oftentimes motivated to minimise their tax burden.[1] This tension between compliance and avoidance is a key aspect surrounding the broader issue of tax law and justice.

* Views expressed in this chapter are the personal views of the authors and do not reflect the views of their respective organisations. Thanks to the chair in Ethical Taxation UHasselt.

[1] According to calculations, the missed tax revenue is substantial: A Cobha and P Janský, 'Global Distribution of Revenue Loss from Corporate Tax Avoidance: Re-estimation and country results: Global Corporate Tax Avoidance' (2018) 30 *Journal of International Development* 206.

Nearly all are in agreement that the need for a just taxation system is more pressing than ever. However, the inquiry of how such a goal can be achieved still eludes us.

There is the widespread belief that such an equitable taxation can be attained by merely designing a comprehensive and just legislative framework. In this chapter, we challenge this one-sided outlook. Such a strict legislative perspective contains certain ethical and political philosophical presuppositions, which neglect crucial facets of the issue at hand. Within this paradigm, it appears that a consensus has emerged, according to which, the establishment of a just taxation system can be accomplished by the mere design of good legislation. Upon completion of said legislation, the arduous task is thought to have been accomplished, and the demand for justice is deemed to have been met. Consequently, citizens, corporations, tax consultants, and all other relevant actors are relegated to the sole responsibility of complying with the law. Thus, tax law is, in this manner, reduced to, and treated solely from, a legislative standpoint. The demand for justice is thus a formality, devoid of real substance.

This vision, which assumes a minimal concept of justice, is comprehensible and reconcilable with a multitude of legal and political philosophical positions and with most narrow theories of the rule of law,[2] and that is precisely what makes it so attractive. It is even consistent with a strict legal positivism that posits that law and ethics are entirely separate spheres.[3] This way of thinking also fits nicely within the framework of the (pluralistic) modern state, which derives its validity from the existence of a social contract, with, amongst others, central notions such as the rule of law.[4] However, translating this vision into practice is not a straightforward endeavour. Despite the efforts of the legislature, supported by supranational institutions,[5] there always seem to be numerous loopholes that can be exploited for tax planning purposes with the aim of significantly reducing the amount of tax paid. The law itself always seems to be one step behind and, with some legal creativity, exploitation of the rules seems unavoidable by those who are willing and looking for far-reaching optimisation. Those seeking aggressive tax optimisation schemes are judged and ruled in the same way as those

[2] This chapter will not deal specifically with the different approaches and definitions of the rule of law (ie 'thick' versus 'thin' conceptions). But, on the whole, it argues predominantly against, and as addition to, the rule of law as defined in a narrow way. For a more comprehensive overview of different rule of law conceptions see Daly and Lindsay, Chapters 2 and 3 in this volume.

[3] Legal positivism has its origin in the writings of Jeremy Bentham. It was further developed by, amongst others, Hans Kelsen, HLA Hart and Joseph Raz. J Bentham, *Of Laws in General* (London: Athlone Press, 1970), H Kelsen, *Introductions to the Problems of Legal Theory* (Oxford: Clarendon Press, 1992), HLA Hart, *The Concept of Law* 3rd edn (Oxford: Oxford University Press, 2012) and J Raz, *The Authority of Law* 2nd edn (Oxford: Oxford University Press, 2009).

[4] The foundation of modern social contract theory is to be found in the works of thinkers such as Thomas Hobbes and Jean-Jacques Rousseau. Social contract theory puts forward a minimal theory of ethics and political philosophy which can serve as the basis of the state. The mechanism of the social contract also plays a fundamental role in the more contemporary thought of John Rawls, wherein it is used as a mechanism to gain insight into the ordering of a just society. JJ Rousseau, *Du Contrat Social: ou Principes du Droit Politique* (Verviers: Marabout, 1974), T Hobbes, *Leviathan* (Cambridge: Cambridge University Press, 1991), J Rawls, *A Theory of Justice* (Cambridge MA: Harvard University Press, 2005).

[5] The European Union's 'Anti-tax Avoidance Directives' (ATAD) and the OECD's 'Base Erosion and Profit Shifting' (BEPS). See also the demand for an even larger institutional framework to conduct taxation at a global level: C Peters, *On the Legitimacy of International Tax Law* (Amsterdam: IBFD, 2014) and C Peters, 'Global Tax Justice: Who's Involved?' in RFW van Brederode (ed), *Ethics and Taxation* (Singapore: Springer Singapore, 2020).

who seek to contribute their fair share. This ties in with the fact that the perception of fairness among taxpayers plays a crucial role. Despite the efforts of lawmakers and supranational institutions, citizens often feel that the tax system is not fair, and that some individuals or corporations are not paying their fair share – even though they are judged and ruled by the same standards. Research shows that this perception is not entirely unfounded, and that tax avoidance and evasion remain pervasive problems in many countries.[6] As a result, taxpayers may become sceptical about the fairness of the system and may feel less motivated to comply with their tax obligations. This undermines citizens' trust in the rule of law and the obligation to pay their fair share, as mere rule of law as a minimum-standard is seemingly inadequate to guarantee fairness between parties. This can lead to a vicious cycle, where non-compliance breeds further non-compliance, and the sense of injustice and resentment grows.[7] Thus, in our opinion, it is not enough to rely solely on legal and technical solutions to achieve a just tax system; we also need to address the ethical factors that shape taxpayers' attitudes and behaviour towards taxes. This requires a deeper understanding of the moral dimensions of taxation, and a more comprehensive approach that considers not only the formal rule of the law, but also the informal norms and values that underpin citizens' sense of fairness and obligation and the way in which different actors relate in different manners to the legal framework.

Hence, we must go *beyond* the typical approach and instead shape this ethical standpoint through the lens of a more encompassing normative ethics which can strengthen and supplement the rule of law as well as *correct* the rule of law. We will do this by taking into consideration a point of view from virtue ethics. By building upon the virtues of the actors involved, rather than the notion of duty on which the focus is generally, we can problematize the hypothesis that a perfect legislative framework is the solution to tax issues. While most rule of law theorists would most likely not disagree with the claim that the rule of law itself is, of course, insufficient, and is itself only one facet of a good legal system,[8] we argue that a coherent exploration of what *exactly* can supplement the rule of law would be beneficial. Also, specific moral frameworks (this chapter will emphasise virtue ethics) might interact with the rule of law in different ways, thus an investigation into the nature of this interaction is advised. We will argue that virtue ethics not only has the strength of supplementing the rule of law, but also of correcting it in certain circumstances (eg actors can differ greatly in their knowledge and context; is there no argument to judge them *differently* as well?). The idea that *genuine* rule of law actually requires putting aside the law as it is, and thus in a way putting aside the rule of law, is also put forward by legal philosopher John Finnis.[9]

[6] According to calculations, the missed tax revenue is substantial: A Cobha and P Janský, 'Global Distribution of Revenue Loss from Corporate Tax Avoidance: Re-Estimation and Country Results: Global Corporate Tax Avoidance' (2018) 30 *Journal of International Development* 206.

[7] A thought which is not entirely unfounded: A Van de Vijver and A Decuypere, 'Tax Fairness in Belgium: The Perspective of Organizational Psychology' (2022) 612 *Tijdschrift voor Fiscaal Recht* 3.

[8] See eg Raz: 'The Rule of Law is Just One of the Virtues Which a Legal System May Possess' in J Raz, *The Authority of Law* 2nd edn (Oxford: Oxford University Press, 2009) 211.

[9] See eg 'Sometimes, moreover, the values to be secured by the genuine Rule of Law and authentic constitutional government are best served by departing, temporarily but perhaps drastically, from the law and the constitution.' J Finnis, *Natural Law and Natural Rights* 2nd edn (Oxford: Oxford University Press, 2011), 271.

Of course, one might argue that most formal rule of law theories do not rule this out, but we hope the examples further down will illuminate this point more clearly.[10]

Concretely, we ask the following questions from a virtue ethics point of view. Given the existing legal framework, how should we, as actors, behave? What does it mean to act virtuously within the confines of the rule of law? And, perhaps most crucially, how can and should we make this framework more virtuous? Thus, rather than advocating for merely a just taxation, we argue for what we call an ethical and even virtuous taxation, which is a broader and more comprehensive perspective that itself includes within its confines justice as a fundamental component. Such a broadening will be achieved by exploring the way in which virtue ethics can enhance the discussion. By broadening the scope to include not just the legislative side but also taxpayers (citizens as well as entrepreneurs), tax consultants, and tax lawyers who must adhere to the law, we can contribute to the discourse. Within this broader perspective, it is not only the development of a loophole-free legislative framework that matters, but also the interaction with this framework. By employing the term 'ethical taxation' we hope to emphasise the potential richness of (theoretical) normative ethics and encourage a more in-depth ethical inquiry into the presuppositions and foundations of the different positions in the debate.

In this chapter, we shall first illuminate the history and central tenets of virtue ethics. Next, we shall explore how virtue ethics offers a distinct perspective on the ethical issues that govern tax law (from an ethical standpoint) and how this, in turn, strengthens the rule of law by necessitating a more contextual approach. Finally, we shall briefly examine how a limited set of virtues can function within a fiscal context and what it truly means to act virtuously in the realm of taxation. We endeavour to capture the essence of an ethical approach to taxation, by exploring how a limited set of virtues can function within a fiscal context, and what it truly means to act virtuously in the realm of taxation.

Virtue Ethics

In contemporary normative ethics, three schools of thought are typically distinguished: utilitarianism (originating from the ideas of Jeremy Bentham), deontology (based on the Kantian concept of rationality),[11] and virtue ethics. At the beginning of the previous century, only the first two of these schools were prominent in the debate. In 1958, with the publication of Elizabeth Anscombe's 'Modern Moral Philosophy,' virtue ethics regained popularity.[12] She argued that normative ethics had reached an

[10] When looking at Raz's principles as well as Lon Fuller's there are at least some tensions with regard to generality, prospectivity, etc. if such similar cases are to be judged differently depending on the actor. For the principles see: J Raz, *The Authority of Law* 2nd edn (Oxford: Oxford University Press, 2009), 214–19. LL Fuller, *The Morality of Law: Revised Edition* (New Haven CT: Yale University Press, 1969) 46–91.

[11] Political philosophers like John Rawls can also be included in this category. Within Rawls' philosophy, a Kantian concept of rationality is at work. J Rawls, *A Theory of Justice* (Cambridge MA: Harvard University Press, 2005) 251–57.

[12] E Anscombe, 'Modern Moral Philosophy' (1958) 33 *Philosophy* 1.

impasse from which there seemed to be no escape.[13] One of the central arguments in her article was that the concepts of 'moral obligation' and 'moral duty' are no longer useful in our time because of their religious origins.[14] This article led to a resurgence in virtue ethics[15] due to its hinting at the usefulness of the classical tradition of virtue ethics as an escape from the impasse, and some of the central texts in this revival include[16] Alasdair MacIntyre's *After Virtue*, Rosalind Hursthouse's *On Virtue Ethics*, and Philippa Foot's *Virtues and Vices: and Other Essays in Moral Philosophy*. Also, Martha Nussbaum's *Creating Capabilities: the Human Development Approach* is strongly influenced by virtue ethics.[17] However, the true origins of virtue ethics date back much further, to ancient Greece, where we find its roots in the works of Plato and Aristotle. One can also distinguish the central tenets of virtue ethics in a non-reflective manner in other places such as ancient China, for instance, in the teachings of Confucius.[18] Throughout Western history, what we now understand as virtue ethics (not necessarily in the Aristotelian sense) has played a central role as almost the only way of thinking in ethics, until modernity as the philosophy of thinkers such as Hobbes drew a stark demarcation between ancient and modern thought.[19]

Even though virtue ethics encompasses a wide and diverse range of theories there are certain central tenets common to all of them, ie there is a conceptual unity,[20] that differentiate it from deontologist ethics and utilitarianism. One could describe virtue ethics as a theory that places emphasis on the question of how one ought to live one's life in the best possible manner. This question, in turn, demands an inquiry into the type of person one should strive to be, leading to considerations of the virtues that guide

[13] It is also interesting to note that the word consequentialism, which is often used to refer to a form of utilitarianism, is used for the first time in this chapter.

[14] Another criticism of deontological and contractual ethics, which operate from a Kantian-inspired concept of duty, can be found in Bernard Williams' *Ethics and the Limits of Philosophy*. In that work, it is argued that the concept of duty in these frameworks ignores the importance of the individual perspective that is fundamental to morality. Unlike others, however, Williams, will argue that philosophy is unable to establish a coherent normative theory. B Williams, *Ethics and the Limits of Philosophy* (London: Routledge Classics, 2011).

[15] There are some other fruitful investigations into virtue ethics before Anscombe in the first part of the twentieth century, see eg J Pieper, *The Four Cardinal Virtues* (Notre Dame: University of Notre Dame Press, 1980).

[16] This list does not claim to be exhaustive, but it provides an overview of the central philosophers responsible for the revival of virtue ethics in the second half of the twentieth century.

[17] A MacIntyre, *After Virtue* 3rd edn (Notre Dame: University of Notre Dame Press, 2007), R Hursthouse, *On Virtue Ethics* (New York:, Oxford University Press, 1999), P Foot, *Virtues and Vices: and Other Essays in Moral Philosophy* (Oxford: Oxford University Press, 2003), M Nussbaum, *Creating Capabilities: The Human Development Approach* (Cambridge MA: Harvard University Press, 2011).

[18] DC Russel, 'Virtue Ethics, Happiness, and the Good Life' in DC Russel (ed), *The Cambridge Companion to Virtue Ethics* (Cambridge: Cambridge University Press, 2013) 1.

[19] L Strauss, *The Political Philosophy of Thomas Hobbes: Its Basis and its Genesis* (Chicago: University of Chicago Press, 1996).

[20] See, eg, what MacIntyre says: 'I am going to argue that we can in fact discover such a core concept and that it turns out to provide the tradition of which I have written the history with its conceptual unity. It will indeed enable us to distinguish in a clear way those beliefs about the virtues which genuinely belong to the tradition from those which do not.' A MacIntyre, *After Virtue* 3rd edn (Notre Dame: University of Notre Dame Press, 2007) 186.

our actions and decisions.[21] Whereas deontological ethics prioritises the concept of duty and utilitarianism the hedonistic calculus, the virtues are the most fundamental building block in a theory of virtue ethics. All forms of virtue ethics listed above are, to a certain extent, neo-Aristotelian, meaning that they rely in some way on a number of basic insights originally formulated by Aristotle.[22] Nevertheless, they also exercise the freedom to deviate from some of the presuppositions made by Aristotle.[23] The central ethical concepts elaborated by Aristotle are set out in his 'Nicomachean Ethics'.[24] The present discussion of virtue ethics shall concentrate on three central notions that are found in all forms of neo-Aristotelian virtue ethics: the first is the key concept of *eudaimonia*. The second crucial concept is that of 'virtue', and the third is 'practical wisdom', or *phronesis*, which also functions as one of the virtues.

This first concept, eudaimonia, which can be translated as happiness or blessedness, is the ultimate goal of a good life. It can be attained through right choices and actions. It is the highest good, in that it does not refer to any other good and as such it is complete in and of itself, it is not an instrument for further goals but the final goal itself.[25] It is crucial to not confuse this concept with the everyday usage of the word happiness, as it does not refer to the fleeting moments of joy one may, for example, experience after completing a task or enjoying a meal. Rather, it points to a permanent state of being, a kind of true happiness. How can one achieve this goal, this state of eudaimonia?

This is where the second key concept, virtue, comes into play. For Aristotle, happiness is an activity of the soul in accordance with virtue.[26] Virtues are character traits that enable us to make the right choices and take the right actions. They are deeply rooted in our personality and can be acquired through cultivation and habituation. When we are faced with choices, these virtues enable us to make correct decisions that are most enabling for our state of happiness. Examples of such virtues include honesty, generosity, courage, justice, and practical wisdom. The virtuous person, therefore, is the morally good person, one who acts rightly and deserves praise.[27]

One virtue demands further attention: practical wisdom. This virtue is both a virtue in its own right and the one that enables us to apply the other virtues correctly. It is practical wisdom that allows us to assess concrete situations and determine the right course of action. Virtue ethics has a certain open-ended nature in the sense that it does not rely on a set of universal laws that are applied in the same way every time. Instead, it is practical wisdom which enables us to respond adequately in a diverse set of concrete situations which each require their own assessment. Thus, the correct assessment of situations requires practical wisdom and, as such, it is an essential virtue that enables the other virtues to be properly applied.

[21] DC Russel, 'Virtue Ethics, Happiness, and the Good Life' in DC Russel (ed), *The Cambridge Companion to Virtue Ethics* (Cambridge: Cambridge University Press, 2013) 7.

[22] Not all forms of virtue ethics are necessarily Aristotelian, see eg the actor-based ethics of Michael Slote: M Slote, *From Morality* to *Virtue* (New York: Oxford University Press, 1994).

[23] For example, there is barely anyone who still argues for Aristotle's very elitist approach to ethics.

[24] See also the 'Eudemian Ethics' which was most likely written earlier in Aristotle's life.

[25] Aristotle, *Nicomachean Ethics*, 1097b 21–22.

[26] ibid, 25–28.

[27] R Hursthouse, *On Virtue Ethics* (New York: Oxford University Press, 1999), 13.

Ethical Taxation and Virtue Ethics

Building upon this theoretical exposition of virtue ethics, we will now analyse its implications within the context of taxation: how do these insights, derived from virtue ethics, reshape the discourse? What implications arise from this prism if we want to re-address certain questions of ethics and taxation? As mentioned before, virtue ethics, in contrast to deontology, dismisses the concept of duty as its foundational locus. In the realm of deontological thought, one arrives at the notion that moral agents can fulfil their fiscal obligations with dutiful compliance, faithfully following the letter of the law and thereby contributing their fair share – provided, of course, that the law is properly formulated. Yet, within the domain of virtue ethics, such facile precepts no longer prove adequate as the sole compass. Duty, after all, does not serve as the foundational element of ethical action within the virtue ethics tradition. The essence of ethical conduct resides in the virtues themselves. And precisely because these virtues always call upon practical wisdom as their guiding light, questions arise such as: 'What is the spirit of the law?', 'What context frames its existence and what purpose does it strive to fulfil?' These queries, inseparably woven into the fabric of virtue ethics, form the necessary conditions for addressing the more fundamental question: 'Which choices should I make, and which actions must I execute within the tax realm?'. This realisation further signifies that reasoning on a case-by-case basis assumes paramount importance. Practical wisdom – the faculty to discern moral quandaries – occupies not only a prominent place but also necessitates active cultivation. However, this does not imply that the concept of duty ceases to play a role within virtue ethics. Indeed, it remains a morally relevant notion, albeit one that is framed within and subordinate to the virtues themselves, which, in turn, point toward the pursuit of the good life as their ultimate end.

This novel perspective of virtue ethics in taxation also bestows upon the non-legislative realm,[28] wherein compliance is expected and demanded, as well as other non-legislative actors, an extensive guide for action that complements other normative positions. Contrary to prevailing assumptions, even if the law were formulated in its most impeccable manner, it is doubtful whether every resolution can be resolved. The rule of law, as such, is not enough for moral behaviour to prevail, something most rule of law theorists undoubtedly agree with. But how precisely does morality interact with rule of law? Indeed, tax legislation itself includes and harbours open norms which demand interpretation from a broader perspective.[29] Practical experience has already demonstrated the formidable challenge of formulating such a flawless, watertight and just legislation, let alone determining the appropriate level of governance.[30] Complex legislation tends to give rise to loopholes and opportunities for contrivances (aimed at

[28] And evidently also on the legislative side, as we speak of a broadening of perspective.

[29] See eg the 'good faith principle'.

[30] Observe, for instance, the discourse on whether this should occur at the supranational level or, conversely, if the sovereignty of the state should remain the fundamental premise. For a respective portrayal of both perspectives, consider C Peters, *On the Legitimacy of International Tax Law* (Amsterdam: IBFD, 2014) and P Dietsch, *Catching Capital: The Ethics of Tax Competition* (Oxford: Oxford University Press, 2015).

reducing the average tax rate),[31] while simplistic legislation risks overlooking crucial contextual nuances and paying inadequate attention to concrete exceptions that have emerged over the years, each with its own justification for existence.[32] The strength of virtue ethics, in our view, lies in its broad applicability. Taking the status quo as a given, with the legislative framework as it is, virtue ethics can help us to determine what we can do, as individual actors, in the fiscal realm. Virtue ethics goes beyond the obligation to contribute our fair share, it operates with the idea wherein the central element becomes the question as to how to lead our life in its totality. Our fiscal choices are no longer confined to the tax realm alone; instead, they form an integral part of a larger whole, namely, the good life in all its facets. The quintessential question in ethical reasoning becomes: 'How would a virtuous person act in this situation?' Fiscal choices can only be morally justified if they align with the choices and actions made by an individual who has cultivated his virtuousness. The virtuous person, by developing the different virtues, possesses a certain finesse and sensitivity to context, and, contrary to the deontological approach, there is no readily available universal law that can be applied as a litmus test.

At present, scant regard is paid to the role of virtues and, perhaps rightfully so, for virtues possess an elusiveness that seems to defy codification.[33] Yet, this does not negate the fact that potential contributions to the discourse may outweigh any perceived deficiencies, for this more contextual approach of virtue ethics may be eminently suited to deal with the complexities inherent in tax law. When one elects to work as a consultant or tax advisor this is generally deemed to be a neutral and amoral choice, ie in a liberal society one is free to take up any job available in the job market (ie as long as it is legal). This implies that, at first glance, this choice harbours no (profound) ethical implications, nor is it linked to matters of ethics. The ethical questions with regard to tax law are generally solely ascribed upon the one who bears the burden of taxes, or may bear them in future, ie from whom we demand compliance to the tax law. All other actors, who may facilitate the optimisation or evasion of taxes, have generally been deemed ethically impartial (as long as they themselves do not incite fraud, ie stay within the legal framework). However, from a virtue ethical standpoint, it becomes clear that this bifurcation is untenable, the emphasis on the taxpayer alone assumes too limited a perspective. The taxpayer is surrounded by other actors and acts within a framework wherein the legislator, the tax authority, the government, and so forth, also wield influence and contribute to the eventual practical result. But as we argued virtuous conduct transcends the bounds of mere compliance and can solely be apprehended within a broader context. In virtue ethics, there exists no rigid demarcation between

[31] Here we refer not only to the renowned structures of large multinational corporations, but also to the comparatively modest optimisations of individuals and smaller companies.

[32] This also raises the immediate question of whether all simplification of legislation is inherently good. There appears to be a tendency to equate simplicity with improvement, but the ease of such simplistic – unexamined – assimilation is questionable. Each alteration from the status quo must be assessed on its own merits. The correlation between simplicity and fairness cannot be established without contextual analysis so presumed breaches of rule of law might not be as problematic upon closer inspection.

[33] This was indicated by Aristotle himself at the outset of the Nicomachean Ethics where he states: 'we would not seek the same degree of exactness in all sorts of arguments alike' Aristotle, *Nicomachean Ethics*, 1094b 13–14.

choices and actions that derive from a moral foundation, and those that are intrinsically amoral.[34] All choices and actions bear the potential for moral implications.[35] This responsibility extends beyond the viewpoint of the taxpayer alone. Virtue ethics, with its goal-oriented approach – namely, the pursuit of happiness – thus alludes to a vision of society wherein a state of being comes to the foreground that may be delineated as the shared good of all actors involved.[36] A strict dichotomy between the professional and personal domains is, therefore, untenable within the confines of a virtue ethical theory. The moral compass within the professional realm exceeds the bounds of code of conduct that governs that in professional life,[37] it is impossible to separate it entirely from the moral fabric of the personal sphere. Assuredly, it is self-evident for other normative theories that moral choices must be made, transcending the strict adherence to the letter of the law.[38] Nonetheless, within virtue ethics, this assumes a more profound character.

An important argument emerges from the perspective of virtue ethics regarding the professional practice that makes clear how virtue ethics operate in practice: one can argue that the embodiment of professional practice in its most perfect form is inherently to the ethically responsible one. The notion suggests that instead of hanging an ethical framework on an external benchmark, such as a universal law detached from the professional activity or personal situation, one should perceive the pursuit of excellence within the professional activity, or personal matter even, as the very essence of the ethical approach to taxation. This approach is not an open door to a relativist interpretation wherein everyone deduces moral values to his liking: virtue ethics contains standards and excellences, but these are internal to the activity itself. What is valuable is that which helps in excelling at a certain activity. Excelling, after all, means doing something well – excelling as a lawyer, therefore, implies being a good lawyer, excelling as a tax consultant denotes being a good tax consultant. However, this notion of what constitutes this goodness, within the professional setting, cannot be arbitrarily defined; ie one cannot argue that maximal tax evasion designates the excellence of a tax advisor. An analogy can be drawn to explicate this matter, for instance, with a table – what constitutes a good table cannot be determined ad hoc either. If someone were to argue that the most essential aspect to speak of a good table is its colour, purple for example,

[34] See also David Bloom on the often-argued difference between the moral and the legal: D Bloom, 'Tax Avoidance – A View from the Dark Side' 39 (2016) *Melbourne University Law Review* 950.

[35] Even if one maintains a strict separation between morality and law, virtue ethics will inevitably exert influence on those matters internal to law. In this context, it is important to mention that Hans Kelsen's legal positivism was driven by a moral scepticism, and in that sense, legal positivism served as a 'rescue' from moral relativism. A similar line of reasoning can even be made in relation to Thomas Hobbes' *Leviathan*. They advocate a minimal standard in case of a loss of moral consensus. Another question, which cannot be addressed here due to its scope, is whether a strict legal positivism (not to be confused with a theory of positive law) is tenable from a virtue ethics perspective.

[36] See also: W Lemmens and J Badisco, 'Taxation and Ethics: An Impossible Marriage?' in B Peeters, JLM Gribnau and J Badisco (eds), *Building Trust in Taxation* (Cambridge: Intersentia, 2017).

[37] The fact that the term 'deontological ethics' is synonymous with 'code of conduct' is related to the notion that these ethical codes find their originating ground within the realm of deontology. J Frecknall-Hughes, P Moizer, E Doyle, B Summers, 'An Examination of Ethical Influences on the Work of Tax Practitioners' (2017) 146 *Journal of Business Ethics* 729.

[38] An example: H Girbnau, 'De Morele Dimensie Estate Planning' (2020) 24 *Kwartaalbericht Estate Planning* 20.

it becomes evident to all that this description does not necessarily capture a good table. One could possess a table with a broken leg, rendering it unable to stand upright, yet it could be purple. Clearly, this is not a good table.[39] Conversely, a good table is one that has a number of legs to ensure stability, a functional surface to place or use objects, and so forth. Therefore, the essence of a good table can only be discerned by contemplating its role. Only when we grasp the purpose of the object we call a table, can we begin to formulate what constitutes a good table. Naturally, the purpose can encompass a certain degree of variation (some tables are meant for work, others for dining, and so on), yet there remains a certain unity that distinguishes a table from a chair. However, it is evident that determining the goodness of a table cannot be arbitrary; it is determined by its purpose. The same line of reasoning can be applied to lawyers, tax consultants, and so on – one cannot simply impose their own definition of what it means to be a good lawyer. Being a good lawyer means understanding the purpose of being a lawyer, a far more complex endeavour than understanding the purpose of a table. It necessarily entails a reference to the entire structure of society within which the lawyer functions as a particular figure or institution. The lawyer, as a professional, is a man-made legal figure or institution that fulfils a specific role within the fabric of society as a whole. It is at this juncture that virtues come into play. Understanding the roles of these institutions and figures requires a comprehension of society in all its contingent facets, a comprehension that can only be attained by someone who is in the possession of virtues. Hence, the good lawyer, tax consultant, and so forth, is the virtuous one.[40] This is an alternative way of deducing standards and measurements of morality compared to duty-based ethics; but it is not subjectivist in nature as these standards and measures are deduced from inside the practice as an objectified undertaking serving a societal purpose.

By means of this argument virtue ethics arrives at the conclusion that excellence in the professional practice entails the virtuous execution of that practice.[41] Thus, one could posit that for example that a tax advisor, when standing at the crossroads of choosing a particular fiscal construction, arrives at the ethical choice precisely when, drawing upon his or her past experiences and insights, strives to handle the matter in the most excellent manner possible, thereby understanding what it means to be a good

[39] Of course, this can be seen as a good table from the perspective of a person at a certain moment when he is specifically looking for such a purple table. But there is an underlying element here before one can look to more specific elements of excellence – for a given person at a given time – this underlying element is that which distinguishes it from other objects.

[40] See also Aristotle: 'We have found, then, that the human function is activity of the soul in accord with reason or requiring reason' and 'And so the human good proves to be activity of the soul in accord with virtue'. Aristotle, *Nicomachean Ethics*, 1098a 7–8, 16–28.

[41] See also MacIntyre on the role of 'practices' which is central in his conceptualisation of the concept of virtue – and an example of an argument from virtue ethics. One could argue the professional activity is a type of practice as defined by him: 'By a 'practice' I am going to mean any coherent and complex form of socially established cooperative human activity through which goods internal to that form of activity are realised in the course of trying to achieve those standards of excellence which are appropriate to, and partially definitive of, that form of activity, with the result that human powers to achieve excellence, and human conceptions of the ends and goods involved, are systematically extended.' And: 'A virtue is an acquired human quality the possession and exercise of which tends to enable us to achieve those goods which are internal to practices and the lack of which effectively prevents us from achieving such goods.' A MacIntyre, *After Virtue* 3rd edn (Notre Dame: University of Notre Dame Press, 2007), 187, 191.

tax advisor within the entirety of our society. Not by emphasising a single facet alone (such as profit maximisation), but by excelling in the role of a tax advisor and, holistically speaking, making the most coherent choice. Of course, profit maximisation is part of the task of a tax professional, to a certain extent. From a virtue ethics point of view, drawing up the concrete balance as to where to draw the line is left to those who stand in the practice and can draw upon years of experience, *and* who have developed and practised the virtues relevant to their profession. Even for the non-professional there is clearly a line where it becomes *too* much. Virtue ethics argues that it is he who is virtuous and well-versed in the profession is most able to deduce precisely where that line is situated: he possesses practical wisdom, *phronesis*. In reality the practitioner or any other person will most likely not harbour a complex reflective thought on the matter, and the identification of concrete goals will not be consciously present but rather implicitly operate in the background. Hence, the immense importance of cultivating a certain ethos at the societal level.[42] Excelling therein also entails considering the place this profession occupies in our society and the purpose associated with it. Fundamentally, this excellence relies upon the presence of virtues, as such excellence can only be attained by someone who possesses the various virtues. Underlying this approach is the idea that if everyone acts in this manner, particularly in the realm of taxation, an ethical taxation is also achieved without the need for imposing grand universal rules. A virtue ethics, then, may well be construed as an 'ethics from the trenches', an uprising from the professional activity itself.

Even though virtue ethics does not deduce universal moral laws, it is not reduced to mere opinion or 'that is what you say'. Deduction of standards and measurements are merely done from a conception of what it means to do something good or well by people experienced in the enterprise of doing these things. The history of philosophy, starting with Aristotle, has brought forth a wealth of information regarding the nature and role of the virtues.

Exploring Virtues in the Tax Realm

In this section, we shall cautiously embark upon the exploration of some of the virtues that can be of relevance for tax law and in which way they operate as an extra layer to the rule of law and thereby strengthen it. We do not argue for a replacement of rule of law by virtue ethics, but merely wish to explore its relationship and see how virtuousness can strengthen a rule of law-based reasoning. Given the vast potential of this intellectual exercise and its inherently exploratory nature, we shall confine ourselves to a core and indispensable constellation of virtues (there are many more than these enumerated here). In our selection, we shall be guided by the classical division of virtues, heeding the footsteps of Plato's classical delineation, subsequently embraced by Aristotle. This leaves us with the following four virtues: *phronesis* (practical wisdom, sometimes also translated as prudence), *sophrosyne* (temperance), *dikaiosyne* (justice), and *andreia* (courage).

[42] See also Aristotle: Aristotle, *Nicomachean Ethics*, 1103a–04b on the acquisition and subsequent application of virtues.

Characteristic of virtue ethics is that it does not necessarily generate grand universal laws, as is often the case with deontological ethics. Instead, it emphasises the individual's room to make decisions that align with the contextual nuances of the situation. The enactment of such choices necessitates the virtue of practical wisdom.[43] Consider, for instance, those employed in the tax sector, who find themselves exposed to moral quandaries on a daily basis within their professional practice. It is plausible that these situations, in practice, often go unrecognised since they are addressed by a pattern of actions ingrained in one's character over time-they have become a habit. Tax law is not always straightforward; it encompasses open norms and its complexity allows for manipulation and utilisation to achieve objectives that may not align with the legislator's intentions. Emphasising universal principles such as 'act in such a way that your behaviour can be universalised'[44] leads to the realisation that such propositions are frequently ambiguous from the perspective of those in the field. They tend to be overly general and arduous to apply to concrete situations. The path from these moral principles to concrete action is not always evident. Practical wisdom, on the other hand, is a virtue that accentuates the complexity of choices and actions in specific circumstances: each situation is unique, and only those intimately acquainted with the practice itself can assess the consequences of certain behaviours. Practical wisdom, in this sense, becomes the ultimate virtue of the tax practitioner – who could be more at home in the labyrinth of tax law than the practitioner? Here, the virtue of practical wisdom reverberates back to the aforementioned pursuit of excellence in professional activity (see no 12). Such excellence can only be attained through the cultivation of practical wisdom. From a rule of law perspective, we see how practical wisdom can help to judge on a case-by-case basis where the law itself is clearly violated yet not immediately eminent by the letter.

When we turn our gaze to the other virtues, we immediately recognise that the virtue of justice is inseparable from the tax realm. As previously indicated, justice is often regarded as the sole guiding principle for a just taxation, which is oftentimes equated it with righteousness itself. Justice is a virtue that can be cultivated both by individuals as well as institutions.[45] The virtue of justice is indispensable for anyone faced with tax dilemmas; it pertains to the individual's capacity to comprehend what constitutes a fair distribution of burdens, how and to what extent income redistribution should ideally occur. It also encompasses determining what constitutes acceptable conduct, where is the rule of law violated and how much should tax practitioners who clearly show avoidance behaviour in contrast with the spirit of the law be addressed. A coherent understanding of justice necessitates the virtue of practical wisdom, as it must be applied in concrete situations.

Courage and moderation are virtues that are not often mentioned in discussions regarding fiscal ethics. Nevertheless, we believe they are indispensable to a truly

[43] For the importance of practical wisdom also see Pieper: 'The guarantee of the goodness of concrete human action is given solely by the virtue of prudence' in J Pieper, *The Four Cardinal Virtues* (Notre Dame: University of Notre Dame Press, 1980) 28.

[44] See one of Kant's formulations of the categorical imperative.

[45] Already, for Plato, it was a virtue of both the individual and the state; justice in the city and justice in the individual can be approached analogously. Plato, *The Republic*, 368d–369b.

ethical tax law. Whether it pertains to the legislative side, the professionals involved, or ordinary citizens, each of them will at some point be confronted with situations where it is apparent that something is just or unjust, but the execution thereof is far from straightforward and demands a measure of courage. Consider, for instance, a tax administration confronted with an individual who is to pay a fine, but it is clear that, ethically speaking, the situation is unjust. Perhaps the citizen could absolutely not have known about something due to the complexity of the matter.[46] Of course, one can argue that the application of the law is always just, as that is the only standard and measure. However, this argument presupposes that there exists no other standards and measures,[47] such as morality (ie a form of moral relativism), a highly questionable claim, one that also runs counter to the everyday understanding of morality that clearly delineates just and unjust behaviour beyond abiding by the law. The situation wherein one would rule certain cases with more leniency does not take away anyone's legal right, so it is entirely unproblematic from that perspective. It would merely be a showing of mildness: a form of moderation that might run counter to rule of law but enhances the morality of the system as a whole.

It is situations such as these that demand courage as they need more than just the rule of law to be alleviated in an ethical manner. Judging these situations in strictly the same manner for everyone is unjust, a tax professional and an average citizen differ greatly in their knowledge regarding tax matters and judging the law in relation to their behaviour would be unjust. But between the awareness of what is unjust and the actual execution of the right action lie numerous obstacles. These situations are not limited to professionals or individuals; even from the perspective of tax lawmakers, one can envision examples of this nature. To resolve a budgetary deficit from the state's side, for instance, they may choose to impose a tax that lacks a good justification, serving only as a budgetary solution and disproportionately affecting certain groups, while perhaps totally within the boundaries of a narrow rule of law conception. Converting this awareness of justice into the action of refraining from implementing such a tax is by no means easy. Both examples require virtues that extend beyond justice; they necessitate courage and moderation, among others. Faced with injustice, it is not enough to possess this awareness – it appears that practical reasoning alone does not necessarily exert an immediate influence upon us regarding the concrete actions.[48] Multiple virtues are required to guide our actions. The accountant or lawyer needs courage to stand up against their client and moderation in the understanding that they may displease the client and even risk losing a portion of their income source. But also the tax administration needs courage to see where the rule of law is lacking.

[46] See eg the following case in Belgium reported by the Vlaamse Ombudsdienst: Vlaamse Ombudsdienst, *Jaarverslag 2022: Transparantie en Verbondenheid*, 49–51.

[47] This is a matter wherein the normative system of law clashes with that of morality. As long as one accepts both give normative reasons for action this sort of situation is unavoidable.

[48] This position has been embraced by the eminent philosopher David Hume. He contends that practical reason – if it exists at all – is impotent, lacking the power to guide our actions. Based on insights like this, Hume himself has forged a distinctive theory of virtue ethics. D Hume, *A Treatise of Human Nature* (Oxford: Oxford University Press, 2011).

Naturally, this approach from virtue ethics raises questions. One essential question, particularly relevant within the realm of tax practice, emerges: how do you quantify virtuousness? How do you measure the presence of these virtues? While one's sense of justice may be inferred to some extent from their behaviour, what about courage, moderation, and the encompassing virtue of practical wisdom? If you seek to strengthen the rule of law with something such as virtue ethics it is necessary stringent checks are made. It is understandable that within a given organisation, one may choose to foster an ethos of virtue, but how does one account for this in the recruitment process? Aristotle already addresses this issue in Ethics, but the answer may prove insufficient: the wise man serves as the measure.[49] Yet, this is not a mere 'that is what you propose' response.[50] The action of the wise man becomes the morally correct action, in an epistemological sense: we know what the virtuous action is when we know what the action or choice of the wise man would be. Faced with complex situations, one may ask what someone who excels would do in such a scenario. The answer to that question, at the very least, points us towards a guide. Ideally, we all have virtuous individuals in our surroundings who can fulfil an exemplary role, and whose own actions and choices can serve as guiding principles.

Concluding Remarks

And, finally, how does all this relate to the rule of law? Virtue ethics has an interaction with the rule of law as one of the supplements which enhance the legal system as a whole. Many rule-of-law theorists argue that the rule of law is just one of the many essential facets of a legal system, we argue virtue ethics – contrary to deontologist ethics and utilitarianism – might also be one of these essential facets. Of course, theorists such as Raz acknowledge that the rule of law is certainly not the only value and discussion as to which values are most important is open: 'It [the rule of law] has always to be balanced against competing claims of other values.' Virtue ethics, we argue, is one of those other values.

It is evident, of course, that virtue ethics will not provide all the answers immediately, but it does open the door to a broader approach to taxes and ethics. It can place central concepts, provide a direction for exploration, and remind us that the ethics we adhere to always bring certain assumptions. It also shows that speaking of a just tax law framework as if it were purely a formal legal dimension is not a simple matter. Therefore, we advocate for an ethical tax system, which entails a more expansive vision, by doing so the rule of law can be strengthened.

In line with this broader perspective, we have attempted to introduce virtue ethics into the discussions concerning tax law. It has shown us that virtues can still play a role in this day and age. Although virtue ethics may not always offer ready-made solutions, it is questionable whether other normative ethical theories can do so either.

[49] Aristotle, *Nicomachean Ethics*, 1113a 30-1113b.

[50] E Voegelin, *Order and History Volume III: Plato and Aristotle* (Columbia MI: University of Missouri Press, 2000).

Unlike these other theories, virtue ethics has a closer connection to practice, as we argued earlier. The explicit mention of phronesis, practical wisdom, as a virtue and as a driving force behind practical reasoning, indicates that virtue ethics is always to some extent a realised element in practice. However, we consider this certainly not a drawback of the theory. After all, taxation does not revolve around 'big questions' like those sometimes found in debates of applied ethics (eg abortion, euthanasia, ecology). On the contrary, the issues that arise in a tax context are often precisely of a nature that emerges during implementation (eg when a client wishes to establish a particular structure, when confronted with dilemmas while filing taxes, when a tax administration is confronted with a case of tax avoidance in direct opposition to the spirit of the law etc.). Taxation often resides in the details, details and contexts that vary significantly each time and where the unambiguousness of the law somewhat diminishes. That is why cultivating virtues, with an emphasis on practical wisdom, is equally relevant to fiscal ethics. It provides a guide to navigate the flux inherent in taxation in a stable and ethical manner.

10

Does the Social Security Tax Violate Rule of Law Principles?

HENRY ORDOWER

'[W]ith law our country will thrive, but with lawlessness it will be laid waste.'[1]

'The fundamental freedom of the legislature ... is limited in tax law, especially income tax law, by two closely related guidelines: the requirement that tax burdens align with the ability to pay principle and the requirement of consistency. Accordingly, in the interest of equality also in tax burdens as the constitution provides ... the goal must be to tax taxpayers with the same ability to pay the same amount (horizontal tax justice), while (in the vertical direction) the taxation of higher incomes must be appropriate in comparison with the tax burden on lower incomes (citations omitted). Although the legislature has a wide range of discretion to select tax subjects and determine tax rates, it must, under the requirement that all taxpayers be burdened as evenly as possible, consistently implement the structuring of tax legislation with the goal of implementing equal burdens. (citations omitted). Exceptions to such a logical implementation require a compelling objective justification.'[2]

[1] EÓ Sveinsson, ed. and annotator, *Brennu-Njáls Saga* (Reykjavik, Hið Íslenzka Fornritafélag, 1954) Ch 70, 172. The quotation has been translated by the author. The original quotation reads: '[M]eð lǫgum ska land várt byggja, en með ólǫgum eyða.'

[2] BVerfGE 107, 27, Beschluss des Zweiten Senats vom 04. Dezember 2002 - 2 BvR 400/98 -, Rn 1–75. Available at: www.bverfg.de/e/rs20021204_2bvr040098.html. The quotation has been translated and paraphrased by the author. The original quotation reads: 'Die grundsätzliche Freiheit des Gesetzgebers ... wird für den Bereich des Steuerrechts und insbesondere für den des Einkommensteuerrechts vor allem durch zwei eng miteinander verbundene Leitlinien begrenzt: durch das Gebot der Ausrichtung der Steuerlast am Prinzip der finanziellen Leistungsfähigkeit und durch das Gebot der Folgerichtigkeit. Danach muss im Interesse verfassungsrechtlich gebotener steuerlicher Lastengleichheit ... darauf abgezielt werden, Steuerpflichtige bei gleicher Leistungsfähigkeit auch gleich hoch zu besteuern (horizontale Steuergerechtigkeit), während (in vertikaler Richtung) die Besteuerung höherer Einkommen im Vergleich mit der Steuerbelastung niedriger Einkommen angemessen sein muss (citations omitted). Zwar hat der Gesetzgeber bei der Auswahl des Steuergegenstands und bei der Bestimmung des Steuersatzes einen weitreichenden Entscheidungsspielraum, jedoch muss er unter dem Gebot möglichst gleichmäßiger Belastung aller Steuerpflichtigen bei der Ausgestaltung des steuerrechtlichen Ausgangstatbestands die einmal getroffene Belastungsentscheidung folgerichtig im Sinne der Belastungsgleichheit umsetzen. (citations omitted). Ausnahmen von einer solchen folgerichtigen Umsetzung bedürfen eines besonderen sachlichen Grundes (citations omitted).'

Abstract

The rule of law as applied to taxation assumes primarily procedural form. If tax rules have developed through adequate legislative and administrative procedures and been applied to taxpayers by unbiased administrators and an unbiased judiciary, they are facially neutral and procedurally rule of law compliant. Yet, the rule of law also has a substantive aspect that focuses on equality in the outcome of the procedures. It asks whether the tax rules as enacted and applied consistently with rule of law procedural criteria nevertheless result in unequal or biased outcomes? If they do not, they must change to meet thicker understandings of the rule of law. This chapter applies this substantive concept to the US social security tax and argues the tax fails to meet rule of law fairness criteria even if it might have when first enacted. The chapter argues that the rule of law is dynamic, and the payroll tax has become obsolete, harmful, regressive, and inconsistent with the substantive rule of law. While public retirement systems are firmly embedded in and critical to the modern economies that characterise the developed world, they should be funded from general revenue rather than a limited, targeted tax that cannot be adequate to the job as the size of the retired population grows.

Introduction

This chapter addresses the intersection of rule of law principles with payroll taxes in the United States of America (US) but may apply as well to payroll taxes in many other countries. Payroll taxes are ubiquitous worldwide and have some structural commonality from country to country so that this chapter's observations are not unique to the US. The range of variations renders the US system an example of, but not necessarily a model for, the payroll tax–social insurance relationship. Many payroll taxes are imposed on the gross wages of employed individuals at a flat rate as in the US; apply to income from performance of services without any significant minimum amount of income that is exempt from the taxes; and have a wage ceiling above which no tax is imposed. Often the employee and the employer pay equal shares of the tax although characterisation of the shares may differ. The employee's share is a gross income tax (whether designated as a contribution or another term) while the employer's share is an excise-type tax since its base is not the employer's income but the gross wages the employer pays. In the US, the tax receipts from the payroll taxes are designated to fund social insurance programmes, including periodic payments – social security benefit payments – to individuals who have reached retirement age.

Nothing procedurally irregular taints the enactment and continuation of the taxes. In the US, as in its counterpart jurisdictions with elected governments, the legislature, with the concurrence of the executive, has imposed taxes following the established procedures for enacting taxing legislation. Accordingly, payroll taxes are consistent with procedural rule of law principles, that is they comfortably satisfy 'thin' or 'narrow' rule of law concepts.[3] The taxes have been adopted with the consent of the governed acting

[3] See Lindsay Chapter 3 in this volume. See also Daly, Chapter 2 in this volume.

through their elected representatives. The taxes apply uniformly to all individuals in the defined, albeit narrow, tax base. The taxes are enforced uniformly through collection by deducting them from the individual's wages and transmitting them to the government via the employer who acts as a withholding agent.

Payroll taxes offer administrative simplicity. The number of points of contact between the tax administrator and the public is smaller because many employers have multiple employees. Withholding at the source of payment simplifies collection. There are severe penalties for failing to deduct the appropriate amount of tax. Those responsible become personally liable for a 100% penalty for failing to deduct and pay over the correct amount of tax.[4] The taxes are computationally straightforward because the tax rate is a flat, positive rate up to a wage ceiling and then zero. No individual variants affect the computation as might some features of the general income tax, for example, itemised deductions,[5] that enable an employee to diminish the amount of income subject to income tax. Exploiting the fluidity of the boundary between wages or self-employment income subject to the payroll/self-employment tax, on the one hand, and distribution of an entity's earnings to its owners on the other hand, enables some taxpayers in the US to limit their payroll tax liability by inserting an entity between the income source and the individual owner/employee.[6] Corporate distributions of their earnings through dividends are not subject to social security tax even if the general income tax is imposed only on the individual owners of the corporation, rather than the corporation itself, because the corporation can choose tax transparency rather than corporate tax.[7]

This chapter argues that a 'broad' or 'thick' rule of law[8] is indispensable to the assertion that a government and a society respect the rule of law. Rule of law principles must transform and adapt to changing societal conditions and understanding of fundamental equality and fairness. Procedural regularity of enactment, uniformity and predictability in collection, and neutrality of language in a taxing statute or regulation are markers of, but insufficient to comply fully with, rule of law principles. Such rule of law indicia do not guarantee the absence of oppression. Oppression of one individual or group by another whether through physical domination or through the legislative or judicial process would seem characteristic of governing structures lacking the rule of law.

Accordingly, this chapter assumes that rule of law principles substantively limit discretion of the legislative body and the judiciary by encompassing broader equality principles. The historical example of the Jim Crow laws in the US illustrates this limitation.[9] These laws that southern states of the US enacted consistently with rule of law procedures required racial segregation in public facilities. Under Jim Crow, discrimination was permissible despite constitutional guarantees of equal treatment.[10] Racially separate, but equal, facilities sufficed under constitutional equality protection guarantees.[11] The US Supreme Court initially accepted the enactment

[4] Section 6672 of the Internal Revenue Code of 1986, as amended, 26 United States Code, referred to throughout as IRC § (followed by a section number).

[5] IRC §63.

[6] W Schwidetzky, 'Is it Time to Give the S Corporation a Proper Burial?' (1996) 15 *Virginia Tax Review* 591.

[7] IRC §1362.

[8] See Lindsay, above n 3. Daly, above n 3.

[9] M Urofsky, 'Jim Crow Law' (*Brittanica*, 2023). Available at: www.britannica.com/event/Jim-Crow-law.

[10] US Const Art XIV (1868).

[11] *Plessy v Ferguson*, 163 US 537 (1896).

and enforcement of such laws as valid practice.[12] From a contemporary perspective, the prevailing view is that such separate facilities serve to oppress a segment of the population and are rarely, if ever, equal. The Supreme Court later rejected these laws as unconstitutional.[13] Jim Crow laws are inconsistent with substantive rule of law principles, even if they comply with procedural rule of law principles and are no longer tolerated – although Professor Dean argues that global tax rules resemble Jim Crow laws.[14] If the tax rules favour some taxpayers over others or create or enhance disparities in income or wealth, they are neither neutral nor consistent with rule of law equality principles.

Biased rules characterise the privileged legal and economic status enjoyed by some under governmental structures that do not ensure the rule of law, including absolute monarchies, dictatorships, and oligarchies.[15] Just as regulatory capture by industry participants results in regulatory agencies failing to serve the interests of the public,[16] informational and political domination of the tax legislative process by the affluent and special interests produces tax legislation that complies with procedural rule of law principles but fails to serve broader public interests or maintain rule of law.

Recent scholarship[17] and governmental studies[18] reveal that facially neutral tax rules may be infused with racial and economic biases favouring white over black and Latin American individuals. This chapter contends, similarly, that the rate structure of the US social security tax expresses a bias in favour of high-income individuals over low- and moderate-income individuals by applying a nominal and effective 6.2 per cent tax rate[19] to each dollar of wage income earned by an employee whose wage income in 2024[20] is less than $168,600 while applying a zero rate to individuals on that portion of their income from services exceeding $168,600 and to all income from sources other than wages. Taxpayers with income only from wages and such wage income less than $168,600 make up the bulk of US taxpayers.

In recommending the unbundling of the social security benefit system from the dedicated payroll tax currently funding the system,[21] this chapter acknowledges that social security is popular under its existing payroll tax funding system[22] despite

[12] ibid.

[13] *Brown v Board of Education of Topeka*, 347 US 483 (1954).

[14] S Dean, *Global Jim Crow: Taxation and Racial Capitalism*, (Oxford: Oxford University Press, forthcoming).

[15] Universal Declaration of Human Rights 1948, Art VII. Available at: www.un.org/sites/un2.un.org/files/2021/03/udhr.pdf.

[16] D Carpenter and D Moss (eds), *Preventing Regulatory Capture: Special Interest Influence and How to Limit It* (Cambridge: Cambridge University Press, 2014).

[17] D Brown, The Whiteness of Wealth: How the Tax System Impoverishes Black Americans – And How We Can Fix It. (New York: Crown Publishers, 2021).

[18] G Leiserson, 'Disparities in the Benefits of Tax Expenditures by Race and Ethnicity' (US Department of Treasury, 20 January 2023). Available at: https://home.treasury.gov/news/featured-stories/disparities-in-the-benefits-of-tax-expenditures-by-race-and-ethnicity.

[19] Some argue that employees bear the burden of the employer's share of the tax indirectly through lower wages and benefits, as well as the employee's share.

[20] The ceiling inflation adjusts annually by the increase in the cost of living.

[21] H Ordower, 'Unbundling Social Security from the Payroll Tax' (2023) 27 *Florida Tax Review* 269.

[22] Eligibility for Social Security in retirement. Available at: www.ssa.gov/retirement/eligibility#:~:text=You're%20eligible%20if%3A,for%2010%20years%20or%20more. Accessed 22 April 2023.

current challenges that threaten its long-term financial viability.[23] Nevertheless, the chapter argues that the payroll tax violates rule of law principles in its regressivity and the interplay of the benefit formula with the payroll tax impedes social security from serving a welfare function and reaching further to help those needing retirement assistance. Although the social security benefit formula favours lower-income participants, it provides no benefit to those who lack adequate tax payment participation in the system. Like benefits under a growing variety of voluntary and primarily private retirement savings plans, benefits are a function of the recipient's payments into the system rather than more general individual need. Social security as the public and mandatory retirement savings plan that was critical when private, voluntary plans were rare is no longer necessary. Social security is duplicative in the existing world of tax-incentivised private and mostly contributory retirement plans. Its better future lies in combatting the impoverishment of individuals who lack adequate retirement plan participation.

In the next part, the chapter briefly explores the dependence of democratic institutions on rule of law principles and the substantive side of those principles. In the following part, the chapter reviews the relationship between the benefit and ability to pay concepts in taxation and tests them against rule of law principles. Then the chapter considers the dynamism of the rule of law in relationship to the development of social security in the US and its funding as the payroll tax has become increasingly significant to government revenue, increasingly regressive, and tax burdens have shifted generally from capital to labour. Next the chapter recommends shifting social security expenditures to general revenue and concomitantly enhancing the progressivity of the income tax overall to provide those revenues through rate adjustments and base expansion. Base expansion would accompany diminution of tax expenditures that benefit more affluent members of the populace. This part also suggests ceasing or phasing-out the distribution of social security benefits to those who otherwise have ample resources for their comfort in old age. The chapter then summarises and concludes.

Rule of Law Principles

Njal's saga[24] is among the best developed and most intricate of the Icelandic family sagas, a body of prose narratives dating to the thirteenth and fourteenth centuries. The sagas relate events transpiring during the initial period of the Icelandic democracy, the eighth to eleventh centuries in Iceland. Among other narratives, the family sagas describe legal proceedings that take place at regional meetings or things and the annual Althing,[25] as the nascent democratic institutions struggled to maintain peace and civil

[23] Soc Sec Admin, Summary: Actuarial Status of the Social Security Trust Funds (2023). Available at: www.ssa.gov/policy/trust-funds-summary.html (showing that the social security trust fund will become inadequate to fund benefits during the next decade).

[24] *Brennu-Njáls Saga* (1954), above n 1. For a translation, W Cook (trans), *Njal's Saga* (London: Penguin Classics, 2002).

[25] H Ordower, 'Exploring the Literary Function of Law and Litigation in Njal's Saga' (1991), 3 *Cardozo Studies in Law & Literature* 41. The regional things met quarterly except for one meeting each year, the Althing, which was a country-wide meeting. The things served both as participatory legislative bodies and courts for the settlement of disputes.

order. In the absence of a monarchy, the governmental structure characterising most of Europe during the period, Iceland's farmers with significant landholdings formed their own small fiefdoms to consolidate their power and influence. Conflicts among the landholders were inevitable and violence and legal trickery often threatened and sometimes thwarted the operation of the democratic institutions and undermined the rule of law.

The quotation at the beginning of this chapter is attributed to Njal,[26] described in the saga as an unusually wise individual with the gift of clairvoyance. Njal expresses in simple terms the critical importance of the rule of law to the development of the fragile, early Icelandic democracy: '… with law our country will thrive, but with lawlessness it will be laid waste'.[27] Emphasising the importance of settling a dispute that otherwise was likely to lead to bloodshed, Njal agreed to arbitrate a settlement between Gunnar and two men named Thorkell who had tried, but failed, to ambush Gunnar. Njal is willing to arbitrate only if the parties grant him full power to determine the settlement terms.

Njal's offer suggests the delicacy of finding terms of settlement that will be sufficiently fair to the settling parties that the risk of a blood feud, always lurking in the background in the family sagas as the alternative to legal settlement of disputes, might be avoided.[28] If granted settlement autonomy, Njal believed he could find those terms. The settlement Njal names is large and requires many other individuals to contribute to the settlement both to raise the necessary funds and to engage them in the settlement to protect the rule of law with their financial commitment. The distribution of payment obligations loosely follows ability to pay principles. In this instance, Njal failed, but his 'rule of law' proposition encompasses not just the procedural element of using a disinterested arbitrator to settle disputes but also the arbitrator's commitment to fairness in the settlement and the participation of the community.

The second quotation at the beginning of the chapter comes from the German Constitutional Court in a case involving the deductibility of the expenses of maintaining two households.[29] The court analyses the substantive side of rule of law embodied in the equality principle of Germany's Basic Law.[30] While some scholars may view substantive equality principles embedded in national constitutions as independent of rule of law principles,[31] this chapter advances the view that constitutional equality and rights principles are essential parts of the 'thicker' versions of the rule of law. Constitutions include such principles because they define the scope of the society's requirements for its legal infrastructure and, hence, its rule of law formulation. Principles of equality are essential elements of rule of law. Their inclusion in a constitution channels the functions of the governmental institutions according to the rule of law so circumscribed. As applied to taxation, the constitutional equality principle

[26] *Brennu-Njáls Saga* (1954), above n 1.

[27] ibid.

[28] W Miller, *Bloodtaking and Peacemaking: Feud, Law, and Society in Saga Iceland* (Chicago IL: University of Chicago Press, 1990).

[29] BVerfGE 107, 27, above n 1.

[30] Grundgesetz für die Bundesrepublik Deutschland. Available at: www.gesetze-im-internet.de/gg/BJNR000010949.html.

[31] Lindsay, above n 3.

requires equal treatment under the law for there to be adherence to rule of law. The substantive rule of law thus limits the legislature's discretion:[32]

> The fundamental freedom of the legislature … is limited in tax law, especially income tax law, by two closely related guidelines: the requirement that tax burdens align with the ability to pay principle and the requirement of consistency. Accordingly, in the interest of equality also in tax burdens as the constitution provides … the goal must be to tax taxpayers with the same ability to pay the same amount (horizontal tax justice), while (in the vertical direction) the taxation of higher incomes must be appropriate in comparison with the tax burden on lower incomes (citations omitted). Although the legislature has a wide range of discretion to select tax subjects and determine tax rates, it must, under the requirement that all taxpayers be burdened as evenly as possible, consistently implement the structuring of tax legislation with the goal of implementing equal burdens. (citations omitted). Exceptions to such a logical implementation require a compelling objective justification (Author's translation and paraphrase).

This decision establishes horizontal equity as the basic tenet of individual income tax and requires legislation to remain consistent with an ability to pay principle as it mandates substantially identical tax treatment of individuals with like means measured by income. While the decision leaves the legislature to choose the tax base and rates, schedularity in taxation[33] with differing tax rates on differing types of income would seem to contradict the stated equality and logical consistency principles underlying taxation in the absence of a compelling justification for the schedularity.

The payroll tax is schedular. Its base reaches only individuals' income from their performance of services. Unless individuals with income from investments differ materially from individuals with income from services or income from services differs materially from income from investment, the payroll tax appears to violate the requirement of taxing like incomes alike. In the US, longstanding disagreements concerning the tension between services and investment income have manifested themselves in the rate structures of the income tax. Capital gain has enjoyed favoured treatment for most of US tax history, except the rate levelled in 1987 during a conservative administration.[34] While equalisation of rates was short-lived, even temporary equalisation suggests the absence of a compelling justification for favouring capital gain. Professor Blum catalogues an array of capital gain arguments but concludes that no argument is compelling.[35] Except for the social security tax and, until 2010, the Medicare tax, as well, investment income generally has been taxed at the identical rates as income from services with periods during which it was taxed at a higher rate to discourage tax sheltering, Thus for several years, there was a maximum tax on earned income[36] and there continues to exist a tax credit for income from services of low income taxpayers but not for income from

[32] BVerfGE 107, 27, above n 2 at [50].

[33] F Vanistendael, 'Legal Framework for Taxation' in V T Thuryony (ed), *Tax Law Design and Drafting*, V 1, (International Monetary Fund, 1996). Available at: www.elibrary.imf.org/display/book/9781557755872/ch02.xml; H Ordower 'Schedularity in US Income Taxation and its Effect on Tax Distribution' (2014) 108 *Northwestern University Law Review* 905.

[34] Tax Reform Act of 1986, Public law: 99–514 (22 October 1986).

[35] W Blum, 'A Handy Summary of Capital Gain Arguments' (1957) 35 *Taxes* 247.

[36] IRC §1348 (repealed).

investments.[37] Recent legislation favouring investment income, including the temporary qualified business income deduction,[38] seems politically motivated rather than a reflection of a compelling justification to favour the deployment of risk capital.

In addition, the wage cap violates ability to pay principles by taxing only the lower band of income from services. Yet, Germany has a payroll tax following the model of taxing service, but not investment, income, and the German payroll tax has a wage cap. A recent OECD economic survey criticises the lack of progressivity in the German tax system and the high tax burden on labour.[39] Perhaps the 'besondere sachliche Grund' (compelling substantive reason)[40] lies elsewhere.

Benefits versus Ability to Pay as Basis for Taxation

Rule of law, as the preceding discussion observes, has substantive characteristics as well as the commonly identified procedural characteristics of public participation either directly or through elected representatives, independent judiciaries, and access to legal process. The substantive features relate primarily to concepts of equal treatment without oppression under law. In terms of taxation, everyone must be subject to the same tax obligations as everyone else, a participation requirement, and like individuals must be taxed the same without some enjoying advantages or suffering disadvantages in tax obligations unless a compelling justification exists for disparate treatment of taxpayers. Tax statutes generally are neutral in their language, so they purportedly apply equally to all taxpayers. On closer examination, however, tax statutes often reveal discriminatory, embedded biases that result in unequal treatment of taxpayers without compelling justifications for so doing.[41]

That relative ability to pay measured by wealth or income, rather than marginal utility, should inform tax rules as well[42] led to development of the progressive income tax. Preventing accumulation and concentration of power through the assembly of dynastic wealth underpinned the estate taxes.[43] Yet, progressive taxation has yielded in recent years to flattening of tax rates on income, the repeal or diminution of estate taxes, and shifts to regressive forms of taxation, especially consumption taxes that find their justification primarily in simplified tax administration. Nevertheless, the general income tax, but not the services income-based social security tax, always has included some progressivity insofar as there always has been a minimum level of income upon which no tax is imposed.

[37] IRC §32.

[38] IRC §199A. Enactment of this provision accompanied the reduction in the corporate tax rate from a maximum of 35% to a flat 21% rate. One justification for IRC §199A is that it in part levelled the advantage corporations gained over unincorporated businesses from the change in the corporate rate under the Tax Cuts and Jobs Act of 2017, Pub L 115–97.

[39] OECD Economic Surveys: Germany 2023. Available at: https://read.oecd-ilibrary.org/economics/oecd-economic-surveys-germany-2023_9642a3f5-en#page4.

[40] BVerfGE (2002), above n 2.

[41] Brown, above n 17.

[42] BVerfGE, above n 2.

[43] T Smith, 'The Greatest Wealth Transfer in History Is Here, With Familiar (Rich) Winners' *The New York Times* (14 May 2023).

One argument favouring that shift in tax burdens is capital mobility, perhaps a false narrative.[44] Absent critical international cooperation to limit capital mobility, exit and continuation taxes, mark-to-market taxation of capital appreciation and other anti-deferral measures are domestic tools that discourage capital flight and could assist in countering the capital mobility argument. Nevertheless, rhetorical devises like calling estate and inheritance taxes 'death' taxes build public support for tax structures benefiting affluent taxpayers. Many people supporting those tax structures themselves never would become subject to such taxes and are advocating for tax structures against their own economic interests as the revenue lost by repeal or diminution of taxes on the affluent must be replaced by taxes on the middle- and lower-income taxpayers. Similarly, at state and local level in the US where state constitutional limitations require referenda to increase taxes, sales and use taxes more frequently receive approval than do income and property tax increases.

Social security, including Medicare, is the only major government programme funded with a discrete, dedicated tax. General revenues provide the funds for other programmes. Income taxes on individuals and companies, estate taxes, and excise taxes provide general revenue for the federal government in the US while in many other countries and in most US states, consumption taxes supply a further source of general revenues. General revenues, as supplemented by targeted user fees, fund some programmes although most user fees provide only sufficient revenue to cover the administrative expense of providing a governmental service or benefit.

The income tax itself is not a singular progressive tax on income from all sources[45] but is and has become increasingly schedular.[46] Income from certain transactions or sources is taxed more lightly than income from other sources. Affluent taxpayers capture the bulk of the benefit of more lightly taxed income.[47] Net capital gain[48] and qualified dividend income[49] is subject to a lower rate of tax than is income from services. Gain on property may go untaxed if the property is sold after the death of the person in whose hands it appreciated in value.[50] A 20 per cent deduction of the amount of qualified business income[51] reduces the effective rate for income in the qualified business income schedule. Some income including interest paid by state or local governments is exempt from tax,[52] a benefit with considerable deadweight loss as high marginal bracket taxpayers receive tax-exempt interest pegged to encourage individuals in lower marginal brackets to invest in state and local bonds. Income earned on investments in life insurance if paid to beneficiaries after the death of the insured[53] is similarly exempt from tax without regard to whether the beneficiaries are companies or individuals or need the insurance proceeds to maintain their

[44] W Cui, 'The Mirage of Mobile Capital' (7 May 2023). Available at: SSRN: https://ssrn.com/abstract=4440596 or http://dx.doi.org/10.2139/ssrn.4440596.

[45] IRC §61.

[46] H Ordower, above n 32.

[47] Leiserson, above n 18.

[48] IRC §1222(11).

[49] ibid §1(h)(11).

[50] ibid, §1014.

[51] ibid, §199A.

[52] ibid, §103.

[53] ibid, §101.

existence or standard of living, as is income earned on investments in certain retirement accounts.[54] For lower-bracket taxpayers, there is an exclusion of social security benefits for which they have paid from their wages that were subject to income tax, including amounts paid to social security.[55]

Each income tax schedule, except social security and Medicare, provides that an aggregate minimum amount of income remains free from income tax.[56] In Germany, this minimal, subsistence exemption is a constitutional corollary to the ability to pay principle.[57] Income from services is taxed, however, from the first dollar earned in the income tax schedule that funds social security[58] and Medicare.[59] In this the social security income tax resembles common consumption taxes that likewise are regressive, first dollar taxes.[60] Even fundamentally regressive consumption taxes are distributionally less egregious than payroll taxes. Consumption taxes remain proportional without limitation. More affluent consumers are likely to spend more than less affluent consumers and pay more tax without regard to their source of income or wealth. Payroll taxes include the embedded limitations of a wage cap and exclusion of non-services income from their base upon which they impose their flat rate. In many jurisdictions, consumption taxes exclude or apply a diminished rate to some non-luxury necessities like many food items and clothing thereby ameliorating their basic regressivity somewhat.

Taxes failing to require substantive equality or ability to pay under the rule of law find their justifications in other policies.[61] Several narrow base, regressive taxes seek to discourage possibly undesirable consumption activities and to modify taxpayer behaviour. Alcohol, tobacco, petroleum, and, more recently, cannabis taxes are examples that target undesirable behaviours either as a penalty for engaging in those activities or with the objective of causing taxpayers to engage in those activities less frequently. If successful, many such taxes would produce a diminishing revenue stream as taxpayers eschew the heavily taxed items.

Similarly, there are occasions on which legislatures have imposed taxes to prevent an individual or discernible group from exercising some right or privilege. Poll taxes were fixed capitation taxes that violated ability to pay principles. States imposed poll taxes to prevent black Americans, who tended to be very poor, and incidentally some poor white Americans, from exercising their franchise. The US Supreme Court determined such impositions to be unconstitutional as discriminatory.[62] A constitutional change while the case was pending prohibited poll taxes in the future,[63] leaving state legislatures to suppress minority voting in other ways.

[54] ibid, §409A.
[55] ibid, §86.
[56] ibid, §§63, 1.
[57] BVerfGE 82, 60, Beschluss des Ersten Senats vom 29 Mai 1990.
[58] IRC §§3111, 1401.
[59] ibid, §§3101, 1401.
[60] A Jurow Kleiman, 'Impoverishment by Taxation' (2022) 170 *University of Pennsylvania Law Review* 1389, 1477.
[61] I Ordower, 'Capital, an Elusive Tax Object and Impediment to Sustainable Taxation' (2020) 23 *Florida. Tax Review* 625.
[62] *Harper v Virginia Board of Elections*, 383 US 663 (1966).
[63] US Const Art XXIV (1964).

Social security taxes may fit the pattern of other regressive, limited base taxes designed to achieve a specific policy objective. Historically, social security taxes served to encourage or compel taxpayers to provide for their own retirement. Unlike other limited base taxes, social security taxes offer taxpayers no opportunity to avoid the imposition short of ceasing to work, a potentially counterproductive impact of the tax. When first enacted in the 1930s in the US, earlier in other locations, a programme to provide a source of income to prevent impoverishment of older individuals was needed. Private retirement plans were scarce and primarily available for the highly compensated. Imposing a tax exclusively on income from services was sensible given that those with income from capital would not age out of income production because their capital would continue to produce income and the owners of the capital would be less likely to need a retirement plan than would those with only income from services.

Within the category of narrow base, policy driven taxes, the social security tax in the US, but possibly not in the UK, for example, remains an outlier because it links directly to and funds a governmental benefit for the taxpayer. This linking causes the social security tax to resemble user fees that also link to specific benefits. Governmental authorities impose many mandatory payments for the use of facilities and services the government provides. Examples include fees for travel on toll roads, trash collection, use of courts or agencies for resolution of civil disputes, passports for travel, and admissions to national parks. Those exactions are in exchange for a direct and immediate benefit to the person who must pay the fee to engage in specific activities. Sometimes the individual without adequate means to pay the fee may use the facilities or receive the service without payment. Courts, for example, waive filing fees for individuals lacking means to pay the fees. Individuals unable to pay passport fees may get a fee waiver. Fees seem unobjectionable under rule of law principles if they do not serve as a means for oppression or favouritism.

With limited exceptions, individuals may choose to refuse governmental services and not pay the fees or consume the taxed items and avoid the tax. In many instances, an alternative opportunity is present that does not require the fee but may be far less convenient than paying the fee. For example, an individual may use a non-toll public road, rather than a toll road, that requires a longer travel time or is less well-maintained than the toll road, or, in the case of energy taxes, use public transportation rather than private vehicles.

Payroll taxes resemble, but are not, user fees despite the possible receipt of an eventual benefit by many who pay the payroll tax. Voluntarily joining the social security system might be a sound election where there is an exemption. The benefit formula for social security requires that an individual has participated in the system and paid tax for a minimum number of pay periods aggregating 40 calendar quarters, even if non-consecutive, to qualify to draw a continuing, lifelong benefit.[64]

But viewed as analogous to a user fee, the payroll tax lacks the immediacy of a direct benefit that accompanies user fees. The benefit, if any, is in the future. Unlike user fees which accompany consumption of the good or service for which the fee is imposed, the future benefit under the social security tax is uncertain. It remains subject to the

[64] Eligibility for Social Security in retirement, above n 21.

legislature's power to alter or even discontinue the programme. The benefit is also subject to the individual's survival causing it to resemble government mandated life insurance for workers but not for other members of the public. Resemblance to user fees also is tenuous in that most user fees are structured so that the user may forego the benefit and not pay the fee. Not so with social security. Income from services as an employee or as a self-employed individual draws the tax which the working individual may not refuse to pay even if the individual is willing to forego the benefit unless the individual is a member of a religious group or sect that refuses to accept government benefits, the Amish, for example, for whom a specific religious exemption exists.[65]

Since the social security tax does not follow the ability to pay principle extracted from the rule of law and resembles, but lacks significant features of, user fees, justification for departure from rule of law principles must be elsewhere. This broad-based, popular, public retirement facility seems to hold the greatest promise for departure from equality and ability to pay principles under a benefit theory of taxation. The benefit theory, unlike ability to pay, seeks to tax according to the measure of governmental benefits a taxpayer receives. Complexity in determining the value of many government benefits, national defence for example, to individual taxpayers renders the general application of benefit-based taxation elusive, but, with respect to specialised programmes like social security, measuring the benefit seems straightforward. Ease of measurement has encouraged some to view social security less as a governmental welfare-type programme than as a compulsory savings plan in which each participant should have a separate account holding the participant's tax payments with accompanying investment rights. The retirement pay-out would be based on the payor's success in investing the account balance. Insofar as a moderately progressive, benefit formula determines the amounts of the payments from social security, individual account ownership and control would undermine the benefit formula and threaten the welfare function of the programme.[66]

The past half century in the US has been a period of increasing regulatory capture by powerful economic interests. Tax structures, rates and benefits have followed. A questionable benefit narrative has produced acceptance of high social security taxes as the narrative has defined the social security benefit as analogous to a retirement plan rather than part of the social welfare system of its origin. This narrative is visible both in the exclusion of those who do not pay the tax from receiving benefits and the increasing benefits, albeit tinged with moderate benefit progressivity at the lower end, for those who have paid more into the system and especially those who have the means to defer the time for commencement of benefits. Benefits under social security may be claimed as early as 62 but the periodic payments reach their maximum if the claimant waits until 70 to commence receiving benefits. More affluent individuals, of course, are generally better able to defer benefits than less affluent individuals.

Identifiable and quantifiable benefits have similarly led to a broad acceptance of high rates for value-added taxes and substantial income taxes for moderate income individuals in many European countries. Delivery of government-provided benefits for all

[65] IRC §§1402(g), 3127.

[66] P Dilley, 'Taking Public Rights Private: The Rhetoric and Reality of Social Security Privatization' (2000) 41 *Boston College Law Review* 975.

directs the focus of discussion away from the necessary tax burden distribution that should apply to all benefits, including tax subsidies for business and investment. If the benefit narrative were legitimate, affluent taxpayers would pay for the tax and direct subsidies they receive that are funded by general revenues, but affluent taxpayers do not.

Dynamism in Rule of Law

Whenever procedural structures fail to protect those who interact with them from unjust outcomes or oppression, change to those structures becomes critical. Both the procedural and substantive principles of rule of law must remain fluid and dynamic. Legal rules that were sensible at one time often cease to be so as societal and economic conditions change. Failure to accommodate to changing circumstances leaves governments, even those with long histories of comfortable compliance with rule of law principles, outside the boundaries of rule of law. Such governments must develop lest they remain outside. For example, before 18 August 1920, the US would have been perceived to be solidly governed by the rule of law even though women were not permitted to vote,[67] yet countries today in which women have no voting franchise lack the rule of law. Rule of law concepts are never stagnant. Societies and their governments must be nimble to change laws, even clearly democratically enacted laws, as soon as they become inconsistent with current conditions and needs of the society as those change over time.

When social security became law in the US in 1935, the rate of tax to fund it was 1 per cent of the employee's wages as an income tax plus 1 per cent of an employee's wages as an excise tax imposed on the employer. The maximum rate of the progressive income tax was 79 per cent at that time. The wage cap of $3,000 meant that employees were not subject to social security tax on any amounts subject to the regular income tax as the exemption from the income tax was $4 000. Retirement plans were rare and primarily for the highly compensated. Families often cared for retired family members as family members tended to live near one another. The Great Depression held the US economy in its grip.

The current social security income tax has increased to 6.2 per cent, with a matching excise tax on employers, the social security tax wage base is $168,600 and is inflation adjusted so employees now are subject to both the social security income tax and regular income tax on their wages. Regular income tax has become less progressive now carrying a maximum marginal rate of 37 per cent.[68] Between the first social security tax enactment and today, income tax rates have fluctuated with the lowest maximum rate being 28 per cent[69] in 1987 while the flat rate, social security income tax has increased. The spread between the rate of social security tax and the maximum regular income tax has narrowed from one-eightieth when introduced to one-sixth now. The regressive structure of the social security tax has become

[67] US Const Amend XIX.

[68] IRC §1.

[69] Subject to a 3% bubble on a portion of income to raise the rate for higher income taxpayers to 31% on a portion of their incomes.

starker as disparities in income and wealth have grown in the US with increasing numbers of higher income wealthy individuals paying an effective social security tax rate approaching or reaching zero.

Social security has corrected some of its departures from substantive rule of law. The exclusion of agricultural and household workers from social security disproportionally affected women and racial minorities under the original social security legislation and has been eliminated. Yet, uncompensated household employment continues to be excluded from social security.[70] Changed economic circumstances characterised by ever-growing concentrations of wealth and escalating economic disparities suggest that re-evaluation of the social security tax and its basic structure is in order. In addition, the trust fund into which social security taxes are deposited is predicted to become insufficient to meet required payments under the programme during the decade beginning in 2030 so an increase in the base or the rate of the tax would be necessary to avoid benefit reductions.[71] An increase in the rate of tax would harm workers further by diminishing their current resources to meet their day-to-day consumption requirements. Price level increases exacerbate that concern. Increase in the wage base may cure the funding shortfall temporarily but fails to address the fundamental inequality in treatment that characterises the payroll tax, and many high-income individuals may discover opportunities to recharacterise income from services as income from property as they have done to capture the qualified business income deduction[72] and avoid Medicare taxes.[73]

Re-evaluation should conclude that benefits must be severed from payroll tax funding and the payroll tax replaced with a tax meeting the rule of law equality and ability to pay principles. The existing social security and Medicare taxes produce roughly one-third of US federal revenue. Shifting the payment of social security benefits to general revenue that the current moderately progressive income tax, the flat corporate income tax, and very limited estate tax provide would address the rule of law shortcomings but leave a very large revenue gap. But unbundling social security from the payroll tax would facilitate modification of the benefit formula to include many needing retirement assistances but currently excluded from benefits under the pay-in requirement while possibly excluding those with ample resources. The next section addresses replacement of that revenue.

Revenue Replacement

Repeal and Rate Adjustment

Repeal of the payroll tax frees most services income from 6.2 to 15.3 per cent tax, depending upon whether the repeal includes repeal of the Medicare tax and the

[70] N Staudt, 'Taxing Housework' (1995–1996) 84 *Georgetown Law Journal* 1571.
[71] Soc Sec Admin (2023), above n 22.
[72] IRC §199A.
[73] J Hughes, *Key Reform in Build Back Better Act Would Close Loophole Used by the Rich To Avoid Funding Healthcare* (ITEP, 2021).

employer share of the wage tax. This chapter recommends eliminating all vestiges of the payroll tax and increasing the marginal rates of the progressive income tax and the corporate tax. The rate increase ought not be equal across the rate brackets but should enhance and follow the tax progression with a small increase at the lowest rates and larger increases at the progressively higher rates. Integration with income tax automatically broadens the base to include income from investment alongside income from services without a wage cap. Tolerance for steep increases in progression is politically limited so the rate increases are unlikely to replace all the revenue lost from payroll tax repeal as many taxpayers at the lower end of the income spectrum will pay lower rates of tax than they did when they were subject to the payroll tax.[74]

Tax Expenditure Adjustments

The US Treasury must maintain a list of tax expenditures. Tax expenditures are defined in the law as 'revenue losses attributable to provisions of the Federal tax laws which allow a special exclusion, exemption, or deduction from gross income or which provide a special credit, a preferential rate of tax, or a deferral of tax liability'. These exceptions may be viewed as alternatives to other policy instruments, such as spending or regulatory programmes.[75] Tax expenditures benefit high income or wealth individuals disproportionally to low income or wealth individuals because they are primarily a function of capital and lower income individuals rarely can assemble capital. The costliest of those expenditures include the net capital gain rate preference, deductibility of charitable contributions, permanent exclusion of gain on property received as a gift from a decedent's estate, exclusion of the rental value of owner-occupied residences from income, and the qualified business income deduction.[76]

There is no inherently compelling justification for any tax, rather than, if appropriate, direct, expenditure although political and historical arguments for one or another expenditure abound. Preferential treatment of capital gain, for example, has a lengthy history and many arguments have sought to justify its continuation.[77] Yet, the 1986 tax reform act temporarily ended the preference.[78] Increase in tax basis at death[79] and exclusion of imputed income from owner-occupied residences are primarily matters of administrative convenience. Repeal or reduction in the tax loss from many of the tax expenditures could replace much of the lost revenue even if compelling policy driven subsidies to replace some tax expenditures may increase direct, but transparent, governmental costs.

[74] Ordower, above n 21.
[75] 'Tax Expenditure' (US Department of Treasury, 3 June 2021). Available at: https://home.treasury.gov/system/files/131/Tax-Expenditures-FY2022.pdf.
[76] Ordower, above n 21.
[77] Blum, above n 34.
[78] Tax Reform Act of 1986, above n 33.
[79] IRC §1014.

Benefit Coverage Modifications

Social security is and should be targeted to individuals who do not have adequate economic resources to maintain themselves in retirement. The vast array of existing retirement plans in the US enables many US taxpayers to fund their retirement with savings accumulated from income earned, but often untaxed, during their working careers. Despite the pleasure that receiving a periodic payment from the government provides, the elimination of social security benefits for many would have minimal adverse impact on their post-retirement living standard. Current US tax law recognises that not all social security recipients need the benefits they receive as current US tax law includes in the incomes of higher income individuals as much as 80 per cent of the social security benefit while excluding all the benefit from the incomes of lower income individuals.[80] And, concomitantly, there are many individuals who fail to meet the participation requirement but are much in need of financial assistance as they age.

The technique of phasing out certain tax-based benefits has become common in the US tax law. The earned income credit for lower income individuals includes a rapid benefit phase-out.[81] The qualified business income deduction limits the deduction for specified service businesses with a phase-out.[82] A phase-out based on the previous year's income was used for the supplement payments necessitated by the recent pandemic. A similar phase-out of the social security benefit would make sense. It would remove the highest-income recipients from social security roles and permit those who are in need, but currently fail to meet the participation requirements to receive benefits. An individual's entitlement to social security would be subject to an annual review based on income from all sources, even income otherwise excluded from tax.[83]

Conclusion

Rule of law is neither a static concept nor one based on the maintenance of appropriate procedures. The concept reaches far deeper into fundamental notions of economic ability, need, and distributional fairness and must change as circumstances and societal expectations change. Social security has failed to meet distributional fairness because it has appropriated an increasing share of workers' wages that they might better be deployed for their current, rather than future, needs. While the benefit side of social security continues to be a much-lauded programme to limit impoverishment for aging individuals, its funding mechanism has become obsolescent and harmful. The payroll tax is no longer an ideal method for funding social security and should be repealed along with social security funding, a necessity of economically developed societies, funded from general revenues as an essential governmental programme.

[80] ibid, §86. Note that inclusion of social security benefits in the incomes of higher income individuals effectively transfers revenue from social security to general revenues rather than returning it to the social security fund to help maintain the solvency of that fund.

[81] ibid, §32.

[82] ibid, §199A.

[83] Ordower, above n 21.

Political reality may be a barrier to this chapter's underlying conclusions and the implementation of its recommendations. Social security taxes are an administratively easy and accepted revenue source. Ease and acceptance militate against change. Repeal risks long-term or even permanent loss of revenue and might compromise the availability of benefits or reduce other governmental services. Nevertheless, the existing tax does appear to violate substantive rule of law principles. As this chapter suggests, when the tax structure lacks the dynamism to change to reflect the compelling needs of society, it requires substantial adjustment.

11

Expert Systems, Access to Information, and the Rule of Law in the Tax Transfer System

HELEN HODGSON

Abstract

The principles of the rule of law include accountability and transparency, particularly in government dealings with its citizens.[1] Tax-transfer systems are rules-based systems that raise revenue and re-distribute a proportion of the revenue raised to those individuals who meet the criteria. The rule of law applies to all parties: protecting the revenue while preserving the rights of taxpayers and welfare recipients. Arguably, the rule of law is fundamental to protect human rights[2] and maintain trust in government.[3]

Public administration is increasingly reliant on data collected through automated systems when determining taxable income and entitlements to welfare payments.[4] These systems ostensibly reduce complexity and improve accuracy,[5] however the use of these systems creates an asymmetry in access to information as individuals may not have access to the same systems to verify the information that has been considered, particularly vulnerable individuals claiming welfare payments.

In Australia, the consequences of a poorly designed system were seen in the 'Robodebt' programme. From 2016 until 2020 this programme applied an averaging algorithm to data-match taxable income as assessed by the Australian Taxation Office on an annual basis, against the income declared by welfare recipients fortnightly for means testing purposes.

[1] World Justice Project, 'What is the Rule of Law'. Available at: https://worldjusticeproject.org/about-us/overview/what-rule-law accessed 9 January 2023.

[2] See Daly, Chapter 2 in this volume.

[3] See Lindsay, Chapter 3 in this volume.

[4] M Zalnieriute, Lyria Bennett Moses and George Williams, 'The Rule of Law and Automation of Government Decision-Making' (2019) 82 *The Modern Law Review* 425.

[5] C Jordan, 'Paving the Way Forward – Working Together to Meet the Changing Needs of Our Clients' (2021 Institute of Public Accountants National Congress, 18 November 2021). Available at: www.ato.gov.au/Media-centre/Speeches/Commissioner/Paving-the-way-forward---working-together-to-meet-the-changing-needs-of-our-clients/, last accessed 9 January 2023.

This is a particularly egregious example of how the use of automated data-matching technology can breach the rule of law. The averaging process was not supported by the legislation, as identified in legal advice prepared at the time of introduction,[6] there was a lack of transparency, and the administrative processes shifted the evidential burden of proof to the recipient to show that the average earnings did not reflect the pattern of actual earnings.

There have been other cases globally that have had similar flaws. AI is now a part of the administrative toolbox. It must be designed in a way that ensures that human decision makers remain accountable, that the processes are transparent and that the rights of affected individuals are respected.

Introduction: The Rule of Law

Earlier chapters in this volume have addressed the nature of the rule of law. It may be looked at through a procedural lens, examining whether the law has been followed; or by taking a more robust approach that considers whether the law respects the rights of those to whom it applies.[7] At its heart, the rule of law expects governments to apply the law in accordance with the principles of accountability, access to justice, and transparency.[8]

In respect of taxation systems, it has been shown that in developed countries there is a positive correlation between tax revenues and the rule of law.[9] The IMF and OECD have highlighted the need for tax certainty, particularly in the context of multinational transactions, as it enables the taxpayer to enter into commercial transactions with an understanding of the outcomes, and ensures that tax administrations are focusing resources appropriately.[10,11]

The distinction between the narrow, or 'thin' and the broader, or 'thick' interpretation of the rule of law has been discussed earlier in this volume.[12] The rule of law is embodied in the principles of administrative law, providing rights and redress to citizens where the government has acted unjustly.[13] The broader interpretation of the rule of law considers the effect on society through the impact of laws and administrative practices on the rights of those affected by those laws, taking human rights into consideration. One of the functions of the rule of law is to provide guidance to citizens.

[6] K Campbell, 'The Royal Commission into the Robodebt Scheme: Final Report' (Commonwealth of Australia 2023) Royal Commission. Available at: https://robodebt.royalcommission.gov.au/publications/report.

[7] Lindsay, above n 3.

[8] World Justice Project above n 1.

[9] T Günel PhD and I Didinmez, 'Relationship between Rule of Law and Tax Revenues: Dynamic Panel Data Analysis' (2022) 46 *Public Sector Economics* 403.

[10] IMF/OECD, '2019 Progress Report on Tax Certainty' (2019). Available at: www.oecd.org/tax/tax-policy/g20-report-on-tax-certainty.htm.

[11] In Australia, the Taxation Administration Act 1953 (Commonwealth of Australia) sets out provisions regarding the publication of rulings that are binding on the Commissioner and provides the right of objection and appeal.

[12] Daly, above n 2; Lindsay, above n 3.

[13] In Australia the relevant Commonwealth legislation includes the Administrative Decisions (Judicial Review) Act 1977 (Commonwealth of Australia); Freedom of Information Act 1982 (Commonwealth of Australia); Administrative Appeals Tribunal Act 1975 (Commonwealth of Australia).

Anything contradictory, retrospective or which cannot be complied with can lead to a loss of trust in government.[14]

Statutory rights are constrained by the legislation that establishes those rights; and legislation cannot keep up with the evolving use of technology. The use of artificial intelligence is now permeating government systems in a way that challenges the rule of law. In response, the OECD has developed a set of principles to ensure that the application of artificial intelligence respects human rights. The five key principles are consistent with the thicker interpretation of the rule of law and include:

- Inclusive growth, sustainable development and well-being
- Human-centred values and fairness
- Transparency and explainability
- Robustness, security and safety
- Accountability.[15,16]

Over the last decade there has been a series of public administration scandals globally where the use of artificial intelligence has resulted in serious harm to humans affected by the system: the UK Post Office scandal, where errors in the accounting system saw users convicted of fraud,[17] the Dutch child care benefits affair resulted in the resignation of the Government; and the Michigan's Integrated Data Automated System in the US branded welfare applicants as welfare cheats.[18] The common thread in these cases is the willingness of administrators to rely on automated processes without adequate supervision by humans.

This chapter will discuss the challenges that the use of artificial intelligence in the tax and transfer systems poses to the rule of law, using the Australian 'Robodebt' scandal as a case study. This case study is grounded in welfare law, rather than taxation law. However, there are important lessons that can be transferred across government systems, particularly in respect of welfare recipients who may be particularly vulnerable by virtue of their circumstances.

Artificial Intelligence

Computer-assisted technology has been employed across business and governments for many years. However, developments in the capabilities of these systems bring new challenges to governments utilising technology to administer laws, particularly where these techniques can be used to impose obligations or liabilities on citizens. The new

[14] Lindsay, above n 3.

[15] Recommendation of the Council on Artificial Intelligence 2019 (OECD/LEGAL/0449).

[16] This framework was endorsed by the Australian Government in 2019 when it established an AI Framework. See www.industry.gov.au/publications/australias-artificial-intelligence-ethics-framework/australias-ai-ethics-principles.

[17] RK Helm, 'Wrongful Conviction in England and Wales: An Assessment of Successful Appeals and Key Contributions' (2022) 3 *Wrongful Conviction Law Review* (WCLR) 196.

[18] SN Giest and B Klievink, 'More than a Digital System: How AI Is Changing the Role of Bureaucrats in Different Organizational Contexts' (2022) *Public Management Review* 1.

capability is changing the culture of the bureaucracy as resources are redirected toward compliance activities.[19]

There is a range of automated tools available to government agencies. These can be broadly classified as decision-support systems that provide a set of principles to ensure that the human decision maker has considered all relevant factors when making a decision, through to expert systems that perform tasks without the assistance of humans. Expert systems can be differentiated based on the way they use data.[20] Constructed knowledge, or 'code-driven'[21] systems construct outcomes by applying a series of rules to circumstances, following the logical path determined by the responses provided to each of the rules. Systems requiring calculations, including tax payable or penalty calculations, are inherently rules based and lend themselves to this form of expert system. They may also aid accountability, with citizens able to engage with such systems to understand obligations and available courses of action.

Learned knowledge, or data-driven systems,[22] develop algorithms that rely on inductive reasoning processes applying learned information to the known facts. Significantly, as the system continues to operate it takes in more information that will be used to inform later decisions. A significant challenge in such systems is the principle of transparency: although the system may have been programmed to take account of specific factors in decision making, as it works and develops the algorithm it becomes more difficult to see how those factors have developed and are applied to particular situations.

Expert systems are welcomed by the community when these systems are useful in dealing with routine tasks. For example, in the personal income tax system automated data collection systems have progressed from reporting inconsistencies against the returns filed by individuals, to pre-filling key information in returns; in some jurisdictions, the taxpayer is required to do no more than review and submit the return.

However, when dealing with automated decision-making processes, it is essential that the algorithms are free of inherent bias. While it is known that all decision makers, whether human or machine, carry a level of inherent bias, machine-based systems present a challenge in understanding how those biases are affecting the processes that the system is using to make the relevant decisions. These may be based on human biases or errors that have been incorporated when setting up the system, as in the Michigan Integrated Data Automated System which sent automated fraud notices without evidence first.[23] Alternatively human bias that is incorporated when the system is initially programmed may be magnified as the algorithms learn from that data until the irrelevant correlations become a key feature in the selection of cases. For example, algorithms in the Dutch childcare benefit case were found to be based on racial profiling that was amplified as the program algorithms developed.[24]

[19] ibid.

[20] Administrative Review Council, Administrative Review Council, 'Automated Assistance in Administrative Decision Making' (2004) (Commonwealth of Australia, 2004) Report to the Attorney General 46. Available at: www.ag.gov.au/sites/default/files/2020-03/report-46.pdf, accessed 19 April 2023.

[21] M Hildebrandt, 'Algorithmic Regulation and the Rule of Law' (2018) 376 *Philosophical Transactions: Mathematical, Physical and Engineering Sciences* 1.

[22] ibid.

[23] Giest and Klievink, above n 18.

[24] ibid.

In the Australian context, in 2004 the Administrative Review Council considered the extent to which decisions were being made using expert systems and set out some 27 principles that should underpin their use.[25] These principles included:

- the need for human involvement in decision-making, particularly in respect of the exercise of discretions, where the expert system should be an administrative tool;
- the expert system must comply with administrative law standards, including privacy and freedom of information standards, to be lawful;
- the integrity of the expert system must be protected to prevent human interference; but
- internal reviews and panels should be implemented to ensure the integrity of the decision-making system.

The 2019 OECD Recommendations[26] also recommended that national governments develop internal frameworks for the use of AI, and the Australian Government released updated guidelines in 2019.[27] Most recently, the federal government released a discussion paper in June 2023[28] to support further discussion on the governance of AI systems in Australia. While the focus of this guidance is not specifically on legal systems or government administration, the outcomes of this process should inform future government practice.

The Privacy Act 1988 (Commonwealth of Australia) applies to Australian data-matching programmes including those run by Commonwealth agencies. The objects of this Act include the protection of the privacy of individuals,[29] and promoting responsible and transparent handling of personal information;[30] with the Information Commissioner authorised to investigate complaints and enforce determinations.[31]

Commonwealth data-matching programmes should[32] comply with rules established by the Commissioner that set out the protocols. These were first established as guidelines in 1994 but were remade as statutory rules in 2021 without substantive changes.[33] The implementing agency must ensure that the programme is published, a protocol and subsequent reports on any 'relevant matter' are filed with the Information Commissioner, and it must monitor, maintain, and report on technical standards.[34]

[25] Administrative Review Council, above n 20.
[26] Recommendation of the Council on Artificial Intelligence, above n 15.
[27] Text at n 16, above.
[28] Department of Industry, Science and Resources, 'Safe and Responsible AI in Australia: Discussion Paper' (Australian Government 2023) Discussion Paper. Available at: https://storage.googleapis.com/converlens-au-industry/industry/p/prj2452c8e24d7a400c72429/public_assets/Safe-and-responsible-AI-in-Australia.pdf, last accessed 6 June 2023.
[29] Privacy Act 1988 s 2A(a).
[30] ibid, s 2A(d).
[31] ibid, Part V.
[32] Programmes that rely on tax file numbers to match data are regulated by the Data-matching Programme (Assistance and Tax) Act 1990 (Commonwealth of Australia). In other cases, the data-matching guidelines are not mandatory.
[33] Data-Matching Programme (Assistance and Tax) Act 1990 – Guidelines (31/10/1994) (Commonwealth of Australia), repealed by Data-matching Programme (Assistance and Tax) Rules 2021 (Commonwealth of Australia).
[34] ibid, Part 4 Data-matching Programme (Assistance and Tax) Rules 2021 (Commonwealth of Australia), Guideline 5.

Safeguards are incorporated to protect the rights of the affected individuals:

- the agency must establish procedures to confirm the validity of the results before relying on them to take action against an individual;
- where the agency goes back to the individual for verification instead of the source, they must provide written notice of the match, the conclusions the agency has drawn and proposed action, and that the agency has not verified the source data; and allow the individual a reasonable period[35] to respond;
- inform the individual of their right to make a complaint under the Privacy Act 1988;
- any written records must be retained on the person's file; and
- the agency must not take any action that would interfere with any rights of review or appeal.

The Federal Register of Legislation[36] shows that around 100 notices of data-matching programmes have been published since 2012, although it is not clear which are still active. They range across portfolios, but the majority of data-matching programmes are run by the Australian Taxation Office (ATO), with the data collected being used for prefilling tax returns as well as in compliance activities. These are well understood in the community, with the ATO regularly reminding taxpayers that it has access to information that will be used to verify tax returns.

Robodebt: The Online Compliance Intervention Programme

The Court has described the Robodebt programme as: '… a shameful chapter in the administration of the Commonwealth social security system and a massive failure of public administration …'.[37]

The Online Compliance Intervention (OCI) programme[38] that came to be known as Robodebt, matched data between the Australian Taxation Office (ATO) and Centrelink, the agency responsible for making welfare payments. For around 20 years, the ATO had provided data to match against the earnings that a welfare recipient had declared to Centrelink to calculate benefits payable.[39] However, from July 2016 the OCI programme changed the way in which that data was handled.

[35] The 1994 Guidelines suggested 14 days as an example, but the 2001 Rules have extended this to 28 days.

[36] Federal Register of Legislation. Available at: www.legislation.gov.au/. (Australian Government) accessed 6 March 2024.

[37] Murphy J in *Katherine Prygodicz & Ors v The Commonwealth of Australia (No 2)* (2021) [2021] FCA 634, 5 (Federal Court of Australia).

[38] The programme was rebadged as the Employment Income Confirmation (EIC) programme in 2017 and in 2018 as the Check and Update Past Information (CUPI).

[39] Senate Community Affairs References Committee, 'Design, Scope, Cost-Benefit Analysis, Contracts Awarded and Implementation Associated with the Better Management of the Social Welfare System Initiative' (Commonwealth of Australia 2017). Available at: www.aph.gov.au/Parliamentary_Business/Committees/Senate/Community_Affairs/SocialWelfareSystem.

The basis of the programme was a 2015–16 Commonwealth Budget measure to

> Strengthen the Integrity of Welfare Payments
>
> The Government will achieve savings of $1.7 billion over five years by enhancing the Department of Human Services (DHS) fraud prevention and debt recovery capability, and improving assessment processes.
>
> From 1 July 2015 DHS will implement an integrated package of compliance and process improvement initiatives including improved automation and targeted strategies for fraud prevention in areas of high risk.[40]

This initiative in respect of the period 2010–11 to 2012–13 was extended to match another two years of data in December 2015.[41] It was estimated that over six years the programme would raise $4.772.

The policy aims appeared unexceptional, but the scale of welfare fraud was significantly overestimated, and assumptions were untested in developing the proposal.[42] There were also a number of significant policy design flaws. The most obvious flaw was a mismatch of purpose and policy between income tax and social security systems. Income tax is reported annually, and tax is paid based on taxable income over the tax year. Social security payments are designed to support eligible citizens at a time of need, and in Australia is means tested based on a fortnightly reporting of income and assets.[43,44] The algorithm adopted under the data-matching programme presumed that income was earned evenly across the year, and where this did not match the details held by Centrelink, OCI action was initiated automatically.

The programme was proposed by the Department of Human Services (DHS), which is responsible for social and health service delivery. Centrelink, as referred to in this chapter, is the service delivery agency under DHS. The Department of Social Services (DSS) is responsible for policy advice on income support and workforce participation, but the distinction between operational policy and broader policy is not well understood, and lack of communication between the two departments contributed to the poor design of Robodebt.[45] Notably, DHS, which operated the OCI system, was focused on operational cost savings as an administrative outcome, whereas by virtue of their engagement in policy and system design, DSS had a more nuanced understanding of the legislative requirements of the Social Security Act 1991 (Commonwealth of Australia).

[40] Treasury (2015) Budget 2015–16: Budget Measures Budget Paper No. 2 2015–16 (Commonwealth of Australia). Available at: https://archive.budget.gov.au/2015-16/bp2/BP2_consolidated.pdf.

[41] Treasury (2015) Mid-Year Economic and Fiscal Outlook 2015–16 (Commonwealth of Australia). Available at: https://archive.budget.gov.au/2015-16/myefo/MYEFO_2015-16_Final.pdf.

[42] Campbell, above n 6, 422.

[43] R Boden and H Hodgson, 'Not-so-Distant Cousins: Family Benefits in the United Kingdom and Australia' (2008) 61 *International Social Security Review* 29.

[44] At the hearings held by the Senate Community Affairs References Committee the representatives of the Australian Taxation Office were questioned on this point. While not permitted to reflect on policy matters, they advised that it was the responsibility of the receiving agency to ensure that the design of the programme is fit for purpose. However, Centrelink did not engage in meaningful discussions with the ATO in the design phase.

[45] Campbell, above n 6, 7.

The key difference between the OCI programme and previous data-matching programmes was the increased automation. Centrelink staff did not verify the matched information before contacting the payment recipient by mail, directing the recipient to a data portal to enter relevant information. The resources that were redirected from service delivery to compliance activities facilitated an increase in the number of investigations that were initiated from 20,000 pa to 10,000 to 20,000 per week.[46]

The scale of the design problems can be seen by the speed with which the complaints snowballed. The programme commenced in July 2016, and between November 2016 and January 2017 it is believed that at least 200,000 people were impacted.[47] In response to numerous complaints the Commonwealth Ombudsman's Office initiated an urgent investigation that reported in April 2017.[48]

This investigation has been criticised as not being sufficiently independent.[49] The legal foundations of the scheme were not considered by the Ombudsman, although the report did identify procedural flaws including:

- A 10% 'recovery fee' was applied automatically to all debts raised under the programme, including those raised automatically where the recipient had not responded to Centrelink.
- Recipients were not advised of the basis of the calculation or that a debt would be raised if the recipient did not respond.
- Letters were sent to incorrect addresses, including deceased persons, as the recipient may not have had reason to contact Centrelink for several years.
- The online portal was inaccessible to many recipients, and the data entry process was laborious and confusing. The initial letter advised claimants to go online to 'confirm' the ATO data, prompting confirmations from recipients who did not understand the consequences.
- Recipients were required to obtain the relevant information going back up to six years. There was no allowance for the difficulties that recipients may have faced in obtaining evidence of actual payments such as uncooperative employers or pay slips that may not have been retained or may now be inaccessible online behind employee log-ins.
- The 21-day period allowed to respond to the initial letter was inadequate considering the information that the recipient was expected to collate.
- There were several points where the automated online system should have directed the matter to human staff, for example where a person stated that they did not work for a nominated employer, but this process did not always occur. Recipients complained that when they tried to contact service staff they were directed to the automated system.

[46] Senate Community Affairs References Committee, above n 39.

[47] ibid, 4.

[48] Commonwealth Ombudsman, 'Centrelink's Automated Debt Raising and Recovery System' (Commonwealth of Australia Ombudsman's Office 2017) 4.

[49] Campbell n 4, 21; Carney T, 'Robo-Debt Illegality: The Seven Veils of Failed Guarantees of the Rule of Law?' (2019) 44 *Alternative Law Journal* 4.

Concurrently the Australian Senate referred the issue to the Community Affairs References Committee.[50] That committee had a majority of non-government members, and the 2017 Report was consistent with the concerns raised in the Ombudsman's report. The majority of the committee recommended that the programme should be suspended until the procedural fairness flaws have been addressed, and until the technology to match fortnightly payments is in place.[51] It further recommended that all debt notices should be reviewed and recalculated manually.[52]

Following the two 2017 enquiries the programme was modified to adopt some of the recommendations and rebadged firstly as the Employment Income Confirmation (EIC) programme and later as Check and Update Past Information (CUPI). The number of manual interventions increased, pay slips were no longer the only form of evidence accepted and the 10% recovery fee was no longer applied without considering individual circumstances. Letters were sent by registered mail to ensure that they were received at the correct address.[53,54] The Ombudsman reported that communication had improved, although more work was required to explain more clearly the basis of the debt and the need to review the data.

However public concern over the programme continued.[55] Following several legal challenges, Robodebt was cancelled in November 2019; in May 2020 the government announced that it would repay moneys collected under the programme. The net cost of the programme, following the settlement of legal matters, is estimated to be around $565m.[56]

Legal Basis of the Debt Notices

In 2017, matters started to appear in the listings for the Administrative Appeals Tribunal. The pre-existing data-matching programme had produced regular reviews, but the first of the Robodebt-generated reviews was heard in March 2017. Professor Carney, at that time a member of the Administrative Appeals Tribunal,[57] heard five matters over the next six months.[58] He determined that these debt notices were not legally sound:

> 29. The legal grounds on which I found Robodebts to be unlawful were:
>
> …
>
> d. The Robodebt methodology of extrapolating fortnightly earnings from Australian Taxation Office (ATO) information about total amounts earned over much longer periods than a

[50] Senate Community Affairs References Committee, above n 39.

[51] Changes to employer reporting obligations that require wages to be reported to the ATO each pay cycle have now been rolled out in stages from 2019, enabling more accurate data matching.

[52] Senate Community Affairs References Committee, above n 39, 6.9, 6.11.

[53] Commonwealth Ombudsman, above n 48, 35.

[54] Commonwealth Ombudsman, 'Centrelink's Automated Debt Raising and Recovery System: Implementation Report' (Commonwealth of Australia Ombudsman's Office 2019).

[55] See, eg the #notmydebt campaign. Available at: www.notmydebt.com.au/, last accessed 9 June 2023.

[56] Campbell, above n 6, 401.

[57] Professor Carney was not reappointed after his term at the AAT expired on 30 September 2017, although he had served in that position for nearly 40 years.

[58] The decisions are unpublished as it is not administratively practical to anonymise the decisions. However, they were tabled at the Royal Commission. See Campbell, above n 6, 556.

fortnight provided no information of any probative value at all regarding earnings across differing social security entitlement periods (at best arguably being an acceptable basis to make enquiries of a recipient), and thus could not enable a decision-maker to be 'satisfied' a debt existed;

e. The 'practical burden of satisfaction/proof' of a debt rested with the Department (the Robodebt scheme essentially reversed that, offering no proofs of its own) and in any event, because of the nature of and potential consequences of an allegation that a citizen purportedly owed a debt, the usual test of 'satisfaction was not the appropriate one, but instead – applying the Briginshaw principles – a much higher burden of proof was borne by the Commonwealth when seeking to evidence a purported debt.[59]

Between 2016 and 2022, the Administrative Appeals Tribunal reviewed 558 matters that arose from income averaging. Of these cases, 431 (77%) were not upheld; 114 were upheld; and 13 were conceded by the applicant. The cases that were upheld did not address the lawfulness of the application of averaging.[60] This was not public knowledge as matters heard by the AAT at level one are confidential, although there was clearly concern within the AAT as tribunal members did request a briefing on the programme.

There were at least two matters (see Masterton and Amato below) that were listed in the Federal Court to determine the lawfulness of robodebts issued in the amounts of $3,725 and $3,215 respectively, however neither proceeded to hearings as the relevant department reviewed and withdrew the debt notices.[61] There were no Court Orders in the *Masterton*[62] matter, but consent orders were issued in the *Amato*[63] matter in which the Commonwealth acknowledged that the demand for payment of the debt and penalty was not valid.

Following the *Amato* consent orders a class action was commenced against the Commonwealth. At this stage all debts had been withdrawn and recipients refunded, so the grounds for the class action were unjust enrichment, and negligence for damages for economic loss and stress, anxiety and stigma. This was also settled by the Commonwealth in November 2020, with an amount of $112 million available to be distributed to members of the class action. The Court approved this settlement in June 2021,[64] although this may not be the end of the legal matters, as the Court gave group members who objected to the settlement a further opportunity to opt out of the settlement.

[59] 'Exhibit 3-3489 – TCA.9999.0001.0059_R_Statement of Emeritus Professor Terry Carney AC, FAAL'. Available at: https://robodebt.royalcommission.gov.au/publications/exhibit-3-3489-tca999900010059-r-statement-emeritus-professor-terry-carney-ao-faal.

[60] Campbell, above n 6, 556.

[61] M Browne and C Brumby-Rendell, 'Victoria Legal Aid' (An in-depth look at our Robodebt test case, 14 April 2020) (Legal Aid, Victorian Government). Available at: www.legalaid.vic.gov.au/depth-look-our-robo-debt-test-case, last accessed 2 June 2023.

[62] 'Exhibit 4-5427 – AGD.0003.0002.6825_R – MASTERTON *Madeleine v Secretary*, DHS – FC VID73-2019 – Report on Case Management Hearing'. Available at: https://robodebt.royalcommission.gov.au/publications/exhibit-4-5427-agd000300026825-r-masterton-madeleine-v-secretary-dhs-fc-vid73-2019-report-case-management-hearing-dlmsensitive-legal, last accessed 6 June 2024.

[63] *Deanna Amato v The Commonwealth of Australia* [2019] Federal Court VID611/2019 (Federal Court of Australia).

[64] *Katherine Prygodicz & Ors v The Commonwealth of Australia (No 2)*, above n 32.

It is striking that the Commonwealth was not prepared to defend Robodebt in the Courts, reassessing debts to prevent the matter coming before the Courts. In evidence before the Royal Commission, it became clear that senior public servants had been advised that the programme was not on a sound legal basis before it was approved as a Budget measure, raising questions over the information presented to Expenditure Review Committee when the programme was approved.[65]

Royal Commission

Following a change of government in 2022 a Royal Commission was established to examine the Robodebt programme. Tabled on 7 July 2023, the Commission report[66] makes it clear that from its inception the programme did not meet the standards expected.

The first recommendation of the Royal Commission strikes at the heart of the flawed programme.

> 10:1: Design policies and processes with emphasis on the people they are meant to serve. That should entail:
>
> - avoiding language and conduct which reinforces feelings of stigma and shame associated with the receipt of government support when it is needed
> - facilitating easy and efficient engagement with options of online, in person and telephone communication which is sensitive to the particular circumstances of the customer cohort, including itinerant lifestyles, lack of access to technology, lack of digital literacy and the particular difficulties rural and remote living
> - explaining processes in clear terms and plain language in communication to customers, and acting with sensitivity to financial and other forms of stress experienced by the customer cohort and
> - taking all practicable steps to avoid the possibility that interactions with the government might exacerbate those stresses or introduce new ones.[67]

The 57 findings of the Royal Commission cover a range of matters that go to the heart of the legality of the programme.

The rule of law expects that administrators act impartially and transparently, and that their actions are consistent with the legislation that authorises their action. Not only was the Robodebt programme not authorised by the relevant legislation, but the administration of the scheme did not meet the standards of professionalism, competence and good faith that are expected under the wide interpretation.

Legality

The requirement that administrative action is within the scope of legislation is fundamental to the rule of law. This was not the case in the Robodebt programme which

[65] Campbell, above n 6, 21.
[66] ibid.
[67] ibid, 232.

was not in accordance with the law governing social security debts. As set out in Professor Carney's evidence above, the Social Security Act requires the Department to prove the debt, but this programme reversed the onus of proof, requiring the recipient to prove their income, and ignoring the requirement for probative evidence before any decision was made. Where the onus of proof is reversed, for example in taxation laws, this must be explicit in the enabling legislation. DHS received legal advice to this effect prior to the programme being presented to the Expenditure Review Committee for approval as a budget measure and at several critical points when decisions were made.[68]

The Royal Commission highlighted the need for cultural reform in in-house legal teams, including the development of internal legal practice standards and further training on professional standards including the obligations of integrity and independence even when working as a government lawyer.[69]

The obligation placed on government agencies to be a model litigant was also ignored in respect of proceedings before the AAT and the Federal Court. There was no systematic review of the outcomes of the matters heard by the AAT, and the lack of systematic oversight allowed the various legal opinions and adverse reports to be ignored.

Accountability

The rule of law expects that government is responsible for the actions of its administrators. The most damning findings of the Royal Commission were in respect of the lack of accountability, in respect of the actions of the senior public servants who were responsible for the design of the programme.[70] The Commission found that the policy was motivated by the desire to reduce budget outlays on social security, and that legal advice that the programme was not soundly based in law was disregarded.[71] The involvement of the two departments, DHS and DSS, with separate legal teams, was a further complication, and it was noted that these teams often failed to share advice that may have raised concerns over the legality of the programme.[72] Although the requirements for the strict rule of law must be balanced against other objectives, acting outside the scope of the legislation is a fundamental breach.

The lack of accountability extended to the failure by the DHS legal team to systematically review the outcomes of the AAT cases. The outcomes and findings in these matters are not generally available to the public as level one matters are confidential, limiting transparency.

The Report also highlighted the failure of the checks and balances that are in place to protect the rule of law. The extent of the engagement with the DHS when

[68] Campbell, above n 6, 526.

[69] ibid, Recommendations 19.2–19.4.

[70] The Final Report included a sealed chapter that includes information that may be relevant to subsequent legal proceedings against certain individuals, whose names have not been released.

[71] Campbell, above n 6, 19.

[72] This is a requirement under the *Legal Services Directions 2017* (Commonwealth of Australia) in respect of overlapping portfolios.

the Ombudsman's Office was drafting reports[73] is an example of regulatory capture: an email from DHS referred to 'co-writing the report'.[74] While there was evidence that the protocols had originally been approved by the Office of the Information Commissioner, as the programme continued the protocols were not updated, and not always followed.

Carney[75] criticises the Ombudsman and other accountability agencies for not taking further action as the problem emerged. He also notes that the political environment contributed to the failure of the rule of law, specifically the lack of funding for Legal Aid and other community organisations to support recipients; the lack of pro-bono capacity to take legal action; and the prevailing culture that tolerated the devaluing of rights of vulnerable welfare recipients.[76] In fact the (then) government senators who were members of the first Senate Committee continued to support the programme, rejecting any findings of continuing procedural unfairness.[77]

Transparency

There was a lack of transparency, and a culture of defensiveness that enabled secrecy. Decisions and discussions were not recorded, with much of the evidence regarding procedural matters being pieced together by the Royal Commission through email trails. The excesses and illegality of the scheme were brought to the attention of the public by academics, journalists and underfunded advocacy and legal aid organisations.

The basis of the debt notice was not transparent, as illustrated in Professor Carney's evidence before the Royal Commission:

> MR GREGGERY:Was there generally some difficulty in identifying, from your perspective, what debts were alleged under the Robodebt Scheme?
>
> PROFESSOR CARNEY:Enormous difficulty. Not so much for myself, because I had been in the game for a long period of time, but the way – and the only accurate way to know whether it's a Robodebt case or has a Robodebt component – because the review officer cover letter never identifies or very rarely ever alludes to that. The only way to identify it is to go to the – one of the two big calculation programmes, the ADEX or the Multical programme, and to look at the columns of what the person who was before you reported fortnight by fortnight as their income, and then look at the column of what the Department is contending was the true income so that the difference became a debt under the relevant section.[78]

If members of the AAT needed specialised reports to be able to confirm whether a debt existed, clearly recipients would have even less information to be able to challenge the debt notice. In fact, many of the debts that were issued were not contested as recipients accepted the basis of the debt notice.

[73] Commonwealth Ombudsman, above n 48; Commonwealth Ombudsman, above n 54.
[74] Campbell, above n 6, 583.
[75] Carney, above n 49.
[76] ibid, 5.
[77] Senate Community Affairs References Committee above n 39 Coalition Senators' Dissenting Report.
[78] 'Evidence, 24 February 2023'. Available at: https://robodebt.royalcommission.gov.au/publications/transcript-hearing-day-24-24-january-2023, last accessed 2 June 2023.

The automated process had a further impact on vulnerable recipients as they were required to respond through a computer interface that was poorly designed. After receiving a debt notice, recipients who attempted to use the interface reported problems in accessing and entering data into the system and a lack of help when they experienced problems, causing significant distress to the recipient and overwhelmed Centrelink support staff. This highlights the need for systems to be designed to be accessible, with the needs of vulnerable users being taken into consideration.

Procedural Fairness

Most significantly, under both the 'thick' and 'thin' conceptualisations of the rule of law, the scheme lacked balance.[79] The policy objective to save revenue was allowed to override procedural fairness. While some of the procedural issues were addressed in the later iterations of the programme, the scheme was fundamentally flawed in a way that impacted on people who were entitled to support.

Administrative law is concerned with procedural fairness, particularly as there is an imbalance of power between the government and those who are governed.[80] For example, in the taxation system the reversed onus of proof is balanced by limits on the time within which the Commissioner of Taxation can amend an assessment, with specific exceptions in the event of fraud or tax evasion, or to give effect to the outcomes of objections and appeals.[81] Unlike the taxation laws, the Social Security Act specifically provides that there is no time limit on debt recovery[82] nor does it establish specific time periods for either the amendment of payments or the retention of documentation.

The procedural flaws in the Robodebt scheme have been outlined above. Some of these were addressed following the Ombudsman's report, but the fundamental premise, that the recipient was required to be able to prove why averaging was not appropriate in their circumstances, remained. Debt notices were issued in respect of payments received up to six years earlier, with debt recovery notices for the 2010–11 year being issued in 2016–17, six years later. Demonstrably the time period initially allowed, 21 days, was not reasonable for people to obtain pay slips going back up to six years, particularly where an employee was no longer in contact with that employer.

Under the reversal of the onus of proof, Centrelink staff no longer engaged with employers to verify payments, leaving recipients to manage the process personally. Prior to the introduction of the OCI programme, the Centrelink website recommended that recipients retain evidence of payment for a period of six months,[83] and would accept bank statements as evidence of income received. This practice was revoked,[84] but was reinstated after the initial Ombudsman's report.

[79] Lindsay, above n 3.
[80] Daly, above n 2; Lindsay, above n 3.
[81] Income Tax Assessment Act 1936 (Commonwealth of Australia), s 170.
[82] Social Security Act 1991 s 1234B.
[83] Commonwealth Ombudsman n 43, 22.
[84] ibid. 3.26–3.27.

It is essential that systems are designed to take account of the citizens that are to be using those systems.[85] Both the narrow and broad concepts of the rule of law expect that citizens should be able to understand their obligations to comply. In respect of welfare recipients, a human-centered focus would take into consideration the vulnerability of welfare recipients. In Australian tax law, the amendment periods provide certainty, particularly for taxpayers with simple tax affairs. In contrast, welfare recipients are frequently more vulnerable yet are treated more harshly under the relevant laws.[86] The Robodebt programme covered a wide range of means-tested income support payments including payments to support unemployed workers, people with a disability that limits their working hours, sole parents and older workers supplementing the age pension. The power imbalance between recipients and Centrelink, purporting to act on information received from the ATO, resulted in many recipients accepting that the information in question was not only correct but had been used appropriately.[87]

The Application of Artificial Intelligence

As the use of artificial intelligence (AI) accelerates, systems are evolving from decision support systems to learned knowledge systems. The public release of ChatGPT has raised the profile of AI systems in the public domain, but many people are not aware of the extent to which AI is already being used in existing systems. The scandals that have emerged globally have shown the challenges that the use of AI in making government decisions raises for Administrative Law, particularly in relation to accountability, transparency and fairness. It is important to examine the process of how the decisions were made and the technology was applied in the programme.[88]

The discussion paper issued in June 2023 by the Australian Government[89] has been informed by work from the office of the Australian Chief Scientist[90] (the Expert Report) that considers 'the opportunities and risks of applying large language models (LLMs) and multimodal foundation models (MFMs) learning technologies over the next two, five and ten years'.[91] LLMs are defined as text-based models, in which the technology is trained on text-based materials, whereas MFMs can incorporate information from other sources including images, numerical data and other code.

The key issues include identifying who is the decision-maker, and who holds the relevant delegated authority. Clearly an AI system must be developed under appropriate authority, but where a system can 'learn' from previous decisions, the concept of

[85] See Badisco, Chapter 9 in this volume.
[86] L Marriott, 'Justice and the Justice System: A Comparison of Tax Evasion and Welfare Fraud in Australia and New Zealand' (2013) 22 *Griffith Law Review* 403.
[87] Senate Community Affairs References Committee, above n 39, 3.1–3.7.
[88] Carney, above n 49.
[89] Department of Industry, Science and Resources, above n 28.
[90] G Bell et al., 'Rapid Response Information Report: Generative AI – Language Models (LLMs) and Multimodal Foundation Models (MFMs).' (Australian Council of Learned Academies 2023).
[91] Bell et al., ibid. 1.

delegated power becomes problematic.[92] This risk was identified early in the Robodebt programme when the Commonwealth Office of Legal Services Coordination noted that 'emerging issues with automated decision-making may have implications for other departments and agencies'.[93]

Advances in AI in a medical context are an example of the capability of systems, and the potential risks. For example, in medical imaging AI may be able to identify an anomaly that is not apparent to the eye of a radiologist, but should AI be relied on for the diagnosis and treatment plan?[94] In the legal profession, AI can be useful in managing documentation,[95] and is already available to generate answers to simple legal questions. However, it is still risky to rely on AI for legal advice, and there is evidence that algorithms used in sentencing decisions amplify bias.[96]

Human oversight and intervention must be built in at critical points in the process. Robotic Process Automation is the set of instructions that are provided to the automated system to achieve the programme outputs and includes the decision automation that drives the process. In this context, the question regarding delegations becomes significant, as the computer programmer who is translating a process into computer instructions is unlikely to have the expertise to be a 'decision-maker' as understood at administrative law.

The decision-maker should be a person who understands not only the issue that is the subject of the decision but also understands the technology making the decision in order to ensure that governments and agencies are accountable for the decisions that are made. Hildebrandt[97] recommends that 'agonistic machine learning' should be adopted by developers to ensure that algorithms are robust and subject to the rule of law, applying a process of adversarial interrogation to ensure that the core principles of the rule of law are integrated within the architecture of the data learning system.

The Expert Report notes the need for 'human-in-the-loop' as part of the risk management protocols for a programme. This extends from the design and pre-tuning of the model, through implementation to post-release monitoring,[98] although it also notes that the scale of a programme may limit the extent of human intervention, and the system needs to be constructed with a human rights perspective.[99]

Robodebt was not an AI system that learned from data inputs but was an expert system that compared data from two sources. It was intentionally designed to reduce the reliance on human intervention in the process to scale up the number of cases that could be processed.

[92] M Perry, 'iDecide: Administrative Decision-Making in the Digital World' (2017) 91 *Australian Law Journal* 29.

[93] Campbell, above n 6, 537.

[94] Bell et al., above n 90 11,13; Department of Industry, Science and Resources, above n 28, 7.

[95] See, e.g. https://lawchatgpt.com/; Spellbook for Law. Available at: www.spellbook.legal/.

[96] M Callahan, 'Algorithms Were Supposed to Reduce Bias in Criminal Justice – Do They?' (*The Brink: Boston University*, 23 February 2023). Available at: www.bu.edu/articles/2023/do-algorithms-reduce-bias-in-criminal-justice/ accessed 6 June 2023; Sourdin T, 'Judge v Robot? Artificial Intelligence and Judicial Decision-Making' (2018) 41 *University of New South Wales Law Journal* 1114.

[97] Hildebrandt, above n 21.

[98] Bell et al., above n 90, Table 1.

[99] ibid. 12.

The programme ostensibly complied[100] with the voluntary data-matching guidelines,[101] which include the requirement for human involvement in decision making. However, the points at which the algorithm directed the process to human intervention were dictated by the policy decision to make administrative savings by transferring the evidentiary burden back to the recipient, for example to enter data into an online system. Given the lack of complexity of the system, the programme failure may have been averted if the threshold for diverting the system to a decision-maker was lower.[102]

In its examination of the automated decision making the Royal Commission made the following recommendations:

> *Recommendation 17.1: Reform of legislation and implementation of regulation*
>
> The Commonwealth should consider legislative reform to introduce a consistent legal framework in which automation in government services can operate.
>
> Where automated decision-making is implemented:
>
> - there should be a clear path for those affected by decisions to seek review
> - departmental websites should contain information advising that automated decision-making is used and explaining in plain language how the process works
> - business rules and algorithms should be made available, to enable independent expert scrutiny.
>
> *Recommendation 17.2: Establishment of a body to monitor and audit automated decision-making*
>
> The Commonwealth should consider establishing a body, or expanding an existing body, with the power to monitor and audit automate decision-making processes with regard to their technical aspects and their impact in respect of fairness, the avoiding of bias, and client usability.[103]

One of the core values of the OECD framework,[104] as endorsed by the Australian Government in 2019, before the Robodebt programme was cancelled, is human-centred values and fairness. The nature of Robodebt, to recover purported overpayments of welfare benefits, resulted in the impact being most severe on vulnerable welfare recipients. Recipients included a cross-section of the community, from people temporarily between jobs to people whose capacity to work was limited by physical or mental illness. There is evidence[105] that the stress of dealing with the unexpected debt and subsequent debt collection activity had a severe impact on the lives of people who were caught up in the programme, to the extent that at least three suicides appear to have had Robodebt as a contributing factor.[106]

[100] Commonwealth Ombudsman, above n 48, 2.63–2.66.
[101] Administrative Review Council, above n 20.
[102] M D'Rosario and C D'Rosario, 'Beyond RoboDebt: The Future of Robotic Process Automation' (2020) 11 *International Journal of Strategic Decision Sciences* (IJSDS) 16–17.
[103] Campbell, above n 6, 488.
[104] Recommendation of the Council on Artificial Intelligence, above n 15.
[105] Senate Community Affairs References Committee, 'Accountability and Justice: Why We Need a Royal Commission into Robodebt' (Commonwealth of Australia 2022). Available at: www.aph.gov.au/Parliamentary_Business/Committees/Senate/Community_Affairs/Centrelinkcompliance.
[106] Campbell, above n 6, 337.

The Australian Human Rights Commission has made a number of recommendations[107] that specifically address the use of AI by government departments of agencies, including:

Recommendation 2:	a human rights impact assessment should be required before a programme is implemented;
Recommendation 3:	legislation should require that a person is advised if AI was a material part of the decision-making process;
Recommendations 5 & 7:	an assessment should not be issued unless a decision maker can generate reasons for the decision, and guidance should be developed to assist decision-makers with the preparation of decisions; and
Recommendations 6 & 8:	the legal rights of a person to an administrative review should be clarified; including a merit review of a decision made using AI.

These recommendations would go some way to addressing the accountability and transparency concerns that emerge from the use of AI systems in government processes, ensuring that an individual can be identified as a decision maker and enabling a merits-based review of a decision that has been generated by an algorithm.

Other risks to the rule of law include the risk to democratic systems. Braithwaite notes that when the government is seen to act without integrity, the community loses trust in government.[108] Survey evidence shows that the Australian community is of the view that AI systems should supplement human decision-making processes, and should not replace them.[109] Notably the survey percentage of respondents who approved of the use of AI in the social services sector was 38.9 per cent compared to a general level of support of 63.1 per cent for AI development, which the authors note may be the result of the publicity surrounding the Robodebt programme.[110] This is amplified by the Experts Report that notes the systemic and economic risks that may result from the adoption of AI,[111] particularly if issues of fairness and transparency are not adequately addressed in the design of systems.

Conclusions

Expert systems have been around for many years, but the capability of such systems has increased exponentially over recent years. These 'big data' systems can be seen as a way to expedite or streamline decision-making processes. However, AI systems must be developed in a way that ensures that they comply with the rule of law. There needs to be

[107] Australian Human Rights Commission, 'Human Rights and Technology' (Australian Human Rights Commission 2021) Final Report. Available at: https://tech.humanrights.gov.au/downloads?_ga=2.220573144.1546570568.1686039037-1724900368.1681282491.

[108] V Braithwaite, 'Beyond the Bubble That Is Robodebt: How Governments That Lose Integrity Threaten Democracy' (2020) 55 *Australian Journal of Social Issues* 242.

[109] S Isbanner et al., 'The Adoption of Artificial Intelligence in Health Care and Social Services in Australia: Findings from a Methodologically Innovative National Survey of Values and Attitudes (the AVA-AI Study)' (2022) 24 *Journal of Medical Internet Research* e37611.

[110] ibid, 22.

[111] Bell et al., above n 90, 11.

an appropriate balance between the efficiency and revenue gains and ensuring accountability, transparency and access to justice.

Specifically, designers must have regard to:

- *Accountability*: Human oversight is essential to ensure that an aggrieved person can seek accountability. Administrative Law systems are built around holding a person to account for decisions and actions that have been made and ensuring that the appropriate authorities are in place. Machine learning systems could overturn this concept of accountability where an algorithm learns from data within the system.

  Legislation should ensure that there is a point of accountability, ensuring that a person can be held accountable for the operation of expert systems and the decisions that are assisted by that technology.
- *Transparency*: In code-based systems an audit trail can be generated showing how the data that has been input is reflected in the final decision. However, as systems are trained on vast amounts of data, audit trails become problematic. Compromises are required to ensure a balance between the rule of law and the ability to fully utilise emerging technology. However, systems must be designed with appropriate checks, balances and audit processes to ensure that they can be interrogated to understand the nature of the data that has been used to create the parameters applied to the matter in question; and how an algorithm has evolved as more data is available to the system.
- *Procedural Fairness*: The understanding of bias in expert systems has been recognised for many years. The right to have decisions and outcomes reviewed must be factored into AI systems in a way that provides checkpoints and alternatives both for vulnerable users, and where there are power imbalances, including access to information.

However applying the broader conceptualisation of the rule of law, procedural fairness is not sufficient: there must be an ethical framework to support the rule of law.[112] Case studies in Australia and other countries that have applied expert systems in decision making show the importance of a human-centered approach, as set out in the OECD principles.[113] As seen in the Robodebt case study, the use of expert systems can lead to a change in culture within government agencies as resources are directed to compliance and maintaining the system instead of providing human support to people caught up in the system.[114]

Staff working in front facing roles see the human cost of policy failures:[115]

> Some of the witnesses who gave evidence before the Commission would make one despair of the Australian Public Service; but there were others, like Colleen Taylor, who restored faith. The shame is that people of her calibre were not listened to.[116]

[112] See Badisco, Chapter 9 in this volume.
[113] Recommendation of the Council on Artificial Intelligence, above n 15.
[114] Giest and Klievink, above n 18.
[115] Campbell, above n 6, 13.
[116] ibid, 657.

Robodebt was an example of a poorly designed programme. Although it was not complex, the legal and administrative processes demonstrated a shocking disregard for the rule of law. The Royal Commission and other enquiries have detailed heart-rending evidence from people whose lives were upended.

The breach of trust between citizens and government also had a political cost. In the 2022 Federal Election the coalition government was resoundingly defeated, and several ministers who held office at different times over the period of the programme are no longer in Parliament. At least one senior public servant is no longer employed in the public service. The Royal Commissioner sealed a chapter of the report to be referred to other bodies with the power to initiate criminal proceedings.

Like similar scandals in other parts of the world, the Robodebt fiasco has shocked policy makers and public servants into taking the challenges of AI seriously and developing protocols around its use. This must include reviewing the safeguards and including human rights in the protections afforded under administrative law.[117]

[117] World Justice Project, above n 1.

12

The Kindness of Strangers; The Bond and FX Markets, the Rule of Law and Fiscal Credibility

ALEXIS BRASSEY

Abstract

This chapter is an examination of the importance of the bond and FX markets (markets) and their impact on fiscal policy development.

The argument presented in this chapter suggests there are interesting parallels between a thin theory of the rule of law and the principles that lie behind good fiscal governance. The parallels drawn out in this chapter are threefold. Firstly, the rule of law promotes procedural orthodoxy over an arbitrary or discretionary approach.[1] This rules-based approach helps to keep the executive in check with an external standard. Secondly, a fiscal rules-based approach also has parallels with a thin theory given the proposal is that decisions ought to be governed by stable, widely promulgated, clear, non-contradictory, credible and prospective rules. These rules are likely to constrain an executive who increasingly promote unrealistic spending programmes without the requisite need to raise taxation. Thirdly, the markets have helped shape the UK constitutional apparatus as governments insatiable appetite for debt have required institutions to become more responsive to international investors. The intra-governmental relationship and conventions form part of the rules-based system that provide markets with confidence to lend to the UK.

Introduction

The ever-present temptation for politicians in the UK has been to increase tax as a percentage of GDP.[2] An aging population with increasingly complex health needs

[1] See Lindsay, Chapter 3 in this volume.

[2] UK tax as a percentage of GDP is at its highest in 70 years. No major political party is calling for reductions in government expenditure. OBR, *The UK's tax burden in historical and international context*, March 2023, *Economic and Fiscal Outlook*, 78. Mark Carney, the ex-Bank of England Governor, referred to the

requires an NHS having to deal with ever greater demands which places pressure on politicians to promise more without necessarily having the means to do so.[3] The term 'crisis' is routinely used to refer to all manner of public sector demands,[4] but ultimately the lessons of history, as discussed in this chapter, teach us that all governments need to live within their means. Living within their means requires having the capacity to raise taxation to fund desired public expenditure or being able to borrow excess balances with a credible plan to service, if not repay that borrowing. It is the markets that impose that discipline and have tutored governments to operate within the boundary of fiscal credibility and a rules-based system is more likely to achieve that objective than one which operates with too much sensitivity to the political demands of the day.

The next part of this chapter sets out the definitions that will be used throughout; what is meant by the 'rule of law' and 'the constitution' and what are the parallels with a rules-based fiscal policy. Although the chapter will focus on the UKs experience, the argument applies to any open economy. The subsequent part of the chapter sets out how the markets work and demonstrates their objective character. This section notes that markets tend to be ambivalent about the overall fiscal mix, ie high tax, high spend or low tax, low spend, but become hostile to governments who put forward programmes that lack credibility. It is then examined how the markets have influenced English constitutional arrangements throughout English history from the establishment of the pound and creation of HM Treasury, the Bank of England (BoE), and the Office for Budgetary Responsibility (OBR). The final section examines two periods in which the UK government lost credibility in both the FX and the bond markets, 1976 and 2022. The economic circumstances surrounding this period were strikingly similar as was the political decision making that led to the crises. The chapter examines how a disregard for the UK institutional framework and the lack of fiscal rules led to a loss of confidence in the markets which led to a reversal of policy. The proposal in this chapter suggests that adherence to a rules-based system would be more likely to avert these sorts of crises.

This chapter concludes by arguing that fiscal policy is ultimately constrained by market assessment and as a result good governance suggests operating within a stable, widely promulgated, clear, non-contradictory, credible and prospective framework to deal with market-sensitive dynamics.

Definitions

This section sets out the terminology used in this chapter. The proposal to introduce fiscal rules is not new.[5] It is, however, a constraint on power and a thin theory of the

financing of Britain's deficit as having to rely on the 'kindness of strangers'. Mansion House Speech, London 20 June 2017.

[3] A Charlesworth, 'Securing the future: funding health and social care to the 2030s' (2018), IFS.

[4] Political campaigns involving calls for greater public spending have included widespread use of the term crisis including; 'NHS crisis', 'cost of living crisis', 'housing crisis', 'social care crisis', 'mental health crisis', 'energy crisis', 'climate crisis' etc.

[5] Gordon Brown proposed fiscal rules in 1997, see: HC Deb 02 July 1997 vol 297 cc303-16. These rules were not adhered to for a variety of political reasons although Starmer's administration does appear to be moving back towards a rules-based system, see: R Hughes, J Leslie and C Pacitti, 'Britannia waives the rules?' (2019), Resolution Foundation Briefing. IEA, 'Binding the Hands of Government – A Credible Fiscal Rule for the

rule of law, as explored below and elsewhere in this chapter, provide a framework that a successful fiscal policy rules could follow.

As discussed in this volume, the 'rule of law' is not a settled term.[6] On the one hand, some conceptions posit the notion that the rule of law is strictly a procedural requirement and relates to the way in which law is formed. Dicey, for example, argues the state may only legitimately act after a clear law has been established and interpreted in accordance with due process.[7] This, so called 'thin' conception does not argue for or against any substantive law, nor does it protect against notions of distributive injustice that might cause wide inequalities in society.[8]

However, thicker conceptions of the rule of law argue towards more substantive content for law to be compliant.[9] That substantive content might include, for example, the protection of human rights, freedoms, health and education.[10] On any analysis of the rule of law the essential feature is the idea of executive constraint, i.e. the governing entity, or executive is required to have regard to some external set of rules, conventions or processes that prevent an arbitrary deployment of power.[11]

This chapter accepts there is a spectrum of content for the rule of law but draws out the parallel between the advantages of a 'thin' theory of law with application of those procedural constraints on fiscal policy formation. As discussed below, the extent to which the executive can hold and deploy power, is a function of its ability to maintain credibility and the confidence of those they seek to govern. Government credibility and adherence to a rules-based system of fiscal policy determination parallels with a thin conception of the rule of law, given it encourages the executive to operate within the confines of stability and prospectivity.

It could be argued that 'thin' rule of law values are not engaged here, given that individual autonomy, human rights and other interests are not directly at stake. However, rules are conductive to good governance which will in turn improve lives.[12]

We now turn to a definition of the constitution bearing in mind this chapter focuses on developments in the UK. What the following section seeks to sketch out is a framework of 'rules' that already exist and through which confidence in policy formation has evolved. If fiscal rules and Office for Budgetary Responsibility (OBR) this provides independent economics forecasts and analysis for government) forecasting are to inform and constrain the executive either through law or convention, it is important to understand how the mechanics of that might work in the context of existing constitutional

UK', (2012), IEA Current Controversies Paper No 36. Rishi Sunak's 'Charter for Budget Responsibility' goals. Available at: https://questions-statements.parliament.uk/written-statements/detail/2022-01-05/hcws513. JP Keppenne, 'Fiscal Rules' in Federico Fabbrini and Marco Ventoruzzo (eds), *Research Handbook on EU Economic Law* (Cheltenham: Edward Elgar, 2019) 35–80.

[6] See Lindsay, Chapter 3 in this volume; J Raz, 'The Rule of Law and its Virtue' (1977) *93 Law Quarterly Review*, 195, 210–11; and I Jennings, *The Law and Constitution* (Oxford: Oxford University Press, 1980).

[7] A Dicey, *Introduction to the Study of Law of the Constitution* 10th edn (1885; London: Macmillan, 1959) 87–95.

[8] ibid. Raz, above n 4.

[9] ibid. Jennings, above n 4.

[10] S Golub, 'Make Justice the Organizing Principle of the Rule of Law Field' (2009) *Hague Journal on the Rule of Law* 61–66.

[11] Lord Bingham 'The Rule of Law' (2007) 66 CLJ 67, 69. See also Lindsay, Chapter 3 in this volume.

[12] D Galligan, 'The Exercise of Discretionary Powers, II' in *Discretionary Powers: A Legal Study of Official Discretion* (Oxford: Oxford University Press, 1990; online edn, Oxford Academic, 22 Mar. 2012); M Elliott and R Thomas, *Public Law* 4th edn (Oxford, Oxford University Press, 2020) 399–417.

arrangements. In the UK, the constitutional arrangements are referred to as a constitutional monarchy.[13] Although the UK constitution is uncodified,[14] the constitution is comprised of law and rules that create the institutions of the state.[15] The rules also regulate the interrelationship between those institutions as well as the relationship between the state and its citizens. The ultimate decision-making body that creates the rules is Parliament which has absolute sovereignty.[16] The exercise of government power is expressed through the executive headed by the Prime Minister (PM) who holds that position in virtue of their ability to carry the confidence of Parliament.[17]

The requirement that a PM, as head of the executive, can command the confidence of Parliament is critical in the analysis below. English history is littered with examples of PMs losing the confidence of Parliament, often because of political decisions that impact on the economy, whether because of war,[18] or more directly relating to economic affairs.[19]

Since at least the Bill of Rights,1689, the constitution required the Crown to seek the consent of the people through their representation in Parliament to rule.[20] Whilst the Crown retained certain prerogative powers,[21] parts of the executive apparatus created by Parliament derives its legitimacy from the confidence placed in it by the people through Parliament. The development of constitutional rules throughout English history has, in part, been influenced by the desire to improve good governance, albeit that those rules have, on occasion, also been developed to protect some elites against others. The proposal for the development of fiscal rules, however, is intended to assist policy makers in providing guardrails against excessive borrowing.

Since 1689, Parliament has created several institutions that benefit from a degree of independence.[22] The degree to which institutions are able to maintain independence, given they rely on Parliament for their legitimacy is a complex and important puzzle.[23] For the purposes of this chapter, the institutions that will be more closely examined are the BoE the OBR and HM Treasury.

[13] Political and Constitutional Reform Committee, The UK Constitution, A summary, with options for reform (HC 2015-3, 5).

[14] Above, n 2.

[15] Above, n 5.

[16] There is a nuanced debate on Parliamentary supremacy: A Geçer, 'The Principle of Parliamentary Supremacy in the UK Constitutional Law and its Limitations' (2013) 6(1) *Ankara Bar Review* 155–168.

[17] Above n 11, 8.

[18] See, eg, Lord North's defeat after the Siege of Yorktown, 1782, see: P Whiteley, *Lord North: The Prime Minister Who Lost America* (London: The Hambledon Press, 1996) ch 15; J Shepherd, 'The Fall of the Callaghan Government, 1979' in T Heppell and K Theakston (eds), *How Labour Governments Fall* (London: Palgrave Macmillan, 2013).

[19] See, eg, Callaghan's defeat in 1979, following the Winter of Discontent. This was the last time a British Government fell to a vote of no confidence.

[20] Bill of Rights 1688 ch 2 (1 Will and Mar Sess 2). Arguably the English arrangements go back further to Magna Carta 1215 and develop through the reign of Henry III.

[21] ibid.

[22] For example, Bank of England Act 1998 (Bank of England) and the Budget Responsibility and National Audit Act 2011 (OBR). It is noted that Parliament has, over the same period, made itself responsible for the regulation of other jurisdictions.

[23] A Stansbury and E Balls (2017), 'Twenty years on: Is there still a case for Bank of England independence', CEPR. Available at: www.cepr.org/voxeu/columns/twenty-years-there-still-case-bank-england-independence. See also: D de Cogan, *Tax Law, State-building and the Constitution* (Oxford: Hart, 2020) 77–80.

The BoE was established by Parliament in 1694, but remained subject to substantive executive control via HM Treasury until 1998.[24] Although the 1998 Act provides for the BoE to independently supervise the banking sector,[25] the Monetary Policy Committee (MPC) which sets interest rates, does so with regard to a target set for it by HM Treasury.[26] There are benefits for allowing the BoE's independence when setting monetary policy; the most important of which is the lower rate of interest investors are prepared to lend to the government as a result of the perception that independence is more likely to lead to a lower rate of inflation. The debate, however, is nuanced and the decision to engage in QE (which might be described as the printing of money to purchase (largely government) securities, thereby lowering the rate of interest for borrowers across timeframes) raised questions about its independence.[27]

The ability of the MPC to set rates independently of the political cycle lies at the heart of why the markets accept the UK's improved credibility to control inflation. In essence, this is because politicians, after 1998, were no longer able to inflate the economy in preparation for an election by using monetary policy. Similarly, the creation of the OBR in 2010, established the provision of an independent assessment of the fiscal position of the UK economy for the purposes of setting out budgetary measures. The independence of the OBR, as with the BoE, provided the markets with an additional degree of confidence that the figures were not being manipulated to achieve political objectives, but reflected a genuine assessment of the economic picture. This is not to say that the BoE and OBR get it right; it is, however, fair to say their processes are less likely to be politically motivated.

Markets now view the independence of the BoE and the OBR as an important consideration in pricing. They form part of the constitutional furniture of the UK state and as the experience sets out below, if the executive acts to erode the perception of independence, the consequences can be a reversal of this advantage.

The Chancellor and Treasury Ministers also benefit from independent advice from HM Treasury's civil service.[28] HM Treasury's permanent staff, along with the BoE and the OBR, have provided the core institutional basis for the UK to present as a credible economy deserving of international investment. The longevity and independence of that institutional support have developed alongside the knowledge that respect for markets is an essential feature of modern government and to that extent it is reasonable to conclude the markets have helped shape the UK constitutional settlement.

The interrelationships between Ministers, HMT, OBR and the BoE, combined with the possibility of a more robust model of fiscal rules all form part of what might be required for government to create a stable environment in which fiscal policy can be formed.

[24] Bank of England Act 1998.

[25] ibid. Part 3A.

[26] ibid. Part II.

[27] Economic Affairs Committee, Quantitative easing: a dangerous addition? (HL 2021-7).

[28] The independence of the civil service can be traced to the Northcote-Trevelyan Report which recommended a permanent bureaucracy to support the development and implementation of government economy policy. True independence is impossible and has recently been eroded by moves such as Sue Gray, ex-senior civil servant at the Cabinet Office, moving to become Chief of Staff for the Labour Party.

Before analysing the strength of influence the markets have on the UK constitutional settlement, this chapter now turns to examine what the bond and FX market are, how they operate and the transmission mechanism to the real economy that exerts such immediate and powerful signals.

The Markets

The purpose of this section is to explain how the bond and FX markets work. An understanding of the mechanics of the market will achieve two objectives. Firstly, it will demonstrate the objective nature of the participants, i.e., the market is disinterested in any particular political or economic outcome. I use the term disinterested in the sense the market is designed to calculate value which changes depending on inputs, rather like a calculator. Secondly it will assist in demonstrating the core requirement of fiscal credibility for the ongoing funding of government. The development of fiscal rules akin to a thin theory of the rule of law would promote more attractive pricing of government debt, ensuring cheaper funding for government services to the benefit of the UK. This section is divided into an exploration of the bond and then the FX markets.

The Bond Market

Although aspects of the market can be extremely complex, the cost of capital is a simple function of two variables. Firstly, how much will an investor earn? This is determined by the (real/inflation-adjusted) interest rate applied to the bond. Secondly, will the investor get their money back? This is largely determined by credit risk, i.e. will the issuer remain solvent until repayment of the debt. This section explains how pricing of interest rates and credit risk are determined. The examination below highlights the importance of confidence in determining the cost of debt.

The bond market is a market in which participants buy and sell debt. Those debts can be sold by issuers to buyers directly in the primary market.[29] Debts can then be bought and sold in the secondary market. The bond market is larger than the equity market. In 2023 the total amount of global debt outstanding was around $120 trillion.[30]

Bonds differ from shares in that they are debt instruments. Shareholders buy shares with a view to participating in the company's profits; bond buyers lend money to companies to earn interest. The most important part of the bond market is the market for government bonds as they are used as the benchmark for all other bonds to price risk from.[31]

[29] Bonds can also be known as notes, securities, or paper.

[30] Securities Industry and Financial Markets Association. Available at: www.sifma.org/resources/research/insights-global-equity-markets-primer.

[31] If there were no government bonds outstanding, the market would price a nominal government bond as a benchmark. See, eg, www.ice.com/products/37650336/Long-Gilt-Future.

Bonds are priced with reference to a coupon rate which is paid periodically. These routine payments are made annually, semi-annually or, in some cases, quarterly. If a bond is issued at £100 with a coupon of 5 per cent, it is said to have a 5 per cent yield. Bonds also have a maturity date when the amount lent will be paid back, this is known as the redemption date or the date of maturity. Finally, bonds are ordered in terms of seniority in the event of an insolvency. Senior bonds are the safest securities and are protected in an insolvency by layers of capital that are subordinated to them. Subordinated debt might be issued in the form of junior bonds, perpetual bonds or convertible bonds. Bonds are senior to shares in a company, so in the event of an insolvency, shareholders lose their investment before bond holders get affected.[32]

Complexity in the bond market arises given there are so many permutations of maturity date, coupon rate, seniority and currency. HSBC, for example has only one share price but dozens of different bond issues.[33]

Bond prices, as mentioned above, are a function of two variables. The first is the interest rate, which is derived from the government bond market. The second is the credit risk assigned to each company. Credit risk can be evaluated by reference to the rating agencies such as S&P and Moody's whose analysts assess the performance of the company with reference to their ability to both service and repay capital. This credit rating is broadly divided into two categories: investment grade bonds and non-investment grade or, to give its market nomenclature, 'junk bonds'.[34] As the risk on a bond increases the amount of return required by buyers also increases. The credibility of an issuer to meet their financial commitments, therefore has a direct bearing on their cost of capital.

Governments issue bonds to assist with public spending.[35] These bonds have a coupon which is paid periodically and mature over different time frames. Although governments can issue bonds in foreign currency, they typically issue bonds in their domestic currency. The exception to this rule is where a country has a history of an unstable exchange rate, in which case the government may issue in hard currency (most often USD) as raising funds in an unstable domestic currency would require an additional premium assigned to the FX risk, driving up the cost of capital. As with corporate bonds, sovereigns are also rated by the credit-rating agencies.[36]

Unlike corporate bonds, sovereigns cannot default if they have been issued in their domestic currency because governments can print the required sums and pay investors. The three main risks when it comes to sovereigns are inflation, interest rates and currency risks. In the case of inflation, an investor might receive a 5 per cent return on their investment in nominal terms, but if inflation is running at 7 per cent then their real return is -2 per cent. Governments do issue index linked bonds to encourage investors

[32] Save for more complex debt instruments such as AT1 securities. See www.bloomberg.com/news/articles/2023-03-23/credit-suise-at1-writedown-needed-for-bank-to-operate-smoothly-says-finma.

[33] See www.hsbc.com/investors/fixed-income-investors.

[34] Investment grade bonds are those rated BBB- or higher by S&P, or Baa3 by Moody's. Ratings run from AAA to D (Moody's), i.e. prime investment grade with extremely strong capacity to meet its financial commitments, to default.

[35] Government bonds are also known as sovereigns.

[36] Fitch, for example, rates UK debt as AA-. See www.fitchratings.com/entity/united-kingdom-80442209.

to buy their debt to obviate this problem. Returns on those bonds are reflective of the markets prospective view about future inflation expectations.

FX risk relates to the possibility of a currency move which will affect the base currency return. If a UK investor earns, for example 5 per cent in US Treasuries (US government bonds), but the GBP/ USD exchange rate rises by 7 per cent, then this investor loses 2 per cent in GBP terms, all other things being equal.

Finally, sovereigns are subject to interest rate risk. If an investor buys a sovereign bond for £100 at 5 per cent with the government able to issue further bonds at 5 per cent, the value of the bond will remain stable. Assuming the government is now able to issue bonds at 4 per cent, the investor who holds the 5 per cent bond is earning 1 per cent more than they otherwise would have been able to earn until the bond matures. Consequently, the bond value will increase above £100 to reflect this benefit. Bond prices, therefore, are inversely correlated with interest rates.

As governments issue bonds for different maturities, it is possible to calculate the price of bonds over those differing periods. The curve which can be plotted, with interest rates on the x-axis and time on the y-axis is known as the 'yield curve' and represents the market price of rates over the time frame. This curve (see Figure 12.1 below) is more than just an estimate, it represents the actual price of capital over time and directly feeds into mortgage rates, bank loan rates, credit card rates, overdraft rate etc. The yield curve, therefore, which is calculated by the price of different maturities of government bonds, will influence the cost of capital and plays a significant role in determining liquidity in the economy. If the cost of capital increases, then the amounts of liquidity in the economy falls as more money is required to service debts. Central banks and governments around the world are constantly monitoring or intervening in the bond market in an effort to achieve wider macroeconomic goals such as the control of inflation or stimulating the economy to promote growth.

Figure 12.1 Yield Curve

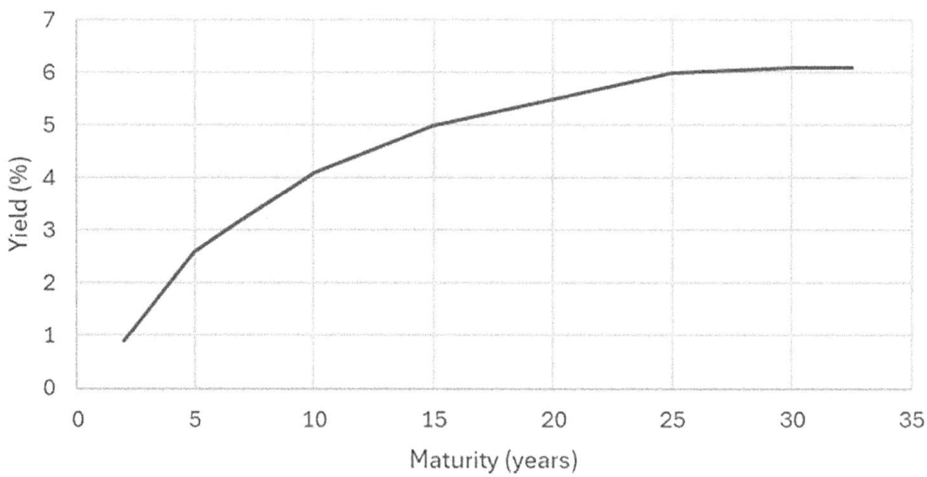

It follows from the above analysis that pricing in the bond market is a mechanical process of taking into account different factors. That process is objective, as opposed to normative, in the sense that the market is not seeking to obtain any particular outcome, it is just the sum total of evaluations of each function that goes into the pricing of a bond. Political commentators often mistake the pricing of financial market securities as having some sort of normative agency, rather than the more mundane, mechanical exercise of risk assessment which better describes the process.[37] Examples of this are often deployed when sovereign states find themselves unable to pay back debts because of government overspending or under taxing.[38]

This is not to say that the bond market is always correct in its forward assessments. The market is constantly moving to reflect new, unknown information. Every data point that is released from government and non-government institutions, whether that is about employment, inflation, economic growth, or balance of payments can have an impact on the pricing of securities as market participants adjust their expectations of the future. In the Covid-19 period of 2020, the bond market pricing for 10-year US government bonds were trading with yields below 1 per cent. By 2022 that rate had increased to more than 4 per cent as the emergence of inflation caused bond market participants to reassess their forecast models given the effects of monetary stimulus that had been deployed during the crisis.

The FX Market

This section sets out how the FX market reacts to government fiscal and monetary policies. The FX market acts in a similar way to the bond market, given it tends to favour credible, stable governments, rewarding their currencies with enhanced value. Unlike the bond market, currencies tend to increase in value when interest rates increase, given money flows move towards higher returns.[39] This effect, however, is tempered by inflation, which can erode real, as opposed to nominal interest returns. A country increasing interest rates to slow down an economy that is performing well is a different proposition from a country raising interest rates to tame runaway inflation or to prevent capital flight.[40]

The FX market has long acted as a bellwether for the economic strength and credibility of governments. Although most global currencies were linked to gold, in 1971 many currencies became free floating or fiduciary.[41] The history of the FX markets is a history of governments attempting to devalue their currency to 'print' their way out of trouble. FX crises have augured changes in governments over millennium,[42] and its

[37] H Ellyatt and C Roth, 'Greece is like "a slave" to lenders with little power left: Varoufakis' (CNBC, 28 September 2016).
[38] ibid.
[39] V Chari and P Kehoe, 'Hot Money' (2003) 111(6) *Journal of Political Economy* 1262–92.
[40] ibid.
[41] C Zoeller, 'Closing the Gold Window: The End of Bretton Woods as a Contingency Plan' (2019) 47(1) *Politics & Society* 3–22.
[42] See, eg K Kleber, D Bezemer, K Butcher, J Castañeda, D Flynn, P Foldvari and J Dercksen, 'Money, Currency and Crisis: In Search of Trust, 2000 BC to AD 2000' (2018) *Routledge Explorations in Economic*

significance can be seen in the same terms as the bond market when it comes to influencing government fiscal and monetary conduct.

Bond market participants consider FX risk when deciding whether to purchase debts of countries who have a history of devaluing their currency by printing money which in turn causes inflation. The consequences of an unstable currency have led to governments issuing sovereign bonds in 'hard currency' before converting proceeds back into local currency for the purposes of public spending. Governments that have raised funds in USD but then suffered further depreciation in their currencies have had to tackle the problem of paying interest and capital back in USD, but only have a local currency base from which to raise the required funds.[43] This has, over the years, precipitated multiple global debt crises.[44]

When assessing government credibility, therefore, the FX market is a more important influence in countries that have large foreign currency debts than countries that have issued bonds in their own domestic currency. Similarly, when assessing the impact of inflation, countries that have inflation linked their debt are far more vulnerable than those that have not.

The mechanics of the FX market are simpler than the bond market, given participants can buy or sell their currency for some other currency. Since the advent of e-banking and online trading, FX changing facilities only available to large international banks in the 1980s can now be accessed on any smart phone. The value of a currency will rise and fall on the volume of supply and demand. It is perhaps the purest market mechanism available in financial markets. Save for those countries that seek to restrict convertibility, the FX market trades 24/7 on every business day in huge volume.[45]

Attempts by governments to control FX rates in free floating currencies have been met with varied success. The most successful instance involved multi-lateral agreements and intervention under the Plaza Accord in 1985.[46] Perhaps the most notorious UK example of failure was Black Wednesday when HM Treasury attempted to prevent GBP from falling out of the Exchange Rate Mechanism (ERM) in 1992.[47]

As with the bond market, it is likely the FX market would reward the UK for following fiscal rules. Prior Sterling crises have tended to be caused by ill-disciplined governments unable to fund their budget spending, as discussed in the 1976 and 2022 crises below.

History 80; R Dornbush, I Goldfajn, R Valdés, S Edwards and M Bruno, 'Currency Crises and Collapses' (1995) 2 *Brookings Papers on Economic Activity*' 219–93 and J Lamb, 'The Paper Age: Currency, Crisis, and Carlyle' (2008) 30(1) *Prose Studies* 27–44.

[43] Operating in USD rather than local currency might be considered in the same way as an extra payment of interest.

[44] Above, n 42.

[45] Daily volumes of $7.5 trillion. BIS 'OTC Foreign Exchange Turnover April 2022', Triennial Central Bank Survey.

[46] The G5 organised concerted intervention to weaken the US Dollar. C Bergsten, and R Green (eds), *International monetary cooperation: Lessons from the Plaza Accord after thirty years* (Peterson Institute for International Economics, 2016).

[47] Although the pound collapsed after exiting the ERM, some viewed the affair as positive: A Budd, 'Black Wednesday-A Re-examination of Britain's Experience in the Exchange Rate Mechanism' (2005) *IEA Occasional Paper* (135).

Market Reactions

Markets respond rapidly to information relating to government fiscal credibility. Typically, the most dramatic market movements occur with changes of government or on the announcement of significant changes to fiscal or monetary policy. These changes can provoke defaults, and there are some countries that are prone to changing government to take advantage of benefits that electorates believe will come from default.[48]

Argentina is a good case study showing how markets respond to significant changes in economic policy. Market assessment is objective and adjust expectations of, for example, a currency's value with adjustments in political approach to economic policy. As a government's credibility erodes, the market prices in the risk of inflation and default which result in falls in the value of the currency and increases in the country's cost of capital and imports.

Some writers believe that default in emerging economies stems from a lack of access to liquidity, resulting from a hierarchical system of currencies with monetary power retained in the creditor nations.[49] In reality, lenders fare worse than borrowers and defaults are broadly a result of misfortune or mismanagement.[50] What is perhaps surprising is the extent to which perennial defaulters are able to repeat the same process, regardless of the increase in risk premia that the borrower is offering.[51]

The likely mismanagement of the incoming Fernandez administration in 2019 was assessed by the market as he followed the Kirchners economic model.[52] Those policies included the nationalisation of private pension funds, and currency controls to prevent the devaluation of the peso. Rather than recognise the inevitability of Argentinians seeking to shift their savings out of the peso, Cristina blamed 'vulture funds' for destabilising the country, describing them as 'economic terrorists'.[53]

Argentina is not unique; sovereign debt defaults and currency crises have littered history with Spain being an early example.[54] In 1998 the financial markets went into turmoil as a series of Far Eastern and Asian countries struggled to service their USD denominated sovereign debts, which were accompanied by dramatic falls in the value of their domestic currencies.[55]

[48] Argentina has defaulted nine times since 1816: R Silva, M Campbell and A Ranieri, 'Lessons from the Argentine Perspective' (Latin Lawyer, 26 August 2022).

[49] K Patrício and F Lima, 'Sovereign Solvency as Monetary Power' (2022) 25(3) *Journal of International Economic Law*, 424–446.

[50] ibid; R Levy, 'Hedge Fund loses $1 billion in One Month on Argentina Bet' (*The Wall Street Journal*, 5 September 2019).

[51] Argentina defaulted once again on its debt in 2020 despite external support from the IMF. This default followed the defeat of Mauricio Marci's administration by Albert Fernandez; R Dube, 'Argentina Defaults on Sovereign Debt Amid Coronavirus Crisis' (*The Wall Street Journal*, 22 May 2020).

[52] Fernandez served as their Chief of the Cabinet of Ministers. The currency fell from 38 peso:1$ to 370 1$ within four years of his election.

[53] S Pisani, 'Cristina characterized the vulture funds as "terrorists" and accused them of destabilization' (*La Nacion*, 25 September 2014).

[54] Between 1557 and 1936 Spain defaulted on 18 occasions, C Reinhart and K Rogoff, 'The Forgotten History of Domestic Debt' (2011) 121(552) *Economic Journal* 319–50.

[55] T Miyakoshi, 'The Causes of the Asian Currency Crisis: Empirical Observations' (2000) 12(3) *Japan and the World Economy* 243–53.

Whether these crises were caused by widespread corruption, economic mismanagement, or external shock, what is common to all these sovereign debt defaults and currency crises is the loss of confidence international investors and domestic citizens undergo as the problem emerges. This loss of confidence leads to a snowball effect of selling, followed by attempts on the part of government to redress, followed by a loss of resource on the part of government, culminating in a new equilibrium rate after a default or devaluation. The explanations for how some countries end up in such dire circumstances are as varied as the crises themselves, but the commonality is a loss of confidence in the system and the attendant loss of credibility in the systems institutions that service that economy.

In all cases, the lack of, or the breaking of fiscal rules lies at the heart of the crisis, namely governments presenting an economic programme that lacks credibility. In other words, poor governance and a failure to produce fiscal policy along the lines of a thin theory of the rule of law. It might be argued that some governments are unlucky in the sense they face hard external shocks necessitating a burgeoning deficit. Examples might include war, energy shocks or pandemics. The markets, however, are less concerned about one-off disaster spending than endemic, systematic, structural deficit spending. The direction of travel, in other words, is nearly always more important than the absolute level of debt.

This section has explained how the markets work; it has explained that the mechanics of the market are simply a function of the assessment of component variables that have no normative power. The default of sovereign bonds has been considered alongside cases of currency crises as resulting from a loss of confidence in the government's capacity to counter the cause of the crisis. This explanation helps us to properly understand the role the markets have played in the development of England and UK institutions as part of the constitutional settlement in 1689 and it is to this we now turn.

English History, how the Market Influenced the Formation of the Constitution

The analysis above suggests markets respond to government policies. Market prices are the sum product of the participants assessment.[56] That assessment is not subject to debate, nor ought it to be considered a view, it is simply the price that 'strangers' are willing to lend at and a price for which 'strangers' are willing to exchange currency. It is not a democratic outcome, nor is it an outcome based on notions of justice; it is, instead, a mechanical outcome. Given this is how markets work, it is unsurprising that governments, including the UK, have developed constitutional arrangements sensitive to how the markets price their currency and bonds.

[56] There are nuances in this debate that revolve around the efficient market hypothesis, but there is little doubt that market prices respond to known information, see: B Malkiel, 'Reflections on the Efficient Market Hypothesis: 30 Years Later' (2005) 40(1) *Financial Review* 1–9.

This section explores how the UK Government has responded to the need to raise debt and maintain a stable currency in the development of its institutions. Although English institutions have not followed prescriptive fiscal rules, its history of stability has endured because it has largely maintained a particular approach to markets, namely fiscal and monetary policy credibility. It is argued a more orthodox approach to these rules would have improved outcomes further.

The section begins by considering the relatively benign period of inflation from the introduction of the pound in approximately 800 CE, to 1694, before turning to the events surrounding the establishment of the BoE. The analysis then turns to the increasing significance of the UK sovereign bond market (gilts)[57] on government decision making which accelerated in the twentieth century as government spending increased in line with democratic demands.

The section suggests that markets can be comfortable in conservatively pricing FX and bond risk in high-tax, high-spend states, but respond negatively when the credibility of government economic planning is undermined. A more detailed analysis of the 1976 and 2022 crises is considered in the final section.

Establishment and Stability

The period between the emergence of the pound around 800 CE and the establishment of the BoE in 1694 saw significant political and social upheaval. England was subject to repeated attacks from Vikings prior to the invasion and establishment of the unitary English state by William I in 1066. The country also suffered repeated national security crises,[58] health crises,[59] and underwent a transformational civil war, briefly operating as a Republic between 1649 and 1660. The English civil war unfolded largely because Charles I refused to live within the constraints set out by Parliament.[60] Charles I was not the only monarch during this extended period which also saw John,[61] and Henry VIII stretch the tax-raising capacity of the feudal system to its limits.[62]

What is remarkable about this period is twofold. Firstly, the relative stability of the pound, in so far as its purchasing value was relatively well maintained. Secondly the state was able to fund itself using revenues derived from taxation without the creation

[57] They are known as gilts as the paper they were originally printed on was gilt-edged.

[58] I Hernon, *Fortress Britain: All the Invasions and Incursions since 1066* (Cheltenham: The History Press, 2013).

[59] J Hatcher, 'England in the Aftermath of the Black Death' (1994) 144 *Past & Present* 3–35.

[60] C Russell, 'Parliament and the King's Finances' in C Russell (ed) *The Origins of the English Civil War. Problems in Focus Series* (London: Palgrave, 1973). Alternative views on Charles I's desire for greater revenue include the position that additional state funding was required and ultimately obtained by Cromwell by force, see M Braddick, *God's Fury, England's Fire: A new History of the English Civil War* (Harmondsworth: Penguin, 2009) chs 4 and 7.

[61] N Barratt, 'The Revenue of King John' (1996) *English Historical Review* 835–55.

[62] G Elton, 'Taxation for War and Peace in Early-Tudor England' (1975) *War and Economic Development: Essays in Memory of David Joslin* (Cambridge: Cambridge University Press, 1975) 33–48.

of a funded national debt, notwithstanding the debts incurred by the Crown prior to 1694.[63]

The stability of the pound may also be due to its value being derived from precious metal.[64] The pound was not entirely stable throughout its history,[65] the metallic base also changed from silver to gold in the thirteenth century, although this led to repeated debasement, particularly by Henry VIII, who used currency management as a source of personal enrichment.[66]

Ultimately, confidence in the pound rested on its capacity to retain its value, which itself became the basis of a medium of exchange. The relative restraint, albeit with notable exceptions,[67] on the part of the English government, by avoiding excessive devaluation and eroding the currency's value, gave rise to the confidence the population of England and eventually the wider British Empire had in the pound.

By way of contrast with the English experience, confidence in other countries led to instances which broke the link between the currency as a medium of exchange, store of value and unit of accounting. Argentina is a good example of this, but there are other more dramatic cases such as the assignat of the French Revolution, the reichsmark of the Weimar Republic and more recently the Zimbabwean dollar and the Venezuelan bolivar.[68] In each of these cases, an abandonment of adherence to some external metric, such as the gold standard or even the US dollar, led to a catastrophic erosion of value.

The BoE and the Growth of the National Debt

The impetus for the issuance of English government bonds came from obligations William III had as leader of the Grand Alliance. William III needed to fund the Nine Years War,[69] but found there were insufficient tax revenues to do so.[70] Consequently, the King borrowed £1.2m from the BoE's private subscribers, thus creating the national debt.

[63] See R Outhwaite, 'The Trials of Foreign Borrowing: The English Crown and the Antwerp Money Market in the Mid-Sixteenth Century' (1966) 19(2) *The Economic History Review, New Series* 289–305; See also M Jurkowski, C Smith and D Crook, *Lay Taxes in England and Wales 1188–1688* (Richmond: PRO Publications, 1998). In this book the authors compare forced loans with taxation. Estimated inflation between 1300 and 1931 was 0.37%, p.a.: M Weale, '1300 years of the pound sterling' (2000) 172 *NIER* 79.

[64] ibid p 80, 240 denarii = 1 pound of silver.

[65] S Deng, *The Great Debasement and Its Aftermath. In Coinage and State Formation in Early Modern English Literature* (New York: Palgrave Macmillan, 2011) 87–102.

[66] Elton, above n 62, 82.

[67] Deng, above n 65.

[68] B Cutsinger, L Rouanet, and J Ingber, 'Assignats or Death: The Politics and Dynamics of Hyperinflation in Revolutionary France'. See: c4e4a991-b47b-4759-88f8-a1e395365b5a-meca.pdf (elsevier-ssrn-document-store-prod.s3.amazonaws.com); A Roselli, 'Hyperinflation, Depression, and the Rise of Adolf Hitler' (2021) 41(2) *Economic Affairs* 300–08; J Coomer and T Gstraunthaler, 'The Hyperinflation in Zimbabwe' (2011) 14(3) *Quarterly Journal of Austrian Economics* 311–46; G Pittaluga, E Seghezza, and P Morelli, 'The Political Economy of Hyperinflation in Venezuela' (2021) 186(3–4) *Public Choice* 337–50.

[69] Fought between 1688–1697.

[70] P Harris, 'Income tax in Common Law Jurisdictions, From the Origins to 1820' in *Income Tax in Common Law Jurisdictions* (Cambridge: Cambridge University Press, 2006) 180–92.

The evidence suggests the national debt developed largely because of war.[71] From 1691 the national debt grew from approximately £3.1m to >£800m in 1856.[72] It spiked because of World War I, with debt rising to £7.4 billion in 1919, representing approximately 170 per cent of GDP. World War II then increased the debt to a record 252 per cent of GDP in 1946 at approximately £21 bn. Debt started to fall as a percentage of GDP in the post-war period to less than 50 per cent of GDP in 1974,[73] but then picked up again in the late 1970s as spending exceeded tax receipts. The result was a rescue package from the IMF in 1976 of £2.3 billion, which came with conditions requiring reductions in spending.

During the Conservative administrations from 1979–1997 debt to GDP fell to below 40 per cent before increasing again under the Blair–Brown administration of 1997–2010. The financial crisis of 2008 was a significant cause of the increase with debt to GDP rising from 36 per cent in 2006 to 66 per cent in 2011. The COVID-19 pandemic in 2020 led to a period of economic decline alongside a sharp increase in government spending. Consequently, the UK national debt stood at >£2.5 trillion or 99.2 per cent of GDP by February 2023.[74]

One might expect a positive correlation between interest rates and the built up of debt, relative to GDP. After all, the higher the percentage of a country's debt, the lower the chance one might expect to get paid back. Experience, however, shows the picture is more complex.

The stability of interest rates, particularly during the period running up to the Second World War and the explosion of debt, is remarkable given the UK had to finance more than 250 per cent of its GDP. Government financing, however, was more opaque than today. Control over rates, currency exchange and media were more extensive than the post-1971 period.[75] Confidence in the system and the ability to raise capital was strong, although there were gaps, notably in the issue of the 1914 War Loan which raised less than a third of its £350 million target.[76]

The ever-growing national debt has not impacted on rates since 1691, given the ability of the BoE to purchase gilts during times of crisis. That was as true in the early twentieth century through two world wars as it was in the post COID-19 period of 2020. The ability of the BoE to maintain confidence in the currency, however, was far more challenging given the consequences of monetising the deficit are inflationary.

[71] F Francis, *History of the Bank of England, Its Times and Traditions, from 1694 to 1844* (San Francisco: Legare Street Press, 1862) 29.

[72] ibid. The national debt began prior to William III's issuance in 1694 with around £3.1m of unfunded debt.

[73] Bank of England, 'A millennium of macroeconomic data'. Available at: www.bankofengland.co.uk/statistics/research-datasets.

[74] This figure does not include the unfunded public sector pensions liabilities which total >£2.19 trillion; HM Treasury, 'Whole of Government Accounts, 2019–20', 6 June 2022.

[75] C Schenk, 'The Sterling Area 1945–1972' (2020) *Handbook of the History of Money and Currency,* 771–790.

[76] M Anson, 'Your country needs funds: The extraordinary story of Britain's early efforts to finance the First World War', (Bank Under Ground, 8 August 2017). Available at: www.bankunderground.co.uk/2017/08/08/your-country-needs-funds-the-extraordinary-story-of-britains-early-efforts-to-finance-the-first-world-war/.

There are several theories about why the inflationary pressures in the post-war period were kept relatively in check.[77] On the one hand, the UK experienced substantial economic growth, with the supply-side of the economy growing alongside improvements in productivity. On the other hand, the pound had been devalued and inflation was running at a faster rate than in previous periods as a result.[78] Throughout the first half of the twentieth century, confidence was maintained in the UK capacity to service its debt, largely because of the success of its institutional framework and the confidence it brought investors. The BoE performed its role well and HM Treasury was able to ensure that the record high deficit reached in 1946 was managed, albeit with significant support from the United States.[79]

There were several reasons why confidence in the pound waned during the 1960s and 1970s. The British Empire was in a state of decline reducing the economic advantages the UK had enjoyed for the previous 200 years.[80] Inflation and the government response to it, post 1974, reduced the confidence of market participants, particularly as spending commitments exceeded the government's capacity to raise sufficient funds through tax. The UK IMF crisis bit particularly hard on the pound which fell from around $2.65 in 1972 to around $1.58 in 1976, further exacerbating inflation.

Similarly, the crisis of confidence in government spiked after the pound fell out of the ERM in 1992 as market participants viewed governments attempts to peg it to the Deutschemark as doomed to failure. On the one hand, it could be argued that the consequences of a rules-based system such as the ERM is reason enough to grant Minister's discretion. On the other hand, a mechanical system of currency control was only as good as a government's intention to stick to the rules which, in the case of ERM, they rarely did.[81]

What can be learned from this selection of English history? It appears that a rules-based system, guided by external mechanisms such as a metallic standard currency and the need to pay attention to unsustainable debt, had largely kept the pound and the gilts markets relatively stable. It seems reasonable to conclude that greater adherence to a rules-based system could have ensured greater stability, whilst deviation from sensible budgetary planning was more likely to cause economic turmoil as evidenced by the two periods under investigation below.

Evaluating the UK Government's Credibility in 1976 and 2022

This section evaluates the performance of the UK Government in two critical periods during which UK institutional credibility came under threat. The crises of

[77] D Laidler, 'Inflation in Britain: A Monetarist Perspective' (1976) 66(4) *The American Economic Review* 485–500.

[78] ibid.

[79] F Rohrer, 'What's a Little Debt Between Friends?' (2006), *BBC News Magazine*, 10.

[80] B Tomlinson, 'The Contraction of England: National Decline and the Loss of Empire' (1982) 11(1) *The Journal of Imperial and Commonwealth History* 58–72.

[81] B Eichengreen, and C Wyplosz, 'The Stability Pact: More Than a Minor Nuisance?' (1998) 13(26) *Economic Policy* 66–113.

1976 and 2022 took place with strikingly similar economic backdrops, namely high inflation precipitated by an energy crisis and a government in danger of over-spending relative to its tax-raising capacity. The section considers the response of the markets to these crises and examines how that transmitted via HM Treasury, Parliament and the BoE, to change government policy. In both cases, markets reacted violently and were the ultimate cause of a radical change. The 1976 crisis changed the way UK economic policy developed for more than 20 years and whilst the consequences of the 2022 crisis are yet to be felt, any government that attempts to spend freely and without reference to external or OBR forecasting is unlikely to remain in power for any significant period.

What the analysis shows in both cases, is that policy was being delivered to achieve a series of ad hoc political objectives rather than forming part of a co-ordinated, stable, and prospective fiscal policy backed by rules-based orthodoxy.

The 1976 Crisis

The seeds of the 1976 crisis were sown some years before the IMF granted a loan to the UK Government, led by then-Prime Minister, James Callaghan.[82] The previous Conservative Government, led by Edward Heath from 1970–1974, had attempted to address an economy suffering from stagflation. The 1972 'Barber Boom' budget was intended to boost demand to improve living standards ahead of an anticipated election.[83] This approach, in light of the existing inflationary pressures, had strong parallels with the intended effect of Kwarteng's 2022 budget, as discussed below. The result, however, was even higher inflation combined with spiralling demands for public-sector pay increases.[84] Although the government attempted to control inflation with a Price Commission and Pay Board,[85] things worsened as a result of the Yom Kippur war and its effects on energy inflation.[86] The Conservatives lost the February 1974 election as the electorate rejected the anti-inflationary proposals from Heath and preferred the proposals from Harold Wilson, Prime Minister from 1974–1976, to run the economy on lines akin to central planning as influenced by Tony Benn.[87] Although Labour won more seats than the Conservatives, the government was unable to command the confidence of Parliament; another election was held in October 1974.[88]

[82] Rohrer above, n 79.

[83] G Steele, 'Inflation Economics: The Heath–Barber Boom, 1972–74' (2010) 30(3) *Economic Affairs* 79–81. The 'Barber Boom' was named after the then Chancellor, Anthony Barber.

[84] ibid.

[85] P Curwen, and P Curwen, 'Prices-and-Incomes Policy Inflation' in P Curwen *Inflation* (London: Palgrave, 1976).

[86] D Schumacher, 'The 1973 Oil Crisis and its Aftermath. In Energy: Crisis or Opportunity?' (London: Palgrave, 1985) 21–41.

[87] B Spittles, 'Who Governs Britain? Britain since 1960: An Introduction' (London: Red Globe Press, 1995) 57–81. Tony Benn occupied several senior positions in the Labour Party and Labour administrations between 1964–1979. He represented the hard left of the Labour Party.

[88] Labour secured a three-seat majority in the October 1974 general election.

Wilson's administration committed to an expansion of the welfare state, with greater spending on the NHS, education and housing.[89] It imposed significant increases in taxation, reaching 98 per cent on the highest incomes.[90] Despite the increase in government spending, unemployment still rose, exceeding 1 million by April 1975.[91] By 1976, the pound fell as Labour government attempted to negotiate economic realities and the consequences of unrealistic spending commitments.[92] As the deficit started to become an insurmountable issue, a radical change in policy appeared to be the only acceptable solution to calm the markets. This occurred as the then Chancellor Denis Healey began to introduce IMF-led spending reductions as part of the conditional $3.9 billion loan that was eventually granted on 15 December 1976.[93]

The PM, James Callaghan, set out the change in approach at the Labour Party conference:

> We used to think that you could just spend your way out of a recession and increase employment by cutting taxes and boosting government spending. I tell you, in all candour, that that option no longer exists, and that insofar as it ever did exist, it only worked by injecting bigger does of inflation into the economy followed by higher levels of unemployment as the next step. That is the history of the past twenty years.[94]

This U-turn was prompted by the realities of market pricing in both the bond and FX markets. The consequences of a market-prompted change in government economic policy in the 1970s forced elected officials to acknowledge the limits of demand management policies and introduced a market compliant orthodoxy. This orthodoxy involved tackling the painful process of reducing inflation and introducing supply side reforms with a view to increasing productivity.[95]

From 1976 the government undertook to constrain spending, regardless of the economic pain the changed approach was to cause.[96] The difficult task of fiscal rebalancing that took place throughout the 1980s, that ultimately brought success in the control of inflation, however, did not extinguish the political desire to expand government expenditure. The Labour Party continued to advocate for expansionary fiscal expenditure in each of the 1983, 1987 and 1992 General Elections, although it was not until the next Labour administration of 1997 before state spending and the global financial crisis of 2008 once again drove up the debt to GDP ratio to troubling levels.[97] The effects of Labour Government spending, combined with the global financial crisis, culminated

[89] C Rogers, 'From Social Contract to 'Social Contrick': The Depoliticisation of Economic Policy-making under Harold Wilson, 1974–75' (2009) 11(4) *The British Journal of Politics and International Relations* 634–51.

[90] IFS, 'Long-Term Trends in British taxation and spending' (2002) *Briefing Note* 25.

[91] ONS, 'Changes in the economy since the 1970s', 2 September 2019.

[92] M Holmes, 'Trade Unions and Governments. Developments in British Politics' in H. Drucker et al., *Developments in British Politics* (London: Macmillan, 1983) 209–21.

[93] Above n 79.

[94] Labour Party Annual Conference Report (LPACR) (1976): 188.

[95] P Hall, 'The Movement from Keynesianism to Monetarism: Institutional Analysis and British Economic Policy in the 1970s' in S Steinmo, K Thelen and F Longstreth eds *Structuring Politics: Historical Institutionalism in Comparative Analysis* (Cambridge: Cambridge University Press, 1992) 90–113.

[96] ibid.

[97] M Carstensen, and M Matthijs, 'Of Paradigms and Power: British Economic Policy Making since Thatcher' (2018) 31(3) *Governance* 431–447, Figure 4.

in a subsequent period of austerity imposed by the Conservative-Liberal Coalition Government of 2010.[98]

In the 46 years from 1976 to 2022, despite precipitous events such as the 1992 ERM currency crisis and the global financial crisis in 2008, global institutions remained confident that UK institutions could manage the gilts market. Gilts soared after 1992 in contrast with the reduced value of the pound. Similarly, in 2008, the falling value of the pound, combined with the reductions in GDP led gilts to move higher with interest rates falling to historically low levels. The UK Government had never been able to borrow at lower levels than after the 2008 crisis, superseded only by the ultra-low interest rates following the pandemic, largely achieved by a programme of quantitative easing (QE), a period during which the largest buyer was the BoE itself.[99]

The 2022 Mini-budget

Liz Truss was declared as Prime Minister on 6 September 2022 having defeated Rishi Sunak in a leadership contest amongst Conservative party members.[100] Truss' policy intentions contrasted with Sunak's proposed approach during the leadership campaign. Sunak's view had been informed by HM Treasury, given he had been Chancellor for the duration of the COVID-19 pandemic. He made clear during the leadership election that tax cutting would only happen once inflation was under control. It was clear that his approach would take account of OBR forecasting and operate within the confines of the constitutional safeguards, such as respecting the independence of the BoE in the fight against inflation. Sunak's proposals, eventually introduced after Truss abruptly left office, had all the hallmarks of fiscal conservativism, bound by a rules-based philosophy, namely to keep budgets within OBR medium-term forecasts.

Truss, on the other hand, adopted a more radical approach to economic management, taking the view that taxes would be cut from 'day one' regardless of the pandemic deficit spending and demands required to mitigate the rising cost of energy. Before the mini budget on 23 September 2023, Truss had announced measures to cap the price of household and business energy bills. This unprecedented government intervention was estimated to cost as much as £130 billion over 18 months.[101] The measures were broadly well received by an electorate desperate for some respite from the rising cost of living. The costs of that decision required funding alongside the existing costs of the pandemic measures, estimated at around £400 billion.[102]

To pay for these measures, Truss and Kwasi Kwarteng, who had been appointed as Chancellor, formulated a tax cutting, pro-growth agenda echoing Barber in 1972. Setting aside institutional advice, Truss and Kwarteng decided to act contrary to market

[98] H Clarke, P Kellner, M Stewart, J Twyman, and P Whiteley, *Austerity and Political Choice in Britain.* (Basingstoke: Palgrave Macmillan, 2016).

[99] W Allen, 'Box A: Quantitative Easing, Government Debt Management and Debt Interest' (2022) 8 (Autumn) *National Institute UK Economic Outlook* 10–12.

[100] Sunak won the vote among Conservative MPs 137–113.

[101] A Wickham, 'Truss drafts £130 billion plan to freeze UK energy bills' (Bloomberg, 6 September 2022).

[102] House of Commons Library, 'Public spending during the Covid-19 pandemic', 29 March 2022.

expectations and began to erode confidence in established processes. Firstly, they rejected the offer from the OBR for a forecast to accompany their proposals, something that had become HM Treasury convention.[103] Secondly, the Permanent Secretary to the Treasury, Tom Scholar was dismissed. Kwarteng then held a series of meetings with the BoE Governor, Andrew Bailey and, although he affirmed the independence of the Bank, he pointedly remarked that independence did not mean immunity from 'discussion'. Both Kwarteng and Bailey would have been aware that the pro-growth Barberesque approach to fiscal policy was likely to create headwinds for an anti-inflationary approach, which was precisely the route that needed to be adopted by the BoE. A clash between government policy and the BoE's remit looked increasingly likely in the run up to the mini budget.

On 23 September 2022 the Truss-Kwarteng 'Growth Plan' was presented to the House of Commons.[104] The proposals contained a series of tax-cutting measures including reductions in the additional and basic rates of income tax, national insurance, a scrapping of the Health and Social Care Levy and a proposed increase in corporation tax.

The market reaction was sharp and immediate. The pound collapsed reaching a record low of $1.0350 on 26 September 2023, breaking a previous 37-year low. Gilts reacted strongly, with the 30-year yield rising 120 bps in three days. The violence of this move in the gilts market had a precipitous effect on several pensions funds that had been engaging in liability driven investments (LDI) which meant forced selling, further increasing yields. On the shorter end of the curve, five-year gilt yields recorded their largest ever increase in a single day.[105] The consequences of these moves in gilts rippled through the mortgage market with banks and building societies withdrawing products from the 27 September as well as raising rates over the following weeks. By the 29 September, around 40 per cent of the available mortgage products had been withdrawn.[106]

More than 45 years after the 1976 crisis, the IMF criticised the mini budget. commenting: 'Given elevated inflation pressures in many countries, including the UK, we do not recommend large and untargeted fiscal packages at this junction, as it is important that fiscal policy does not work at cross purposes to monetary policy.'[107] The UK's debt was also affected because of scepticism from credit-rating agencies who noted the measures 'could more permanently weaken the UK's debt affordability'.[108]

Truss' approach appealed to a majority of the Conservative party membership but relied on unrealistic assumptions about how markets would react. Similarly, naivete about the markets was shared by sections of the right-wing media.[109] The budget

[103] K MacLellan, 'UK finance minister Kwarteng: BoE independence is a cornerstone' (Reuters, 7 September 2022).

[104] HM Treasury, 'The growth plan 2022', (2022), CP743.

[105] P Aldrick, 'UK's biggest tax cuts since 1972 trigger crash in pound, bonds' (Bloomberg, 23 September 2022).

[106] S Taaffe-Maguire, 'Mortgages withdrawn from sale as market reels after mini-budget' (Sky News, 27 September 2022).

[107] C Smith, 'IMF urges UK to 're-evaluate' tax cuts in biting attack on fiscal plan' (*Financial Times*, 28 September 2022).

[108] W Cole, 'Moody's warns UK unfunded tax cuts are 'credit negative' (*Reuters*, 28 September 2022).

[109] A Heath, 'This was the best budget I have ever heard a British chancellor deliver' (*Daily Telegraph*); A Brummer, 'The boldness and courage of Kwasi Kwarteng's debut budget is seismic' (*Daily Mail*); M Littlewood,

was described as 'right wing', however, it sharply contrasted with the more cautious economic management of the Thatcher administrations of 1979–1991. As Sunak pointed out, earlier administrations understood the importance of dealing with inflationary pressures and careful government deficit management before embarking on fiscal expansion.[110]

It took a week for Truss and Kwarteng to recognise they would need to U-turn. The loss of credibility had required an emergency BoE intervention in the gilts market on 28 September offering to buy long-dated gilts.[111] This was contrary to their stated intention to unwind QE measures that had been undertaken as part of the pandemic response.[112] The intervention succeeded in preventing a total market panic. By 30 September an emergency meeting was held with the OBR with an announcement made that it would deliver an initial forecast on 7 October 2023. This was later moved to 23 November with a more detailed report.[113] Both Truss and Kwarteng failed to recognise the urgency of the situation and market reaction became the catalyst for change. By 2 October, Kwarteng had reversed the additional rate tax reduction and moved the OBR forecast to be released on 31 October 2023.[114] The markets remained in turmoil with sterling remaining below its Brexit lows and gilts still presenting extreme stress.

Truss dismissed Kwarteng on 14 October after just 38 days. He was replaced by Jeremy Hunt who had been given the remit to reverse large parts of the mini budget in an attempt to stabilise the markets. In his Autumn Statement to Parliament, stability was stated as his first priority, acknowledging the fact that market confidence was the most important priority for economic management.[115] Hunt's appointment and remit to reverse nearly all of the changes introduced by the mini budget was widely acknowledged as a necessary measure.[116] Truss' resignation on 20 October further indicated that the market reaction to her fiscal policies were the ultimate cause of her decision. She stated, 'I recognise that given the situation, I cannot deliver on the mandate on which I was elected by the Conservative Party',[117] in other words the mandate could not be implemented without market support, therefore, a new administration would need to introduce fiscal policy measures that were considered acceptable.

Director General of the Institute for Economic Affairs, 'This isn't a trickle-down budget, it's a boost-up budget. It's refreshing to hear a chancellor talk passionately about the importance of economic growth'. All were quoted in 'Great divide: Pundits' reaction to mini-budget run from alarmed to delighted' (*The Guardian*, 25 September 2022).

[110] Ben Riley-Smith, 'Rishi Sunak exclusive: I'll run the economy like Thatcher if I win the Tory leadership', (*Daily Telegraph*, 12 July 2022).

[111] Bank of England, 'Bank of England announces gilt market operation', 28 September 2022. Available at: www.bankofengland.co.uk/news/2022/september/bank-of-england-announces-gilt-market-operation.

[112] R Lea, 'The MPC raises the Bank Rate to 0.5% in February: and more increases to come' (2022) Arbuthnot Banking Group, 7.

[113] W James, 'UK Treasury: OBR's economic forecast to be published on Nov. 23' (*Reuters*, 30 September 2022).

[114] House of Commons Library, 'The 17 October 2022 fiscal statement: Summary and background', 17 October 2022.

[115] HM Treasury, 'The Autumn Statement 2022 speech', 17 November 2022.

[116] Institute for Government, 'Five things we learnt from Jeremy Hunt's 2022 Autumn Statement', 17 November 2022.

[117] Prime Minister's Office, 10 Downing Street, 'Prime Minister Liz Truss's statement in Downing Street: 20 October 2022'.

Sunak was subsequently elected as leader of the Conservative Party on 24 October 2022, having stood unopposed. He implemented a fiscal plan endorsing Hunt's measures alongside a series of tax increases and cuts to public expenditure. In his first speech as Prime Minister, Sunak promised to 'place economic stability and confidence at the heart of this government's agenda',[118] recognising the importance played by markets in providing him with the opportunity to implement a viable fiscal plan.

The events of 1976 and 2022 followed a similar path, in similar circumstances with both administrations having to reverse fiscal policy because of market reaction. The clash between a popularist, fiscally expansionary economic plan and market responses demonstrating in both cases the limits of government power and the requirement to operate within unspoken constraints. Stability in 2022 was ultimately achieved, as it was in 1976, by providing the market with confidence that a market sensitive approach to fiscal responsibility would be adopted. This chapter contends that fiscal rules would further strengthen market confidence, removing the ability of short-term political expediency to cause chaos in the markets that reduce the living standards of everyone in the economy.

Conclusions

This chapter has set out the mechanics of the bond and FX markets. In doing so, it explains how pricing is simply a function of calculating interest rates, inflation and capital default. The market does not propose any normative fiscal position, and it is ambivalent about whether economies want higher or lower levels of tax and social welfare, rather, it responds to risk.

The fiscal institutional framework in England/the UK has developed in response to market pricing, particularly so after the establishment of the BoE in 1694 and the need to service and expand the funded national debt. HM Treasury advice to Ministers has also taken account of market responses that have influenced and delineated the boundaries of popularist attempts to spend. The chapter has argued that the development of more robust fiscal rules would assist in improving governance and adherence to these rules might have prevented the crisis faced by Ministers who felt bound to act in a politically expedient manner rather than one that might accord with a stable, rules-based system in the interests of everyone.

The chapter has explored the events of 1976 and 2022 to demonstrate the consequences for politicians who were not prepared to listen to the market's concerns about credible governance. Without stable fiscal rules, the markets drove up the cost of interest rates for the UK, depreciated the currency and exacerbated inflation, all of which worsened the cost-of-living crisis for millions of people. Those consequences, mediated through the institutions of HM Treasury, the BoE and, latterly, the OBR, ultimately resulted in a complete reversal of government policy until it accorded with market

[118] BBC News, 'Rishi Sunak's first speech as UK Prime Minister in full'. Available at: www. bbc.co.uk/news/uk-63386413.

pricing. The evolution towards a more robust rules-based fiscal system, given the events of 2022, now appear more likely and it is a development that we should all welcome going forward.

The parallels with a thin theory of the rule of law and the principles that lie behind good governance are striking. More ought to be done to encourage governance that displays stable, widely promulgated, clear, non-contradictory, credible and prospective rules.

PART III

The Rule of Law in EU and International Context

13

Limitations to the Rule of Law Argument in International Tax Law

BASTIAAN VAN GANZEN, DIRK BROEKHUIJSEN, HENK VORDING AND JAN VLEGGEERT

Abstract

Several concerns that have been raised about new international tax initiatives such as Pillar 2 explicitly or implicitly invoke values related to the rule of law. For instance, it has been argued that the international law-making process is undemocratic; that the new rules create too much legal uncertainty; or that they conflict with customary international law or human rights. We argue that in those arguments, rule-of-law values such as prospectivity, clarity, stability, democracy and human rights should not be invoked as strict and supreme criteria. Instead, they are based on complex concepts that are open to divergent interpretations, and always require trade-offs with other values and goals. This applies particularly in the international realm that lacks one overarching definition of the rule of law. Both 'thick' versions of the rule of law based on democracy and human rights and 'thin' versions based on the legality principle are interpreted differently across countries. Therefore, their international application is hard to separate from power, persuasion and politics.

Introduction

The landscape of international tax law has been changing considerably over the last decade and will likely continue to do so over the next, driven by a commitment among states to reduce MNE tax planning. The scope of the measures implemented or under consideration is broader than just anti-avoidance rules; it includes, for instance, new allocation rules (Pillar 1) and a minimum effective tax rate (Pillar 2). Those new rules have raised several concerns, many of which relate to some conception of the rule of law.

Pillars 1 and 2 and likely more initiatives to come depart from the ideas that underly current international tax law. They create interactions and potential conflicts with existing domestic laws, EU law and bilateral tax treaties. This increases complexity and contributes to a rapidly changing, uncertain legal environment for internationally mobile taxpayers.[1] A specific example is that according to some authors, the Under Taxed Payments Rule (UTPR) of Pillar 2 is contrary to principles of customary international law, in particular against 'well established principles' of 'nexus' that underpin residence and source taxation.[2] A concrete rule-of-law concern with respect to that particular conflict is that taxing someone without a factual link with the state imposing the tax would be 'unreasonable, excessive or arbitrary'.[3] And as the concrete legal repercussions of this conflict are unclear, legal uncertainty increases.

Another concern is that the source of legal changes is shifting from the domestic legislative process to international agreements and pressure. Indeed, it can be argued that Pillars 1 and 2 and future initiatives represent multinational[4] tax legislation, only formally endorsed in national legislative procedures. This raises 'taxation without representation'-style questions that are relevant in a more substantive version of the rule of law going beyond mere legality. Finally, even more substantive rule-of-law values are invoked in arguments that Pillar 2 may infringe the right to property when it leads to disproportionate tax burdens on an entity level,[5] or, though unconvincingly substantiated, that it may conflict with 'rights to health, social security, and food … if it results in reducing … tax revenues for developing countries'.[6]

The concept of the rule of law limits the political discretion of lawmakers by legal means.[7] Whether the values invoked in the arguments above are indeed rule-of-law values depends on the particular definition of the rule of law one adheres to – and many alternative definitions exist.[8] But regardless of the width of one's definition, the meanings of its values are usually established within legal communities that take the shape of a national state.[9] That is only natural, as laws (including implementation of

[1] See P Hongler, IJ Mosquera Valderrama, F Debelva, V Chand and J Chaisse, 'UTPR: Potential Conflicts with International Law' (2023) 111 *Tax Notes International* 141; F Debelva and L De Broe, 'Pillar 2: An Analysis of the IIR and UTPR from an International Customary Law, Tax Treaty Law and European Union Law Perspective' (2022) 50 *Intertax* 898.

[2] See, for an overview, G Kofler, SCW Douma, A Kardachaki, P Bräumann and M Tumpel, 'The UTPR and International Law: Analysis from Three Angles' (2023) 110 *Tax Notes International* 857 and RS Avi-Yonah, 'UTPR's Dynamic Connection to Customary International Tax Law' (2022) 108 *Tax Notes International* 951; J VanderWolk, 'The UTPR: Taxing Rights Gone Wild' (2022) 108 *Tax Notes International* 1369.

[3] Debelva and De Broe, 'Pillar 2', above n 1, 899.

[4] The emerging body of international tax law and legal norms that is substantively formed in a multi-jurisdictional setting of design, pressure and compromise (such as the BEPS minimum standards and the Pillar 2 rules) is still lacking a good descriptive label. 'Tax coordination' usually refers to legal instruments like EU Directives. Multinational tax legislation produces results that are neither legally binding nor enforceable; yet those results are perceived as politically binding or as inevitable restraints on national policy choices. 'Transnational legal ordering' seems to cover all forms of legal regulation of transnational issues, and hence does not particularly focus on multinational decision-making versus national legislation: G Shaffer, 'Theorizing Transnational Legal Ordering' (2016) 12 *Annual Review of Law and Social Science* 231.

[5] Hongler, above n 1.

[6] Letter from four experts appointed by the United Nations Human Rights Council to the Director of the Centre for Tax Policy and Administration at the OECD, AL OTH 21/2022. Available at: https://spcommreports.ohchr.org/TMResultsBase/DownLoadPublicCommunicationFile?gId=27165&idp=https%3A%2F%2Fengine.surfconext.nl%2Fauthentication%2Fidp%2Fmetadata (accessed 16 May 2024); but see P Baker, 'Human Rights and the Two-Pillar Solution' (2022) 50 *Intertax* 574.

[7] J Waldron, 'The Rule of Law', *Stanford Encyclopedia of Philosophy* (Summer edn, 2020) [2].

[8] BZ Tamanaha, *On the Rule of Law: History, Politics, Theory* (Cambridge: Cambridge University Press, 2004).

[9] 'The rule of law, then, is an ideal that strives to achieve an effective legal ordering within a community': BZ Tamanaha, 'Why Sovereigns Are Entitled to the (Horizontal) Benefits of the International Rule of Law' (2023) 8 *UC Irvine Journal of International, Transnational, and Comparative Law* 5, 15.

international agreements) are enacted by national states and adjudicated by national courts.[10] Hence, a practicable view is that any rule of law argument concerning taxation of cross-border income can only be raised in the national setting of legislation and legal procedure. This is, however, an uneasy conclusion. It provides no ready answer to the abovementioned rule-of-law concerns related to multinational tax law. The question is, therefore, whether the limits put by the rule of law to national lawmaking also apply to the project of multinational lawmaking.

Indeed, there is a tendency to widen the application of rule-of-law values to rules, norms and procedures at the international level. For instance, the UN General Assembly decided in 2012 that the rule of law applies to all states equally, and to international organisations. Such a statement may have a variety of meanings. One is that the relations among states are or should be governed by the rule of law.[11] A more controversial one is that every state is governed by the rule of law, or even more controversially, by the same rule of law. The pluralistic nature of the international arena – many domestic legal orders mean many rule-of-law conceptions – may be problematic in this respect. To illustrate, several countries would probably object to a world-wide, substantive rule of law that includes democracy as a core value.[12]

The issue that specifically concerns us here is the impact of multinational tax agreements on taxpayers – should they enjoy the protection of the rule of law? Prima facie, it is not quite clear what the rule of law can mean for taxpayers in the absence of world-wide legislation, administration and legal protection. Is this only due to implementation difficulties; or are those values indeed less relevant to multinational tax law? If so, is this the case only with substantive rule-of-law versions or also with formal versions?

We will first set out the different conceptions of the rule of law that will be referred to in this chapter. We will do this briefly because we believe that the distinction between those conceptions is semantical in the context of our argument: even under a 'thin' and uncontroversial rule-of-law definition based on the legality principle, conformity to the rule of law is a matter of degree and entails a trade-off with other values; and this trade-off is determined politically. More substantive values such as democracy and human rights logically require trade-offs that are at least as complex and political. As these trade-offs are normally made domestically, the application of rule-of-law values in the international sphere can only be more political.

We will present the latter argument in a subsequent section that first underscores the political nature of all international law in general and then zooms in on the supposed conflict between Pillar 2 and international customary law. We argue that this conflict

[10] 'National' may be replaced by 'EU' – but that only underscores the point, as the EU is an important source of legislation and adjudication for its Member States.

[11] Tamanaha, above n 9.

[12] In fact, the UN Secretary General in 2004 described the rule of law as: 'a principle of governance in which all persons, institutions and entities, (…) including the State itself, are accountable to laws that are publicly promulgated, equally enforced and independently adjudicated, and which are consistent with international human rights norms and standards. It requires, as well, measures to ensure adherence to the principles of supremacy of law, equality before the law, accountability to the law, fairness in the application of the law, separation of powers, participation in decision-making, legal certainty, avoidance of arbitrariness and procedural and legal transparency': Secretary-General of the United Nations, *The rule of law and transitional justice in conflict and post-conflict societies*, S/2004/616. When this definition would have had significance for legal and political practice, quite a number of UN Member States would have found reason to object to it.

has an inevitable political dimension and that, as a result, its legal analysis can never be watertight. This weakens the claims that this conflict increases complexity and legal uncertainty, and that taxation based on the UTPR is excessive or arbitrary. We argue that a similar conclusion can be drawn with respect to the application of any other rule-of-law value at the international level.

We give two illustrations of this core argument. First, we examine the supposed democratic deficit in multinational tax law making. Insofar as the rule of law should incorporate substantive values, democratic decision making is particularly relevant, especially in the field of multinational tax law. In this field, there is a trade-off between the amount of democratic deliberation and the substantive tax policy outcome. In line with the preceding section, we will argue that taking a position in that trade-off is a political decision rather than a supreme Rule-of-Law value. Second, we examine one 'thin' or formal rule-of-Law value, namely the predictability of legal change. We will argue in the context of Pillar 2 that conformity to this value, again, is a matter of degree.

The Rule of Law

Waldron's discussion of the rule-of-Law concept shows that its content is not fixed.[13] Some authors use it to underscore the value of traditional customary law against legislative activism, while others connect it to human rights and social justice; yet others stick to formal requirements to laws and law making. Many of those elements map onto the distinction between 'thin' and 'thick' versions of the rule of law.[14]

The thinnest version is defined by Bingham as the notion 'that all persons and authorities within the state, whether public or private, should be bound by and entitled to the benefit of laws publicly and prospectively promulgated and publicly administered in the courts',[15] and by Tamanaha simply as '[t]he rule of law exists in a society when government officials and the populace are generally bound by and abide law'.[16] Others, especially Fuller and Raz, add formal requirements that the law should be able to meet, such as being general and stable, prospective, clear and practicable.[17]

What Fuller and Raz also did was to underscore the normative underpinning for a 'thin' concept of the rule of law in terms of personal freedom. The idea is that a free society does not require the rule of man, but generally applicable rules that are suited

[13] Waldron, above n 7.

[14] See, for an overview of the demands of 'thin' versions, S Daly, Chapter 2 in this volume. A different distinction is made by Lindsay, Chapter 3 in this volume, between a narrow scope rule of law (requiring legal norms to be general, prospective and impartial) and a wide scope rule of law (which 'concerns whether the government rules through law or through some extra-legal method').

[15] T Bingham, 'The Rule of Law' (2007) 66 *Cambridge Law Journal* 67, 69. Bingham himself went beyond pure formalism. He added sub-principles aimed at the functioning of the state, eg that the state should ensure the adequate protection of human rights.

[16] BZ Tamanaha, 'Functions of the Rule of Law' in J Meierhenrich and M Loughlin (eds) *The Cambridge Companion to the Rule of Law* (Cambridge: Cambridge University Press, 2021).

[17] Drawn from L Fuller, *The Morality of Law* (revised edn, New Haven CT: Yale University Press, 1969) 39, Raz has partially overlapping criteria that focus more strongly on legal protection by courts: J Raz, *The Authority of Law: Essays on Law and Morality* (Oxford: Oxford University Press, 1979) 214–18.

to guide people's choices as to their legal consequences. That is, a free society cannot exist without the rule of law in a formal sense: 'the law must be capable of guiding the behavior of its subjects.'[18] 'Law as guidance' entails that laws should be accessible to all, prospective, and reasonably stable. Predictability is key.[19]

Raz argued that this basic requirement has nothing to do with democracy or human rights.[20] But of those thicker values, democracy lies relatively close to the core concept of 'law as guidance'. Tamanaha's two-dimensional classification of rule-of-law values distinguishes between formal and substantive definitions, and identifies 'thin' versus 'thick' definitions in both categories.[21] In this scheme, democracy is not a substantive rule-of-law value but a formal one, insofar it is merely a political procedure and is not judged on the basis of its substantive outcomes.[22] A rule of law that includes democracy is the thickest of three formal definitions, the thinnest being 'rule by law' (that is, the mere exercise of control through positive law) and the middle one being legality (which includes the values stipulated by Raz and Fuller). When not prescribing any substantive outcomes such as negative and positive rights and social welfare, democracy is merely a formal criterion to be met by the legislative process, one step away from the commonly accepted legality requirement.[23]

That step can be defended on multiple grounds. For instance, whereas legality boils down to 'law as guidance', actual law-making is not necessarily aimed at or concerned with guidance – a government might want to signal some goal or concern without actually being prepared to commit to a clear norm.[24] A 'thin' concept of rule of law may offer some protection against such poor legislation by underscoring the value of the predictability of law. However, an inclusive law-making process would offer more protection because it better captures the intentions of the community – a point that is not usually reflected in legal analysis (which tends to construe monolithic legislative 'intent').[25]

[18] Raz, above n 17, 214.

[19] When we believe the rule of law to require that laws offer guidance, the implication could be that legal rules which do not meet that requirement cannot be law. Indeed, Fuller comes close to the normative statement that law should be predictable to constitute valid law. Fuller, above n 17, 39.

[20] Raz, above n 17, 211: 'A non-democratic legal system, based on the denial of human rights, on extensive poverty, on racial segregation, sexual inequalities, and religious persecution may, in principle, conform to the requirements of the rule of law better than any of the legal systems of the more enlightened Western democracies.'

[21] Tamanaha, above n 8, 91.

[22] Democracy is, in fact, often judged on its outcomes. In order to be called democratic, tax policy should arguably not only be legitimised by the democratic process but also effectuate the preferences of the demos: see J Jaakkola, 'A Democratic Dilemma of European Power to Tax: Reconstructing the Symbiosis Between Taxation and Democracy Beyond the State?' (2019) 20 *German Law Journal* 660.

[23] Tamanaha later moved democracy to the category of substantive definitions: B Tamanaha, 'A Concise Guide to the Rule of Law', St John's University School of Law Legal Studies, Research Paper Series No 07-0082, as noted in J Møller and SE Skaaning, 'Systematizing Thin and Thick Conceptions of the Rule of Law' (2012) *The Justice System Journal* 33, 136, 138.

[24] JA Grundfest and AC Pritchard, 'Statutes with Multiple Personality Disorders: The Value of Ambiguity in Statutory Design and Interpretation' (2002) 54 *Stanford Law Review* 627. In legal theory, the related concept is legislative intent. Intent can be understood as the will to express a (new) rule, as the will to give a text the status of law, or as the wish to achieve some result through the instrument of legal rules. M Matczak, 'Three Kinds of Intention in Law-making' (2017) 36 *Law and Philosophy* 651.

[25] There is an extensive jurisprudential literature on the identification of the purposes of the legislator. See, eg KA Shepsle, 'Congress Is a "They", not an "It": Legislative Intent as an Oxymoron' (1992) 12 *International*

Alternatively, in a liberal tradition where freedom is the underlying goal of the rule of law, one may argue that the rule of law requires democracy because one can only be free as a co-author of the laws one is subject to.[26] Even more fundamentally, echoing Habermas, one may stress that the rule of law requires a source of authority to be universally accepted. While its authority has long been anchored in the supremacy of natural law, our modern loss of faith in natural law leaves us with only democracy as a source of legitimacy of the legal order.[27]

Regardless of whether democracy (or even human rights) should be added to the definition of the rule of law, its core meaning remains 'law as guidance' and builds on predictability. However, in practice, laws cannot always meet the test of predictability. For instance, income tax law may be too complex to offer guidance to people who lack legal training. Apparently, we are able to live with some level of technicality and opaqueness in our laws. Homo economicus is not a fully informed agent, as it is costly to acquire and digest information.[28] In dealing with our legal environment, we probably assume that laws are generally reasonable, and only start paying closer attention when we need to. Predictability of how the law regulates choices, therefore, cannot be an all-overriding concern of the legislator. This may explain why Bingham added to his definition as quoted previously: 'I doubt if anyone would suggest that this statement, even if accurate as one of general principle, could be applied without exception or qualification. But it seems to me that any exception calls for close consideration and clear justification.' The reason is that we always need to balance rule-of-law requirements with other demands, such as effectiveness. As Raz put it: 'Conflict between the rule of law and other values is just what is to be expected. Conformity to the rule of law is a matter of degree, and though, other things being equal, the greater the conformity the better – other things are rarely equal. A lesser degree of conformity is often to be preferred precisely because it helps realization of other goals.'[29]

'Thick' versions of the rule of law build on and hence retain the elements of 'thinner' versions. Although there is no clear hierarchy between them,[30] all 'thick' versions have the 'thin' element of 'law as guidance' at their core. Hence, Raz's observation that '[c]onformity to the rule of law is a matter of degree'[31] logically applies to both 'thick' and 'thin' versions. Furthermore, the requirements added by 'thicker' versions, such as democracy or human rights, can only increase the complexity of the trade-off between the rule of law and other values.

Review of Law and Economics 239; JF Manning, 'Textualism as a Nondelegation Doctrine' (1997) 97 *Columbia Law Review* 673.

[26] See I Kant, *Political Writings* (Cambridge: Cambridge University Press, 1991) 78–80; J Habermas, *Between Facts and Norms: Contributions to a Discourse Theory of Law and Democracy* (William Rehg tr, Cambridge MA: MIT Press, 1996) 408.

[27] Habermas, above n 26.

[28] 'Rational choice' implies decision-making on the basis of limited information (up to the point that the marginal benefit of evaluating more information is exceeded by the marginal cost of acquiring it).

[29] Raz, above n 17, 228.

[30] Møller and Skaaning, above n 23.

[31] See text to n 29.

International Law as a Political Project

This trade-off also becomes no less complex on the international level. In fact, as we will argue in this section, the rule of law on the international level is hard to separate from politics. Koskenniemi,[32] well-known to international law scholars,[33] shows that international legal argument moves between two poles: between 'concrete' or 'apologetic' arguments on the one hand, and 'normative' or 'utopian' arguments on the other. Normative arguments represent the aspiration for a more just (cosmopolitan?) world order. The more normative an argument, the more political it is because the weaker is its reference to the real-world social context.[34] Concrete arguments, on the other hand, refer to actual state practice, meaning that a particular rule can be defended by pointing at actual (and perhaps contingent) state behaviour. But this then equates the law with the will of a state, making the law infinitely flexible. International law is then used as an apology for state power.[35] These normative and concrete arguments exclude each other.

Many international tax arguments, like arguments generally in international law, as Koskenniemi shows,[36] work this way.[37] We apply his insights to core issues of international tax. We first examine two issues related to fiscal sovereignty: unilateral tax competition and the division of taxing rights between countries. These issues do not directly relate to the rule of law but are intended as general examples that illustrate Koskenniemi's reasoning and at the same time highlight the normative tension that is present within all multinational tax initiatives. We then focus on the potential conflict between Pillar 2's UTPR and customary international law that may lead to rule-of-law concerns. Our analysis of those rule-of-law concerns is illustrative of our broader argument, namely that any international application of the rule of law is inseparable from political values.

Fiscal Sovereignty

Fiscal sovereignty is understood as the power to tax those with a 'nexus' or 'genuine link' to a territory; and to be able to design tax policy according to national preferences.[38] Under increasing externalities, it suffers from the 'sovereignty paradox': in order to be able to exercise their fiscal sovereignty, states have no choice but to cooperate – that

[32] M Koskenniemi, *From Apology to Utopia: The Structure of International Legal Argument* (Cambridge: Cambridge University Press, 2009).

[33] See, eg E Jouannet, 'Koskenniemi: A Critical Introduction' in M Koskenniemi (ed) *The Politics of International Law* (Oxford: Hart Publishing, 2011).

[34] ibid, 8.

[35] ibid, 7–9.

[36] Koskenniemi, above n 32.

[37] Koskenniemi's more general point with respect to international law is that it is impossible 'to make substantive decisions within the law which would imply no political choice': M Koskenniemi, 'The Politics of International Law' (1990) 1 *European Journal of International Law* 4, 31.

[38] D Ring, 'Democracy, Sovereignty and Tax Competition: The Role of Tax Sovereignty in Shaping Tax Cooperation' (2009) 9 *Florida Tax Review* 555; P Dietsch and T Rixen, 'Tax Competition and Global Background Justice' (2014) 22 *Journal of Political Philosophy* 150.

is, to limit their freedom in setting competitive tax rates so as to protect the freedom of all states in designing tax policies according to national preferences.[39] In the frame of Koskenniemi's dichotomy, the fiscal sovereignty argument is either normative or concrete.

On the one hand, we cannot define a state's fiscal sovereignty without a notion of the fiscal spheres of other states; it requires delimitation. Unilateral tax policy autonomy thus requires an external theory that attaches normative weight to the interests of other jurisdictions.[40] For instance, Risse and Meyer argue that '[a]ny state should design its fiscal policy to advance justice, both domestic and global'.[41] But such theories can be criticised for being detached from reality, for being utopian or infeasible, closer to natural law than to social facts, and hence political. On the other hand, we cannot speak of fiscal sovereignty with reference to an external theory, without losing what 'makes up the fiscal state'. Fiscal sovereignty protects important notions such as self-determination, consent and equality. It requires respecting individual states' (democratic) justification for certain tax policy choices and hence refers to the concrete status quo. But abandoning the normative, utopian, external theory and relying on the status quo instead is a political decision as well: one would then opt for a world in which states are sellers of investment and residence opportunities, where their competitiveness is determined by pre-established divisions in state power, resources and wealth, and where inequality between taxpayers is affected by their ability to enjoy the fruits of global mobility.[42] That choice is vulnerable to the critique that 'the law' is not driven by principle, but forms an apology for a structural bias of power and interests.

The discussion concerning fair international distribution of taxing rights works in a similar way. States' fiscal sovereignty currently allows them to conclude bilateral tax treaties as they see fit – somewhat analogously to freedom of contract between individuals. The result, a territorially based international tax system that favours taxation by the residence state, is mainly shaped by the parties with the most bargaining power: capital exporting (OECD) nations who prefer limitations on source-country withholding taxation. This fundamentally restricts the rights of source (capital importing) countries.[43] A change to a more equal division of the international tax base cannot be construed on the intellectual basis of fiscal sovereignty and contract freedom alone. Freedom of contract itself provides no normative guidelines on how to deal with structural differences in negotiating power between treaty partners, or with the effects of tax treaties on third parties.[44] Fiscal sovereignty in this sense becomes vulnerable to

[39] Dietsch draws an analogy with individual liberty: that 'has to be limited in order maximise the analogous liberty of everyone else': P Dietsch, 'Rethinking Sovereignty in International Fiscal Policy' (2011) 37 *Review of International Studies* 2107, 2117; P Hongler, *Justice in International Tax Law* (Amsterdam: IBFD, 2019) 277–78.

[40] Dietsch, ibid, 2115.

[41] M Risse and M Meyer, 'Tax Competition and Global Interdependence' (2019) 27 *The Journal of Political Philosophy* 480, 492.

[42] T Dagan, 'Klaus Vogel Lecture 2021: Unbundled Tax Sovereignty – Refining the Challenges' (2022) 76 *Bulletin for International Taxation* 318.

[43] See A Christians and L van Apeldoorn, *Tax Cooperation in an Unjust World* (Oxford: Oxford University Press, 2022) ch 2.

[44] BN van Ganzen, DM Broekhuijsen and H Vording, 'Contract Theory as a Guide to Fairness in Tax Treaties' in I Lindsay (ed) *Fairness in International Taxation* (Oxford: Hart Publishing, forthcoming).

the critical theory that the current international tax system is hegemonic and distributionally biased towards existing structures of power and expertise (that is, favouring residence taxation claims).[45] Instead, any theory of tax base distribution that departs from fiscal sovereignty and contract freedom in bilateral tax treaties in order to reduce these persistent injustices (for instance, entitlement based on location of economic activities; 'inter-nation equity';[46] or the 'equal benefit principle'[47]) requires a cosmopolitan 'world tax regime' and negates a nation's right to liberty and self-determination. Most comprehensive 'tax cooperation' theories are hence open to the critique of being too far from social context, infeasible, utopian and political.[48]

Validity of the UTPR under International Custom

The same argumentative structure exists in discussions of a more concrete legal nature, as illustrated by the recent argument on the validity of the OECD's (and the EU's) work on Pillar 2 as regards the UTPR under international custom. Some authors hold that the UTPR is contrary to principles of customary international law, in particular against 'well established principles' of 'nexus' that underpin residence and source taxation.[49]

Customary international law is based on the presumption that there is a material practice of states (the objective element), grounded on those states' belief that this practice is obligatory (*opinio juris*, the subjective element).[50] As there are no independently applicable criteria for ascertaining international customary law, it is based on the intensity of evidence in favour of state practice and *opinio juris*.[51] Finding a customary law argument is at the same time a normative affair and an infinitely flexible affair, because the subjective element is analogous to what Koskenniemi calls the 'normative' argument, whereas the objective element is 'concrete' or 'apologetic'. The problem is that those arguments are incommensurable: on the one hand, international customary law is based on the practices of states, but on the other hand serves to regulate those very practices.

[45] TD Magalhães, 'What Is Really Wrong with Global Tax Governance and How to Properly Fix It' (2018) 10 *World Tax Journal* 499; and his PhD Thesis: *Critical Theory of International Tax Law, Teoria Crítica Do Direito Tributário Internacional* (Belo Horizonte: Letramento, 2020).

[46] RA Musgrave and PB Musgrave, 'Inter-nation Equity' in RM Bird and JG Head (eds) *Modern Fiscal Issues: Essays in Honor of Carl S. Shoup* (Toronto: University of Toronto Press, 1972) 63.

[47] Christians and van Apeldoorn, above n 43.

[48] Exemplary in this regard is T Dagan, *International Tax Policy: Between Competition and Cooperation* (Cambridge: Cambridge University Press, 2017): Dagan oscillates between the two poles and aims to find a compromise.

[49] See n 2.

[50] The argument is drawn from Koskenniemi, above n 32, ch 6.

[51] Koskenniemi, above n 37, 26. According to the International Law Commission, this 'involves a careful examination of available evidence .... To establish that a claim concerning the existence or the extent of a rule of customary international law is well-founded thus entails a search for a practice that has gained such acceptance among States that it may be considered to be the expression of a legal right or obligation': International Law Commission, *Draft conclusions on identification of customary international law, with commentaries* (A/73/10; GE.18-13644) 125.

Evidence of a practice as regards 'nexus' – for instance, residence and source state taxation as evidenced by almost all tax treaties – is used by scholars to criticise the legal validity of the UTPR under the 'common approach'.[52] The goals of this 'newer' Pillar 2 consensus as regard taxing nexus, are, however, put forth by the same states, as they want the Pillar 2 rules to work and be widely implemented. Evidence of the widely shared *belief* of states that the 'old' nexus principles are legally binding, must somehow be harmonised with a statement of states contrary to that belief. The argument that the new consensus on UTPR runs against existing nexus principles of customary international law, is, in other words, an 'I-know-you-better-than-you'-argument.

The opposite statement, namely that the UTRP does not run against customary international law, can be similarly deconstructed. To argue that Pillar 2's UTPR is valid, a new nexus link is introduced, which is said to form customary law. Under this new customary nexus link, any jurisdiction hosting a constituent entity that is part of the MNE group is said to have a customary connection with the MNE group's income.[53] But this argument conflates the (informal and even partial) consensus under Pillar 2's 'common approach' with the first requirement of international customary law: state practice. If states consider the 'new' nexus rule binding, why do they not explicitly say so? It raises the question why we would need treaties, and state consent to treaties, if we could do with any form of state consensus to establish binding international (tax) law. It makes the argument defensible only on the basis of the political importance of the subject matter.

Thus, the political consensus regarding Pillar 2 and its UTPR is at the same time the object that is precluded or limited by customary international law; and the very criterion to test whether customary international law should preclude it. As a result of this paradox, neither of the two positions above can be based on watertight reasoning. This weakens any claims that taxation based on the UTPR is excessive or arbitrary.

While the supposed conflict of the UTPR and customary international law is a very specific example of how multinational tax rules may lead to rule-of-law concerns, we think that the paradox of customary international law as described above is analogously present in the rule of law in general. The rule of law on the one hand serves to limit political choices by legal means in order to protect individuals from arbitrary decisions by lawmakers, but on the other hand, its definition is a political choice itself – absent a belief in natural law. The intensity of this problem increases with the substantivity or thickness of its definition. For instance, the questions whether Pillar 2's tax burdens on individual entities violate the right to property[54] and whether its minimum rate violates the right to social security[55] are essentially political: what is an excessive tax burden; what is the appropriate minimum rate? Defining a substantive rule of law is a challenge

[52] The 'common approach' stands for informal international consensus on Pillar 2 and is used by the OECD to envisage implementation of Pillar 2 rules in domestic law systems. It is hence not a treaty and is perhaps unlikely to turn into one. See, for this argument, J VanderWolk, 'The UTPR is Inconsistent with the Nexus Requirement of Tax Treaties' Kluwer International Tax Blog, 26 October 2022. On the implementation of Pillar 2: OECD, *Tax Challenges Arising from the Digitalisation of the Economy – Global Anti-Base Erosion Model Rules* (2021).

[53] Avi-Yonah, above n 2.

[54] See text to n 5.

[55] See text to n 6.

already on the national level, but an additional problem with its application on an international level is that we would require one overarching, global definition. Echoing Koskenniemi, that scenario is utopian. Alternatively, the rule of law may be domestically defined. But then, we run into the problems of legal pluralism, making it hard to separate the rule of law from power, persuasion and politics at the international level.

Hence, there is a case for more formal rule-of-law definitions on which countries can more easily agree. However, we aim to show in the next two sections that the international application of formal versions may similarly depend on political considerations. We first focus on the value of democracy, which, we have argued, can be seen as a 'thick' but formal rule-of-law value that lies relatively close to the legality principle. We then examine the value of predictability, which is an unequivocally 'thin' value.

Democracy as an International Rule-of-Law Value

An analysis of democracy as an international rule-of-law value begins with the question whether democracy is indeed a rule-of-law value. This chapter has listed several arguments in favour of that position, and indeed, the incorporation of democracy into the Rule-of-Law concept has been gaining some momentum recently, as evidenced, for instance, by a communication of the European Commission and by a 'rule of law checklist' of the Venice Commission of the Council of Europe.[56] Still, a quick look at the definitions by Fuller, Raz and Bingham shows that the inclusion of democracy is not uncontroversial; and there are good reasons to limit oneself to a purely formal definition based on the legality principle.[57] However important, democracy may well be a separate value instead of being part of 'the' rule of law. But that discussion is semantical here. In many concerns expressed recently about democratic deficits in multinational tax law making, democracy in fact functions in a similar way as 'the' rule of law: it is invoked as a criterion to test whether a certain tax policy, or the governance process behind it, is acceptable. Formulated differently, it serves as a supreme value that limits certain political outcomes.

The starting point of most worries about the democratic nature of multinational tax legislation is that parliaments are less involved in its drafting process than they are in drafting domestic laws. For instance, Lind expects that global tax cooperation 'will require tax administrations to be more active in the law-making process as the implementation of the toolboxes provided by the OECD and EU becomes more of

[56] European Commission, *Further strengthening the Rule of Law within the Union. State of play and possible next steps* (COM/2019/163), underscoring that 'all public powers always act … in accordance with the values of democracy and fundamental rights …' and that '[t]he rule of law includes … principles such as legality, implying a transparent, accountable, democratic and pluralistic process for enacting laws'. Relatedly, the Venice Commission of the Council of Europe spells out various criteria for a 'transparent, accountable, inclusive and democratic' process for enacting law, including the supremacy of Parliament and a meaningful opportunity for the public to provide input to draft legislation: European Commission for Democracy Through Law (Venice Commission), *Rule of Law Checklist* (711/2013) 13.

[57] As argued by Lindsay, Chapter 3 in this volume, incorporating 'thick' values into the rule of law blurs the meaning of the concept and reduces consensus about its normative significance. Furthermore, it encourages debates over which values to include, and those debates distract from direct analyses of the values as such.

a tax technical implementation unlike past practices where the domestic legislatures have taken their own initiatives based on the needs and traditions of respective individual nations'.[58] Similarly, Wiman observes that international tax law is increasingly made not by states but by groups of experts: civil servants working at domestic and international (tax) administrations who seem to rely on the public input of (mostly commercial and non-governmental) stakeholders.[59] Relatedly, Essers argues that 'the present debate on international tax justice is polluted by power play and deception.'[60] The OECD and G20, and their output such as the BEPS Action Plan, suffer from democracy deficits. What is required, says Essers, is more 'Habermas', that is, 'deliberative democracy' between peoples, in which 'a true dialogue with national parliaments and citizens will be necessary'.[61] The point of all three authors is not that democratically elected parliaments should be able to formally endorse multinational tax rules, which they are, but that elected representatives of the people should be actively engaged with the legislation that implements multinational tax rules.[62] As Peters argues, that engagement diminishes once governments delegate the matter to the OECD.[63]

Peters refers to Scharpf's distinction between input legitimacy (the government system itself, which should be 'by the people') and output legitimacy (the actual policy output, 'for the people').[64] Scharpf himself underlines the trade-off between these concepts in the EU: the unanimity required for many decisions on an EU level (the input side) results in an extensive bargaining process that stands in the way of an effective resolution of problems caused by European integration, such as tax competition (the output side).[65] A similar trade-off is mentioned by de la Feria.[66] Peters notes that Pillar 2 is rooted in the same thinking because the OECD apparently accepts a defective democratic input – relying solely on expert knowledge – in order to effectively resolve the collective action problem of tax competition.

Echoing Scharpf, Peters suggests that sole reliance on output legitimacy requires a form of normative consensus about the policy output in question, which, he argues, does not exist with respect to the global minimum tax.[67] This argument seems to suffer from Koskenniemi's paradox explained in the previous section. The trade-off between input legitimacy and output legitimacy implies that we can legitimise a policy based on its effective solution to a collective action problem, while reducing the standards

[58] Y Lind, 'Blurring the Separation of Powers. A Legal and Political Study of the Phenomenon of Tax Administrations Moving from the Executive Branch towards the Legislative Branch' (2023) 21 *eJournal of Tax Research* 383, 405.

[59] B Wiman, 'Klaus Vogel Lecture 2022: Who Should Be in the Driver's Seat in Developing International Tax Norms – Civil Servants or National Parliaments?' (2023) 77 *Bulletin for International Taxation* 157.

[60] P Essers, Klaus Vogel Lecture 2013, 'International Tax Justice between Machiavelli and Habermas' (2014) 68 *Bulletin for International Taxation* 54, 55.

[61] Essers, ibid, 65. See also C Peters, *On the Legitimacy of International Tax Law* (Amsterdam: IBFD, 2014).

[62] See also S Hemels, 'Tax Autonomy from a Member State Perspective: Are We Faced with a Democratic Deficit?' Erasmus University Rotterdam, 29.

[63] C Peters, 'The Legitimacy of the OECD's Work on Pillar Two: An Analysis of the Overconfidence in a 'Devilish Logic'' (2023) 51 *Intertax* 554, 561.

[64] F Scharpf, *Governing in Europe: Effective and Democratic?* (Oxford: Oxford University Press, 1999), as cited in Peters, above n 63, 559.

[65] ibid.

[66] R de la Feria, 'Pillar 2, Fiat, and the EU Unanimity Rule on Tax Matters' (2023) 32 *EC Tax Review* 2.

[67] Peters, above n 63, 566.

of democratic consensus-building (for the reason that tax competition is a multilateral Prisoners' Dilemma where it takes only a few defectors to render the outcome greatly sub-optimal). Here, formulated in terms of Koskenniemi's dichotomy, democratic consensus is limited by a 'normative' argument. At the same time, it is part of a 'concrete' argument: following Scharpf and Peters, the existing amount of consensus would be the very criterion on the basis of which we are allowed to make this trade-off. The consequence of this dual role of democratic consensus is that we cannot invoke it as a supreme value to judge the normative right of the OECD to implement Pillar 2; this judgement is instead political.

Peters also argues that insofar we do make a trade-off between input legitimacy and output legitimacy, a precondition is that 'the governance process of the OECD should meet burdensome standards of 'good' governance including accountability', which he and Schmidt call 'throughput legitimacy'.[68] Throughput legitimacy requires, for instance, that stakeholders can evaluate the work of technical experts and that national parliaments are more involved in the process than merely rubber-stamping the outcome. Although we are very sympathetic to these goals, we again find it hard to view them as absolute and independent touchstones of the acceptability of the policy, and of the authority of the policymaker, as several authors seem to do.

Hemels, for instance, argues that we need 'fully democratically legitimized legislation' (with which she would mean input and/or throughput legitimacy) 'that has been discussed openly, and not just on a technical level behind closed doors, by national parliaments in the presence of journalists and the broader public',[69] even if this reduces the quality of the policy outcome; otherwise 'we might end up in a technocratic dictature'.[70] Instead, we would argue that democratic deliberation, like conformity to other rule-of-law values, is a matter of degree, and that the amount of input and throughput legitimacy required in multinational policy making is a political choice. We would also argue that throughput legitimacy is part of the political trade-off between input and output legitimacy, rather than an independent criterion outside this trade-off. For one thing, if all national parliaments had the right to evaluate and amend the Pillar 2 proposal at every stage of the process, there probably would have been no output at all.

The argument above applies to a greater extent on the international level than on the national level, where the requirements for the democratic process might be stricter. The underlying reason is legal pluralism regarding the definition of democracy as a rule-of-law value. Barring the fact that countries take divergent stances towards democracy as such, the point is that different countries have different preferences for policy output, such that their input/output/throughput trade-offs will also be different and not necessarily commensurable. Thus, while technical accountability and involvement of national parliaments in Pillar 2 certainly are desirable goals, it is infeasible to use a particular minimum level of accountability and involvement as an independent touchstone of the legitimacy of the OECD's Pillar 2 project.

[68] ibid, 554; V Schmidt, *Europe's Crisis of Legitimacy. Governing by Rules and Ruling by Numbers in the Eurozone* (Oxford: Oxford University Press, 2020) 31.

[69] Hemels, above n 62, 28.

[70] ibid, 30.

Whatever trade-off between input, output and throughput legitimacy is made, the formal democratic requirement remains intact: national parliaments must approve the new legislation. Therefore, the trade-off should not be put on a slippery slope towards a 'technocratic dictature' insofar the outcome does not maximise the levels of input and/or throughput legitimacy.[71] To most rule-of-law theorists it is obvious that none of its values are absolute, internationally as well as nationally. To repeat Raz, 'other things being equal, the greater the conformity the better', but 'other things are rarely equal'.[72] In the words of Bingham, any deviation still 'calls for close consideration and clear justification'. Closely considering and justifying the governance process behind Pillar 2, we should take as a benchmark the democratic nature of national tax law making and, in particular, the situation before the Pillar 2 project was launched.

Although direct parliamentary involvement in tax law making is greater on the national level than on the international level, it does not seem fair to lament the technocratic nature of multinational tax law without any reference to how national tax law is often made: we may safely assume that it is also largely written by unelected civil servants. Perhaps, this process behind closed doors even may have the incidental advantage that it reduces the influence of lobby groups, such that the outcome is based on a fairer weighing of everyone's interests. Another point is that in a world with unrestricted tax competition, countries have no option but to act as competitive sellers of investment and residence opportunities, such that their national processes of law-making are distorted by non-domestic interests and concerns. The resulting unequal concern for mobile and immobile constituents is arguably a grave violation of input legitimacy.[73] One could even argue that the categorisation of legitimacy into input, throughput and output becomes semantical in the first place, because regardless of the democratic control exercised by national parliaments, a wide range of policy options are out of the question because capital mobility renders them unaffordable – namely those policies that significantly raise the effective unilateral tax rate on corporate income. Again, we acknowledge that parliaments have more direct influence on the drafting of national tax laws than on the new multinational rules aimed at curbing tax competition. However, given the above problems of democratic legitimacy that exist without those new rules, we would be hesitant to say that Pillar 2 significantly worsens the democratic legitimacy of tax policy compared to the situation ex ante.

As in the previous section, this particular policy issue can also be seen as an illustration of a broader point. We have argued that democracy is often invoked as a Rule-of-Law value, because it serves as a touchstone for the acceptability of a policy and of the legitimacy of policy making. As with any other Rule-of-Law value, conformity to it is already a matter of degree on the national level. But its international application adds another dimension: countries define the value nationally, and their different conceptions of what the value entails might not be commensurable on the international level. This makes it difficult to appeal to Rule-of-Law values internationally, however important these values are.

[71] See text to n 70.

[72] See text to n 29.

[73] See generally T Dagan, 'The Tragic Choices of Tax Policy in a Globalized Economy' in Y Brauner and M Stewart (eds) *Tax, Law and Development* (Cheltenham: Edward Elgar Publishing, 2013).

Predictability as an International Rule-of-Law Value

Finally, to show that even 'thin' Rule-of-Law values may run into the problem of being political, we briefly highlight a debate on the value of predictability. This debate hinges upon 'legitimate expectations'.

Ignoring definitional issues, the core question is: when tax law changes, should losers be compensated?[74] The notion that legal subjects should not suffer retroactive effect is old. As Thomas Hobbes put it: 'No Law, made after a fact done, can make it a Crime: because … a Positive Law cannot be taken notice of, before it be made; and therefore cannot be obligatory'.[75] And indeed, '(t)he principle that the legal effect of conduct should ordinarily be assessed under the law that existed when the conduct took place has timeless and universal human appeal'.[76] The underlying argument is that legal subjects should be able to rely on the law, or the law loses its capacity to offer guidance. Therefore, the issue of predictability does not merely involve laws that inherently have retroactive effects, but also overlaps with the issues of complexity and legal uncertainty: when rules are very complex or when conflicts between new rules and existing laws and treaties are still unresolved, subjects will find it difficult to understand the legal consequences of their actions ex ante. Exactly these concerns have been raised with respect to current initiatives in international tax law.[77]

In opposition to the traditions that the ex-post legal consequences of one's actions should always be predictable, a New View on retroactivity has developed, starting with Graetz and Kaplow.[78] The New View is clearly rooted in the law-and-economics tradition with economic efficiency of legal rules as the key concept, and free market transactions as the benchmark.[79] The core of the New View is the idea that the risks of legal transitions are best borne by market parties rather than by the government (that is, the community of taxpayers at large). People make their best decisions when they take into account all relevant information; this includes information about all types of risks that they may face. And changes in the law are risks – from the taxpayer's perspective comparable to business cycles or natural disasters. In principle, there should be no relief for losses caused by changing law because it would discourage taxpayers to anticipate socially desirable changes in the law. The New View rejects the 'reliance' argument for being circular – people's reliance on old rules should be protected because they rely on those old rules. This circularity of the reliance argument is reminiscent of Koskenniemi's paradox applied in the previous sections, which we will not repeat here. Instead, the New View replaces reliance by expectations.

[74] For an analysis of the prospectivity requirement, see generally Gillis, Chapter 4 in this this volume.

[75] T Hobbes, *Leviathan* (first published 1651, R Tuck ed, Cambridge: Cambridge University Press, 1992) XXVII, 203. Note that Hobbes only refers to ex-post changing the law.

[76] *Kaiser Aluminium Chemical Corporation v. Bonjorno* [1990] 494 US 827, Scalia, concurring, para 67.

[77] See text to n 1.

[78] MJ Graetz, 'Legal Transitions: The Case of Retroactivity in Income Tax Revision' (1977) 126 *University of Pennsylvania Law Review* 47; L Kaplow, 'An Economic Analysis of Legal Transitions' (1986) 99 *Harvard Law Review* 509.

[79] Some recent overviews of the discussion: M Doran, 'Legislative Compromise and Tax Transition Policy' (2007) 74 *University of Chicago Law Review* 545; RL Revesz and AL Westfahl Kong, 'Regulatory Change and Optimal Transition Relief' (2010) 105 *Northwestern University Law Review* 1581.

Taxpayers should be taught not to rely on the improbable (that is, unalterable law) but to expect the reasonable (that is, adaptation of law to changing preferences and circumstances). In that way, the transaction costs of legal change are reduced to a minimum.

The ensuing debate has generated some conclusions that seem to express a certain level of consensus. One is that the level of legal certainty to be provided always requires trade-offs, especially against any need to adapt laws to changing priorities, preferences and circumstances.[80] And the second is that an evaluation of the legitimacy of taxpayers' expectations may be required to decide whether they should receive protection from retroactivity. Could they believe bona fide that the tax law would not change – or should they have picked up signs that legal norms would be adapted to changing social perceptions?[81]

Applying these considerations to the uncertainty created by multinational tax law-making, the core issue is what MNE taxpayers may legitimately expect as the architecture of cross-border tax law is being adapted. If changing circumstances require new rules, if complexity is required for these rules to function properly, and if conflict with existing laws and treaties is unavoidable, can the rule of law be invoked in arguments against these new rules? We doubt it. While the above considerations do not negate that 'thin' rule-of-law values such as predictability, prospectivity, clarity and stability are very much desirable, it again becomes clear that conformity to these values is a matter of degree and involves political choices. As a result, the extra dimension of complexity added on the international level also applies in the case of 'thin' values: as the rule of law is politically defined, we either need one overarching theory or must rely on the problematic reality of legal pluralism. As there is no international theory on what taxpayers may legitimately expect from new initiatives in tax law, it is hard to invoke 'law as guidance' as an argument against these new rules.

Conclusion

The concept of the rule of law limits the political discretion of lawmakers by legal means. Conformity to the rule of law is a matter of degree and entails trade-offs with other values, such that, paradoxically, the concept itself is to some extent political. This observation primarily applies to 'thick' or substantive rule-of-law definitions; but even the interpretation of 'thin' versions based on legality and predictability may require political choices. As countries have different value systems and no single international conception of the rule of law exists, the use of rule-of-law values in the international realm, like all other international law, is often hard to separate from power, persuasion and politics.

[80] D Shaviro, *When Rules Change: An Economic and Political Analysis of Transition Relief and Retroactivity* (Chicago: Chicago University Press, 2000).

[81] JE Fisch, 'Retroactivity and Legal Change: An Equilibrium Approach' (1997) 110 *Harvard Law Review* 1055, 1119; J Prebble, R Prebble and C Vidler Smith, 'Legislation with Retrospective Effect, with Particular Reference to Tax Loopholes and Avoidance' (2006) 22 *New Zealand Universities Law Review* 17.

In analyses of multinational tax initiatives, authors should therefore be cautious in asserting that the law-making process is 'undemocratic'; that the new rules create too much legal uncertainty; or that they conflict with customary international law or human rights. Instead of functioning as strict and supreme criteria, these concepts are multifaceted and open to divergent interpretations. Although multinational tax law should be as prospective, clear, stable and democratic as possible, deviations from these criteria should be possible, provided that they are closely considered and clearly justified.

14

The OECD as a Lawmaker, the Rule of Law and the Instructive Case of New Zealand

MICHAEL LITTLEWOOD*

Abstract

The New Zealand government has been a wholehearted supporter of the OECD's BEPS (Base Erosion and Profit Shifting) project since its inception in 2012. In some instances, it has taken the traditional approach of enacting legislation putting the OECD's recommendations into its own words. In others, however, it has enacted legislation that incorporates in New Zealand law documents, or parts of documents, produced by the OECD – most importantly, the *Model GloBE Rules*. Consequently, these documents, or parts of them, are now part of New Zealand law. This approach to legislative drafting – called 'incorporation by reference' – has several advantages and its use in various other contexts is well established; using it to define the scope of a tax system, however, seems to be jurisprudentially and constitutionally novel, and perhaps contrary to the rule of law.

Introduction

The New Zealand government has been a wholehearted supporter of the OECD's BEPS project since its inception in 2012 and it has amended the country's tax legislation to implement most of the OECD's recommendations relating to BEPS. For Parliament to enact rules aimed at preventing avoidance is of course nothing new.[1] What is new,

* I am grateful to Casey Plunket, Carmel Peters and Trish Ieong, all of the New Zealand Inland Revenue Department, for sharing with me their views on some of the matters the subject of this chapter. They obviously bear no responsibility whatever for my conclusions or interpretations and probably disagree with at least some of them. I am grateful also to Alex Raskolnikov for some helpful suggestions and to Lauren Aspoas, Alex McClintock and Kelly Ding for their assistance with the research upon which the chapter is based.

[1] On the relationship between tax avoidance and the rule of law, see especially Lindsay, Chapter 3 in this volume.

however, is that some of these amendments refer expressly to documents produced by the OECD in such a way that they, or, at least, parts of them, are now part of the law of New Zealand – a drafting technique called 'incorporation by reference'.[2]

In particular, first, the Income Tax Act 2007 now contains rules dealing with hybrids, and these rules incorporate-by-reference parts of the OECD's two hybrids reports (the *Hybrids Mismatch Report* and the *Branch Mismatch Report*).[3] Secondly, the transfer-pricing rules contained in the Income Tax Act have been amended so as to incorporate-by-reference parts of the OECD's Transfer Pricing Guidelines.[4] Thirdly, the Tax Administration Act 1994 has been amended so as to incorporate-by-reference parts of the Country-by-Country reporting recommendations set out in the Transfer Pricing Guidelines.[5] Fourthly, and most importantly, the Income Tax Act has been amended so as to incorporate-by-reference not only the whole of the OECD's Pillar Two Model GloBE Rules (the Model GloBE Rules or the Model Rules)[6] (subject to some minor qualifications) but also the whole of the Commentary on them.[7]

The incorporation in domestic tax law of text produced by an organisation such as the OECD is novel and its appropriateness is not self-evident. The first aim of this chapter, therefore, is to examine its likely efficacy, as a matter of tax law reform. Moreover, whereas some of the legislation's references to OECD materials are static (referring to documents published prior to the enactment of the legislation), others are ambulatory – that is, the reference is to the document as amended from time to time by the OECD. This ambulatory approach will mean that any revision of the document by the OECD will of itself constitute an amendment of New Zealand law.[8] This might be a good idea, but for the New Zealand Parliament to have effectively delegated legislative power to a body over which it has no control whatsoever seems to be jurisprudentially and constitutionally novel, and to require some refinement of the notion of the rule of law, as traditionally understood – especially since it seems safe to assume that the OECD would be barely even aware that, in revising its documentation, it would be changing New Zealand law. The second aim of the chapter, therefore, is to examine this aspect of the amendments.

[2] See generally JM Keyes, 'Incorporation by Reference in Legislation' (2004) 25 *Statute Law Review* 180; Legislation Design and Advisory Committee (an agency of the New Zealand Government), *Legislation Guidelines: 2021 edition* (New Zealand Government, 2021) [15.3].

[3] OECD, *Neutralising the Effects of Hybrid Mismatch Arrangements, Action 2 – 2015 Final Report*, OECD/G20 Base Erosion and Profit Shifting Project (Paris: OECD Publishing, 2015 (the *Hybrids Mismatch Report*); OECD, *Neutralising the Effects of Branch Mismatch Arrangements, Action 2: Inclusive Framework on BEPS*, OECD/G20 Base Erosion and Profit Shifting Project (Paris: OECD Publishing, 2015) (the *Branch Mismatch Report*); Income Tax Act 2007 (NZ) ss FH 1 and FH 11.

[4] OECD, *OECD Transfer Pricing Guidelines for Multinational Enterprises and Tax Administrations*, OECD Publishing, Paris, 2022 (the Transfer Pricing Guidelines); Income Tax Act 2007 (NZ) ss GC 6 and GC 13. See also Income Act 2007 (NZ), ss GB 54 and YD 4B(4).

[5] Tax Administration Act 1994 (NZ), s 78G(1)(a).

[6] OECD, *Tax Challenges Arising from the Digitalisation of the Economy – Global Anti-Base Erosion Model Rules (Pillar Two)* (OECD Publishing, Paris, 2021); Income Tax Act 2007 (NZ), subpart HP.

[7] OECD, *Tax Challenges Arising from the Digitalisation of the Economy – Commentary to the Global Anti-Base Erosion Model Rules (Pillar Two), First Edition* (Paris: OECD Publishing, 2022) Income Tax Act 2007 (NZ), subpart HP.

[8] Inland Revenue (NZ), *OECD Pillar Two: GLoBE Rules for New Zealand: An Officials' Issues Paper*, May 2022 [10.6]–[10.14].

Incorporation by Reference

Incorporation by reference is a well-established drafting technique. One distinguished commentator – John Mark Keyes – has explained it as follows: 'This technique involves providing in a legislative text that material expressed elsewhere is part of the text, even though it is not reproduced in the text itself.'[9] The consequence is that the material referred to 'has the same binding legal effect as the legislative text and is judicially enforceable'.[10]

It is necessary to distinguish between incorporation-by-reference and where a statute refers to material *without* incorporating it.[11] As will be seen, the New Zealand Parliament has used both approaches; in some instances the legislation refers to OECD materials so as to incorporate them; in others it refers to OECD materials without incorporating them – mainly to confirm that the materials, whilst not having the force of the statute, are nonetheless relevant as a guide to its interpretation.

According to Keyes, there are four main types of cases in which the incorporation-by-reference technique is used.[12] The first is where a provision in a legislative text refers to another provision in the same text, to avoid replicating it. This is common and unexceptional, including in tax statutes. For example, section YA 1 of New Zealand's Income Tax Act provides (among other matters) that 'assessable income' 'is defined in section BD 1(5)' of the same Act. Secondly, a statute might refer to 'some other legislative text enacted in the same jurisdiction'.[13] This, too, is common and unexceptional, including in tax statutes. For example, New Zealand's GST statute provides that the term 'resident' has the same meaning under that Act as under the Income Tax Act.[14] The third type of case is where a statute refers to a legislative text enacted in some other jurisdiction. Keyes gives examples showing that this is common. It would seem to be unusual in tax, but examples can be found in the US, where it is common for state income taxes to 'piggyback' on the federal income tax. For example, the Tax Code of the US State of Virginia § 58.1-301 states:

> Any term used in this chapter shall have the same meaning as when used in a comparable context in the laws of the United States relating to federal income taxes, unless a different meaning is clearly required.

Fourthly, some statutes refer to 'non-legislative texts, such as technical standards or international agreements'.[15] It is perhaps worth noting that this fourth category seems potentially problematic, in that Keyes's two examples of it – technical standards and international agreements – have very little in common. An example of the incorporation-by-reference of an international agreement might be where an EU member state

[9] Keyes, above n 2, 180.
[10] ibid, 182. See eg, *R v Secretary of State for Social Services, ex p Camden London Borough Council* [1987] 2 All ER 560 (CA).
[11] *Reference re Manitoba Language Rights (No 3)* [1992] SCR 212, 288, quoted in Keyes, above n 2, 180–181.
[12] Keyes, above n 2, 181.
[13] ibid.
[14] Goods and Services Tax Act 1985 (NZ), s 2.
[15] Keyes, above n 2, 181.

has incorporated in its domestic law materials produced by the European Union;[16] and an example in tax is where a statute incorporates a double tax agreement (DTA) in domestic law (though in the case of New Zealand that is invariably done by incorporation-by-repetition rather than incorporation-by-reference – that is, the entire text of the DTA is repeated in a schedule to the legislation).[17]

The incorporation-by-reference technique seems traditionally to have been used in subordinate legislation for the purpose of giving legal effect to technical standards, such as those governing vehicles and construction.[18] Many countries, however, have incorporated various OECD materials in their domestic law. In particular, most countries have networks of DTAs closely based on the OECD Model; most countries rules relating to transfer pricing are closely aligned to the OECD's transfer pricing guidelines; and many countries have enacted rules implementing the OECD's recommendations relating to hybrids. It might be said, then, that what the New Zealand Government has done is nothing new; or, at least, that it is no more than another step along a road already taken. But the New Zealand Government's incorporation of the *GloBE Rules*, in particular, seems more like a quantum leap forward. The reason is that the *GloBE Rules*, once they take effect as New Zealand law, will impose two entirely new taxes; and for a tax to be imposed by incorporation-by-reference seems, to say the least, unusual.

Hybrids: Subpart FH

Subpart FH of the Income Tax Act comprises 15 sections (FH 1 to FH 15) added to the Act in 2018.[19] It is aimed at 'hybrid mismatches', meaning arrangements that are either (a) treated as an entity in one jurisdiction and as transparent or 'look through' in another jurisdiction or (b) treated as equity in one jurisdiction and as debt in another jurisdiction. For example, such an arrangement might be treated as a company in one

[16] See eg, V Miller, *Legislating for Brexit: Statutory Instruments Implementing EU Law*, House of Commons Briefing Paper 7867, 16 January 2017; Geringer, Chapter 15 in this volume; and Pantazatou, Chapter 16 in this volume.

[17] See eg, Income Tax Act 2007 (NZ), s BH 1; Double Tax Agreements (China) Order 2019 (NZ).

[18] S Argument, 'The Incorporation by Reference of Technical Standards in Legislation: A Developing Issue' (2017) 28 PLR 277; ES Bremer, 'Incorporation by Reference in an Open-Government Age' (2013) 36 *Harvard Journal of Law and Public Policy* 131. See eg, Interpretation Act 2019 (NZ), s 64, which expressly provides for subordinate legislation to incorporate by reference any 'standard, framework, code of practice, recommended practice, or requirement of an international organisation or a national organisation' or 'any other written material that deals with technical matters'.

[19] See also Income Tax Act 2007 (NZ), s YA 1, for the definitions of 'hybrid mismatch report' and 'branch mismatch report'. The Income Tax Act 2007 (NZ) has an innovative structure that has proved outstandingly successful. See Ivor Richardson, 'Simplicity in Legislative Drafting and Rewriting Tax Legislation' (2012) 43 *Victoria University of Wellington Law Review* 517. Sir Ivor Richardson was the President of the New Zealand Court of Appeal from 1996 to 2002. He was preeminent in the field of tax, delivering many important judgments (eg *Commissioner of Inland Revenue v McKenzies Ltd* [1988] 2 NZLR 736 CA) and he was also a key figure in the rewrite project that led to New Zealand's income tax legislation taking its radically improved form. See also Adrian Sawyer, 'New Zealand's Tax Rewrite Program – In Pursuit of the (Elusive) Goal of Simplicity' [2007] BTR 405; Adrian Sawyer, 'Moving on from the Tax Legislation Rewrite Projects: A Comparison of the New Zealand Tax Working Group/Generic Tax Policy Process and the United Kingdom Office of Tax Simplification' [2013] BTR 321; and Inland Revenue (NZ), *The Generic Tax Policy Process and the Tax Policy Work Programme* (2017).

jurisdiction and as a partnership in the other. In the absence of rules preventing their abuse, hybrid mismatches can be used to produce various tax advantages.

Section FH 1(4) states that each of ss FH 3 to FH 11 'implements' one or other of the recommendations made by the OECD in the *Hybrid Mismatch Report* and the *Branch Mismatch Report*.[20] This is reference *without* incorporation; that is, s FH 1(4) refers to the two reports but without incorporating them in the Act. The thinking behind this was presumably that, if difficulties arise in interpreting subpart FH, the two reports might assist in resolving them – and that might be helpful.

Section FH 1(4) may be compared with s FH 11(5), which provides that, in the circumstances in which it applies, the taxpayer is to be denied a deduction of an amount 'determined consistently with the approaches described in Chapter 8 of the *Hybrid Mismatch Report* and Chapter 5 of the *Branch Mismatch Report*'. This is incorporation by reference. Section FH 1 merely requires the reports to be referred to as *guiding the interpretation* of ss FH 3 to FH 11, whereas s FH 11(5) requires the taxpayer's liability to tax to be *determined* on the basis of the two reports. In other words, the report *is the law*, not merely a guide to the interpretation of the statute.

Transfer Pricing: Sections GC 6 to GC 19

Prior to 2018, the Income Tax Act listed the five standard methods of determining arm's length prices (comparable uncontrolled price, resale price, cost plus, transactional profit split, and transactional net margin),[21] and required taxpayers to use whichever of them, or whichever combination of them, would 'produce the most reliable measure of the amount that completely independent parties would have agreed upon after real and fully adequate bargaining'.[22] But the Act neither defined the five methods, nor even described them, so there was considerable scope for disagreement as to how they were to be interpreted and applied.[23]

Those called upon to interpret the legislation (taxpayers, the Inland Revenue and the courts) generally looked to the relevant case law. Disputes were common but they were virtually all resolved by negotiation, so there were hardly any New Zealand cases.[24] New Zealand's transfer pricing practitioners therefore turned to the decisions of the courts of other countries, mainly Australia, the United States and the United Kingdom,[25] and also the literature.[26] Last, but not least, there were the *OECD's Transfer Pricing Guidelines*.

[20] OECD, *Hybrid Mismatch Report*, above n 3; OECD, *Branch Mismatch Report*, above n 3.

[21] See generally OECD, *Transfer Pricing Guidelines*, above n 4; and RS Collier and JL Andrus, *Transfer Pricing and the Arm's Length Principle after BEPS* (Oxford, Oxford University Press, 2017).

[22] Income Tax Act 2007 (NZ), s GC 13.

[23] See Krever and Sadiq, Chapter 18 in this volume, who argue that transfer pricing rules are 'particularly problematic in terms of rule of law principles'.

[24] *Commissioner of Inland Revenue v ER Squibb & Sons (NZ) Ltd* (1992) 14 NZTC 9,146 (CA).

[25] See eg, *Chevron Australia Holdings Pty Ltd v Federal Commissioner of Taxation* [2017] FACFC 62; *Abbey National Treasury Services Plc v The Commissioners for Her Majesty's Revenue and Customs* [2015] UKFTT 0341 (TC); *Bausch & Lomb Inc v Commissioner of Internal Revenue* 933 F 2d 1084 (1991); *Amazon.com Inc v Commissioner of Internal Revenue* 934 F 3d 976 (9th Cir 2019).

[26] For example, the International Bureau of Fiscal Documentation publishes a periodical called the *International Transfer Pricing Journal*. See also Collier and Andrus, above n 21.

As a matter of New Zealand law, the status of the *Guidelines* was unclear. On the one hand, there was little precedent for treating a document published by an organisation such as the OECD as a guide to the interpretation of a New Zealand statute. It was true that the OECD's *Commentary* on the *Model Tax Convention* was widely regarded as authoritative as to the interpretation of DTAs, but it was also widely seen as being in a class of its own.[27] On the other hand, the OECD was an important organisation, New Zealand was a member of it and very supportive of its work on international tax, and the *Guidelines* were comprehensive, detailed and very competently crafted.

Nonetheless, the uncertainty as to the *Guidelines*' status, as a matter of law, persisted; and that uncertainty was among the matters that the amendments to the Income Tax Act were intended to resolve. Most importantly, s GC 13(2) provides that arm's length prices are to be determined 'by performing a comparability analysis as required by the OECD transfer pricing guidelines, chapter III, using any 1 or a combination' of the five prescribed methods.[28] Again, this is incorporation by reference; that is, the Act has turned the sections of the Guidelines referred to into *rules of law*.

Whether this is the best way of addressing the mischief is debatable but on the whole it seems sensible. There would seem to have been only two other plausible courses of action. First, Parliament could have done nothing, which would have meant that uncertainty would have persisted, where an arm's length price was required, as to the method by which it was to be calculated. Secondly, Parliament could have enacted detailed rules prescribing how the five methods were to be used. That, however, would have required legislation of considerable complexity, the drafting of which would have been fraught with difficulty. It would seem reasonable to conclude that the approach taken by the New Zealand Parliament is probably at least as good as any.

The Tax Administration Act 1994 and Country-by-Country Reporting

In 2017 the OECD recommended that governments should expand the obligations imposed on a company, if it is a member of a 'large multinational group' (defined as a group with annual revenues of €750 million or more), to supply information to the tax authorities of the jurisdictions in which it operates. The recommendations were originally set out in Chapter 5 of the 2017 version of the *Transfer Pricing Guidelines* and the several annexures to that chapter, and are now in the same sections of the 2022 version. They include that states should require large multinational groups to produce

[27] See *Commissioner of Inland Revenue v JFP Energy Inc* [1990] 3 NZLR 536 (CA); *Lin v Commissioner of Inland Revenue* [2017] NZHC 969, reversed *Commissioner of Inland Revenue v Lin* [2018] NZCA 38; *Commissioner of Inland Revenue v Chatfield & Co Ltd* [2019] NZCA 73; Hugh J Ault, 'The Role of the OECD Commentaries in the Interpretation of Tax Treaties' [1994] *Intertax* 144; JF Avery Jones, 'The Effect of Changes in the OECD Commentaries after a Treaty is Concluded' (2002) 56 *Bulletin for International Taxation* 102.

[28] See also Income Tax Act 2007 (NZ) ss GC 6(1B) and GC 13(1C); compare the Taxation (International and Other Provisions) Act 2010 (UK), s 164.

a standardised 'country-by-country report', containing the information described in chapter V, Annex III.[29]

In 2019 the New Zealand Parliament duly amended the Tax Administration Act 1994, so as to provide:

> A large multinational group with an ultimate owner that is a New Zealand resident must provide to the Commissioner a report, for each period set by the Commissioner, that includes–
>
> (a) the information described in the OECD transfer pricing guidelines, Chapter V, Annex III ….[30]

As with most of the other recent amendments, this seems sensible. The alternative would presumably have been to amend the Tax Administration Act so as to set out what was required. But incorporating the text of Annex III in the Act by repetition would seem to serve no purpose, unless the wording was changed; and that might have raised difficult questions as to the significance of the differences between the wording of the Annex and the wording of the statute. All in all, incorporating the text of the Annex, or a rewritten version of it, in the Act would have lengthened and complicated it for no advantage.

The GloBE Rules

The basic idea of the *GloBE Rules* is that large multinational enterprises or MNEs (again, those with annual gross revenues of €750 million or more) should pay tax at a rate of at least 15 per cent on their worldwide profits; and that this should be achieved by participating countries enacting legislation implementing the *Model Rules* produced by the OECD.[31] The *Model Rules* comprise two main components: the Income Inclusion Rule (IIR) and the Undertaxed Profits Rule (UTPR). The OECD's plan is for each participating jurisdiction to impose these rules by means of domestic legislation.

The IIR will impose a 'top-up tax' on the 'Ultimate Parent Entity' (UPE) of any MNE whose group profits are taxed at less than 15 per cent. This top-up tax will be charged at whatever rate is necessary to bring the total tax on the group's profits up to 15 per cent. The IIR is thus similar in its effect to CFC rules. It is assumed that it will incentivise countries to tax corporate profits at a rate of at least 15 per cent – because, if they do not, the profits will be taxed in the UPE's jurisdiction of residence.

The IIR will solve the problem where the UPE is resident in a jurisdiction that has such a rule. Where that is not the case – that is, where the UPE is resident in a jurisdiction that has not enacted an IIR – the jurisdictions in which its subsidiaries are resident will be able to correct the under-taxation of the group under the UTPR, which will impose an appropriate share of the top-up tax on each subsidiary.

The IIR is a 'top down' rule, imposing the top-up tax on the UPE, so as to correct the under-taxation of its subsidiaries; and the UTPR is a 'bottom up' rule, imposing an appropriate share of the top-up tax on each of the MNE's subsidiaries, so as to correct

[29] *OECD Transfer Pricing Guidelines*, above n 4, para 5.24.
[30] Tax Administration Act 1994 (NZ), s 78G(1)(a).
[31] OECD, above n 6.

the under-taxation of the group as a whole. The IIR is the simpler of the two rules, because it entails only determining whether any top-up tax is payable and, if so, how much. The calculation is therefore essentially:

$$T = (P \times 15\%) - C$$

where:

- T is the top-up tax payable;
- P is the group's profit; and
- C is credit for tax already paid by the group's members.

The UTPR is more complex because it also entails allocating an appropriate share of the top-up tax to each of the group's subsidiaries. The UTPR will only apply where the under-taxation of an MNE is not solved by an IIR in the UPE's jurisdiction of residence (or by an IIR in the jurisdiction of residence of an intermediate holding company). For that reason, it is described by the OECD as a 'backstop'.[32]

Some countries, for example the United Kingdom, are planning to implement the *Model Rules* by what might be called the traditional approach: that is, they plan to enact legislation that gives effect to the OECD's recommendations, but accords with their usual style of legislative drafting (and that does not incorporate any of the text produced by the OECD).[33] The New Zealand Government, however, has again used incorporation by reference: it has enacted a relatively skeletal statute incorporating in New Zealand law both (a) the *Model Rules* and (b) the *Commentary*. As the government explained:

> New Zealand legislation provides the legal scaffolding necessary to support the OECD rules but gives effect to them by reference to the rules themselves, rather than re-writing them in the legislation.[34]

The legislation came in the form of a new subpart HP, added to the Income Tax Act in 2024. The charging section is s HP 1, which provides: 'A constituent entity … that is required to pay an amount of tax under the applied global anti-base erosion rules must pay the amount to the Commissioner.' Section HP 2 provides that constituent entities must generally pay the tax within 16 months of the end of the fiscal year. These sections are supported by s HP 3, which provides (a) that the *Model Rules* apply as New Zealand law, except for a small number of exceptions, (b) that the *Model Rules* apply 'in accordance with … the most recent [version of the *Commentary*]', and (c) that, in the case of conflict, the *Commentary* prevails over the *Model Rules*. The Act does not define 'constituent entity' but s HP 4 provides that any term defined in the *Model Rules* and used in the Act has the same meaning as in the *Model Rules*; and the *Model Rules* define 'constituent entity' as meaning basically a member of a MNE within the scope of the *Model Rules*.[35] The Act (as amended) defines 'global anti-base erosion model rules' as meaning the *Model Rules*, 'as amended from time to time' by the OECD;[36] and it defines

[32] OECD, above n 7, ch 1, para 6.
[33] Draft Finance Bill 2022–23 (UK). Available at: https://assets.publishing.service.gov.uk/government/uploads/system/uploads/attachment_data/file/1092586/Draft_legislation.pdf.
[34] Inland Revenue, above n 8, [10.6].
[35] Arts 1.3 and 10.1.
[36] Income Tax Act 2007 (NZ), s YA 1 (as amended), definition of 'global anti-base erosion model rules'.

'applied global anti-base erosion rules' as meaning 'the global anti-base erosion model rules as applied by section HP 3'.[37]

The *Model Rules* are complex (62 pages), novel (the IIR resembles CFC rules, but nothing like the UTPR has ever been tried before), and not only technically difficult (at least as dense as most other tax legislation) but also politically fraught (it seems possible that the US will not only renege on its agreement to participate, but will also retaliate against countries that do). It seems probable, therefore, that the OECD will amend the *Model Rules* or the *Commentary* or both, and that such amendments will be contentious.

Advantages

According to Keyes, incorporation by reference has five advantages and seven disadvantages.[38] The first advantage is that it 'reduces the amount of legislative text that has to be published'.[39] This is clearly true of the New Zealand legislation's references to the instruments produced by the OECD. Moreover, given the length and complexity of the OECD materials, the reduction is substantial: hundreds of pages. Certainly, anything that might slow down the rate at which the Income Tax Act has been growing should at least be considered. Compared to some other countries' income tax legislation, it is succinct and straightforward,[40] but it is the lengthiest statute ever enacted in New Zealand. It is currently 3,852 pages and is growing at a rate of 100 pages or so per year, with no end in sight.

Secondly, incorporation by reference 'promotes harmonisation with laws of other jurisdictions'.[41] This, too, is true of the New Zealand legislation's references to the OECD materials. At the very least, there is no room for arguments as to the significance of differences between the OECD's wording and New Zealand law: since the OECD text *is the law*, there are no differences. Moreover, if other countries were to take the same approach – that is, if they were to incorporate the OECD materials in their legislation – there would obviously be more harmonisation than if they were to draft their own rules. In the field of tax law that might be especially advantageous, because the types of tax planning engaged in by MNEs largely depend on discovering and exploiting gaps between two or more countries' tax rules;[42] to the extent that different countries adopt identically worded rules, there would be fewer such gaps.

Thirdly, incorporation by reference 'might avoid having to translate the incorporated material'.[43] New Zealand is fortunate in that its legislation is generally in the English language; so, too, are the materials produced by the OECD.[44] The question of

[37] ibid.
[38] Keyes, above n 2, 194–195.
[39] ibid, 194.
[40] See the materials referred to in n 19 above.
[41] Keyes, above n 2, 194.
[42] For a recent example, see *Frucor Suntory New Zealand Ltd v Commissioner of Inland Revenue* [2022] NZSC 113.
[43] Keyes, above n 2, 194.
[44] Although New Zealand's legislation is generally in English, some of it is also in te reo Māori; and in some instances, in the case of conflict, the Māori version prevails: Te Ture mō Te Reo Māori 2016/Māori Language Act 2016, s 12(2). The legislation relating to taxation is in English only.

translation therefore does not arise. How countries that use other languages will go about implementing the *Model GloBE Rules* remains to be seen. It is notable, though, that the *Model Rules* include a de minimis threshold of €750 million; the OECD has gone to considerable trouble to explain how countries that are reluctant to adopt a rule referring to a foreign currency should go about reformulating it using their own currency.[45] Presumably a number of countries were reluctant to use the euro; they might be even more reluctant to incorporate a foreign-language text into their domestic law.

The fourth advantage of the incorporation-by-reference technique is that, if an ambulatory approach is used, 'it might avoid updating the incorporated material'.[46] As explained above, some of the New Zealand legislation's references to OECD materials are static and some are ambulatory. Specifically, the references in the hybrid rules are static; they refer to the *Hybrids Mismatch Report* (published in 2015) and the *Branch Mismatch Report* (published in 2017).[47] Similarly, New Zealand's transfer-pricing rules originally referred to the version of the *Transfer Pricing Guidelines* published in 2017, and have now been amended to refer to the 2022 version;[48] the Country-by-Country reporting obligations are likewise static.[49]

The references to both the *Model GloBE Rules* and the *Commentary*, however, are ambulatory. Consequently, any amendments made to either the *Model Rules* or the *Commentary* by the OECD will automatically amend New Zealand law. As Keyes says, that might be advantageous. However, he also emphasises that it might also be disadvantageous in that 'the legislator has less control over the content of its legislation'.[50] This aspect of the legislation is examined further below.

The fifth advantage of the incorporation-by-reference technique is that 'the incorporated material might already be familiar to those who are governed by it'.[51] That would seem to be so of the OECD materials incorporated in New Zealand law: the MNEs whose liabilities to New Zealand tax are to be determined by reference to those materials will no doubt be familiar with them. Moreover, if other countries were to adopt New Zealand's approach, their laws would be to that extent identical, which would tend to minimise the burden of compliance.

Disadvantages

As for Keyes's seven disadvantages of incorporation by reference, the first is that '[t]he law is fragmented between legislative text and incorporated text published elsewhere'.[52] In the case of New Zealand's incorporation-by-reference of OECD materials, this is

[45] OECD, above n 7, Introduction [17]–[24].
[46] Keyes, above n 2, 194.
[47] Income Tax Act 2007 (NZ), subpart FH.
[48] ibid, ss GC 6–GC 14.
[49] Tax Administration Act 1994 (NZ), s 78G(1)(a).
[50] Keyes, above n 2, 194.
[51] ibid.
[52] ibid.

true, but insignificant. In order to find out what the law is, it is necessary to look at the relevant legislation (the Income Tax Act and the Tax Administration Act) and also at the relevant OECD materials – but that is hardly burdensome, since it can be assumed that everyone who practises in the area, either in New Zealand or anywhere else, will be familiar with this.

Secondly, 'the incorporated material might not be in an official language'.[53] In the case of New Zealand, this problem does not arise: both the legislation and the OECD materials are in English. Many other countries' legal systems operate in English also, so following New Zealand's approach might be similarly straightforward for them. Most countries, however, mostly or exclusively use languages other than English. They therefore face a dilemma: if they want to follow the OECD's recommendations, either they must use materials in a foreign language, or they must translate them. It seems likely that the governments of many small countries and some large ones lack the resources to do either.

Thirdly:

> [T]he legislator has less control over the content of its legislation since the incorporated text is made by someone else (especially in cases of ambulatory incorporation by reference since the text can be changed without any further action by the legislator) ...[54]

This is the most serious problem presented by New Zealand's approach. In particular, the New Zealand legislation's references to the *Model GloBE Rules* and the *Commentary* on them are ambulatory.[55] Consequently, any changes made by the OECD to the *Rules* or the *Commentary* will automatically change New Zealand law, unless Parliament legislates to prevent that from happening. The use of the incorporation-by-reference approach in tax law is novel, and may seem dangerous, unconstitutional and contrary to the rule of law. It is possible, though, that this problem is more hypothetical than real, because it may be that the OECD is unlikely to produce a version of either the *Rules* or the *Commentary* that is not to the government's liking. But the government's plan is to keep a close eye on the OECD's future revisions of the *Rules* and the *Commentary*, so that, if any of them effects a change in New Zealand law that it regards as undesirable, it can arrange for Parliament to amend the legislation to negate the amendment.[56]

Conversely, the New Zealand legislation's static references to OECD documents present another obvious problem: that the statute will become out of date as soon as the OECD publishes a revised version of the document in question. That has, indeed, already happened: amendments to the Income Tax Act enacted in 2018 incorporated in New Zealand law the version of the OECD's *Transfer Pricing Guidelines* published in 2017; in January 2022 the OECD published a revised version; and in 2023 Parliament amended the Act so as to refer to the 2022 version.[57] On balance, the ambulatory approach seems better; the advantages outweigh the disadvantages.

[53] ibid.
[54] ibid.
[55] Income Tax Act 2007 (NZ), subpart HP.
[56] Inland Revenue (NZ), above n 8, ch 10.
[57] Income Tax Act 2007 (NZ), s YA 1, definition of 'OECD transfer pricing guidelines', as amended.

The fourth disadvantage of incorporation-by-reference, as identified by Keyes, is that 'the drafting style or terminology of incorporated material might be incompatible with the legislative text that incorporates it'.[58] It is certainly the case that the OECD's drafting style is different to that of New Zealand's legislation generally and its tax legislation in particular. That is so of the *Model Rules*, even though they are at least in the form of rules. As for the *Commentary* on the *Model Rules* and the *Transfer Pricing Guidelines*, they are not in the form of rules at all, so the contrast in style between them and the legislation is more marked. That is true also of the *Hybrids Reports*. It seems unlikely, though, that the OECD's drafting style will prove problematic; at any rate those currently drafting legislation for the New Zealand Government seem not to be troubled by it.[59]

Fifthly, 'the incorporated material might be subject to interpretation in some external forum'.[60] This, too, is true of the OECD materials but, again, it is not necessarily a problem. On the contrary, assuming the OECD's BEPS project to be basically sound (which is the New Zealand Government's position), it would obviously be beneficial if every country were to adopt rules as close as possible to those promulgated by the OECD. Moreover, the New Zealand courts, when called upon to interpret New Zealand tax law, routinely refer to materials produced elsewhere, in particular the decisions of other countries' courts (especially those of the UK, Australia, Canada and the US) and the OECD's Commentary on its Model DTA.[61]

Further, the ambulatory references in the legislation stipulate that, if the OECD were to amend the document referred to, the resulting change in New Zealand law will not take effect until the following tax year;[62] thus, if the New Zealand Government does not want the OECD's amendment of its document to change New Zealand law, it has a window, albeit possibly brief, to legislate so as to prevent that from happening.

Sixthly, Keyes, says, 'it might be hard to obtain the incorporated material'.[63] Since the OECD has made all the relevant materials available on its website and will presumably continue to do so, this problem does not arise.

Seventhly, 'the incorporated material might be subject to copyright and charges for copies'[64] – and some of the OECD's materials are indeed behind a paywall. It might be said that the only people to whom these laws apply are MNEs – which can obviously afford the OECD's relatively modest charges. But it is obviously in the public interest that everyone should be able to discover what the law is. It would be helpful, therefore, if the OECD were to remove its paywall and make all its tax-related materials available free of change to anyone, anywhere, wanting to look at them.

[58] Keyes, above n 2, 194.
[59] See Legislation Design and Advisory Committee, above n 2.
[60] Keyes, above n 2, 194.
[61] See eg, *Commissioner of Inland Revenue v Lin* [2018] NZCA 38, where the New Zealand Court of Appeal referred to both the *OECD Commentary* and the decision of the UK Supreme Court in *Anson v Commissioners for Her Majesty's Revenue and Customs* [2015] UKSC 44.
[62] Income Tax Act 2007 (NZ), ss HP 3(3) and YA 1 (definition of 'global anti-base erosion model rules').
[63] Keyes, above n 2, 195.
[64] Keyes, above n 2, 195.

Maybe Some of the OECD's Publications are Law Anyway?

It might be said that the courts, in numerous other countries and also New Zealand, have already adopted the practice of referring to the *OECD Commentary* when called upon to interpret a DTA; that they routinely refer not only to the version of the *Commentary* current at the time the DTA in issue was entered into but subsequent versions also; and that the statutory references to OECD documents are therefore unproblematic.[65] A subtler argument is that some of the documents published by the OECD would have been regarded by New Zealand's courts as relevant to the interpretation of the legislation anyway, even if it did not expressly refer to them; and, that being the case, it is better that their relevance should be expressly provided for. This would seem to be so for the *Hybrid Reports* and the *Transfer Pricing Guidelines*, but not the *Model GloBE Rules* or the *Commentary* on them.

More specifically, subpart FH (the hybrids rules) was enacted to give effect to the recommendations made in the *Hybrid Mismatch Report* and the *Branch Mismatch Report*; and everyone who works in the field knows that the OECD produced the two reports, and that Parliament's purpose, in enacting subpart FH, was to give effect to the recommendations they contained. Subpart FH is extremely complex, even by the standards of the income tax legislation. It is likely, therefore, that difficulties will arise in interpreting it, and the obvious way of resolving such difficulties would be to refer to the two reports. That is, since the subpart was intended to give effect to the reports, the reports are presumably a good guide to what Parliament intended the subpart to mean. It seems unlikely that a court, in the absence of an express statutory reference to the reports, would decline to look at them as a guide to interpretation,[66] but the express reference would seem to remove any doubt.

Much the same could be said of the references to the OECD's *Transfer Pricing Guidelines* in ss GC 6 and GC 13 (the transfer pricing rules). That is, even if the statute did not expressly refer to them, the *Guidelines* would be an obvious point of reference for resolving matters of interpretation. As with the *Hybrids Reports*, it seems unlikely that a court, in the absence of an express statutory reference to the *Guidelines*, would decline to look at them as a guide to interpretation, but the express reference would seem to remove any doubt.

But the reference to the *Guidelines* in ss GC 6 and GC 13 (the transfer pricing rules) is more important than the reference to the *Hybrids Reports* in subpart FH (the hybrids rules). The reason is that it would have been obvious, even without the legislation spelling it out, that subpart FH was intended to give effect to the *Hybrids Reports*. As explained above, however, the relationship between ss GC 6 and GC 13 (on the one hand) and the *Transfer Pricing Guidelines* (on the other) was less clear. The reason is that

[65] For a New Zealand example, see *Commissioner of Inland Revenue v Lin*, above n 27. See also Ault, above n 27, and Avery Jones, above n 27.

[66] *Pepper v Hart* [1992] UKHL 3; *Attorney-General v Taylor* [2017] NZCA 215 [120]; Parliamentary Privilege Act 2014 (NZ), s 13.

the five methods of determining arm's length prices (listed in s GC 13(2) and recited above) were not devised by the OECD. Rather, they were developed over a period of decades, mainly, it would seem, by the US Internal Revenue Service;[67] and then they were adopted and refined by numerous other governments (including the New Zealand Government) and also by the OECD.

Consequently, the five methods are the subject of a large body of complicated case law[68] and an even larger and more complicated literature.[69] The materials to which one could turn for guidance on the five methods of setting arm's length prices are consequently vast and diverse. The OECD's *Guidelines*, however, are coherent, comprehensive and, not least, drafted from a governmental perspective. It makes obvious sense, therefore, for Parliament to have intended that any questions as to the interpretation of ss GC 6 to GC 14 should be resolved by reference, in the first instance, to the *Guidelines*, rather than to the cases and the literature; and it also makes sense for Parliament to have spelt that intention out in the legislation, so as to remove any doubt. It is probable that taxpayers and their advisers will continue to refer to the cases and the literature as bearing on the interpretation of the *Guidelines* and thus as bearing indirectly on the interpretation of the statute; but to give priority to the *Guidelines*, as Parliament has done, seems sensible.

This analysis does not apply, however, to the *Model GloBE Rules*. The reason is that, in the case of the *Model GloBE Rules*, the statute itself does not define the scope of the tax; it prescribes neither who is obliged to pay, nor how their liability is to be calculated. In other words, it is impossible to determine even the basic scope of the tax without referring to the *Model Rules*.

Constitutionality and the Rule of Law

The New Zealand Parliament is said to be supreme.[70] That is, there are supposedly no limits whatever on its legislative competence. Moreover, it is unicameral, so there is not even the constraint of an upper house.[71] The orthodox view thus seems to entail that, if Parliament wants to incorporate documents produced by someone else in New Zealand law, it is absolutely free to do so. At any rate, that is evidently Parliament's own view, since that is what it has done. Further, the orthodox view would seem to extend to the proposition that, if Parliament wants to confer on some other body the power to amend one of its own acts, it is absolutely free to do so. Again, that is evidently Parliament's own view, since that is what it has done.

[67] Collier and Andrus, above n 21, chapter 2.

[68] See eg, *Chevron Australia Holdings Pty Ltd v Federal Commissioner of Taxation* [2017] FACFC 62; *Commissioner of Taxation v Glencore Investment Pty Ltd* [2020] FCAFC 187; *The Coca-Cola Company v Commissioner of Internal Revenue* 155 TC No 109, 18 November 2020; Joined Cases C-885/19 P and C-898/19 P *Fiat Chrysler Finance Europe v European Commission* ECLI:EU:C:2022:859 1.

[69] See eg, Collier and Andrus, above n 21 and the *International Transfer Pricing Journal*.

[70] Compare Oats and Ormeño-Pérez, Chapter 8 in this volume.

[71] See generally P Joseph, *Joseph on Constitutional and Administrative Law* 5th edn (Wellington: Thomson Reuters, 2021).

On the other hand, as in the United Kingdom, there is a tradition of speculation in New Zealand over questions such as whether Parliament can bind itself by entrenching legislation; and whether, if Parliament were to enact a statute repugnant to natural law, the courts would be bound to enforce it. For example, in *Taylor v New Zealand Poultry Board* Cooke P (later Lord Cooke of Thorndon) said:

> I do not think that literal compulsion, by torture for instance, would be within the lawful powers of Parliament. Some common law rights presumably lie so deep that even Parliament could not override them.[72]

As in the United Kingdom, however, such speculation has so far come to nothing, because Parliament has neither purported to repeal an entrenched statute by a simple majority nor enacted a statute alleged to be repugnant to natural law (though the Supreme Court has taken what some see as an excessively robust approach to the interpretation of some statutes; see in particular *Fitzgerald v R*, in which the Court held that the apparently plain language of a statute imposing a sentence of at least seven years' imprisonment should not be interpreted as requiring that, if it would 'shock the conscience of properly informed New Zealanders').[73]

Similarly, there is said to be a constitutional principle, in Westminster-derived systems, that it is for Parliament to impose taxes; and that Parliament should not delegate that function. This is said to be based on Magna Carta and the Bill of Rights 1689, parts of both of which supposedly apply in New Zealand.[74] Moreover, section 22 of the Constitution Act 1986 (NZ) provides:

> It shall not be lawful for the Crown, except by or under an Act of Parliament,–
>
> (a) to levy a tax; or
> (b) to borrow money or to receive money borrowed from any person; or
> (c) to spend any public money.

But the point of Magna Carta, the Bill of Rights and section 22 is to preclude the Crown from levying taxes without Parliament's consent; neither Magna Carta, nor the Bill of Rights, nor section 22 would seem, on its terms, to preclude Parliament from imposing a tax by means of incorporating in a taxing statute a text produced by somebody else.

Anecdotally, lawyers in other common-law countries, when told of the New Zealand Parliament's approach, seem commonly to regard it as outrageous, and something that would not be countenanced in their own countries. When pressed as to the reason, they seem unable to offer anything, other than vague references to Magna Carta and the Bill of Rights. As for the New Zealand legal profession, its members seem unconcerned. The Tax Law Committee of the New Zealand Law Society made submissions on the legislation incorporating the *GLoBE Rules*, suggesting that the references to the OECD

[72] *Taylor v New Zealand Poultry Board* [1984] 1 NZLR 394 (CA), 398. See also A Ross, 'Diluting Dicey' (1989) 6 *Auckland University Law Review* 176; and M Harris, 'Is New Zealand Law Ready for a *Marbury v Madison* Moment?' (2012) 25 *New Zealand Universities Law Review* 210. As regards the United Kingdom, see *Jackson v Attorney General* [2005] UKHL 56 [102] per Lord Steyn.

[73] *Fitzgerald v R* [2021] NZSC 131 [3].

[74] Imperial Laws Application Act 1988 (NZ), s 3 and Sch 1; see generally Joseph, above n 71.

materials should be static rather than ambulatory;[75] but Parliament ignored them, and the legal profession and the public at large generally remained silent. The reason, perhaps, is that the *GLoBE Rules* will make no difference to the overwhelming majority of New Zealand taxpayers; they will only apply to a very small number of New Zealand firms; even those firms might benefit from the application of the rules to their foreign competitors.

As for 'the rule of law', everyone agrees that it is an important constitutional principle constraining the legitimate role of government, and that breaches of it are undesirable.[76] For example, s 3(2) of the Senior Courts Act 2016 (NZ) provides 'Nothing in this Act affects New Zealand's continuing commitment to the rule of law and the sovereignty of Parliament.' The concept is, however, contested.[77] The 'thin' notion of the rule of law is simply that the law must meet certain formal requirements. At the very least, it entails that 'laws should be passed in the correct legal manner'.[78] But it seems to be generally agreed that the rule of law entails also that the law should be 'prospective, not retrospective';[79] that it should be 'relatively stable'; that 'particular laws should be guided by open, general and clear rules';[80] that 'there should be an independent judiciary'; that people should have 'access to the courts'; and that 'the discretion which law enforcement agencies possess should not be allowed to undermine the purposes of the relevant legal rules'.[81]

The 'thick' notion, in contrast, is that the rule of law entails not only formal requirements, but also substantive elements such as recognition of human rights.[82] Dame Susan Glazebrook, a judge of the New Zealand Supreme Court, has recently sparked controversy by extrajudicially insisting that the rule of law necessarily also entails 'redress for historical disadvantage', such as that suffered by the Māori people as a result of colonisation and the forcible confiscation of their land.[83]

Most governments, even those widely regarded as repugnant, manage to comply most of the time with the principle that laws should be enacted 'in the correct legal manner'. That is, however, a low bar: as Joseph Raz says, it is 'compatible with gross

[75] New Zealand Law Society, 'Submission on the Taxation (Annual Rates for 2023–24, Multinational Tax, and Remedial Matters) Bill 2023', 13 July 2023.

[76] T Bingham, *The Rule of Law* (London: Penguin, 2010).

[77] See eg, Daly, Chapter 2 in this volume; Lindsay, above n 1; and Gerald Postema, *Law's Rule: The Nature, Value, and Viability of the Rule of Law* (Oxford: Oxford University Press, 2022).

[78] P Craig, 'Formal and Substantive Conceptions of the Rule of Law: An Analytical Framework' [1997] PL 467, 469.

[79] See Gillis, Chapter 4 in this volume; and H Meachen, 'Retrospective Tax Legislation: A Solution to an Enduring Problem' (2023) 29 *New Zealand Journal of Taxation Law and Policy* 269.

[80] See eg, Tandon and Rao, Chapter 6 in this volume; and Lindsay, above n 1.

[81] Craig, above n 78, 469, selectively paraphrasing J Raz, *The Authority of Law: Essays on Law and Morality* (Oxford: Clarendon, 1979), 214–18.

[82] Bingham, above n 76, chapter 7.

[83] S Glazebrook, 'The Rule of Law: Guiding Principle or Catchphrase?'. Available at: www.courtsofnz.govt.nz/assets/speechpapers/Rule-of-law-Guiding-Principle-or-Catchphrase.pdf. For rebuttals of this interpretation, see G Judd, 'The Humpty Dumpty Approach to the Rule of Law' *LawNews* (the weekly magazine of the Auckland District Law Society), 30 March 2023; and B Wilkinson, 'Where is our Supreme Court on the Rule of Law?' *New Zealand Herald*, 13 April 2023. See also P Gowder, *The Rule of Law in the Real World* (Cambridge: Cambridge University Press, 2016) and, especially, P Gowder, *The Rule of Law in the United States: An Unfinished Project of Black Liberation* (Oxford: Hart, 2021).

violations of human rights', and slavery could be instituted without offending it.[84] The assertion that a government has breached the rule of law is generally, therefore, based on some more refined 'thin' notion of the concept (such as that the judiciary is not independent) or a 'thick' notion (such as that the government has infringed the human rights of the populace, or a sector of it).

In the case of the New Zealand legislation's incorporation-by-reference of OECD materials, however, the reverse is true. That is, the legislation seems to satisfy all of the requirements mentioned above, except perhaps the first: the legislation is 'prospective, not retrospective'; it seems reasonable to expect it to be 'relatively stable'; the rules are 'open, general and clear'; there is no reason to doubt the independence of the judiciary; the legislation only applies to MNEs, whose access to the courts is unproblematic;[85] and it confers hardly any discretion on the Inland Revenue, the courts, or anyone else. Further, if the rule of law is seen as entailing rules-based good governance,[86] the incorporation by reference of OECD materials could be seen as contributing to it.

The manner in which the legislation was produced, however, was radically divergent from the norm. That is, whilst the incorporation-by-reference technique has been used in various other contexts in New Zealand, it is only recently that it has been used to impose a method of determining liability to an existing tax (the *Transfer Pricing Guidelines* and the *Hybrids Reports*) or to impose an entirely new tax (the *Model GloBE Rules*).[87] Whether it constitutes a breach of the rule of law is debatable.

Conclusion

The incorporation in New Zealand law of instruments, or parts of instruments, produced by the OECD seems, on the whole, to be sensible because it seems to have enabled Parliament to amend the law to deal satisfactorily (or, at least, less unsatisfactorily than before) with undesirable taxpayer behaviour, whilst keeping the additional complexity of the statute itself to a minimum. Moreover, it would seem to be advantageous for the law of different countries to be more or less the same in areas such as the tax treatment of large MNEs, hybrids, transfer pricing and country-by-country reporting. But it is a notable jurisprudential and constitutional development, and it will be interesting to see how it works in practice. It will also be interesting to see whether it is repeated and whether it becomes routine. It is difficult to say, at this early juncture, which of the two approaches Parliament has taken – static or ambulatory – is better. Or perhaps static references will prove better in some circumstances and ambulatory in others. Time will tell.

[84] Raz, above n 81, 221.
[85] See also Hodgson, Chapter 11 in this volume.
[86] See Lindsay, n 1; Brassey, Chapter 12 in this volume; Broekhuijsen, van Ganzen and Vording, Chapter 13 in this volume; Geringer, above n 16; Pantazatou, above n 16.
[87] See also Sawyer, Chapter 7 in this volume.

15

Preserving the Rule of Law in the Interpretation and Application of Union Law by the Member States Through CJEU Jurisprudence: The Case of VAT

STEFANIE GERINGER

Abstract

While the European Union (EU) legal order provides a common legal framework for all 27 Member States, frictions may nevertheless arise in the transposition of secondary legislation into national legal systems and/or in the decentralised enforcement of EU law by national administrations and courts. Especially at a time of multiple crises and corresponding financial constraints on national budgets, the rule of law may be threatened in the implementation and application of EU law for a variety of reasons. Seen in this light, supranational and thus comparatively neutral institutions such as the Court of Justice of the European Union (CJEU) can fundamentally be assigned a particularly important role in safeguarding the full effectiveness and correct application of EU law in the Member States. However, its powers in this regard are equally limited, especially due to significant restrictions on access to the Court and relevant limitations on its scope of action. Beyond that, although this is often presented as a 'golden bullet', it seems questionable whether it is indeed sensible to seek salvation in CJEU jurisprudence for each case of problematic conduct from an EU-specific rule-of-law perspective. The aim of this chapter is thus to provide a comprehensive and critical analysis of the CJEU's role in upholding the rule of law in the interpretation and application of Union law by the Member States, using VAT law as a representative example.

Introduction

Similar to national legal systems, the idea of the rule of law is also inherent in the supranational legal order of the European Union (EU).[1] The EU's foundation in (inter alia) the rule of law was first recognised by the Court of Justice of the European Union (CJEU) in *Les Verts v Parliament*.[2] Meanwhile, Article 2 of the TEU[3] explicitly identifies the rule of law as one of the values 'common to the Member States in a society in which pluralism, non-discrimination, tolerance, justice, solidarity and equality between women and men prevail'. The EU's rule-of-law concept should thus principally incorporate the features ascribed to this notion in national contexts,[4] while the EU's particularities as a construct *sui generis* between an international organisation and a state require the use of a reading adapted for its purposes. This particularly includes the fact that EU substantive law is broadly harmonised and either directly applicable in the Member States or its transposition into Member States' legal systems mandatory. Its enforcement is usually entrusted to Member States' authorities and courts.[5] As a result, the EU-specific rule-of-law concept has been understood to especially include an obligation for Member States to ensure the application of and compliance with EU legislation on their respective territory. To this end, they must moreover provide remedies sufficient to ensure effective judicial protection in the fields covered by Union law.[6]

Full realisation of these principles in the transposition and application of EU law would, of course, be the ideal. However, experience has shown that acceptance and preservation of the EU-relevant rule of law cannot be taken for granted.[7] After all, the Member States' legislators, administrations and courts routinely responsible for implementing and enforcing Union law (also) represent national interests (and presumably also varying rule-of-law standards). Tendencies to test the limits of acceptable national legislative, administrative and judicial action under the EU-relevant rule-of-law concept have possibly even increased in recent years, which have been significantly shaped by the occurrence of multiple crises and corresponding financial constraints in national budgets.[8] This reality affects, first and foremost, the addresses of Union law, ie

[1] On the potential applicability of the rule of law in an international tax context, see Broekhuijsen, Van Ganzen, Vleggeert and Vording, Chapter 13 in this volume.

[2] Case 294/83 *Les Verts v Parliament* EU:C:1986:166, [1986] ECR 01339.

[3] Consolidated Version of the Treaty on European Union (TEU) [2016] OJ C202/13.

[4] Which may, however, vary in quantity, depending on the construction of the rule of law based on a 'thin' or 'thick' concept; see Lindsay and Daly, Chapters 3 and 2 respectively of this volume. In terms of the understanding relevant to EU law, the need to apply a 'thick' concept, with implications at both individual and institutional (in the sense of good governance) levels, appears to be the dominant view, as evidenced, inter alia, by the definition used by the European Commission; Commission, 'Strengthening the rule of law within the Union: A blueprint for action' (Commission Communication Blueprint) COM(2019) 343 final, s I. In the same vein, see Pantazatou, Chapter 16 in this volume.

[5] See eg, K Lenaerts and P Van Nuffel, *European Union Law*, 3rd edn (London: Sweet & Maxwell, 2011) 524–25 and 623–24.

[6] See eg, Case C-64/16 *Associação Sindical dos Juízes Portugueses* EU:C:2018:117, [2018] para 34; see also TEU art 19(1)(2). The requirements under the EU rule-of-law concept also extend to the Union's institutions, so that their compliance is similarly examined by the CJEU (a recent example concerning VAT law is Case C-695/20 *Fenix International* EU:C:2023:127, [2023]).

[7] Commission Communication Blueprint, above n 4, s I.

[8] See also Commission, 'Enforcing EU law for a Europe that delivers' (Commission Communication Enforcing) COM(2022) 518 final, s VII: 'Under difficult circumstances, there may be a temptation to favour

entrepreneurs (taxable persons) in business-related areas such as value added tax (VAT) law. The resulting deficiencies in legal certainty, predictability of the tax burden and/or guarantees of fundamental (procedural) rights in the event of tax disputes may discourage them from operating in Member States with such problematic patterns of application of the rule of law. This obviously has a negative impact on the internal market and thus goes to the very heart of the EU idea.[9] Due to the highly interconnected nature of the EU's legal ecosystem, non-compliance with the rule of law has moreover an important cross-jurisdictional dimension in the specific EU context. Hence, its affects mutual trust between Member States, possibly leading to equally problematic reactions from peer countries.[10]

Member States' legal systems usually dispose of adequate instruments to counter eventual questionable actions in this regard.[11] Given the augmenting pressure on democracy and other achievements of modern societies (including the standards reflected by the idea of the rule of law), the existence of supranational and thus comparatively neutral instances such as the CJEU has yet arguably gained in importance. Through its case law, the Court has indeed contributed significantly to levelling out legislative, administrative and judicial practices in the Member States that stood in conflict with the EU's rule-of-law concept. However, certain decisions have also memorably illustrated the CJEU's clear limits in upholding the principles of the EU-relevant rule of law, which arise from restrictions on access to the Court, the scope of its review powers and certain characteristics of its own decision-making practice.

Against this background, this contribution aims to discuss the CJEU's role in protecting the EU-relevant rule of law in the Member States, using VAT law as an example. Representative cases from jurisprudence are used to trace the areas in which the Court can effectively contribute to the achievement of these objectives. The limitations under current Union law, as well as the shortcomings of judicial practice, are subsequently elucidated. This forms the basis for an analysis of potential, and maybe even desirable, avenues for improvement.

The Member States' Room for Manoeuvre in the Context of the Broadly Harmonised VAT

The free movement of goods without border controls and customs duties has been at the heart of EU integration.[12] The introduction of a common legal framework for a

domestic considerations over the proper application of EU law'. Specifically, on the loyality of national authorities rather to the respective Member State than the EU, see M Bobek, P Bříza and J Komárek, *Vnitrostátní aplikace práva Evropské unie* (Prague: CH Beck, 2011) 218.

[9] See also Commission, 'Further strengthening the rule of law within the Union: State of play and possible next steps' (Communication) COM(2019) 163 final, s I.

[10] See also L Pech, 'The Rule of Law' in P Craig and G de Búrca (eds), *The Evolution of EU Law*, 3rd edn (Oxford: Oxford University Press, 2021) 318–19.

[11] P Craig and G de Búrca, *EU Law: Text, Cases, and Materials*, 7th edn (Oxford: Oxford University Press, 2020) 46–47.

[12] This is best illustrated by the fact that the European Coal and Steel Community – hence, the earliest predecessor of today's EU – was mostly concerned with the orderly supply of coal and steel in the common market, equal access to production and fair prices, while prohibiting the imposition of customs duties, the

multi-stage VAT intended to burden final consumption was thus seen from the outset as an important prerequisite for achieving this objective, given 'the direct influence of this tax on the formation of prices and consequently on the conditions of competition'.[13] Related efforts culminated in a comprehensive package of secondary legislation with today's VAT Directive[14] as the centrepiece of harmonisation.

Notwithstanding the significant developments to date, VAT in the EU is not fully harmonised. Mandatory provisions exist mainly for those (predominantly substantive) elements of the tax that necessarily need to be defined in a uniform manner for the common system to function.[15] Conversely, setting the rules for the effective and efficient administration of VAT[16] falls principally[17] and explicitly[18] within the competence of the Member States.[19] Leaving eventual divergences in statutory law aside, it should further be borne in mind that VAT law is enforced by the tax administrations and courts of the 27 Member States, which in itself is likely to lead to different interpretation and application practices.[20]

The leeway left to the Member States – a reflection of the degree of fiscal sovereignty retained in the area of VAT[21] – has arguably become increasingly important in recent years, as the realities of life and public perceptions of taxes have changed considerably. On the one hand, an ever-decreasing tolerance for disloyal behaviour has put pressure on national governments to ensure that everyone pays their 'fair' share of taxes.[22] Rising public debt, fuelled by the onset of several crises, has provided additional impetus for the introduction of stricter tax rules and more rigorous enforcement of existing ones, so as to raise the revenues needed to rebuild national economies and adequately fund welfare systems.[23] These are probably the more obvious types of situations capable of sowing the seeds for legislative, administrative and judicial practices at national

introduction of charges having equivalent effect and those that would otherwise distort competition in this segment (particularly state aid).

[13] 'The Report of the Fiscal and Financial Committee' in the *EEC Reports on Tax Harmonization* (Amsterdam: IBFD, 1963) 123 (referring to the gross and net turnover taxes that still existed at that time; however, the argument is analogously valid in the context of VAT).

[14] Council Directive 2006/112/EC of 28 November 2006 on the common system of value added tax (VAT Directive) [2006] OJ L347/1.

[15] Such as the taxable event, the taxable amount and a taxable person's fundamental entitlement to deduct input VAT; see also Recitals 24, 25 and 39 VAT Directive.

[16] Examples include provisions on the taking of evidence (Case C-430/19 *C.F. (Tax Inspection)* EU:C:2020:429, [2020] para 45) and time limits for the submission of supporting documents (Case C-294/20 *GE Auto Service Leasing* EU:C:2021:723, [2021] para 59).

[17] Procedural aspects have not yet been subject to comprehensive harmonisation. Nevertheless, some rules for the streamlining of procedural handling do exist. To name but one example: According to art 263(1) and (1a) VAT Directive, recapitulative statements must be prepared and submitted within one month from the end of the relevant period (one month or one calendar quarter).

[18] VAT Directive, art 273.

[19] Case 34/67 *Lück* EU:C:1968:24, [1968] ECR 00359.

[20] On practical issues leading to different tax treatment (such as capacity constraints and mock compliance), see generally S Geringer, 'Differing abuse concepts in double tax conventions: At what level and to what extent can equality be realized?' (2022) 5(1) *Nordic Journal on Law and Society* 1, 52.

[21] A van Doesum, H van Kesteren, S Cornielje and F Nellen, *Fundamentals of EU VAT Law*, 2nd edn (Alphen aan den Rijn: Wolters Kluwer, 2020) 13.

[22] MJ Graetz, 'Bringing International Tax Policy Into the 21st Century' (2016) 83 *Tax Notes International* 315.

[23] M Stewart, *Tax and Government in the Twenty-First Century* (Cambridge: Cambridge University Press, 2022) 5.

level that are in some tension with the EU-relevant rule of law. However, the introduction and application of national (implementing) provisions which do not comply with the requirements of VAT law and which, on the contrary, tend to benefit the taxpayers concerned,[24] are likewise problematic from the perspective of the beneficiary-neutrally defined EU rule-of-law concept.[25] Their relevance may similarly increase at present, as they contribute to a generally favourable (tax) environment and thus principally encourage foreign investment and/or resettlement, at a time when countries – and especially also Member States among each other – are competing particularly fiercely to attract genuine economic activities to their respective territories.[26]

There are myriad ways in which rule-of-law issues can manifest themselves in VAT law, and it is not the aim of this chapter to address them in an exhaustive manner. Indeed, this is not even necessary because, taking into account the above observations on the level of harmonisation and the Member States' remaining margin of discretion in VAT matters, the relevant situations can be categorised according to common general characteristics. How the CJEU can contribute to upholding the principles of the EU-relevant rule of law in these situations, will be explored in the following section, using representative examples from the case law for each of the identified groups.

The Role of the CJEU as a Supranational Body to Preserve Compliance with the EU-Relevant Rule-of-Law Concept in the Member States

National courts and the CJEU share the duty of ensuring respect of the law in the interpretation and application of EU law (with the primary responsibility resting with the Member States' institutions).[27] However, at a time when we may perceive a mushrooming of national practices testing the limits of the rule of law (for very different reasons),[28] it is arguably all the more important that the CJEU – as a supranational and thus comparatively neutral institution – has been awarded the competence to review the conformity of Member States' actions with the requirements of EU law and, where appropriate, to sanction non-compliance. It is thus vested with authority to take up EU-relevant rule-of-law issues arising at national level.[29] For this purpose, the infringement procedure

[24] An example of this group of cases is the application of a VAT exemption to the supply of intra-group services of financial institutions, insurance companies and pension funds. While not being in line with the requirements of the VAT Directive (see in detail s III), such a measure proves beneficial to the taxable persons concerned in that they are not exposed to a lingering VAT burden due to their typically absent or rather limited entitlement to deduct the VAT on input supplies. Such a measure may then even qualify as state aid that is incompatible with the internal market (TFEU, art 107(1)), which is a question currently pending before the CJEU (see n 81 below).

[25] See s I.

[26] A Cédelle, 'The EU Anti-Tax Avoidance Directive: A UK Perspective' (2016) 63 *British Tax Review* 490, 495.

[27] See eg, Case C-64/16 *Associação Sindical dos Juízes Portugueses* EU:C:2018:117, [2018] para 33.

[28] See s II.

[29] See eg, Case 294/83 *Les Verts v Parliament* EU:C:1986:166, [1986] ECR 01339, para 23.

(TFEU, Article 258)[30] and the preliminary ruling procedure (TFEU, Article 267) can be considered to be of particular importance.[31] Their scope of action and their possible interaction in certain situations will be addressed in the following analysis devoted to the specific possibilities of the Court to uphold the rule of law in the interpretation and application of VAT law in the Member States.

Insofar as the relevant directives contain mandatory rules, the Member States are obliged under Article 288(3) of the TFEU to transpose these provisions into their national VAT legislation, whereby they are bound 'as to the result to be achieved'. Frictions between the Member States' VAT systems and the requirements of EU VAT law could therefore, quite fundamentally, stem from a wrongful or even an absent transposition of these rules.[32] Since the rule of law is defined in a beneficiary-neutral way,[33] deviations from the prerequisites of Union law are to be regarded as problematic regardless of whether they work in favour of the taxpayers or, conversely, deprive them of rights granted to them under EU VAT law.

There may be differences, however, in the consequences that the CJEU deems appropriate for each of these two groups of cases. There is a fundamental obligation to read national provisions as far as possible in conformity with Union law, so as to achieve EU-compatible interpretation and application results.[34] This requirement applies equally to all types of national transposition measures[35] and particularly satisfies the ideals of full effectiveness of EU law and equal treatment of taxpayers within the Union territory irrespective of in which country they are established.[36] An interpretation in line with the requirements of Union law is arguably a workable solution above all if the wording of the relevant national provision is rather too broad and may therefore be read restrictively. For instance, the Austrian provision transposing Article 203 of the VAT Directive – which introduces a VAT liability due to incorrect invoicing – was originally not limited to cases where there is a risk of loss of tax revenue.[37] Following the CJEU's findings in *Finanzamt Österreich*,[38] the referring

[30] Consolidated Version of the Treaty on the Functioning of the European Union (TFEU) [2016] OJ C202/47. It is acknowledged that other Member States may also initiate infringement proceedings under Article 259 TFEU. However, given their very limited practical relevance, the focus will be on infringement proceedings initiated by the European Commission in the following.

[31] In addition, the Court may also address such issues when reviewing decisions of the European Commission in state aid cases under TFEU, art 263. Problematic state aid practices from a rule-of-law perspective may also be addressed in preliminary ruling procedures, as illustrated by the *Heiser* case discussed below.

[32] Regulations, on the other hand, are directly applicable in the Member States (TFEU, art 288(2)). In their context, rule-of-law issues may therefore manifest themselves specifically in problematic application practices (see below). In the field of VAT law, this may concern Member State action within the scope of Council Regulation (EU) No 904/2010 of 7 October 2010 on administrative cooperation and combating fraud in the field of value added tax (recast) [2010] OJ L268/1.

[33] See s I.

[34] See eg, Case C-844/19 *INSS* EU:C:2021:378, [2021] para 53.

[35] On the requirement of an interpretation in conformity with Union law – if necessary also to the detriment of the taxpayer concerned – see Case C-321/05 *Kofoed* EU:C:2007:408, [2007] paras 43–46.

[36] See eg, Commission Communication Enforcing, above n 8, s I.

[37] This has been changed because of the Court's decision described below. Accordingly, as of 22 July 2023, a tax liability does not arise in cases of incorrect invoicing under Austrian VAT law if the recipient of the supply is a final consumer who is not entitled to deduct input VAT.

[38] Case C-378/21 *Finanzamt Österreich (TVA facturée par erreur à des consommateurs finals)* EU:C:2022:968, [2022].

Federal Fiscal Court (*Bundesfinanzgericht*, BFG) considered a correspondingly restrictive reading of Austrian VAT law to be appropriate.[39]

Whenever an EU-compliant interpretation of national VAT provisions would go beyond the utmost possible literal sense (and therefore not be permissible for reasons of legal certainty),[40] it is necessary to distinguish the measures in question according to their effect on the addressees of the law to be able to identify the relevant consequences. If non-compliant national VAT rules prove disadvantageous for the taxpayers concerned, the Court may recognise the direct effect and primacy of the relevant beneficial secondary legislation in the context of a preliminary ruling under the conditions of its long-standing related jurisprudence.[41] This especially allows for safeguarding taxpayers' rights and their equal treatment within the Union territory and, where appropriate, countering any abuse of power by national institutions. In *GMAC UK*,[42] for example, the Court demanded that the UK-based leasing company in question be allowed to reduce the taxable amount in the event of total or partial non-payment by the lessee even in the absence of a national measure by transposing what is now Article 90 of the VAT Directive.[43]

Conversely, when national VAT laws grant legal subjects beneficial treatment contrary to the requirements of EU law, the CJEU is principally willing to protect legality, legal certainty and predictability[44] by refusing both a direct application of unfavourable directive provisions and a *contra legem* EU-compliant interpretation to the detriment of taxpayers. In *DNB Banka*,[45] for instance, the Court rejected the application of the exemption for intra-group supplies under Article 132(1)(f) of the VAT Directive to financial services. Notwithstanding this, it further held that if a Member State has nonetheless established an exemption for these supplies in the statutory national law, the financial authorities could not rely on the opposing legal situation under secondary legislation.[46] These well-established principles, however, do not apply if the relevant benefit constitutes state aid pursuant to Article 107 of the TFEU. Since the Austrian transitional rules under scrutiny in *Heiser*[47] did not impose input VAT adjustments on medical practitioners when they changed to the exempt status under the EU VAT regime and thus conferred a selective advantage to them, that beneficial treatment amounted to state aid and consequently had to be denied.[48]

The occurrence of rule-of-law issues is, however, not limited to situations where the Member States have not (correctly) transposed mandatory provisions of secondary

[39] BFG 27 January 2023, RV/7100930/2021. The Austrian tax authorities appealed against this decision to the Administrative Supreme Court (*Verwaltungsgerichtshof*, VwGH), which brought a follow-up preliminary request before the CJEU (Case C-794/23).

[40] See eg, Case C-844/19 *INSS* EU:C:2021:378, [2021] para 54.

[41] That is, that these provisions, apart from not having been implemented in time or having been implemented incorrectly, are unconditional and sufficiently clear and precise, so that they can be invoked by individuals against the Member State before national courts; eg Joined Cases C-108/14 and C-109/14 *Larentia + Minerva* EU:C:2015:496, [2015] para 48.

[42] Case C-589/12 *GMAC UK* EU:C:2014:2131, [2014].

[43] ibid, para 49.

[44] See eg, Case C-326/15 *DNB Banka* EU:C:2017:719, [2017] para 42.

[45] Case C-326/15 *DNB Banka* EU:C:2017:719, [2017].

[46] ibid, para 41.

[47] Case C-172/03 *Heiser* EU:C:2005:130, [2005] ECR I-01627.

[48] ibid, para 58.

VAT legislation. After all, from a rule-of-law perspective, it is not sufficient to comply with the requirements of Union law only pursuant to the letter of the law. Statutory law also needs to be interpreted and applied accordingly if legality, rather than arbitrariness, were to materialise. In this respect, the EU rule-of-law concept particularly prohibits the use of 'bold' interpretations of principally EU-compliant national provisions which typically reflect a fiscal[49] approach and are often rooted in VAT fraud or abuse allegations. In the illustrative case *Climate Corporation Emissions Trading*,[50] the Court accordingly held that even the reality of downstream fraudulent activities cannot justify a shift of the place of supply to Austria and thus a unilateral change in the allocation of tax jurisdiction in clear breach with the wording of Article 44 of the VAT Directive and the materially identical national transposition provision.[51]

Insofar as VAT secondary legislation does not stipulate binding rules, but 'merely' provides a legal framework for optional schemes, the above observations apply *mutatis mutandis*. When Member States decide to make use of directive options, they are thus bound by the concepts set out in the VAT Directive. In *Norddeutsche Gesellschaft für Diakonie*,[52] for example, the Court recalled the Member States' discretion in introducing VAT grouping under what is now Article 11 of the VAT Directive, but moreover the authoritativeness of a harmonised understanding of the criteria of financial, economic and organisational links. Member States may hence not generally require a majority of capital *and* the voting rights to establish a sufficient financial link, as was seemingly the case under German case law.[53]

Finally, there are areas of VAT law where secondary legislation remains silent, especially for most VAT procedural law.[54] This does not mean, however, that Member States have been given carte blanche to determine freely whether and under what conditions taxpayers can claim their rights under the VAT Directive and, if necessary, challenge acts of tax administrations and courts. On the contrary, the CJEU can still review the use of the Member States' remaining fiscal autonomy in these contexts to ensure that the relevant measures respect, most notably, the VAT-inherent neutrality principle,[55] state aid rules,[56] but also the fundamental rights and the general principles of Union law. The latter two include, among others, the principles of equivalence and effectiveness,[57] the rights of the defence,[58] the principle of equality of arms,[59]

[49] In the sense that tax authorities and courts eventually favour a reading that increases VAT revenue in the respective Member State, regardless of the treatment in other (Member) States.

[50] Case C-641/21 *Climate Corporation Emissions Trading* EU:C:2022:842, [2022].

[51] ibid, paras 43–4 and 52–3.

[52] Case C-141/20 *Norddeutsche Gesellschaft für Diakonie* EU:C:2022:943, [2022].

[53] ibid, paras 44 and 71.

[54] See s II.

[55] Case C-518/14 *Senatex* EU:C:2016:691, [2016] para 38.

[56] According to the case law in other areas of Union law, national procedural rules could prove problematic from a state aid perspective especially when they give national authorities too much room for manoeuvre; eg, Case C-241/94 *France v Commission* EU:C:1996:353, [1996] ECR I-04551, paras 23–24.

[57] See eg, Case C-8/17 *Biosafe – Indústria de Reciclagens* EU:C:2018:249, [2018] paras 27 and 37.

[58] See eg, Case C-189/18 *Glencore Agriculture Hungary* EU:C:2019:861, [2019] para 39.

[59] See eg, Case C-543/14 *Ordre des barreaux francophones and germanophone and Others* EU:C:2016:605, [2016] paras 40–1.

the principle of proportionality,[60] the principle of sound administration,[61] and the principle of legal certainty.[62] By assessing national VAT procedural rules in the light of these standards, the Court thus gives what it refers to as the 'principle of the procedural autonomy of the Member States' an increasingly clear shape[63] while protecting legitimate claims of taxpayers under VAT law. In *Glencore Agriculture Hungary*,[64] for instance, the Court clarified that Article 47 of the Charter[65] forbade the introduction of national rules binding tax administrations and courts to the results of final decisions in connected cases. It further prohibits the use of evidence gathered in proceedings to which the taxable person concerned was not a party, where the latter has not been given access to the documents, but merely a summary of the main findings.[66]

The application of the primacy of EU law, direct and indirect effect and *contra legem* doctrines and the assessment of national VAT procedural rules in the light of the requirements of Union law in preliminary rulings hence enable the Court to take account of certain key aspects of the EU's rule-of-law concept. However, it cannot, in itself, eliminate another fundamental rule-of-law issue that permeates all these cases, namely the unchanged incompatibility of the relevant national measures with the requirements of Union law. Once the CJEU has recognised this circumstance in a decision, it is thus incumbent upon the Member States to adjust the national law or practice accordingly.[67] If they remain inactive – but possibly even before the Court has raised this issue – the European Commission has the power to launch infringement proceedings to address failures to (correctly) implement and apply EU law.[68] If not already resolved at Commission level, these may be decided before the CJEU, and eventually lead to financial penalties.[69] For example, the Commission's action against a German administrative practice of systematically refusing input VAT refund to foreign-based taxable persons if they provided the relevant evidence after the deadline set in Article 15(1) of the Directive 2008/9/EC[70] led to the Court's judgment in *Commission v Germany*,[71] which confirmed the incompatibility of this practice with the requirements of EU law.[72]

[60] Case C-576/15 *Maya Marinova* EU:C:2016:740, [2016] para 44.
[61] Case C-446/18 *AGROBET CZ* EU:C:2020:369, [2020] paras 43–44.
[62] Case C-294/11 *Elsacom* EU:C:2012:382, [2012] para 29.
[63] For a critical view, see X Taton and O Van der Haegen, 'Le droit européen des recours juridictionnels en matière de regulation: un recul de l'autonomie procédurale des États membres' (2011) 19 *Journal de droit européen* 157, 158.
[64] Case C-189/18 *Glencore Agriculture Hungary* EU:C:2019:861, [2019].
[65] Charter of the Fundamental Rights of the European Union (Charter) [2000] OJ C364/1.
[66] Case C-189/18 *Glencore Agriculture Hungary* EU:C:2019:861, [2019] paras 50, 58 and 67.
[67] Joined Cases C-231/06 to C-233/06 *Jonkman* EU:C:2007:373, [2007] ECR I-05149, para 38.
[68] In the specific context of the Commission's competence to monitor Member States' compliance with CJEU jurisprudence, see Commission Communication Enforcing, above n 8, s III.
[69] TFEU, art 260.
[70] Council Directive 2008/9/EC of 12 February 2008 laying down detailed rules for the refund of value added tax, provided for in Directive 2006/112/EC, to taxable persons not established in the Member State of refund but established in another Member State [2008] OJ L44/23.
[71] Case C-371/19 *Commission v Germany* EU:C:2020:936, [2020] (German and French versions available).
[72] ibid, para 88.

Limitations on the Court's Ability to Uphold the Rule of Law in the Implementation and Application of Union Law in the Member States

As demonstrated in the previous section, the CJEU may well be afforded a meaningful role in preserving the rule of law in the context of VAT law. Nevertheless, its possibilities in this regard are severely limited in several respects.

The first limitation relates to the restricted access to judicial review by the Court. It has already been explained above that the CJEU may be involved in the assessment of potential rule-of-law issues particularly through preliminary ruling and infringement procedures.[73] Preliminary rulings may be requested by any court or tribunal of a Member State if it considers that the interpretation of the Treaties or the validity or interpretation of secondary legislation requires clarification (TFEU, Article 267(2)). For courts and tribunals against whose decisions there is no judicial remedy under national law, it is even mandatory to make a request (TFEU, Article 267(3)) provided that the question raised is not immaterial to a given case, the *acte claire* and *acte éclairé* doctrines do not apply, and the correct application of Union law is not otherwise perfectly obvious.[74] In any event, it is solely up to the judge(s) deciding in the specific matter whether or not to make a reference to the CJEU for a preliminary ruling. Taxpayers may steer them in this direction by pointing out relevant issues, but they have no means of forcing the Court's intervention.[75] Failure to make a reference to the CJEU may be for a plethora of reasons, ranging from reluctance to allow a supranational body to intervene in one's 'own affairs', to sheer ignorance of the existence of potential EU law issues, to a strategic move to defuse a potentially damaging conflict between the EU and the respective Member State. If the rule of law is found to be generally threatened in a particular Member State, the deficiencies of the existing mechanisms become even more apparent. After all, it seems fairly unlikely that national courts which do not respect the requirements of Union law in their judgments would be willing to have their practice challenged by the Court.[76]

As far as infringement procedures are concerned, taxpayers can at least interact directly with Union institutions by lodging a complaint with the European Commission.[77] However, the Commission enjoys full discretion as to whether or not to take action against potentially unlawful Member State practices and to eventually bring a matter before the CJEU.[78] Indeed, the policy pursued by the 'Guardian of the Treaties' in this respect does not always seem straightforward and sometimes displays patterns that are somewhat difficult to comprehend. Regarding the

[73] See s III.

[74] Case 283/81 *CILFIT v Ministero della Sanità* EU:C:1982:335, [1982] ECR 03415, paras 10, 13–14 and 16.

[75] Case 93/78 *Mattheus v Doego* EU:C:1978:206, [1978] ECR 02203, para 5. Eventually, taxpayers may claim compensation based on the Court's case law on state liability (albeit under very restrictive conditions; Case C-224/01 *Köbler* EU:C:2003:513, [2003] ECR I-10239).

[76] Craig and de Búrca, above n 11, 47.

[77] See www.ec.europa.eu/assets/sg/report-a-breach/complaints_en/index.html.

[78] See Case 247/87 *Star Fruit v Commission* EU:C:1989:58, [1989] ECR 00291, para 11.

above-mentioned VAT exemption for intra-group supplies under Article 132(1)(f) of the VAT Directive, for instance, the Commission apparently took a hard line on the then German VAT rules.[79] In contrast, the Austrian approach of applying this tax exemption to intra-group supplies by financial institutions, insurance companies and pension funds[80] has not been subject to further scrutiny by the Commission.[81] Such inconsistencies not only raise rule-of-law issues in themselves,[82] but further undermine the Court's ability to contribute to upholding the rule of law in the field of VAT law.

Stakeholders, therefore, fundamentally depend on national courts and the European Commission to act to bring rule-of-law issues to the CJEU's attention. Even if this hurdle has been cleared, there are additional factors that may have a noticeable impact on the Court's ability to strengthen compliance with the EU-relevant rule of law in the Member States. First, under Article 267 of the TFEU, the CJEU is vested with the specific authority to 'provide national courts, in their capacity as courts responsible for the application of EU law … with the points of interpretation of EU law which they need in order to decide the disputes before them'.[83] According to its powers in the preliminary ruling procedure, the Court may thus address questions of Union law, but must refrain from interpreting and applying national law and from finding and assessing the facts of the individual case.[84] In *DuoDecad*,[85] the CJEU further clarified that it may not act as an arbitrator between national tax administrations and thus decide on a specific case. This applies even if the relevant legal issues have already been discussed by the EU judges,[86] the tax authorities involved have exchanged information via the relevant EU legal framework[87] and the situation at hand is nevertheless assessed differently, so that the underlying supply is made subject to VAT in two different Member States.[88] This case memorably illustrates that the CJEU may indeed provide helpful and valuable guidance on the interpretation and application of Union law. However, if national tax authorities and courts are unable (or unwilling) to find a common solution to prevent

[79] Case C-616/15 *Commission v Germany* EU:C:2017:721, [2017].

[80] Whereby the CJEU has meanwhile confirmed the incompatibility of such national provisions with the VAT Directive; see s III.

[81] Which has not followed up on a related request made to the Austrian government; I Rattinger in S Melhardt and M Tumpel (eds), *Umsatzsteuergesetz Kommentar*, 3rd edn (Vienna: Linde, 2021) art 6 para no 696. However, this provision might ultimately become a subject of further investigation of the European Commission in the near future, triggered by a request for a preliminary ruling by the BFG whether a related exemption amounts to a state aid (TFEU, art 107(1)). At the time of finalisation of the manuscript, this case was pending under C-460/24 (*Schoger*). The expected scrutiny of this Austrian particularity by the CJEU and the Commission was likely the main driver behind the Austrian lawmakers' recent decision to abolish the latter exemption as of 2025 (which, however, is irrelevant to situations until that date in which the potential state aid has been granted).

[82] Because of the unequal treatment of violations of EU law across Member States for which a reasonable explanation cannot be identified.

[83] Case C-561/19 *Consorzio Italian Management and Catania Multiservizi* EU:C:2021:799, [2021] para 30.

[84] ibid, para 35.

[85] Case C-596/20 *DuoDecad* EU:C:2022:474, [2022].

[86] As a matter of fact, *DuoDecad* was the follow-up to Case C-419/14 *WebMindLicences* EU:C:2015:832, [2015].

[87] See n 32.

[88] Case C-596/20 *DuoDecad* EU:C:2022:474, [2022] paras 36–37.

a legal assessment that is manifestly at odds with the fundamentals of VAT law,[89] the effects of the CJEU's case law could effectively run dry.[90]

Beyond the institutional limitations under the current EU legal order described above, it should not be forgotten that the Court's jurisprudence may itself, even if unintentionally, be at the root of rule-of-law issues in the Member States. Like any other legal source, judgments may be understood differently by their readers, depending in particular on their educational, social and political backgrounds, but also, very importantly, on their motivation.[91] As far as the latter is concerned, it is hard to deny that the CJEU's increasingly tough stance against VAT evasion and fraud[92] has had the effect of confirming, and probably even reinforcing, the corresponding – sometimes questionable – practices of national tax authorities and courts.[93]

Leaving aside factors that are predominantly related to the sphere of the addressee, a careful observer of the CJEU jurisprudence in the field of VAT law can easily identify certain inconsistencies that are similarly prone to effectuate legal uncertainty, unpredictability of the legal assessment, unequal treatment of the taxpayers concerned and divergent judicial practices within the Union territory. This assertion applies, for example, to the Court's case law on the procurement of a fixed establishment by a separate legal entity in another Member State.[94] The reasoning in *Welmory*[95] hence still suggested that the existence of computer servers, software, servicing and the system for concluding contracts with consumers and receiving income from them could be sufficient to establish a fixed establishment of an online auction house abroad.[96] However, in more recent relevant decisions – *Berlin Chemie A. Menarini*[97] and *Cabot Plastics Belgium*[98] – the CJEU (re)emphasised the importance of technical *and* human resources being available to the foreign-based taxpayer in the same way as if they were their own.[99] As the judges did not contextualise their findings with the previous jurisprudence, it is unclear whether *Welmory* should be considered an 'outlier', whether the findings therein were simply misleading, whether the differences in the underlying business models (digital versus brick-and-mortar) were relevant, etc. What can be considered certain, however, is that such patterns in judicial practice are able to create additional rule-of-law issues and/or exacerbate existing ones.[100]

[89] Instructively, Case C-276/18 *KrakVet Marek Batko* EU:C:2020:485, [2020] para 50: '[T]he correct application of Directive 2006/112 makes it possible to avoid double taxation and to ensure fiscal neutrality'.

[90] On the importance to counter systematic non-compliance with action at the level of the European Commission, see s V.

[91] See, for more detail, Cramwinckel, Chapter 5 in this volume.

[92] As demonstrated in *Ferimet*, where the Court ruled that input VAT deduction ought to be denied even in cases where the reverse charge applies; Case C-281/20 *Ferimet* EU:C:2021:910, [2021] para 56.

[93] Such as that underlying *Climate Corporation Emissions Trading* (see s III). Similar concerns had already been previously expressed by the European Commission; R Lyal, 'Compatibility of National Tax Measures with EU Law: The Role of the European Commission in Tax Litigation before the European Court of Justice' (2015) 24 *EC Tax Review* 5, 12.

[94] S Geringer, '*Cabot Plastics Belgium SA v Belgium*: Procurement of a Fixed Establishment by a Legally Independent Entity' (2024) 70 *British Tax Review* 534, 535.

[95] Case C-605/12 *Welmory* EU:C:2014:2298, [2014].

[96] ibid, para 61.

[97] Case C-333/20 *Berlin Chemie A. Menarini* EU:C:2022:291, [2022].

[98] Case C-232/22 *Cabot Plastics Belgium* EU:C:2023:530, [2023].

[99] Case C-333/20 *Berlin Chemie A. Menarini* EU:C:2022:291, [2022] para 41; Case C-232/22 *Cabot Plastics Belgium* EU:C:2023:530, [2023] para 35.

[100] T Bingham, *The Rule of Law* (London: Penguin Books, 2010) 47.

Avenues for Policy, Administrative and Judicial Action to Reduce Shortcomings in the Future – Feasibility and Desirability

The analysis in the previous section has clouded the rather positive picture drawn earlier. This section therefore aims to identify ways in which the current deficits described above could be overcome. This will be flanked by a discussion of whether the related measures are further to be considered feasible and desirable.

Solving the issues arising from limited access to the CJEU would require a change in the relevant Treaty provisions, which would presuppose a corresponding unanimous political will in the Member States.[101] Even if this were to become a reality, such a move would undoubtedly lead to an increased workload at the level of the CJEU, regardless of what specific changes would actually be made.[102] It is unclear whether this could be dealt with satisfactorily within the existing structures without risking excessively lengthy proceedings (due to an expectable backlog). In this respect, the recent agreement to transfer certain agendas – including VAT – to the General Court (GC)[103] could prove to be a 'game changer'. It remains to be seen, of course, to what extent this measure will effectively be able to live up to the underlying expectations.[104] However, if it turned out to actually result in a more efficient and nonetheless high-quality handling of preliminary requests, this could be an additional and perhaps particularly convincing argument[105] for facilitating access to the EU courts. Such changes would fundamentally improve the situation of taxpayers in cases of non-compliance with the EU-relevant rule of law concept where the competent national courts (of last instance) are unwilling, for whatever reason, to refer the matter to the CJEU.[106]

Notwithstanding the above considerations, there are also ways in which the current practice in the Member States could be improved to raise national judges' awareness of potential legal issues under Union law and of the possibility or obligation to refer questions for a preliminary ruling to the CJEU. This should already be addressed by relevant courses in the education and training of judges at national level. From an EU-centred rule-of-law perspective, it would be even more important to take appropriate measures (also) at Union level, to safeguard a uniform and generally high level of commitment

[101] TEU, art 48.

[102] Such as the introduction of an obligation to make preliminary requests also for lower national courts or even a possibility for taxpayers to bring actions directly before the CJEU.

[103] Regulation of the European Parliament and of the Council amending Protocol No 3 on the Statute of the Court of Justice of the European Union, 2022/0906 (COD) PE-CONS 85/23 JUR 761 COUR 30 INST 515 CODEC 2526.

[104] Most importantly, the conditions for referring cases to the proposed specialised chambers of the GC could easily be circumvented – especially by including questions relating to fundamental rights and/or the general principles of Union law – so that a large number of cases could nevertheless remain before the CJEU (which would render the reform somewhat superfluous).

[105] To the extent that reservations about expanding the Court's review competences have been directed to its limited capacity.

[106] It is acknowledged here that opening up this procedure to taxpayers entails the risk of misuse of the preliminary ruling system. However, this assertion also applies to national courts. It has already been observed in academic scholarship that national judges might likewise abuse their rights, for example, to obtain the repeal of undesirable national legislation; D-U Galetta, *Procedural Autonomy of EU Member States: Paradise Lost?* (Berlin: Springer, 2010) 77.

and compliance throughout the Union territory. It would therefore be welcome if the European judicial training strategy[107] were to be extended to include a specific offer for practitioners in the area of VAT law.[108] However, this would also require the introduction of a corresponding legal basis at an upstream (Treaty) level. Moreover, it is recognised that such an initiative would only find fertile ground with those judges who are actually unaware of the possibilities and obligations under Union law, but conversely would be doomed to failure where the national judiciary is simply unwilling to involve the EU courts.

In terms of factual analysis, it seems both unrealistic and impractical to change the law to enable the CJEU to decide individual cases itself, let alone do the preparatory work such as gathering evidence.[109] Arguably, such changes would not even be necessary, as the Court has already developed a subtler solution to overcome its limited jurisdiction in this respect. By indicating, based on factual assumptions, what it considers to be an appropriate application of its interpretative findings, the CJEU can thus to some extent anticipate the decisions of national courts. This appears to be what the Court did in *Berlin Chemie A. Menarini*, when it held that if the services provided by the Romanian sub-subsidiary had actually been received by the German grandparent company, and if the latter had used its human and technical resources situated in Germany for the supply of goods in Romania (which was for the referring court to verify), the German company could not be considered to have a fixed establishment in Romania.[110] Although the CJEU has thus carefully avoided formulating a final decision, it has provided such clear guidance that it would arguably be difficult for the referring Romanian court to depart from its findings without committing a rather obvious breach of its obligations under Union law.[111]

Such a comparatively extensive use of the CJEU's competences under Article 267 of the TFEU might be seen as laudable in situations where the argument of national authorities seems rather thin and might even have the 'smell' of a misuse of official powers. Nevertheless, this approach sits somewhat uncomfortably with the Court's positioning in cases such as *DuoDecad*, where it refused to settle a dispute between a taxpayer and *two* national tax authorities.[112] Indeed, it is not apparent why more importance should be attached to the idea of case-by-case justice (*Einzelfallgerechtigkeit*) in bilateral disputes than in multilateral ones. If an individual decision turns out to reflect systematic misconduct at national level,[113] it would be upon the European Commission anyway to take the necessary (and arguably more powerful) steps to ensure respect of the EU-relevant rule of law in the Member States, including the eventual initiation of

[107] See in detail Commission, 'Ensuring justice in the EU – a European Judicial Training Strategy for 2021–2024' (Communication) COM(2020) 713 final.

[108] So far, it covers only civil and criminal matters (TFEU, arts 81(2)(h) and 82(1)(c)).

[109] Similarly, F Barth, 'Enforcing EU Law Rights as a Taxpayer – The Case for Better Access to the CJEU', *SSRN Working Paper* 1, 9, papers.ssrn.com/sol3/papers.cfm?abstract_id=4395765.

[110] Case C-333/20 *Berlin Chemie A. Menarini* EU:C:2022:291, [2022] paras 55–56.

[111] See also J Korving, 'Interpretation of EU (Direct) Tax Directives: The Judges Will Decide' in J Lindholm and A Huldqvist (eds), *The Power to Tax in Europe*, Swedish Studies in European Law vol 16 (Oxford: Hart Publishing, 2023) 211: 'When the CJEU ultimately gives a clear interpretation of a concept used, Member States should apply the uniform interpretation as of that moment onwards.'

[112] See s IV.

[113] Case 21/84 *Commission v France* EU:C:1985:184, [1985] ECR 01355, para 13.

an infringement procedure.[114] Moreover, such a judicial practice is likely to effectively go beyond what the CJEU is allowed to do in the context of preliminary rulings (ie to interpret Union law),[115] thereby raising rule-of-law issues in its own right.

In the light of the above observations, issues stemming from a possible misappraisal of the facts of a particular case in cross-border situations[116] could arguably be addressed most effectively by the legal anchoring of two other procedural mechanisms. On the one hand, the problem could be tackled at source by replacing the current voluntary pilot project for cross-border advance rulings in VAT law[117] with a corresponding mandatory regime. On the other hand, and perhaps even more importantly, a system of compulsory dispute resolution, such as that introduced for direct taxation purposes,[118] could do away with issues that may remain, especially even after the CJEU has been consulted in the context of a preliminary ruling procedure.[119] A particular strength of the approach proposed above can be seen in the fact that it pays tribute to the idea of the principle of the procedural autonomy of the Member States[120] and, more fundamentally, to the Treaty-based principles of subsidiarity,[121] proportionality[122] and respect for national identities.[123] But here, too, it would be up to the Union legislator to take action.

By contrast, the rule-of-law issues arising from the CJEU's own judicial practice in VAT law could be eliminated comparatively easily. To this end, it is of the utmost importance that the Court's jurisprudence is as consistent as possible. However, if the CJEU considers that the specificities of an individual case or changes in the living and economic realities (in particular due to increasing globalisation, digitalisation and

[114] While it is acknowledged here that the Commission should choose the approach that it assumes to be the most effective, also from a political perspective (including attempts to resolve issues through informal dialogue under the EU Pilot). In any way, the European Commission should avoid giving the impression of cherry-picking when investigating potentially non-compliant practices, as may have been the case with its approach to national provisions transposing EU VAT Directive, art 132(1)(f) (see s IV).

[115] See s IV.

[116] For purely national situations, it has been argued above that preference should be given to actions at the level of the European Commission (see also n 114).

[117] In which 18 of the 27 Member States currently participate; see in detail Commission, 'Test Case for Privat Ruling Requests Relating to Cross-Border Situations' (Information Notice), taxation-customs.ec.europa.eu/system/files/2021-10/cbr_info-notice-to-the-public_en.pdf.

[118] Council Directive (EU) 2017/1852 of 10 October 2017 on tax dispute resolution mechanisms in the European Union [2017] OJ L265/1.

[119] As in the situation underlying *DuoDecad* (see s IV). Any of the proposed amendments would not necessarily coincide with the emergence of new rule-of-law issues rooted in the possible development of alternative interpretative approaches in, eg, a dispute settlement commission in parallel with those of the CJEU. Such threats to the EU rule-of-law concept could be prevented by appropriate safeguards, such as dialogue channels between the relevant institutions; *see*, for related proposals, K Spies, 'Dispute Resolution in VAT: status quo under the EU VAT Directive and Room for Improvement' in M Lang, P Pistone, A Rust, J Schuch, C Staringer and D Raponi (eds), *CJEU – Recent Developments in Value Added Tax 2016* (Vienna: Linde, 2017) 124.

[120] See s II.

[121] TEU, art 5(3). On the importance of taking due account of subsidiarity issues, see recently S Geringer, 'A Change in the Law or a Guideline from the EU VAT Committee? Evaluating Soft Law Instruments for Clarifying EU VAT Law Through the Lens of Legitimacy' (2024) 52 *Intertax* 251.

[122] TEU, art 5(4). On the requirement under the principle of proportionality to tailor EU action sufficiently narrowly to minimise the impact on national (procedural) autonomy, see G Davies, 'Subsidiarity: The Wrong Idea, in the Wrong Place, at the Wrong Time' (2006) 43 *CML Rev* 63, 81.

[123] TEU, art 4(2). For an elaborate argument for applying this principle to determine EU competences, see B Guastaferro, 'Sincere Cooperation and Respect for National Identities' in R Schütze and T Tridimas (eds), *Oxford Principles of European Union Law*, vol I (Oxford: Oxford University Press, 2018) 380–82.

cross-border mobility) require a different treatment in an individual case or a general change in the case law,[124] this should be clearly expressed in the respective judgments. This would enable taxpayers as well as national tax administrations and courts to correctly assess the scope of its decisions.[125] Similarly, the Court should set clear(er) limits on the instruments available to the Member States to combat VAT evasion and fraud, in order to prevent national tax administrations and courts from overstepping the mark.[126] Increased legal certainty and clarity in the case law would further help the European Commission to take more effective action, if necessary, against national practices that conflict with the requirements of Union law (as any infringement should then be particularly obvious).

Concluding Remarks

The above analysis has shown that the CJEU obviously attaches great importance to the EU-relevant rule-of-law concept in its jurisprudence on VAT law. In its related case law, the Court thus seeks to uphold ideals such as the respect for EU law by national tax administrations and courts, the predictability of legal consequences, the equal treatment of taxable persons and the safeguarding of taxpayers' rights. To this end, it has made use of various instruments and techniques. First, the Court has developed the primacy of Union law, direct and indirect effect and *contra legem* doctrines and, where appropriate, prescribed their application. Second, it has charted the authoritative course for Member States' interpretation and enforcement practice by assessing national legislative, administrative and judicial action in the light of EU primary and secondary law. Third, it has, where necessary, established the incompatibility of national (implementation) provisions and application practices with the requirements of EU law and even imposed financial sanctions on the Member State concerned.

Based on this analysis, it has been concluded that the CJEU jurisprudence has arguably made a significant contribution to upholding the rule of law in the application of VAT law in the Member States. Notwithstanding these achievements, several factors have been identified which have limited the Court's possibilities in this regard: the requirement of action by national judges and/or the European Commission (or other Member States) at an upstream level for the CJEU to be able to intervene (and their inconsistent approaches in doing so); the Court's inability under the current legal framework to assess the relevant national law or the facts of an individual case; but also the impact of the CJEU's own jurisprudence as a result of the judges' increasingly tough

[124] This may indeed be necessary to live up to other ideals, such as treating unequal situations differently or avoiding distortion of competition.

[125] Similarly, R de la Feria, 'On the Evolving VAT Concept of Fixed Establishment' (2021) 30 *EC Tax Review* 201, 205–06.

[126] As in the situation underlying *Climate Corporation Emissions Trading* (see s III). In this context, it is politely suggested that the CJEU should also reconsider its approach of allowing the refusal of input VAT deduction as a sanction in fraudulent and abusive situations (see s IV). After all, the deduction of the VAT on input supplies should not be considered as a right granted to (compliant) taxable persons, but 'simply' as a mechanism baked into the fundamental system of VAT.

stance on VAT evasion and fraud, as well as seemingly wavering lines of reasoning in certain contexts.

Several measures have been presented and discussed to address the existing shortcomings. Overall, it has been suggested that preference should be given to instruments other than extending the Union courts' jurisdiction. Cases of systematic misconduct at national level can arguably be addressed most effectively by the European Commission, which has various tools at its disposal to ensure full compliance with the requirements of EU (VAT) law in the Member States, notably the infringement procedure and the EU pilot as its informal 'sibling'. Ideally, its actions would be guided by clear and transparent communication on the initiation and continuation of these procedures, including the reasons for the choice of a particular instrument. Disputes in cross-border situations, on the other hand, could be meaningfully prevented and resolved through mandatory advance ruling and dispute resolution systems. Within its scope of action, the Court has been encouraged to explain openly and sufficiently the reasons for its findings. In particular, it would be helpful if the CJEU made it a habit to contextualise its decisions with existing relevant jurisprudence and to explicitly communicate any change in (or any rejection to change) the case law. Implementing these recommendations would represent a significant step forward in confirming or possibly even restoring confidence in the rule of law in the implementation and application of EU (VAT) law within the Union territory.

16

Can the Single Tax Principle be Justified under the Rule of Law in an EU Context?

KATERINA PANTAZATOU

Abstract

This chapter commences by exploring the rule of law concept in EU law. It argues that while the term is used differently in different contexts and across different EU institutions, one can observe that several elements of the 'thick' concept of the rule of law can be found in EU law. If this is the case, the chapter investigates whether substantive equality and the ability to pay principle can be read in the 'EU rule of law' and if so, whether they mandate the so-called single tax principle. After analysing primary and secondary EU law as well as the EU Courts' case law, the chapter concludes that while the single tax principle finds some applications in EU law, it cannot be considered as an overarching principle that applies in a consistent and holistic manner.

Introduction

The rule of law is a principle fundamental for all liberal democracies but at the same time it is a concept, a term that can be over encompassing, that can be malleable or one that can be used for different political or ideological objectives. In this sense, the rule of law remains an elusive and highly contested concept. Despite the several interpretations as to its content it appears reasonable to assume that 'the rule of law necessarily involves a claim in principle about the centrality of law to the enterprise of living together – about law's title to rule, so to speak'.[1]

In Hayek's words the rule of law

> […] means that government in all its actions is bound by rules fixed and announced beforehand – rules which make it possible to foresee with fair certainty how the authority will use

[1] G Palombella and N Walker (eds) *Relocating the Rule of Law* (Oxford: Hart Publishing, 2009) xi.

> its coercive powers in given circumstances and to plan one's individual affairs on the basis of this knowledge.[2]

For Tamanaha, the minimal characteristics of the rule of law include that law must be set forth in advance (be prospective), be made public, be general, be clear, be stable and certain, and be applied to everyone according to its terms.[3]

Respect for the rule of law as enshrined in Article 2 Treaty on European Union (TEU), is one of the foundational values of the EU. Article 2 provides that

> [t]he Union is founded on the values of respect for human dignity, freedom, democracy, equality, the rule of law and respect for human rights, including the rights of persons belonging to minorities. These values are common to the Member States in a society in which pluralism, non-discrimination, tolerance, justice, solidarity and equality between women and men prevail.

The rule of law, thus, stands out as an EU value shared among Member States.

The Court of Justice of the European Union (CJEU) has been one of the forerunners in interpreting and enforcing rule of law and its constituent elements, in an EU law context.[4] To do so it has used several different tools that go beyond the mere reference to the rule of law in Article 2 TEU, but instead can be found in other provisions of primary law, including the fundamental freedoms and the non-discrimination principle (Article 18 Treaty on the Functioning of the European Union (TFEU)).[5]

The present chapter aims to explore the EU concept of the rule of law in a tax law context. It will commence by analysing the current inconsistent understanding of the rule of law in an EU context. It will then apply its 'thick', or broad understanding that is endorsed by part of the literature and some EU institutions to inquire whether the single tax principle can be read in such a stretched concept of the rule of law in the EU.[6]

The Rule of Law as an EU Concept?

Unsurprisingly, the rule of law forms one of the cornerstones of the European Union (EU) since its establishment. It is part of the values upon which the EU has been founded, as per Article 2 TEU, together with human dignity, freedom, democracy, equality and respect for human rights. It also figures in the context of the general provisions on the Union's external action (TEU Article 21).

The vague, at first sight, enumeration of the founding values of the EU in Article 2 TEU becomes much more meaningful in the context of Article 7 TEU, which provides

[2] FA Hayek, *The Political Idea of the Rule of Law* (Cairo: National Bank of Egypt 1955) 34.

[3] BZ Tamanaha, 'A Concise Guide to the Rule of Law' in G Palombella and N Walker (eds), *Relocating the Rule of Law* (Oxford: Hart Publishing, 2009) 3 and BZ Tamanaha, *On the Rule of Law: History, Politics, Theory* (Cambridge: Cambridge University Press, 2004).

[4] FG Jacobs, 'The Lisbon Treaty, the Court of Justice and the Rule of Law' in N Nic Shuibhne and L Gormley (eds), *From Single Market to Economic Union: Essays in Memory of John A Usher* (Oxford: Oxford University Press, 2012) 377–78.

[5] See, for instance, CJEU judgment of 18 June 2020, *Commission v Hungary* (Transparency of associations), C-78/18, EU:C:2020:476 and CJEU judgment of 6 October 2020, *Commission v Hungary* (Higher education/ Soros Private University) C-66/18, EU:C:2020:792.

[6] For the distinction between 'thin' and 'thick' concepts of the rule of law, see Lindsay, Chapter 3 in this volume, as well as the section below.

that '[o]n a reasoned proposal by one third of the Member States, by the European Parliament or by the European Commission, the Council, acting by a majority of four fifths of its members after obtaining the consent of the European Parliament, may determine that there is a clear risk of a serious breach by a Member State of the values referred to in Article 2 […]'. A breach of Article 2 may, thus, lead to an investigation against a Member State and, in exceptional circumstances, may lead to the suspension of its voting rights in the Council.

Although Article 7 TEU aims to establish a sanctions mechanism when a Member State seriously breaches one of the values enshrined in Article 2 TEU, it has been repeatedly criticised as an insufficient legal basis for a successful intervention by the Union, including the rule of law.[7] Several reasons can explain the lack of sanctions in the context of Article 7 TEU, including the political unwillingness and the bargaining behind the decision-making procedure and the institutional patterns of behaviour and interactions that it determines.[8] The limited use of Article 7 'in the most outrageous and acute factual constellations'[9] seems to suggest that there is a pressing need to look elsewhere for potential enforcers of the rule of law throughout the Union.

Despite the allegations that Article 7 TEU is an 'empty provision', the discussion on the rule of law (re-)gained prominence recently, following alleged breaches of judicial independence and the separation of powers by different Member States.[10] At the political level, the European Parliament issued a Resolution calling on the Council to determine, pursuant to Article 7(1) TEU, the existence of a clear risk of a serious breach by Hungary of the values on which the Union is founded, most notably the rule of law.[11] As a result of the political developments in Hungary and Poland, on 16 December 2020, the European Parliament and the Council adopted a Regulation that establishes a general regime of conditionality for the protection of the Union budget in the case of breaches of the principles of the rule of law in a Member State.[12] In order to ensure all Member States' compliance with the rule of law *desiderata*, the Regulation allows the Council, on a proposal from the Commission, to adopt protective measures such as the suspension of payments to be made from the Union budget or the suspension of the approval of one or more programmes to be paid from that budget.[13]

[7] C Closa, D Kochenov and JHH Weiler, 'Reinforcing Rule of Law Oversight in the European Union', EUI Working Papers, RSCAS 2014/25, 7.

[8] C Closa, 'Institutional Logics and the EU's Limited Sanctioning Capacity under Article 7 TEU' (2020) *International Political Science Review* 1–15.

[9] Closa et al, above n 7.

[10] See for instance, CJEU, judgment of 24 June 2019, case C-619/18, *Commission v Poland* (Independence of the Supreme Court); CJEU, judgment of 5 November 2019, case C-192/18, *Commission v Poland* (Independence of ordinary courts).

[11] European Parliament Resolution of 12 September 2018 on a proposal calling on the Council to determine, pursuant to Article 7(1) of the Treaty on European Union, the existence of a clear risk of a serious breach by Hungary of the values on which the Union is founded (2017/2131(INL)), OJ C 433, 23.12.2019, 66–85. See also Proposal for a Council Decision on the determination of a clear risk of a serious breach by the Republic of Poland of the rule of law, COM/2017/0835 final – 2017/0360.

[12] Regulation 2020/2092 of the European Parliament and of the Council of 16 December 2020 on a general regime of conditionality for the protection of the Union budget OJ L 433I, 22.12.2020, 1–10.

[13] Note that the Regulation was adopted based on, art 322(1) TFEU and was found to be compatible with the procedure laid down in art 7 TEU by the CJEU in Cases C-156/21 *Hungary v Parliament*, EU:C:2022:90 and Council and C-157/21 *Poland v Parliament and Council*, EU:C:2022:98.

In light of these developments, it comes as no surprise that in a CJEU context, the most contemporary and popular understanding of the rule of law deals with two constituents of the 'thin' understanding of the rule of law; the separation of powers and judicial independence. This focus draws from relatively recent CJEU case law that treated Article 19 TEU as giving concrete expression to the value of the rule of law of Article 2 TEU and as guaranteeing (more explicitly than the general Article 2) judicial independence at EU and national levels.[14] Additionally, the Court has ruled that '[t]he very existence of effective judicial review designed to ensure compliance with EU law is *of the essence of the rule of law*. In that regard, as provided for in the second subparagraph of Article 19(1) TEU, it is for the Member States to establish a system of legal remedies and procedures ensuring for individuals compliance with their right to effective judicial protection in the fields covered by EU law' (emphasis added).[15]

However, the CJEU has gone beyond the obvious and most expected expressions of the rule of law, like legality, legitimacy and accountability, and it has read in it also respect for certain fundamental rights. The Court, thus, is not only shaping the concept of the rule of law but is also unifying within it a set of common characteristics that should apply to all Member States. At the same time, the rule of law is applied and interpreted by all other EU institutions (for instance, the European Commission and the European Parliament) across all EU policies. Due to the different institutions that interpret and apply the rule of law, one may argue that multiple rule of law 'versions' exist within the Union.[16]

In its recent 'Rule of Law Report', the European Commission attempted to provide a definition of the rule of law:

> Under the rule of law, all public powers always act within the constraints set out by law, in accordance with the values of democracy and fundamental rights, and under the control of independent and impartial courts. The rule of law includes principles such as legality, implying a transparent, accountable, democratic and pluralistic process for enacting laws; legal certainty; prohibiting the arbitrary exercise of executive power; effective judicial protection by independent and impartial courts, effective judicial review including respect for fundamental rights; separation of powers; and equality before the law.[17]

According to the Commission, equality before the law and respect for fundamental rights are constituents of the rule of law. On the other hand, equality – in its non-discrimination sense, as a general principle of EU law enshrined in Article 18 TFEU – is simultaneously a self-standing principle, a fundamental right and a fundamental constituent of the rule of law. This statement may seem odd from a classical understanding of the rule of law, especially compared to the formal approach of Raz[18]

[14] See indicatively, CJEU judgments of 18 May 2021, *Asociația 'Forumul Judecătorilor din România' and Others*, C-83/19, C-127/19, C-195/19, C-291/19, C-355/19 and C-397/19, EU:C:2021:393 [188].

[15] CJEU judgment of 11 May 2023, *Inspecția Judiciară* (C-817/21, EU:C:2023:391) [40].

[16] T Konstadinides, *The Rule of Law in the European Union – The Internal Dimension* (Oxford: Hart Publishing, 2020) 19.

[17] European Commission, Communication: 2020 Rule of Law Report, The rule of law situation in the European Union, COM(2020) 580 final (30.09.2020) (hereinafter the 'The first Rule of Law Report'), 1. See also European Commission, 'Communication: Further strengthening the Rule of Law within the Union State of play and possible next steps' COM (2019) 163 final (03.04.2019).

[18] J Raz, 'The Rule of Law and its Virtue', in *The Authority of Law* (Oxford: Oxford University Press, 1979), and subsequently, J Raz, 'The Law's Own Virtue' (2019) 39 *Oxford Journal of Legal Studies* 1.

or Fuller[19] who, in general, do not find substantive equality before the law among the constituents of the rule-of-law concept.[20]

Despite the fact that the principle of equality would not be recognised as part of a formalist theory of the rule of law,[21] several other voices attribute to the rule of law a more substantive content in that it (should) be 'imbued with certain norms, standards or principles' that would protect, inter alia, the individual citizen's autonomy.[22] This 'thick' concept suggests that the rule of law cannot coexist with unfairness and injustice.[23] In this view, the normative shortcomings of 'thin' theories are remedied by incorporating particular conceptions of human rights and other features of political morality into the concept of the rule of law.[24] In Craig's view, the principles undergoing the rule of law should 'embrace, in addition to its formal attributes, ideals of equality and rationality, proportionality and fairness, and [in particular] certain substantive rights'.[25]

At the same time, equality in the sense of non-discrimination may appear an unusual element of the rule of law also from a systematic reading of Article 2 TEU; equality is a separate value in the provision, standing next to the rule of law. Should this be understood as a separate value (or right), distinct from the rule of law? The 'conditionality' Regulation repeated the Commission's definition of the constituents of the rule of law. The preamble provides that '[t]he rule of law requires that all public powers act within the constraints set out by law, *in accordance with the values of democracy and the respect for fundamental rights* as stipulated in the Charter of Fundamental Rights of the European Union (the 'Charter') and other applicable instruments, and under the control of independent and impartial courts' (*emphasis added*).[26] An official document of the EU, thus, suggests that the rule of law requires all public powers (at national and supranational level) to act in compliance with fundamental rights, including the equality principle.

Similarly, the CJEU often relies on the rule of law to interpret and enforce procedural rights, like the right to a fair trial and an effective remedy. For instance, in the famous *Berlioz* case AG Wathelet observed that '[where] a person seeks to challenge a decision adversely affecting him, the applicability of Article 47 of the Charter appears to be the condition sine qua non of a Union subject to the rule of law. As I have observed above, a Union subject to the rule of law means that neither the Member States nor the institutions of the Union can avoid review of the conformity of their acts'.[27] Accordingly, a fundamental right as enshrined in the Charter constitutes a precondition for the application of the rule of law. This Opinion was followed by the Court that affirmed that an

[19] LL Fuller, *The Morality of Law* 2nd edn (New Haven CT: Yale University Press, 1969).

[20] For more on this see, Lindsay, above n 6 and Daly, above n 6.

[21] Lindsay, ibid.

[22] J Laws, *The Constitutional Balance* (Oxford: Hart Publishing, 2021), 19. Similarly, TRS Allan, *Law, Liberty, and Justice* (Oxford, Oxford University Press, 1993).

[23] On the distinction between the 'thin' and the 'thick' concept of the rule of law, see Lindsay, above n 6. For the 'thick' version's 'supporters' see T Bingham, *The Rule of Law* (Allen Lane, 2010); FA Hayek, *The Constitution of Liberty* (Chicago: The University of Chicago Press 1960).

[24] R Peerenboom, 'Human Rights and the Rule of Law: What's the Relationship? University of California, Public Law and Legal Theory Research Paper Series, Research Paper No 05–31, 1–152, 20–1. Available at: http://ssrn.com/abstract=816024.

[25] P Craig, 'Theory and Values in Public Law: A Response' in C Harlow, P Craig and R Rawlings (eds), *Law and Administration in Europe: Essays in Honour of Carol Harlow* (Oxford: Oxford University Press, 2003) 31.

[26] Regulation 2020/2092, Preamble, Recital 3.

[27] Opinion of Advocate General Wathelet 10 January 2017, C-682/15, *Berlioz Investment Fund*, EU:C:2017:2 [66].

intermediary (information holder) should have legal standing to require that the judiciary of the requested state checks that tax authorities have conducted mutual assistance in line with the rule of law.[28]

Therefore, in EU tax law, the rule of law appears to have been rendered to the 'the main umbrella principle applicable to tax procedures'.[29] Beyond procedural rights, however, the rule of law has also been understood – from a tax law perspective, in its substantive form, including the protection of taxpayers' rights to confidentiality, privacy and the right to participate in the exchange of information.[30]

All this shows that there is no one clear understanding or definition of the rule of law concept under EU law. Neither is a 'thin' or 'thick' version preferred at EU institutional level or case law. The CJEU has clearly articulated that the separation of powers and judicial independence are enshrined in the rule of law but beyond that, neither the judiciary nor the Commission or any other EU institution apply a consistent interpretation of this concept. There are cases where an EU institution clearly states the respect for fundamental rights (including equality) as constituents of the rule law[31] and there are also instances where the rule of law appears as separate from but strongly connected to human rights' protection.[32] Even in academic literature however, the rule of law has been linked to the value of justice itself – of which equality is an element, and the prevention of any arbitrary exercise of taxing powers.[33]

Having thus, in mind a 'thick' version of the rule of law, that encompasses equality as a substantive right, this contribution will attempt to understand whether the single tax principle can derive from the equality principle and if so, whether it can be read in EU law. To do so, it will commence by explaining the single tax principle as this was first developed in the international tax context. Then, the single tax principle will be connected to the non-discrimination (and the concomitant ability to pay) principle and finally, it will be reviewed in the context of relevant CJEU case law and secondary EU tax law.

Single Taxation: Origins and the International Discussion

Although the discussion on whether to address double taxation or tax evasion at international level, was already present at the League of Nations' discussions and reports,[34]

[28] CJEU judgment of 16 May 2017, *Berlioz Investment Fund*, case C-682/15, ECLI:EU:C:2017:373, see also, K Pantazatou, 'Luxembourg: Fundamental Rights in the Era of Information Exchange – The Berlioz Case (C-682/15)' in M Lang et al (eds), *CJEU – Recent Developments in Direct Taxation 2017* (Linde Verlag, 2018) 127–152.

[29] J Kokott and P Pistone, *Taxpayers in International Law: International Minimum Standards for the Protection of Taxpayers' Rights* (Oxford: Hart Publishing, 2022) 206.

[30] I Mosquera Valderrama, A Mazz, LE Schoueri, N Quiñones, J Roeleveld, P Pistone, and F Zimmer, 'The Rule of Law and the Effective Protection of Taxpayers' Rights in Developing Countries', WU International Taxation Research Paper Series no 10, (2017), ssrn.com/abstract=3034360.

[31] E.g. European Commission, the first Rule of Law Report (above, n 17).

[32] The text of TEU art 2 speaks in favour of this approach. See also Kokott and Pistone, above, n 29, who suggest that the protection of taxpayers' rights is a corollary of the rule of law, at 206 et seq. See also the *Berlioz* case, above n 28.

[33] See Kokott and Pistone, above n 29, 493.

[34] See, for instance, *Technical Experts to the Financial Committee of the League of Nations, 'Double Taxation and Tax Evasion: Report and Resolutions Submitted by the Technical Experts to the Financial Committee of the League of Nations* (1925).

the single taxation principle in its current formulation and understanding was first attributed to Reuven Avi-Yonah. Avi-Yonah argued that 'income from cross-border transactions should be subject to tax once', at a rate that corresponds to/is determined by the benefits principle.[35] This idea that, according to some, encompasses the foundations of the international tax regime,[36] has since then generated a lot of discussion,[37] which was revamped, especially after BEPS and the alleged transformation of international tax framework.[38]

Part of the discussions on the single taxation principle have focused on whether single taxation should be interpreted as a principle that requires the absence of double taxation or whether it (also) necessitates the absence of double non-taxation, that is, an effective taxation at some point and somewhere.[39] The question of the interpretation of the principle requires some contextual analysis in the realm of Double Tax Conventions (DTCs) that cover bilateral cross-border situations. Two questions arise in this regard; first, what should be the content of the principle, ie whether the emphasis should be put on the tax being levied once only, or whether the emphasis should (also) be put on the tax being levied (at least) once. The two possibilities are not mutually exclusive as, indeed, the objective of preventing double taxation has increasingly been connected to the objective of preventing double non-taxation.[40] However, regardless of whether one understands the single tax principle in its full scope (both no-double taxation but also no double non-taxation) or reads it in a narrower manner (only no-double taxation), a distributive rule is required to determine which state has the right to tax said income. In Avi-Yonah's mind, this distributive rule should derive from the benefits principle, and thus, active income should be taxed at the source state, whereas passive income should be taxed (primarily) at the residence state.

While, as already explained, Avi-Yonah understands the principle of single tax (or single taxation) as mandating that income from cross-border transactions should be subject to tax *once*, that is, *neither more nor less* than once, this understanding was not unanimously shared. Thus, in 2004 – long before BEPS, but much later than 1997 when Avi-Yonah pitched his idea, it was believed that it could not generally be assumed that DTCs aimed at preventing double non-taxation but they rather aimed to allocate taxing rights between the contracting states, without (necessarily) obliging them to actually exercise those rights.[41] An exception to this 'rule' could be found to some bilateral rules, which aimed at achieving single taxation insofar as they made the waiver of the right to tax provided for in the convention subject to the other contracting state actually

[35] RS Avi- Yonah, 'International Taxation of Electronic Commerce' (1997) 52 *Tax L Rev* 507, 517.

[36] See, for instance, Y Brauner, 'An International Tax Regime in Crystallization' (2003) 56 *Tax L Rev* 259, 264.

[37] RS Avi-Yonah has been considered in tax literature as the pioneer behind the discussions on the single tax principle. J Wheeler's edited book that is entirely devoted on 'Single taxation' makes extensive references to Avi-Yonah's research and understanding of the principle. RS Avi-Yonah, 'International Tax Law as International Law' (2004) 57 *Tax Law Review* 4; RS Avi-Yonah, 'Who Invented the Single Tax Principle? An Essay on the History of U.S. Treaty Policy' (2014/15) 59 *New York Law School Law Review* 306.

[38] See, for instance, R Mason, 'The Transformation of International Tax' (2020) 114 *Am J Int'l L* 353.

[39] Avi-Yonah, above n 35, 509.

[40] See also M Lang, *General Report: Double Non-taxation*, IFA Cahiers 89a (2004), 81.

[41] M Lang, ibid, suggesting specifically that '[t]he reporters were accordingly critical as they pointed out – each with a different emphasis – *that DTCs are by no means based on the idea of preventing double non-taxation* and that this is true only for certain cases at the most'.

exercising the right to tax assigned to it by the DTC.[42] The objective of double non-taxation was certainly not perceived by most as an interpretative guide when interpreting DTCs and the overall feeling at the time was that the DTCs based on the OECD MC did not intend to exclude double non-taxation.[43] Hence, the objective of preventing double non-taxation could be of significance only insofar as it was demonstrably expressed in the treaty provision to be interpreted.[44]

Post-BEPS, however, the focus has shifted from ensuring no double taxation through DTCs, to also dealing with abusive situations and cases of double non-taxation. Yet, as Parada notes 'contrary to a pure idea of single taxation, the prevention of double non-taxation is contingent on the fact that artificial (abusive) structures are used to achieve it'.[45] In the words of the BEPS report: '[n]o or low taxation is not per se a cause of concern, but it becomes so when it is associated with practices that artificially segregate taxable income from the activities that generate it'. Thus, if one assesses the single tax principle from a contextual and evolutionary perspective, has the single tax principle become about achieving a fair rate of taxation, rather than ensuring tax at least once through a proper allocation of taxing rights? In other words, does the single tax principle mandate *no under taxation* (however this is to be defined)? Such an interpretation would justify the recent policy developments, not only BEPS but also the Pillar 1 and Pillar 2 initiatives, but the role and the purpose of the principles is not necessarily to transform to be in line with their times.

Single Taxation in EU Law

The single tax principle in an EU law context can be understood as deriving from the equality principle which, often constitutes under EU law, the legal basis for the ability to pay principle.[46] The legal construction of the EU does not allow for much deference to DTCs and the 'international tax regime' (if such exists).[47] Thus, the single tax principle in the EU context, has to be analysed within its own legal framework and, therefore, neither its meaning nor its significance necessarily coincide with those presented before in the DTCs context.

In this context, thus, the question arises whether the single tax principle exists at all, and if so, in which form. In other words, in the assumption of the absence of a DTC

[42] ibid.

[43] ibid.

[44] ibid.

[45] L Parada, 'Full Taxation: The Single Tax Emperor's New Clothes' (2021) 24 *Flo Tax Rev* 729, 735. Parada cites the OECD BEPS Action Plan (2013) according to which '[n]o or low taxation is not per se a cause of concern, but it becomes so when it is associated with practices that artificially segregate taxable income from the activities that generate it'.

[46] On this see, G Bizioli and E Reimer, 'Equality, ability to pay and neutrality' in C HJI Panayi, W Haslehner, and E Traversa (eds), *Research Handbook on European Union Taxation Law* (Cheltenham: Edward Elgar, 2020) 51–74. The ability to pay principle is, itself, enshrined in some Member States' Constitutions.

[47] This holds true regarding the primacy of EU law over DTCs and the obligations that arise therefrom but certainly, not so much regarding the political context of the impact the international/OECD developments have had on the EU legal framework (see for instance the Anti-Tax Avoidance Directive, the GloBE Directive).

between Member States or under the premise of the primacy of EU law over DTCs,[48] is there an obligation to single taxation – to tax income at least/only once, and if so, where does this obligation derive from and how well is it applied?

As already stated, the only way the single tax principle could find its way into EU law is through the non-discrimination principle, which, arguably, encompasses the ability to pay principle, which, in turn, connects to the single tax principle. Several derivations need to be made in this case, in an area like direct taxation where harmonisation in the EU is quite limited, despite recent major steps in the opposite direction.[49] But in this case – if indeed, the only foundation in EU law to guarantee the single tax principle is the non-discrimination principle, then, only one of its elements can be fulfilled, that the taxpayer must pay tax only once (and not necessarily *at least* once).

Secondary EU tax law explicitly provides for the elimination of double taxation in at least two cases, the Parent Subsidiary Directive (PSD)[50] and the Interest and Royalty Directive (IRD)[51, 52] However, the scope of these directives in quite narrow and, thus, a general principle of single taxation cannot be deduced within these confines. In line with international developments, these directives were subsequently amended to include elements of the elimination of double non-taxation. Specifically, the PSD was amended in 2014 to include a provision to prevent situations of double non-taxation resulting in unintended benefits for groups of companies in different Member States compared to domestic groups.[53] A General Anti-Abuse Rule (GAAR) was added to the PSD in 2015.[54] The IRD also includes a provision to prevent situations of double non-taxation (but only partially through a 'subject-to-tax' requirement for permanent establishments).[55] However, given the very narrow scope of the application of these provisions, they could only be characterised as 'incidents' of single taxation.

In contrast, the CJEU case law is ample in analysing the non-discrimination principle in light of the fundamental freedoms in cross-border situations. A very usual situation is this of a resident in an EU Member Stater and a non-resident who are treated differently and thus, the non-resident's respective freedom (eg freedom of establishment, free movement of capital) is restricted. The most common restriction that arises from the different treatment is double taxation, and should the single taxation indeed derive from the non-discrimination principle then the EU judiciary should ensure that it is eliminated, unless it is justified and proportionate.

[48] In reality, bilateral DTCs exist between almost all pairs of Member States. However, the question posed here is not merely rhetorical as, in case of conflict, primary and secondary EU law has primacy over the DTCs (at least those that were concluded after the States' accession to the Union, as per art 351 TFEU).

[49] See, for instance, Council Directive 2016/1164 ('ATAD') and Council Directive (EU) 2022/2523 ('GloBE Directive'), both of which are considered to be the EU implementation of certain BEPS Actions.

[50] Council Directive 2011/96/EU ('Parent Subsidiary') (recast), OJ L 345, 29.12.2011, 8–16.

[51] Council Directive 2003/49/EC ('Interest and Royalty), OJ L 157, 26.6.2003, 49–54.

[52] I am not including here safeguards in other directives to avoid the double taxation that could arise because of these directives' implementation.

[53] See Parent Subsidiary Directive, art 4(1)(a) (Linking rule): Prevention of double non-taxation deriving from mismatches in the qualification of distributed income (equity – debt).

[54] Parent Subsidiary Directive, art 1(2).

[55] Interest and Royalty Directive, art 1(5)(b).

Single Taxation as Tax *Only Once*

While double taxation in cross-border situations is clearly an obstacle to individuals and corporations' freedom to move, there are several conceptual layers applied by the Court before eliminating double taxation. After all, such an exercise, as pointed out earlier, would entail allocating taxing rights between the involved Member States which goes not only beyond the Court's mandate, but also beyond the scope of EU law altogether. The underpinning in these cases is quite evident: in a purely domestic situation double taxation does not arise, or is relieved, whereas in a cross-border one, double taxation ensues.

There are three main caveats in the application of the single taxation in the EU, other than the obvious lack of a harmonised framework of allocation of (single) taxing rights. The first one relates to the comparability of the taxpayers – the test whether two taxpayers, usually a resident and non-resident, deserve to be in the same situation and be taxed in the same way. While there is no clear 'formula' in the application of this test, the Court departs from the (default) premise that residents and non-residents are not in a comparable situation. The comparability test has not been applied by the Court in a consistent manner, although one could say that the Court often looks at the purpose of the national legislation in question and whether this purpose is (also) satisfied in a cross-border scenario. In case of a positive answer, then, the situations would be comparable. But the Court has gone beyond a pure formalistic approach and has decided that residents and non-residents can be in a comparable situation under certain circumstances, especially in cases when the majority of the taxpayer's income is derived at the source state and no income is produced at residence,[56] or in cases of relief from economic double taxation domestically but not for cross-border situations.[57]

The second caveat in this case is the possibility of Member States attempting to justify, on public interest grounds, the different treatment of residents and non-residents (even if the two are in a comparable situation). The Court has accepted justifications relying, inter alia, on the 'balanced allocation of taxing rights' between Member States,[58] the need to combat tax avoidance,[59] and the coherence of the tax system(s).[60] Thus, a Member State may not be obliged to ensure single taxation when one of the aforementioned justifications is successfully invoked before the Court.

The last 'obstacle' in the application of the single tax principle emanates exactly from the interaction of the different tax systems within the EU and the absence of an EU-wide (or EU-generated) allocation of taxing rights among Member States, a *disparity* in the Court's words. Disparities do not, as a rule, fall within the ambit of the fundamental freedoms because they stem from the mere interaction of two taxing systems.[61]

[56] See the Schumacker line of case law, Case C-279/93 *Schumacker* [1995] ECR I-225.

[57] See eg, Case C-35/98 *Verkooijen* [2000] ECR I-4071 and Joined Cases C-436/08 and C-437/08 *Haribo Lakritzen Hans Riegel and Österreichische Salinen* [2011] ECR I–305.

[58] See especially loss relief cases eg, Case C-446/03, *Marks and Spencer* [2006] ECR I-2283.

[59] See especially abuse cases eg, Case C-196/04 *Cadbury Schweppes and Cadbury Schweppes Overseas* [2006] ECR I-7995.

[60] See for instance cases relating to social security/pension contributions and corresponding deductions, eg Case C 204/90 *Bachmann* [1992] ECR I 249 and Case C 300/90 *Commission v Belgium* [1992] ECR I 305.

[61] See AG Geelhoed in Case C-374/04 *Test Claimants in Class IV of the ACT Group Litigation* [2006] ECR I-11673.

Consequently, in cases of juridical double taxation, for instance, whereby the residence state treats the income dividends in the same way as the domestic dividends (e.g. same tax rate), the Court has decided that it does not have to provide relief for the tax withheld at source. Instead, the Court has ruled that 'the adverse consequences which might arise from the application of an income tax system [...] result from the exercise in parallel by two Member States of their fiscal sovereignty' and since EU law does not lay any general criteria for the attribution of areas of competence between the Member States in relation to the elimination of double taxation within the Union, this burden of the 'apportionment of fiscal sovereignty' falls, inevitably, on the DTCs.[62] Accordingly, EU law cannot be relied upon to enforce single taxation in this case.

The CJEU has followed the same approach in cases of a higher tax burden in a cross-border situation due to the different tax rates between the two Member States. The Court, for example, ruled in the *Gilly* case that the higher tax burden the taxpayer had to incur due to his cross-border activity (and the provision of a credit by the residence state that did not result in full relief) was only the consequence of a disparity between the systems of the two states. Thus, in absence of relevant EU law, it remained within the sovereignty of the Member States to determine their own policies in respect of rates.[63] In this context, the Court also provided an interesting understanding of the single tax principle in the DTC context. It specifically held that 'the object of a convention such as that in issue *is simply to prevent the same income from being taxed in each of the two States*. It is not to ensure that the tax to which the taxpayer is subject in one State is no higher than that to which he or she would be subject in the other' (emphasis added).[64]

Accordingly, the CJEU does not appear to vest the non-discrimination principle with the right to single taxation (even in cases that are decided to be comparable) and, consequently, it does not give the taxpayers an enforceable right not to be subject to double taxation,[65] except in cases where the aforementioned conditions are fulfilled (comparability, absence of successful justifications, discriminatory treatment/restriction and *not* disparity but discrimination instead). In essence, in the Court's case law, the conditions for the entitlement of the taxpayer to single taxation, in the sense of the elimination of double taxation in cases where (i) the residence state eliminates economic double taxation domestically and thus, on the basis of the non-discrimination principle and the relevant applicable freedom it has to provide 'equal treatment' to incoming dividends; (ii) the source state imposes a withholding tax to income but does not impose such a tax domestically; on the basis of the non-discrimination principle and the relevant applicable freedom, it has to eliminate the withholding tax that applies only in a cross-border situation. It is doubtful whether the Court's case law that has invented the 'always somewhere principle' that ensures that negative income must be taken into account somewhere is of relevance in the context of single taxation. The same question applies regarding the obligation (or the lack of it, thereof) to provide full relief or partial relief.

[62] See eg, Case C-513/04 *Kerckhaert and Morres* [2006] ECR I-1096.

[63] See Case C-336/96, *Gilly* [1998] ECR I-2793.

[64] ibid, para 46.

[65] J Wheeler, 'Do Taxpayers Have a Right to DTR?' in J Wheeler (ed) *Single Taxation* (Amsterdam: IBFD, 2018) 165.

These questions obviously depend on the concept of the single tax principle itself and the question whether single taxation intends to completely eliminate cases of double taxation or if it aims to *reduce* the double taxation that may arise. In the latter scenario it is questionable whether the principle would be satisfied because of the persisting higher tax burden in a cross-border situation (as opposed to a purely domestic one). The understanding of the Court that found no discriminatory treatment in a *Gilly*-type scenario,[66] is compatible with a 'narrower' understanding of the single tax principle that leaves outside its scope the fairness (and results) of different tax rates. This is understandable also from a certainty and administrability perspective as otherwise the principle would risk becoming too vague,[67] too partitioned and in need of granularisation.

Single Taxation as Tax *at Least Once*

The principle of single taxation in the sense of subjection to tax *at least once* has never been expressly accepted by the Court as a justification of the prevention of base erosion, or as a justification of national anti-abuse measures. The Court specifically argued in *Eisenstadt*, that

> in several cases … in which a Member state has attempted to counterbalance its inability to impose tax on another taxpayer … the Court considered … the argument that national legislation was intended to issue single taxation of certain income in the Member State. In none of these cases, however, did the Court recognise the principle of single taxation as a

Indeed, as Vanistendael argued, if the Court accepted the single tax principle (in its 'at least once' sense) as a justification for anti-abuse, it would, effectively, render the principle into a budgetary safeguard to ensure that the tax base of the invoking Member State is not eroded, and, by implication, that the corresponding revenue is not lost.[68] However, the Court has traditionally rejected justifications based on a Member States' loss of revenue.[69]

In contrast, however, to this rejection the Court has repeatedly accepted national CFC rules when they target *wholly artificial arrangements* and upon the fulfilment of certain other conditions (including the lack of a general presumption of tax avoidance and the actual demonstration of the lack of substance/artificiality of the CFC). Under these circumstances, the Court agrees that freedom of establishment allows a Member State to apply its CFC rules to prevent abuse and tax avoidance. In this sense, as opposed to the previous scenario, the Court does not impose tax at least once, but, instead, it imposes a *certain level of tax* at *least once.* Whether this can be linked to the single tax principle is a question of interpretation and pertains to whether the single tax principle covers indeed (fair) tax rates and whether it can be 'partitioned' to allow for some/more/less tax.

[66] A scenario where the residence state gives a credit for the tax paid at source, which however, due to the different tax rates between source (higher) and residence (lower), does not completely eliminate double taxation.

[67] E CM Kemmeren and F De Lillo, 'International Single Taxation: A Misguiding Notion' in Wheeler (n 67).

[68] F Vanistendael, 'A Single Tax Principle for a Single Market?' in Wheeler (n 67) 192.

[69] See eg, CJEU judgment of 16 July 1998, ICI, C-264/96, EU:C:1998:370.

In the context of fundamental freedoms, thus, the application of the single tax principle in its 'at least once' sense can only apply indirectly (if at all) and assessed on an *ad hoc* basis (is there indeed a wholly artificial arrangement? How does the national CFC rule apply and what will the top up tax be)? Accordingly, it would be very difficult to fit this top up liability into the single tax principle that would require a certain degree of generality and abstraction.

However, if one looks at Article 7 of the ATAD, a more concrete obligation 'to tax' arises, in the sense that Member States are since the implementation of the ATAD under the obligation to apply CFC rules if the tax rate in the Member State of the CFC is less than half of the tax rate in the Member State of the parent company. Accordingly, this means that for certain categories of (passive) income, there is now a minimum tax rate above zero in every Member State and that these specific categories of income to which Article 7 of the ATAD applies are now subject to a variable minimum tax that will be due in the state in which the headquarters of a permanent establishment or the parent of a subsidiary are located. The same result, combatting double non-taxation with regard to a certain type of income is achieved through the ATAD's anti-hybrid rules. This comes as no surprise as the ATAD effectively transposes the BEPS Action Plan in EU law.[70]

Similarly, the ATAD imposes an obligation to Member States to levy an exit tax in case the taxpayer transfers their residence or business or assets to another Member State or third country.[71] This exit tax shall be levied on the difference between the market value of the transferred assets and the value of the assets for tax purposes. While Article 5(5) of the ATAD provides a mandatory step-up in order to avoid double taxation of the unrealised capital gains, the exit tax provision should be considered as a provision that aims to ensure that these capital gains are taxed at least (and only) once. While the discriminatory nature of such a tax is obvious as the exit tax only arises in cross-border scenarios, both the directive and the CJEU case law have developed a framework to make these taxes compatible with primary EU law.[72]

While, hence, secondary legislation appears to agree, *under specific conditions*, with the single tax principle in its no double non-taxation sense, the CJEU has not explicitly recognised the need for income to be subject to tax at least once in its case law. It has to be acknowledged, however that the fundamental freedoms case law does touch upon Specific Anti-Avoidance Rules (SAARs), such as domestic CFC rules and thin capitalisation rules, to ensure that a certain *degree* of taxation applies, under conditions.[73] This requirement, however, does not seem to fit within the meaning of the single tax principle because the Court, in the context of the CFC rules has effectively allowed that only in cases of abuse can a Member State overcome the nexus requirement (as with CFC rules in general) and impose a top-up tax which, only in very specific cases, would amount to a tax on said income for the first time ('at least once').

[70] See Parada, above n 45.

[71] ATAD, art 5.

[72] See eg, CJEU judgment of 29 November 2011, C-371/10, *National Grid Indus*, EU:C:2011:785; CJEU judgment of 11 March 2004.

[73] For example, one requirement in settled CJEU law case law is that the national rule at issue does not generally presume tax avoidance. See CJEU judgments of 4 March 2004 in *Commission v France* (C-334/02, EU:C:2004:129) [27] and 12 September 2006 in *Cadbury Schweppes and Cadbury Schweppes Overseas* (C-196/04, EU:C:2006:544) [50]–[51].

Despite the explicit rejection by the Court of the no double non-taxation element of the single tax principle, the advent of the GloBE directive could force the Court to reassess this view, especially in light of the compatibility of the Directive with freedom of establishment. A first indication towards this direction could be identified in the Opinion of AG Kokott who connected the prevention of non-taxation to the efficiency of the collection of taxes.[74] The case concerned the compatibility with fundamental freedoms of the taxation by Portugal of a 'foreign' fund (UCITS) in comparison to a domestic fund that was exempted from tax but subject to a 'stamp duty'. AG Kokott opined in this context that 'the application of a deduction at source as a taxation technique to non-resident taxpayers – while resident taxpayers are not subject to such a deduction at source – can be justified by the need to ensure the efficiency of the collection of the tax. *The avoidance of non-taxation ultimately also serves the efficiency of the collection of the tax*' (emphasis added).[75]

The Court, however, did not follow AG Kokott's line of thought that tried to link the avoidance of non-taxation to the collection of taxes. Instead, it relied on its settled case law to rule that as long as Portugal has chosen not to tax the resident shareholders of the dividends originating from the domestic UCITS, it cannot rely on the need to ensure a balanced allocation of taxing rights to justify the taxation of a foreign UCITS and its beneficiaries, not even under the pretense of the danger of the dividends escaping taxation altogether.[76] It is true that this argumentation is consistent with existing CJEU case law and that AG Kokott's link of the avoidance of non-taxation to the efficiency of the collection of tax alludes to the potential base erosion and the concomitant loss of revenue that has been repeatedly rejected by the Court. It is also possible that this obiter dictum serves as a nudge to the Court by AG Kokott to re-consider the single tax principle in its 'taxation at least once' aspect.

Relevance of State Aid Rules?

For the sake of completeness, it must be considered whether the state aid provision (Article 107 TFEU) and the burgeoning case law in fiscal aids could allude to a recognition by the General Court (GC) and/or the CJEU of the 'taxation at least once' principle. Article 107 contains a general prohibition of financial assistance that would favour certain undertakings over others. Articles 107(2) and 107(3) TFEU provide the conditions under which aid may be compatible with the internal market. One obvious expression of the rule of law in state aid matters is the prohibition of the recovery of the aid already paid, if the principle of legal certainty has not been met, that is when the legal effects of state aid law were considered unforeseeable.[77] Beyond that, however, it is doubtful whether the EU Courts' interpretation of Article 107 TFEU could signify or even mandate the single tax principle.

[74] Opinion AG Kokott of 6 May 2021, *Allianzgi-Fonds*, Case C-545/19, ECLI:EU:C:2021:372.

[75] ibid at [91].

[76] CJEU judgment of 17 March 2022, *Allianzgi-Fonds*, Case C-545/19 at [83].

[77] See Regulation 2015/1589, art 16(1) 'the Commission shall not require recovery of the aid if this would be contrary to a general principle of Union Law'.

In the Court's case law, state aid includes measures that 'mitigate the charges which are normally included in the budget of an undertaking'.[78] Several steps in the assessment of the existence of state aid, especially the finding of selectivity, make this a difficult task for the Court. The measures applicable to the domestic undertakings (or to a category of these undertakings) must derogate from the so-called 'reference framework', to be found selective, and to not be justified by the nature or general scheme of the system. The idea behind this system is to identify whether 'foreign' undertakings are discriminated against 'domestic' ones.

It is true that in certain cases the CJEU (or the GC) have found the non-taxation or the lower taxation, or the conditional 'beneficial taxation' of certain undertakings as incompatible with Article 107 TFEU.[79] The result of such a finding is that the aid provided to these undertakings must be recovered and the particular scheme at issue must be discontinued. It is true that such a result could fit within the imposition of 'taxation at least once'. However, that would be a very bold statement to make. The particular cases brought by the Commission before the Court and the very specific facts at hand (tax system at issue, undertakings affected, material and geographical scope and policy objectives) prevent any possible identification of such a pattern that could form the basis of the single tax principle.

Issues of double non-taxation may, however, also arise in the context of hybrid mismatches between Member States. In these cases, Member States treat transactions in an inconsistent manner that may result in 'double non-taxation'. In a state aid context, the Commission and the Court have confirmed that measures to avoid double taxation are regularly justified by the nature of tax systems, but the relief measures cannot go beyond what is necessary (proportionality test). If so, they may result in unjustified advantages for certain undertakings. While, as already stated, the ATAD includes specific rules to address hybrid mismatches, it remains questionable whether state aid rules also prevent cross-border hybrid mismatch arrangements. The Commission's negative decision in the *McDonald's* case suggests that state aid rules are not the appropriate tools to tackle hybrid mismatches relating to permanent establishments.[80] The same result was later confirmed by the CJEU in its *Engie* case where the GC and upon appeal, the CJEU were called to answer whether Luxembourg may have been infringing the EU State aid rules by not preventing, through its anti-abuse rules, the effects of cross-border hybrid mismatch arrangements.[81] In fact, the Court found that the General Court erred in interpreting the Luxembourg provision in an over-expansive way, as including that the relevant income should be taxed at least once.[82] Accordingly in both the general line

[78] See eg, CJEU judgment of 14 January 2015, *Eventech*, C-518/13, EU:C:2015:9 [33].

[79] See eg, CJEU, Judgment of 21 December 2016, *World Duty Free*, Joined Cases C-20/15 P and C-21/15 P, ECLI:EU:C:2016:981.

[80] Commission Decision (EU) 2019/1252 of 19 September 2018 on tax rulings SA.38945 (2015/C) (ex 2015/NN) (ex 2014/CP) granted by Luxembourg in favour of McDonald's Europe [2019] OJ L 195/20.

[81] CJEU, Judgment of 5 December 2005, *Engie*, Joined Cases C-451/21 P and C-454/21 P, ECLI:EU:C:2023:948. Note that the transactions at issue and the facts of the case took place before the adoption of the ATAD.

[82] *Engie* case, ibid, [60]: 'The General Court, in the first place, while recognising that Article 166 of the LIR does not make the grant of the exemption of income from participations at the level of a parent company formally dependent on the prior taxation of distributed profit at the level of its subsidiary, nonetheless held that the grant of such an exemption could be contemplated only if the income distributed by a subsidiary had been taxed beforehand, short of there being double non-taxation of profit in a purely internal situation.'

of fiscal aid case law and the tax rulings case law, the specific facts and the Courts' assessment at issue make it impossible to deduce a certain degree of abstraction that could confirm by the judiciary a consistent application of the no double non-taxation principle.

Conclusion

A 'thick' reading of the rule of law would consider equality principle in its substantive form as a constituent of it. The purpose of this chapter has been to examine whether the single tax principle, in both its 'taxation *only once*' and 'taxation *at least once*' aspects, has been understood by the CJEU as being part of the equality principle and, subsequently, of the rule of law.

As this chapter has shown, the case law of the CJEU and EU secondary law provide *segments* of both facets of the single tax principle. The case law of the CJEU appears to apply consistently the no double taxation element, under specific conditions. The same applies in secondary EU law that is aimed at eliminating double taxation (directly or indirectly). However, one cannot ignore that *instances* of double taxation (both economic and juridical) continue to exist in EU law and are considered acceptable restrictions in the free movement of persons and capital.

The requirement to tax at least once is less expressed in EU law. As argued above, the subjection to some degree of taxation has been evinced in EU law in the anti-abuse doctrine, as this is developed in the CJEU case law and. in secondary EU law, like the CFC rules, the anti-hybrid rules and the exit taxes in the ATAD. However, again, if the income escapes taxation altogether, this does not pose a problem from a fundamental freedoms' perspective. While this may appear at odds considering the recent, post-BEPS anti-tax avoidance wave, AG Kokott's subtle reference to the need to avoid non-taxation may be perceived as a nudge to the CJEU to follow an 'evolutionary' approach with regard to the single tax principle, that would be compatible with BEPS and Pillar 2.

This chapter suggests that the single tax principle cannot be found in EU law in a consistent and comprehensive manner. This is partly because EU direct tax law remains largely unharmonised and there is no EU rule to allocate taxing rights among Member States. The development of the single tax principle as a concept in the DTC framework that encompasses such distributive rules explains this difference. The analysis above shows that the existence of such distributive rules is a prerequisite for the single tax principle (in its most rudimentary form) to work. At the same time, the single tax principle itself may suffer from a certain degree of abstraction and generality, the so-called indeterminism, that may make it hard to apply in practice. As Ruth Mason has observed,

> [...] the concepts of full taxation and double taxation are indeterminate – there is no way to specify the tax base or rate that would satisfy them. Although commentators using terms like "double non-taxation" may have in mind an approximate tax base (perhaps financial accounting income with adjustments for tax) and an approximate tax rate (something like

> the OECD average rate), such vague notions are too imprecise to generate clear policy prescriptions.[83]

Accordingly, the single tax principle cannot be considered part of the EU law framework in either of its facets. This may be paradoxical considering both that the ability to pay principle is often perceived as part of the equality principle enshrined in the TFEU; and that in the context of Pillar 2, the EU may require a minimum tax when the conditions of the GloBE directive are met, while it does not have in place a rule or a principle to guarantee a/some tax in general.

[83] Mason, above n 38, 385.

17

Challenges to the Rule of Law in Taxation of the Digital Pornography Industry

GIEDRE LIDEIKYTE HUBER*

Abstract

The chapter examines the largely and regrettably unstudied issue of the rule of law in the taxation of the digital pornography industry. Digital pornography is a sophisticated global business that has developed over the last two decades and is dominated by large multinational enterprises (MNEs) using innovative organisational structures and revenue models. It is precisely this type of business that the Organisation for Economic Co-operation and Development (OECD) Pillar 1 reform proposals target. However, policy debates on comprehensive tax reform for the digital economy have completely neglected this sector, focusing on more conventional digital multinationals. This chapter seeks to fill some of these research gaps. It highlights both the general challenges of the digital economy, which are particularly evident when studying this industry, and the specific challenges that this industry faces, especially under Swiss domestic tax law. Such challenges often undermine the rule of law in tax policy, either from the perspective of the taxpayer or in terms of the proper administration of a tax system. The paper calls for legislative intervention, either at the national or international level, and argues for a closer examination of the digital pornography industry to develop a fairer and more effective corporate tax system.

Introduction

This chapter analyses the concept of the rule of law in relation to the taxation of the digital pornography industry. This industry, that has radically changed[1] with the

* I would like to thank greatly the participants of the Sixth Tax Policy Conference of the Centre for Tax Law, University of Cambridge and their valuable comments and suggestions.

[1] I refer to the research of Betzler and Leuschen who, taking as example Swiss market, analyze the megatrend of digitalisation in film and gaming industries referring to them as 'cultural and creative industries'. However,

widespread digitalisation of the economy, is one of those industries that seem to be able to reap extreme tax benefits from the outdated international corporate tax frameworks. Using revenue models that are radically different from those used in the twentieth century,[2] such multinational enterprises (MNEs) often have no physical presence in the jurisdictions in which they operate (eg streaming adult content) and thus escape most or all corporate income tax. Similar novel business models were also adapted, for instance, by Google and Facebook, two MNEs that control around two-thirds of the global digital advertising income.[3] Tax-related problems in relation to those two MNEs were constantly analysed in the OECD's BEPS reform proposals.[4] However, the digital porn industry was completely overlooked in the BEPS debate, both at international and domestic (for instance Swiss) levels. This is unfortunate because, firstly, pornography appears to take up a huge amount of space on the Internet, so its links with digitisation are significant, and secondly, it appears to have its own specific business characteristics which merit separate consideration in legislative discussions.

In this context, the present chapter focuses on two aspects in relation to the rule of law. Firstly, I study how the fact that the digital porn industry is effectively untaxed is compatible with 'thin' and 'thick' concepts of the rule of law. The key question is how we qualify a situation where the economy and business models are changing radically, but the tax laws are not adapting and therefore failing to capture new ways of generating business income. Secondly, I question the absence of legislative scrutiny related to this industry in the process of the international corporate tax reform. I discuss the extent to which the new economic reality needs to be understood and considered when legislators (national or international) create new tax rules.

The chapter is structured as follows: Section 2 deals with the application of the rule of law in tax law and specifically in Swiss law. Section 3 discusses the emergence and functioning of the digital porn industry and its specificities. Section 4 focuses on general issues that may arise in the taxation of digital porn, both from a national and international perspective. Section 5 provides a critical evaluation.

Rule of Law and Swiss Tax Law

The principle of the rule of law is a multifaceted concept that is often left undefined in national legislation (eg in Switzerland). It can be described as a moral–political philosophy on the objectives and ideals that the law should promote.[5] The interpretation of this

I use the term 'audiovisual industries' without entering the debate as to whether pornography should be classified as a cultural or creative industry. D Betzler and L Leuschen. 'Digitised Value Chains in the Creative Industries: Is there a Convergence of Swiss Film and Game Production?' (2021) 14 (3) *Creative Industries Journal* 226–44.

[2] M Köthenbürger, 'Taxation of Digital Platforms' in S Cnossen and B Jacobs (eds) *Tax by Design for the Netherlands* (Oxford: Oxford University Press, 2022) 169–80, 170.

[3] C Fuchs, *The Online Advertising Tax: A Digital Policy Innovation* (London: University of Westminster Press, 2018). Available at: www.jstor.org/stable/j.ctv5vddvv 5, 7.

[4] OECD Addressing the Tax Challenges of the Digital Economy, Action 1 – 2015 Final Report, OECD/G20 Base Erosion and Profit Shifting Project, (Paris: OECD, 2015). Available at: https://doi.org/10.1787/9789264241046-en.

[5] A Marmor, 'The Rule of Law and Its Limits' (2004) 23(1) *Law and Philosophy* 1, 2, quoting J Raz, *The Authority of Law. Essays on Law and Morality* (Oxford: Oxford University Press, 1979) 210–26, 221.

concept[6] often pits two versions of the rule of law against each other: 'thin' and 'thick'.[7] In the following, I analyse how these standards are delineated in Swiss tax law.

The 'thin' interpretation of the rule of law is that the function of the law is to act as a guide to action.[8] It has two components:[9] procedural (political authorities rule by law[10]) and formal (rule of law describes a 'good law' that could effectively guide human behaviour[11]).

In Swiss law, procedural components of the rule of law are essentially contained in a constitutional norm, stating that all activities of the state are based on and limited by law.[12] It is called 'principle of legality'.[13] It comprises two aspects: (i) the supremacy of law; and (ii) the requirement of a legal basis.[14] In the domain of taxation, the principle of legality strictly limits governmental action: the main structural features of any tax, in particular those liable to pay tax, the object of the tax and its assessment, are regulated by law'.[15] All significant tax provisions that establish binding legal rules must be enacted in the form of a federal act; this includes essential aspects of taxation: the taxpayer, the object of the tax, the amount and the taxable base.[16] In addition, the fundamental modification of an existing tax, as well as the introduction of any new tax, should be submitted to an obligatory referendum.[17] All in all, a formal law is a prerequisite for the action of the state in the field of taxation.[18]

[6] On many aspects of the rule of law, a consensus can be observed between various scholars' jurisdictions. Marmor, ibid, 5.

[7] For a detailed theoretical overview, see Daly, Chapter 2 in this volume; one can also refer to 'narrow' and 'broad' versions of the rule of law – see Lindsay, Chapter 3 in this volume.

[8] Daly, ibid.

[9] Marmor, above n 5, p 2 et seq.

[10] This criterion might seem easy to interpret, but some authors caution against quick judgement. In fact, from a practical point of view, people will always be ruled not by law, but by other people (Members of Parliament adopt laws, judges interpret them, etc.). Nor does this mean that all governmental actions are authorised by law – by definition, any unauthorised governmental acts are illegal. Marmor, above n 5 at 3 citing Raz. It is also difficult to define what government could not rule by law as such an answer depends on the theory of what the law is (Marmor indicates that in the command theory of law, any order backed by sanction of the sovereign would be law.).

[11] Raz, above n 5, 214. In this respect, law must meet certain conditions, on which there is theoretical consensus: generality, promulgation, no retroactivity, clarity, no contradictory rules, no impossible prescriptions, stability, consistent application. Marmor, above n 5 at 5. Even though the observance of these criteria is a matter of degree (no legal system can be perfectly clear and coherent), the law is no longer able to guide human conduct if they fail fundamentally. Marmor at 3 with reference to L Fuller, *The Morality of Law* (New Haven CT, Yale University Press, 1964) 39.

[12] The Federal Constitution of the Swiss Confederation of 18 April 1999, AS 1999 2556 ('Cst.'), art 5 para 1.

[13] Cst art 5 is entitled 'Rule of Law' in unofficial English translation. In the official Swiss languages, art 5 is called 'Grundsätze rechtsstaatlichen Handelns' (DE) and 'Principes de l'activité de l'État régi par le droit' (FR). The literal translation of this title would be 'principles of the State government by law'.

[14] T Tanquerel, *Manuel de droit administratif* (Schulthess éd. romandes, 2011) 15.

[15] Cst, art 127 al. 1.

[16] ibid. art 164, para 1(d). Interpreting those constitutional norms, the Swiss Federal Supreme Court ('the Court') has confirmed on several occasions that the state can levy no tax or any other public contribution (except in some rare cases) if they do not have a sufficient legal basis, identifying at least those three elements. ATF 131 II 562, 56 and cited references; see also G Lideikyte Huber, *Conceptual Problems of the Corporate Tax: Swiss–US Comparative Analysis* (IBFD: Amsterdam, 2019) 1–373, 10.

[17] Cst, arts 140(1)(a), 142(2) and 195; A Auer, G Malinverni and M Hottelier, *Droit constitutionnel suisse*, Vol I (Stämpfli Editions SA, 2013) 404.

[18] S Weerts. 'The Law and the Principle of Legality' In: *Swiss Public Administration: Making the State Work Successfully*, A Ladner, N Soguel, Y Emery, S Weerts and S Nahrath (London: Palgrave Macmillan, 2019) 69–86, 72, 83.

Formal aspects of the rule of law are expressed through various norms. The requirement of defined normative content of a norm derives from the principle of legality (Cst, art 5, para 1), however, according to Federal Supreme Court, it also comes at least from the requirement of legal certainty and equality before the law.[19] Constitutional norms in the field of the rule of law also indicate that the state's activities must be conducted in the public interest and be proportionate to the ends sought; state institutions and private persons must act in good faith.[20] The principles of administrative law, such as proportionality and generality, which reflect the description 'good' law, are applicable to tax law.[21]

The 'thick' version of the rule of law is broader, and contain a moral component, requiring the law (in addition to the standards of 'thin' rule of law) to adhere to more substantive legal standards. It requires for the law to be 'just', protecting, for instance, human rights and dignity, as well as equality, and is concerned with questions of political economy.[22] According to the 'thick' version, if the laws exist and are enforced, but they lack moral content, the concept may be referred to as rule *by* law, rather than rule *of* law.[23]

This 'thick' version of the rule of law is particularly interesting in the present analysis, where a formal legal framework for corporate taxation exists, but some companies (digital porn MNEs) seem to effectively escape it. In tax law, the 'thick' rule of law would generally mean enforcing the moral dimension of taxation. The discussion of morality in tax law and policy could be very diverse. For example, the contributors to this volume look beyond the formal rule of law to the informal norms and values that underpin citizens' sense of fairness and obligation and consider tax morality from a virtue ethics perspective (Badisco/Van de Velde). In the present chapter, I take a purely legal standpoint and argue that the moral element in tax legislation depends on compliance with the constitutional principle (in Switzerland) of the ability to pay. This principle, derived from the humanist philosophy of the Age of Enlightenment, is a fundamental justification for the definition and collection of taxes in Western legal systems.[24] Its meaning remains consistent across Western nations: every taxpayer should be subject to fair taxation, with this fairness embodied in the principles of horizontal and vertical equity.[25] This consensus on what constitutes fairness in a tax law forms the moral core of tax laws; if the principle of ability to pay is not respected, taxation loses its meaning.

The interpretation of some aspects of the principle of ability may differ between jurisdictions and between authors, but these differences do not create substantial gaps in the theory as a whole. One example is the application of this theory in

[19] ATF 123 I 112, para 7(a), 124; Lideikyte Huber, above n 16, 10.
[20] Cst, art 5, paras 2–4.
[21] Lideikyte Huber, above n 16, 10.
[22] R Stein, 'Rule of Law: What Does It Mean' (2009). *Minnesota Journal of International Law* 250, citing F Hayek 'The origins of the rule of law'. In *The Constitution of Liberty* (1960): 162–75, 299 (citing Justice Kennedy). Available at: https://scholarshiatlaw.umn.edu/mjil/250, 297. See Lindsay, Chapter 3 in this volume.
[23] Stein, ibid. 299.
[24] I analyse this principle in a comparative perspective in G Lideikyte Huber, above n 16.
[25] RA Musgrave and PB Musgrave, *Public Finance in Theory and Practice* (London: McGraw-Hill, 1989) 218–19.

corporate taxation: Swiss law holds that the principle applies to both individuals and corporations,[26] whereas some Anglo-Saxon scholars argue that the ability to pay principle can only be applied to individuals.[27] Despite this seemingly large difference, the US and Switzerland have very similar corporate tax systems. This discussion is therefore not very relevant here: in all jurisdictions based on the ability to pay principle, we accept that both companies and their shareholders should be subject to laws that tax their income.

The compatibility of the current taxation of highly digitised porn MNEs with 'thin' and 'thick' concepts of the rule of law will be further developed in this chapter. The main problem here is not that there is no legal framework applicable to porn MNEs – there is indeed one which defines many tax-related aspects for them (their tax residence, etc.) as for other companies. However, the application of these rules, by and large, never leads to the taxation of these companies (at least not sufficiently) due to outdated international tax standards. I will develop this point in the following sections.

Emergence and Structure of the Digital Porn Business

The pornography[28] industry is one of the audiovisual industries that have been the most radically transformed by digitalisation. It's traditional twentieth-century forms – tapes and cinemas – have nearly disappeared and have given way to digital content.[29] Thus, many aspects in the value chain, including distribution, have radically changed as well: instead of being physically sent to or picked up by a user in a specific location, audiovisual product may be digitally transferred in a matter of seconds across the globe. The size of the digital pornography industry has not been estimated by serious academic studies, but rare, usually non-academic, attempts to estimate the economic importance of this sector suggest a billion-francs scale[30] and that it occupies a large part of the internet.[31] This is plausible, because it is widely acknowledged in technology circles that

[26] The Swiss Federal Constitution states that the principle of ability to pay applies to 'all taxes', without specifying whether it applies to all taxpayers (art 127, para 2). However, the Federal Supreme Court highlighted that the existence of economic double taxation is based on the idea that legal entities have their own ability to pay that is independent from that of their owners (see ATF 102 Ib 151, para 6).

[27] Musgrave and Musgrave, above n 23, 218–19.

[28] I use the definition of here pornography as sexually explicit media that are primarily intended to sexually arouse the audience, with a typical content of nudity and/or various sexual acts. N Malamuth, *International Encyclopedia of the Social & Behavioral Sciences* (Amsterdam/New York: Pergamon 2001). However, the definition of pornography is far from being unanimous; this subject is particularly researched in psychology, but less so in other scientific branches. T Kohut et al. 'Surveying Pornography Use: A Shaky Science Resting on Poor Measurement Foundations' (2020) 57(6) *The Journal of Sex Research* 722–42.

[29] Analogue production has become rare as most audiovisual content is now stored as a digital code; the final product in most cases is no longer embodied in a physical form such as videotape, CD or cassette (those products still exist but have become a niche market. D Hesmondhalgh and LM Meier. 'What the Digitalisation of Music Tells Us About Capitalism, Culture and the Power of the Information Technology Sector' (2018) 21(11) *Information, Communication & Society* 1555–70.

[30] J Naughton 'The growth of internet porn tells us more about ourselves than technology', *The Guardian*, 30 December 2018. Available at: www.theguardian.com/commentisfree/2018/dec/30/internet-porn-says-more-about-ourselves-than-technology, last accessed 23 November 2021.

[31] K Buchholz 'How Much of the Internet Consists of Porn?' 11 February 2019, *Statista*. Available at: www.statista.com/chart/16959/share-of-the-internet-that-is-porn/, last accessed 31 January 2022.

pornography has greatly contributed to the development of the internet in general.[32] Adult websites like xvideos, PornHub, and xnxx rank at respectively 11 to 13 of the most visited websites in the world in 2022, meaning that they outrank such websites as Amazon (14), TikTok (15) OpenAI (17).[33] Digitalisation has also brought big changes to other sexual industries, such as prostitution – the live cam industry has been booming during the last decade (with numerous tax aspects to resolve).[34] Overall, it appears that there is a big market with important global revenue streams and supply chains.[35]

Our knowledge of porn's legal structures, business models and markets is scarce and often based on the information provided by porn companies themselves.[36] It is, however, known that a significant part of global porn websites are held by two multinational enterprises named Aylo (previously MindGeek) and Web Group Czech Republic (WGCZ).[37] With headquarters in Luxembourg, this enterprise operates multiple porn websites (including Pornhub) and holds dozens of subsidiaries around the world (including low-tax jurisdictions like Cyprus and Ireland), with its effective siege in Canada. It also possesses companies operating in related areas, such as age verification software, as well as its own ad placement network, TrafficJunky, which exclusively serves the adult industry.[38] Web Group Czech Republic, based in Prague, is a rival company to MindGeek according to an investigation by the *Financial Times*; WGCZ tube sites XVideos and XNXX host about 6bn visits a month. That's roughly the same as Twitter and much more than MineGeek's flagship site Pornhub.[39] Almost nothing is known about this apparently huge second MNE, which keeps its business very secret.[40]

In terms of the reach of digital porn, little official information is available about its markets[41] or other data on consumption.[42] For instance, in Switzerland, local porn

[32] D Tynan, 'Thank You, Porn! 12 Ways the Sex Trade Has Changed the Web', *PCWorld*, 21 December 2008. Available at: www.pcworld.com/article/532547/porn_on_the_web.html, last accessed 11 September 2023.

[33] Similarweb, top worldwide websites, May 2023. Available at: www.similarweb.com/top-websites/, last accessed 18 June 2023.

[34] S Donzallaz and O Crevoisier. 'Digitalisation, innovation and territorial forms: commercial sexual activities between soliciting and livecam.' Working paper 2- 2020/E, The circulation of wealth.

[35] B McNeill. 'An interview with Jennifer Johnson on how pornography influences and harms sexual behavior', 26 January 2015. Available at: https://news.vcu.edu/article/An_interview_with_Jennifer_Johnson_on_how_pornography_influences#.Vp8d6AKozxU.twitter, last accessed 21 January 2022.

[36] Pornhub, for instance, is releasing certain information about its worldwide traffic. Available at: www.pornhub.com/insights/yir-2021#Countries-by-Traffic.

[37] P Nilsson and A Barker 'Knocking on the door of a porn empire' *Financial Times*, 20 January 2023. Available at: www.ft.com/content/cc9ab3c5-bfe1-40d0-862d-c35123ceaf1c.

[38] P Nilsson, 'MindGeek: the secretive owner of Pornhub and RedTube', *Financial Times*, 17 December 2020. Available at: www.ft.com/content/b50dc0a4-54a3-4ef6-88e0-3187511a67a2, last accessed 29 March 2021; K Nicholas, 'The Children of Pornhub. Why does Canada allow this company to profit off videos of exploitation and assault?' *The New York Times*, Opinion, 4 December 2020.

[39] Nilsson and Barker, above n 35.

[40] ibid.

[41] It is possible that Aylo sites target western Europe markets (as well as the North American market), whereas WGCZ dominates emerging markets, especially South America and Asian countries, providing lower-resolution products due to poorer internet connections in those jurisdictions. However, this information has not been confirmed by scientific research. Informal interview with Patricia Nilsson a *Financial Times* journalist, who carried out the investigation 'Hot Money' on the porn industry. Available at: www.ft.com/content/762e4648-06d7-4abd-8d1e-ccefb74b3244.

[42] For instance, in Switzerland. Personal interviews with the Swiss Federal Office of Statistics and the Swiss Federal Office of Telecommunications, December 2021.

production and distribution companies are very rare, and operate not as limited liability companies but as associations.[43] It is thus safe to say that Swiss digital porn consumption is dominated by foreign enterprises. Pornhub, for instance, indicates that porn consumption in Switzerland is high.[44] Websites that belong to either Aylo (Pornhub) or WGCZ (xnxx, xvideos) are in the top 20 most visited websites by traffic share in Switzerland (surpassing Netflix, Amazon, etc.).[45]

In terms of revenue models, a rare study of the digital pornography industry suggests that mainstream digital pornography is largely based on the provision of significant amounts of free content.[46] Companies that adopt such business models use so-called two-sided digital platforms that capitalise on user contributions resulting from indirect network effects and generate a huge amount of advertising revenue.[47] Adopted by some of the largest multinationals such as Google and Facebook, this business model is radically different from traditional twentieth-century approaches.[48] It is particularly important from a tax perspective, as I will discuss later in this chapter.

Overall, it appears that digital porn has become a huge cross-border industry, with at least two significant MNEs – Aylo and WGCZ – operating globally. These MNEs bear similarities to the largest tech giants that are at the centre of the discussion on reforming the international tax framework. At first glance, digital pornography companies seem to resemble companies such as YouTube or Google, whose revenue models are based on the collection of anonymous user data. However, there are many differences between these companies and digital porn. Porn's product is – obviously – very specific. It is neither a social media platform nor a search engine (its form, most closely resembles YouTube, which is owned by Google). Digital porn sites are not allowed to collect and reuse user data in the same way as many multinational companies, because data about a person's sex life or sexual orientation is sensitive and requires additional protection.[49] And, of course, the porn industry is highly stigmatised and therefore does not receive as much scrutiny as other (legitimate) industries.

Current (Non-)Taxation of the Digital Porn Industry

In general, the field of pornography – digital or otherwise – is poorly regulated. Researchers note that many general laws and regulations that are enforced in other industries are ignored in pornography due to its specificity.[50] Many countries, including

[43] A rare example is an ethical porn company Oil Productions: https://oilproductions.ch/. See also: www.letemps.ch/societe/sciences-humaines/melanie-boss-porn-star-ethique, accessed 11 June 2023.

[44] See www.pornhub.com/insights/switzerland, accessed 13 June 2023.

[45] Similarweb. Top Websites Ranking – Most Visited Websites in Switzerland. Available at: www.similarweb.com/top-websites/switzerland/, accessed 1 June 12023.

[46] K Darling, 'IP without IP: A Study of the Online Adult Entertainment Industry.' 17 *Stan Tech L Rev* (2013) 709.

[47] Köthenbürger, above n 2, 170.

[48] ibid.

[49] Regulation 2016/679 of the EU Parliament and the Council of 27 April 2016 on the protection of natural persons with regard to the processing of personal data and on the free movement of such data, and repealing Directive 95/46/EC (General Data Protection Regulation), art 9.

[50] Mellish, 35.

Switzerland, do not define the term 'pornography' in law.[51] Porn-specific regulation is essentially done through criminal laws. In this respect, a basic distinction could be made between legislation that bans production, distribution and/or consumption of *all* pornographic content using criminal law countries that ban only *certain* types of 'harmful' pornography,[52] which has been criminalised in most Western countries.[53] In the latter, other 'adult content' is usually not subject to any restrictions.[54] In countries where some types of porn are legal, the supervision of this industry appears to be relatively open to various infringements. For instance, in Switzerland, access to pornography websites is virtually unregulated (for instance, unrestricted to minors).[55]

Tax law, as the most other branches of law, largely overlooks the existence of the digital porn industry and, except in very rare cases, the legislator does not create specific provisions for it, nor does it discuss this opaque industry specifically during corporate tax reforms. However, if one ventures into the analysis of its tax aspects, the starting point would be determining whether this business in a specific jurisdiction is legitimate.

In a significant number of countries even the consumption of porn (not to mention production and distribution) is *illegal*.[56] However, one could safely guess that digital porn is still certainly produced, distributed and consumed in many (if not all) of these countries. This leaves porn operating in a grey area of semi-legality, where authorities tolerate, or at least cannot eradicate, this business activity. In such countries, the porn industry appears to be simply untaxed. For instance, in a rare empirical study on the issue, companies in the Romanian livecam industry[57] have raised the issue of wanting to pay taxes. Notwithstanding, this was not possible due to the illegal (but nonetheless

[51] The definition of child pornography exists in the Optional Protocol of 25 May 2000 to the Convention on the Rights of the Child, on the Sale of Children, Child Prostitution and Child Pornography, in force in Switzerland since 1 December 2006 (AS 2006 5437 5440; BBl 2005 2807). On the US, see P Gewirtz, 'On I Know It When I See It' (1995) 105 *Yale Law Journal* 1023; *Jacobellis v Ohio*, 378 US 187 (1964).

[52] Harmful pornographic content is often defined as including (1) child or (2) violent pornography or (3) animal abuse (see for instance the Swiss Criminal Code (SCC), art 197, para 4).

[53] In Switzerland, the content that is considered the most harmful, ie pornography offences involving prepubescent children, is not subject to a time limit concerning the right to prosecute and impose penalties. Cst, art 123b.

[54] This debate has not disappeared. It emerged and was most prominent in US legal circles in 1980s. It was led by notorious feminist scholars CA MacKinnon and A Dworkin, who defined pornography as a civil rights violation and argued that pornography reinforces patriarchal structures by making gender hierarchy sexy. CA MacKinnon 'Pornography, Civil Rights, and Speech' (1985) 20(1) *Harvard Civil Rights–Civil Liberties Law Review* 1–70.

[55] For instance, until 2023, entering the term 'porn' in a Google search engine directed users to porn websites that are accessible without confirming legal age (parental control could censure porn but it has been shown that most children have it on their phones or PCs). Federal Council acknowledged that there are no specific legal regulations, other than criminal provisions, to protect children and young people from inappropriate content on the Internet or via on-demand or platform services (Dispatch 2020: 7926). A new Federal Act on the protection of minors in the sector of movies and video games (LPMFJ) adopted only in September 2022, requires age verification systems to be put in place for 'unsuitable content' defined largely (Art. 8). Ordinance on the Protection of Minors in the Film and Video Game Industries (OPMFJ) – Draft under consultation. Recently, accessing pornographic websites in Switzerland mandates clicking a confirmation button affirming legal age, commonly stating 'I am 18 or older'. However, its effectiveness remains debatable.

[56] See https://en.wikipedia.org/wiki/Pornography_laws_by_region, accessed 30 June 2024.

[57] In this chapter, I consider livecam business as online prostitution, not pornography, due to its non-reproducible content and live interaction. However, it appears to be qualified as pornography by the Romanian authorities.

tolerated) nature of the 'pornographic' business activity.[58] Overall, such a situation clearly deviates from the principle of the rule of law in the sense that, in such jurisdictions, not all companies are subject to (tax) law, the tax law is not capable of guiding human behaviour (inconsistent application between different companies) and not all taxpayers are taxed according to their ability to pay.

Such situations are difficult to resolve from tax perspective. As such business activities are illegitimate, criminal law applies, and proceeds from illegal activities should be forfeited, not taxed.[59] However, forfeiture is a lengthy and costly task, difficult to enforce and inefficient regarding widespread illegal activities and foreign perpetrators (and its overall aim is altogether different from taxation). The only other option is taxation of income from illicit sources – an approach recognised by many countries, such as the USA and the Netherlands. Those countries encourage declaring income from *certain* illegal activities, for instance, from dealing illegal drugs[60] (in those two jurisdictions, however, the porn industry is not illegal). Understandable from a public finance perspective, such a tax policy raises multiple inconsistencies in a legal system, which are hard to resolve (eg, a taxpayer's right to non-self-incrimination).[61]

In countries where mainstream porn is *legitimate* – which is all the Western countries – such businesses are theoretically either subjected to a general corporate tax regime or a specific regime with controversial 'porn taxes' (usually an add-on of special tax dispositions on the general corporate tax regime, those taxes are quite rare[62]). However, with the digitalisation of porn, this industry became increasingly difficult to tax. In the present work, I will focus on this second category, as the jurisdiction which I study more closely – Switzerland – falls into it.

As mentioned above, local porn production and distribution companies are rare in Switzerland, and the Swiss market appears to be dominated by foreign digital porn multinationals. As Switzerland has not introduced specific porn taxes, general corporate tax rules apply to the activities of foreign companies on its territory. As in most countries in the world, corporate income taxation in Switzerland follows the 'classic' territoriality principle: legal entities are subject to unlimited Swiss tax jurisdiction if they have their registered office or effective management in Switzerland (DFTA, Art 50). They are subject to limited taxation based on their economic connection if they are associated with a company domiciled in Switzerland, if they operate a permanent establishment in Switzerland or if they own real estate and/or rights related to real estate in Switzerland (DFTA, Art 51(1)). The term 'permanent establishment' is defined in Articles 4(2) and 51(2) of the DBA in its traditional sense, ie it requires a fixed place of business in Switzerland. Corporate profits are subject to profit tax at the federal,

[58] Donzallaz and Crevoisier, above n 35, 8.

[59] SCC, art 70, para 1.

[60] IRS 2021.

[61] Those questions are, to a certain extent, researched in relation to other domains, for instance the taxation of drug trade income (Van Der Veen) or financial criminal sanctions in Switzerland (A Opel 'Ist Besteuerung von Unrecht rechtens?' (Basler Juristische Mitteilungen, 2016) *Basler Juristenverein*, 1–37).

[62] Those taxes consist of imposing a higher rate on profits of porn companies or higher indirect taxes on distribution of pornographic content. OECD, *Tax challenges arising from digitalization – interim report*, 16 March 2018. Italy currently has such a tax, France had it until 2021 and it is under discussion in certain US states.

cantonal and, in some cases, municipal level.[63] Unlike some countries,[64] Switzerland has not introduced a Digital Services Tax (DST) or similar taxes in any other form.

Under the corporate tax rules described above, a foreign digital pornography provider that has neither a registered office nor effective management in Switzerland and that offers large quantities of free digital material on the Swiss market and generates revenue by placing foreign advertisers' content on its websites does not have a physical taxable nexus in Switzerland. Under the limited taxation regime, a mere digital presence is not considered a sufficient permanent establishment. As a result, companies using the two-sided digital business models described in the next section escape any corporate income tax in Switzerland. As their service is free of charge, despite the (arguably) huge volume of market activity, they are also likely to escape VAT altogether (the same applies to advertisers).[65]

Critical Assessment in the Light of the Rule of Law

Domestic Context

Unlike other tech giants such as Google and Facebook, porn companies do not appear to have any taxable nexus in Switzerland. This analysis could be applicable to other industries that operate in a similar manner to digital porn and are based in Switzerland. However, I did not identify any similar situations.[66]

This lack of taxation raises concerns about the rule of law that could be interpreted under 'thin' and 'thick' versions of it.

Firstly, porn MNEs can be seen as businesses that are so different from others, in terms of their structure and operations (not in terms of the business content), that they simply do not fall within existing (outdated) tax law norms and should be subject to specific tax rules. As such rules do not exist, they essentially operate in a rule-free environment, which is unacceptable from the 'thin' perspective of the concept of the rule of law.[67]

Such a situation may be treated as a loophole. It is difficult to deal with loopholes in tax laws because of the first aspect of the rule of law, in particular the strict approach to the principle of legality. Theoretically, 'proper' loopholes can be corrected through judicial review (although the interpretation of tax law is intended to avoid the creation of new cases of tax liability, new taxable entities or new events giving rise to taxation).[68]

[63] Federal Direct Tax Act (FDTA), arts 1 and 57. LHID corporate profits apply the rules of FDTA, art 58. At the federal level, net corporate profits are taxed at a fixed proportional rate of 8.5%. At the cantonal level, corporate tax rates are mostly proportional; however, certain cantons apply a mixed-rate system or even progressive rates, with minimum and maximum limits. Lideikyte Huber, above n 14, 175.

[64] R Avi-Yonah, YR Kim and K Sam. 'A New Framework for Digital Taxation' 63 *Harv Int'l LJ* (2022) 279.

[65] Swiss VAT Act; interview with the Federal Tax Administration, personal communication, December 2021.

[66] In informal discussions with the federal Tax Administration, we concluded that the only (rather tiny) industry truly resembling digital porn is the streaming of pirated videos.

[67] Brassey (see Chapter 12 in this volume) analyses a similar situation in a different context.

[68] ATF 131 II 562 567 and cited references.

It is, unfortunately, almost impossible to envisage that a question of such substantial dimension as the taxation of digital presence could be resolved through judicial review. Furthermore, the fact that the Federal Supreme Court is unable to examine the constitutionality of federal laws, including those that contain corporate tax provisions, such as the Federal Direct Tax Acts, further complicates the matter. The Court is unable to challenge such laws and to control whether they are compatible with the constitution (for instance, the principles of equality or of the ability to pay).[69]

This situation also contravenes the formal aspect of the 'thin' conception of the rule of law. A 'good' law should be such that it could guide human behaviour in a logical manner, and I would particularly cite its aspects of generality and consistent application. The principle of generality requires that legal norms must be issued at some level of generality. No legal system can function by addressing its prescriptions to individuals, one by one, or by addressing each act separately.[70] I would like to reverse this argument by proposing that a law should also not be excluding certain specific businesses. The law cannot guide human conduct if actual deviations from it are not treated as such, namely, as deviations from the rule.[71] The digital porn industry currently stands out as completely untaxed, even in comparison with similar enterprises (in terms of revenue generation) like Google or Facebook. This situation is not explicitly treated as an exception to corporate taxation, making the law unclear and its philosophy (even more) confusing to taxpayers. Such inconsistent legal treatments have not only made the law obscure, but also eroded the public's general trust in corporate tax system.

Secondly, the situation could be interpreted as compliant with the 'thin' concept of the rule of law (ultimately, porn MNEs do adhere to the corporate tax law norms). However, it is lacking essential components of the 'thick' concept of the rule of law. The moral aspect of the rule of law requires just and equitable taxation. One possible approach to measuring this is through the principle of ability to pay. In this respect, the fact that a business, generating substantial amounts of internet traffic and using Swiss high-level IT infrastructure to generate its income, does not contribute anything in taxes, is problematic in comparison to other businesses deriving income from the Swiss territory, via more traditional approaches. It is evident that, in accordance with the prevailing tax regulations, digital porn providers based abroad are not considered Swiss taxpayers and, consequently, are excluded from horizontal and vertical equity comparisons. However, the reason why such market players are not considered Swiss taxpayers is that the revenue models have undergone a radical transformation (even though pornographic distribution and consumption remained within the Swiss territory, and perhaps even increased) and the tax laws failed to adapt to this change. Interpreting tax law[72] from a teleological perspective, nothing suggests that

[69] What further complicates the matter is that in Swiss law, the Federal Supreme Court cannot examine the constitutionality of federal laws, meaning it cannot challenge such laws (such as Federal Direct Tax Acts, that contain corporate tax provisions). The Court assumes, however, that the federal legislator does not propose a solution which would be incompatible with the Constitution. Cst, art 191; ATF 130 II 65 consid. 4.2 at 71; ATF 129 II 114 consid. 3.1 118; ATF 129 III 55 consid. 3.1.1 56/57 and cited cases.

[70] Marmor, above n 5, 6.

[71] ibid.

[72] In Swiss tax law cases, the Federal Supreme Court refers to the general interpretation principles: literal, historical, teleological, and systematic interpretations. If several interpretations are permissible, the one chosen must be consistent with the Federal Constitution. ATF 131 II 562 567 and cited references.

the legislator intended, decades ago, to exempt specific business domains or business models from taxation, notably porn. On the contrary, from a historical perspective, porn enterprises operating in Swiss territory (through cinemas, published media, etc) were taxed as other businesses. Concerning the novel digital business models, the legislator could not have mindfully excluded them while creating basic corporate tax laws in Switzerland, as such business models did not yet exist. Again, the situation with digital porn today amounts to a so-called 'proper' or 'apparent' loophole in Swiss tax law,[73] which undermines the principle of ability to pay.

In summary, the non-taxation of digital porn operating in Switzerland is incompatible with the principle of rule of law, that could be analysed both from 'thin' and 'thick' perspectives. As this loophole cannot be corrected by judicial review, this situation must be resolved by the legislator. It would require amending its corporate tax system – either unilaterally, by adapting DTS or similar levies on the digital presence of foreign companies (an option that Switzerland has considered and refused, at least for now) or by following an international tax reform which could be joined by Switzerland, provided that this addresses the specificities (if any) of this industry – which might be unlikely, as discussed below.

International Context

A study of the taxation of the digital porn industry reveals another issue in connection with the rule of law in an international context (although the discussion below could also hold true in certain domestic contexts). In particular, the fact that the analysis of this huge industry is not included in the international discussions about taxing the digital economy exposes the problems in the process of law-making.[74] In the present chapter, I want to highlight the substantive inclusiveness – the need to thoroughly analyse the subject to create rules that are fair (as much as possible) to all taxpayers.

The digital porn industry provides an interesting case study concerning highly digitalised MNEs, where the issue of deficient taxation has been subject to decades-long discussions. To address the problems of under-taxation, a multilateral solution was recently proposed by the OECD through its Base erosion and profit shifting project (BEPS),[75] specifically through its so-called 'Two Pillar solution' announced in 2021. The extent to which ongoing international reforms will affect digital porn taxation remains unclear, given that this significant industry has been overlooked in previous studies.

In its attempts to reform international taxation, the OECD has consistently highlighted the lack of knowledge about digital industries. It has been acknowledged multiple

[73] A 'proper' loophole is a situation where the legislator has failed to settle a point that should have been settled, and no solution is apparent from the text or interpretation of the law. ATF 131 II 562 568.

[74] van Ganzen, Broekhuijsen Vording and Vleggeert (see Chapter 13 in this volume) analyse the rule of law in the law-making process from the inclusiveness of the stakeholders' perspective; The 'Rule of Law Checklist' authored by the Venice Commission of the Council of Europe and cited by those authors, sets recommendations in this respect.

[75] OECD (2013), Action Plan on Base Erosion and Profit Shifting, OECD Publishing. Available at: http://dx.doi.org/10.1787/9789264202719-en, accessed 1 September 2022; OECD, above n 4.

times that BEPS concerns are better identified and addressed by analysing the existing structures adopted by MNEs together with new business models and by focusing on the key features of the digital economy and determining which of those features raise or exacerbate tax challenges. Only in this way can approaches be developed to address those challenges. In certain areas, the OECD has indeed adopted a methodology of analysing specific MNEs and their business models. Different digital industries, such as online gambling, video games, paid streaming (music and video) and social media, were scrutinised. The OECD concluded that the MNEs were diverse and would adjust to tax reforms in a different way. Notwithstanding those studies, researchers and the OECD have continued to emphasise the lack of empirical evidence regarding various facets of the operation of MBEs (a point that was reiterated as late as 2023). The digital porn industry has not been included in any analysis of this nature. Indeed, it is absent from the thousands of pages of OECD documents on this question.[76]

To ignore such an extensive industry within the context of international reform discussions, particularly those which focus on specific industries, is, at the very least, regrettable. To establish efficient tax regulations, a comprehensive understanding of the diverse functions of various digital businesses is crucial, as the OECD itself acknowledges.[77] The digital porn industry appears to exhibit characteristics that would classify it as a targeted business.

Firstly, it fits the description of an extremely mobile digitalised business that is capable in exploiting various loopholes in international corporate tax rules (as current corporate profits are taxed only if a company has a physical presence in a market (source) jurisdiction). One of the aims of the BEPS project, and currently the focus of Pillar Two reforms, is to reduce aggressive business tax planning and tax evasion, where MNEs, using various tax techniques, shift profits from high-tax to low-tax jurisdictions.[78] This was especially easy for highly digitalised businesses like porn, because of the fact that its product is completely digital; those MNEs are likely using extensively modern corporate assets such as software and other intellectual property of an intangible and easily transferrable nature.[79] In rare publications on the subject, scholars argue that, in industries like pornography and gambling, global digital commerce has probably played a role in the growth of controlled foreign corporations' arrangements.[80] Even though we do not have financial data from MNEs such as Aylo, the fact that it has its headquarters in Luxembourg and many subsidiaries in offshore jurisdictions hints to this 'classical' aggressive international corporate planning that was heavily used before

[76] I have gone through the main OECD documents from 2013, the launch of the BEPS project, searching documents for the key terms 'porn', 'pornography', 'adult', 'sex'.

[77] In its 2014 analysis, the OECD highlights the eight 'most common' revenue models in the digital economy: (1) advertising-based revenues; (2) digital purchases or rentals; (3) selling of goods (including virtual items, overlaps in part with (1); (4) subscription-based revenues; (5) selling of services; (6) licensing content and technology (overlaps with (4) and (5)); (7) selling user data and customised market research; and (8) 'hidden' fees and loss leaders. OECD (2014), Addressing the Tax Challenges of the Digital Economy, OECD/G20 Base Erosion and Profit Shifting Project, OECD Publishing. Available at: http://dx.doi.org/10.1787/9789264218789-en, accessed 1 May 2023, 83–84.

[78] Avi-Yonah, Kim and Sam, above n 62.

[79] ibid; OECD 2015, above n 4; 2017.

[80] A Cockfield, W Hellerstein and M Lamensch *Taxing Global Digital Commerce* (Alphen aan den Rijn: Kluwer Law International BV, 2019) 197.

BEPS.[81,82] Such tax planning will be likely to be reduced with the reforms of the Pillar 2 – provided that porn MNEs reach the €750,000 of turnover required for Pillar 2 rules to kick in. However, do porn MNEs reach this threshold? This question remains unanswered, even though I could speculate that due to their business models, discussed below, porn MNEs are significant.

Secondly, and more relevantly, the digital porn industry encompasses MNEs that, like Google or Facebook, use completely new revenue models based on value creation by users (even though the tax-avoidance preferences of companies using such business models are the same as the ones of more traditional businesses).[83] During the last decade, it was increasingly argued that such business models have implications for tax policy and the OECD acknowledged that they present even bigger challenges in taxing the digital economy in comparison with other industries.[84] In such models, as labour and capital are not the prime input factors in generating the added value, traditional rules of international corporate taxation become meaningless.[85] Such ad-based business models become a crucial reference in discussing how taxing rights could be redefined in digital economy, focusing on Google and Facebook.

Analysis of digital porn could give precious insights into this debate, which is still unresolved and is conceptually the most complicated in the discussion about taxation of digital economy.[86] The current Pillar 1 proposal, even being a fresh approach, is very limited in scope and is essentially still proposing taxing business income. Nevertheless, it remains to be seen whether this is the optimal approach to such intricate business models. Moreover, it is evident that a global consensus on this matter is yet to be reached. Other innovative proposals have been put forth by scholars, which, at least at first glance, appear to be more forward-thinking and better suited to taxing digital pornography and similar industries. For example, the conceptual framework for data tax is based on a novel interpretation of the ability to pay.[87] It proposes that data can act as a proxy for this ability, removing concepts of source and residence. Consequently, the user of the data is subject to a tax.[88] The concept is undoubtedly intriguing. However, to implement it, it is essential to conduct a comprehensive analysis of the operational dynamics of the industries in question. It would be prudent to commence with the most significant ones, including digital pornography.

[81] OECD (2013), *Action Plan on Base Erosion and Profit Shifting.* Available at: http://dx.doi.org/10.1787/9789264202719-en, accessed 1 September 2022.

[82] J Vella, R Collier and M Devereux. 'Comparing Proposals to Tax Some Profit in the Market Country' (2021) 13(3) *World Tax Journal* 405–39; European Commission. (2014). Report of the Commission Expert Group on Taxation of the Digital Economy. Available at: https://ec.europa.eu/taxation_customs/system/files/2016-09/report_digital_economy.pdf, accessed 9 June 2022; OECD 2014, above n 73, Action 1; Avi-Yonah, Kim and Sam above n 72, 279 et seq.

[83] Köthenbürger, above n 2, 170.

[84] OECD, above n 4.

[85] Köthenbürger, above n 2.

[86] ibid.

[87] O Marian, 'Taxing Data' (2021) 47 *BYU L. Rev* 511.

[88] ibid, 652.

Conclusions

The digital pornography industry has radically changed in the last decades. Due to the development of the internet and the digitalisation of its product, it has expanded massively and is currently dominated by large MNEs who use novel organisational structures and revenue models based on value creation by users.

The transformation of this industry presents many tax challenges. This chapter showed that under domestic Swiss tax law rules, foreign digital porn MNEs streaming free porn and targeting Swiss-based users escape all taxation. Such an activity does not create the taxable nexus in Switzerland. This tax situation is unique, in comparison with the other dominant companies using ad-based business models, like Facebook or Google, who have a physical presence.

Such a situation is incompatible with the rule of law principle in tax law, both under its 'thin' and 'thick' versions, looking into the domestic Swiss and international contexts.

In terms of 'thin' conception of the rule of law, the question arises whether the porn MNEs, being so different from other corporations in terms of their structure and operations, must not be subjected to separate tax rules. As such rules do not exist, they currently operate in the effectively rules-free environment, which is unacceptable. This situation might be treated as a loophole, requiring legislative intervention. It is also contrary to formal component of the 'thin' rule of law, and the interpretation *a contrario* of the principle of generality: a law should be general enough and not exclude specific businesses. It cannot guide human conduct if actual deviations from the law are not treated as such. The non-taxation of digital porn operating in Switzerland is also incompatible with the 'thick' interpretation of the rule of law in tax law, whose goal, I argue, is applying the principle of ability to pay and treating all taxpayers equally.

This situation can only be rectified by the legislator, either unilaterally or in the framework of an international reform. With respect to the latter, the shortcomings of the international discussions on these intricate business models, which failed to include an analysis of digital pornography, give rise to concerns regarding the rule of law in legislative processes. Due to such deficiencies, porn industry remains opaque, and it is not clear to what extent the ongoing legal proposals, such as Pillar One, could affect it – even though porn MNEs seem to fit into the description of novel businesses reaping extreme profits from digitalisation. Leaving a huge industry out of studies on the taxation of the digitalised economy denies us a better understanding of how the digital economy works in general, and therefore how to tax it more effectively. As a result, this could lead to important (new) loopholes in tax systems.

Other academic proposals, such as taxing data, seem promising, but could only be used if a deeper knowledge of this industry is gained. A closer analysis of digital porn would thus contribute to development of a more efficient corporate tax system – with rules that are 'just' and 'good' for all businesses.

18

International Tax Law and the Rule of Law – An Aspirational Goal or Ironic Compound Oxymoron?

RICHARD KREVER AND KERRIE SADIQ

Abstract

Common to the many popular understandings of 'rule of law' are two benchmark principles – a sharp dichotomy between the body that makes laws (the parliament) and the body that administers them and a guarantee of certainty in laws that impose liabilities and potential penalties on persons. The former provides protection to taxpayers from arbitrary imposition of laws made up by the agency responsible for administering the law and the latter provides both the persons subject to laws and persons who administer them with clear boundaries to potential liability under the laws. Tax laws generally satisfy the two principles, with legislation passed by the parliament providing explicit guidance in many areas and (in Anglo jurisdictions) judicial doctrines built on the doctrine of precedent, implicitly accepted by the legislature or overruled where the legislature rejects judicial concepts, filling in the gaps. The notable exception to the observation is the system for allocating profits of multinational enterprises adopted unilaterally by almost all countries hosting parts of these enterprises and reinforced by treaties built on two models that also incorporate the almost universally used system. The system first artificially deems each element of a multinational enterprise to be a separate economic entity and then requires taxpayers and tax administrators to construct imagined commercial arrangements between the parts of the enterprises based on hypothetical prices that would be used if arm's-length parties were to enter into similar arrangements. As the arrangements in question will only happen within consolidated multinational enterprises, the hypotheticals are entirely imagined, providing no elements of certainty for the parties and effectively providing the agencies that administer the law with the opportunity to make it as well or at least negotiate an outcome based on their idea of what the law should be. An alternative system for allocating profits is available and has been adopted in other national profit allocation systems. Moving to that system would lead to a fairer system that honoured rule of law principles.

Introduction: The Rule of Law and Tax Law

There is no requirement for laws, including tax laws, to be fair, consistent or even sensible in any way. Parliament is supreme and, absent constitutional prohibitions, can enact any measure as a law, however capricious and unprincipled it may seem. The requirement that laws be enacted by Parliament is sacrosanct, however, and will broach no compromise. The executive responsible for administering the laws cannot create the laws it enforces, a principle that appears in no law or constitutional provision and yet is rigorously enforced by the courts as a fundamental feature of the law, the foundation of the 'rule of law' principle. Only Parliament, and not administrators, can make laws that impose obligations on subjects of the law and actions by administrative bodies such as the revenue service will be ultra vires and of no legal effect if not based on Acts of Parliament.[1]

This blanket assertion must be read subject to a proviso. While the government can only legitimately, in conformity with rule of law principles, require payment of taxes based on statute or imprison subjects based on criminal statutes, under the common law system, courts will enforce laws created entirely by the judiciary including pursuing damages for tort or contract law, and enforce orders for compensation, injunctions and specific performance based on equity law and trust law. In these cases, the court-made law is implicitly endorsed by the Parliament to the extent that it could, but chooses not to, interfere or overrule the judge-imposed law.

Tacked on to this bedrock rule of law principle in some, but not all, quarters, are two supplementary principles: the law should ensure consistent outcomes for different persons in the same situation, and citizens' obligations under a law should be set out with sufficient certainty to enable citizens to comply with the law. Advocates of the wider view of rule of law principles feel strongly about the importance of these further qualities, particularly the principle of certainty, regarded by proponents as a foundation of a state governed by the rule of law,[2] nowhere more so than in respect of tax law.[3]

Tax law, on its face, measures poorly when evaluated against both the narrowest and broader understandings of rule of law. The phrase 'tax law' implies the imposition of a fiscal requirement on persons based on a clear set of rules that can be used to impose tax on persons deriving income, in the case of an income tax law, or spending income and savings, in the case of a consumption tax law such as the value added tax (VAT) law. The reality of tax law is quite different, however. In many instances, ambiguous, but foundational, terms are left undefined, with responsibility delegated to the courts to fill in the meaning of terms used in the legislation.[4]

[1] For a recent discussion of the evolution of the doctrine of sovereignty of Parliament in the UK, see eg, S Sedley, *Lions under the Throne: Essays on the History of English Public Law* (Cambridge: Cambridge University Press, 2015) ch 7.

[2] B Leoni, *Freedom and the Law*, 3rd edn (Indianapolis: Liberty Fund, 1991).

[3] AV Demin, 'Certainty and Uncertainty in Tax Law: Do Opposites Attract?' (2020) 9(4) *Laws* 30, section 2.2.

[4] TC Hartley, 'Five Forms of Uncertainty in European Community Law' (1996) 55(2) *Cambridge Law Journal* 265.

Consequent judicial interpretations of tax law terms, more often than not on the basis of transplanted meanings borrowed from other, and more often than not wholly unconnected, areas of law,[5] provide neither absolute certainty nor clearly visible consistency. This alone does not necessarily undermine rule of law principles, however. Judicial doctrines may be broadly stated and their application to particular fact situations open to discussion or debate, but disputes over their meaning in different circumstances takes place within the boundaries and guidance afforded by a rich tapestry of precedents that illustrate how the courts apply the rules they have developed. The legislature, in turn, implicitly accepts the rules and guidance by its silence or overrules the judicial interpretations with legislation if it concludes the judicial approach is inconsistent with the legislature's policy goals.

Although tax policy theoreticians may weep in despair over the seemingly irrational, from a policy perspective, consequences of the application of definitions, concepts and doctrines imported from other areas of law, the borrowed terms and tests provide sufficient guidance to bring tax law generally under the rule of law umbrella. There is, to be sure, scope for varied interpretations of the law and the tax authority and taxpayer may offer their differing views in what amounts to a negotiation regarding the application of authority to particular circumstances but these discussions take place in the context of articulated judicial principles based on actual fact situations. In one area, however – the transfer pricing rule that allocates the profits of multinational enterprises to separate parts and separate jurisdictions for tax purposes on the basis of 'arm's-length prices' for transactions between related businesses – tax law is particularly problematic in terms of rule of law principles.[6]

On its face, the application of transfer pricing rules and the arm's-length principle appears to transgress all components of both the narrow and broad conceptions of rule of law, providing room for administrators to create and then enforce law, denying taxpayers certainty, and yielding inconsistent results between taxpayers in not dissimilar circumstances. The problems are caused by the ambiguous language of the international tax rules on the allocation of profits within multinational groups that provides no clear guidance for taxpayers or administrators. This is a consequence of the fact that the rules are built on a reference to a wholly hypothetical transaction that will never exist in the real world, a construction that makes it impossible to adopt ordinary interpretation processes that rely on a body of precedent and principles developed by reference to actual events.

[5] The phenomenon is now known as the 'fallacy of the transplanted category'. See further N Brooks, 'The Responsibility of Judges in Interpreting Tax Legislation' in G Cooper (ed), *Tax Avoidance and the Rule of Law* (Amsterdam: IBFD Publications in association with the Australian Tax Research Foundation, 1997) 93, 122–23.

[6] It has been suggested that a second exception to this general assertion is the case of general anti-avoidance rules which authorise administrators to impose tax where taxpayers have prima facie complied with tax legislation but done so, it is alleged by administrators, in a way that is motivated by the aim of minimising their tax liability; see further T Jain, '"GAAR" and the Rule of Law: Mutually Incompatible?' (2013) 43 *Chartered Accountant Practice Journal* 424; R Krever, 'General Report: GAARs' in M Lang, J Owens, P Pistone, A Rust, J Schuch and C Staringer (eds), *GAARs – A Key Element of Tax Systems in the Post-BEPS World* (Amsterdam: IBFD Publications, 2016) 1.

The Structure of Tax Law

A feature of much tax law is its many bright lines. The acceptable ratio of debt to equity in foreign-funded enterprises is usually set in stone. The tax value of employer-provided automobiles, loans, and even parking may be specified in detail.[7] Detailed safe harbour depreciation rates are provided in primary or secondary legislation or rulings. The list of bright lines is long. At the same time, however, many parts of the tax law are deliberately based on uncertainty, employing vague terms that have no common meaning or understanding in the community at large. The income tax assesses 'income' derived by a taxpayer, for example, and does not allow the taxpayer an upfront deduction for 'capital' expenses but neither core term is defined in the law or ordinary usage. Similarly, the tax statute requires taxpayers to withhold tax from payments to those who provide labour services to them in the capacity of 'employees' but not those who provide the same services as independent contractors, undefined terms that have no single understanding in the community.

Flesh is added to these bare bones by interpretative decisions issued by the courts, the institution to which the task of defining the uncertain terms in the income tax law was originally delegated by the legislature. Judicial precedents are used by taxpayers and tax authorities to understand the terms in the law, making it possible, for example, to identify in broad terms the difference between capital gains and income receipts, capital and revenue outgoings, and employees and contractors. The judicial tests and doctrines on which they are built, transplanted from other areas of law unrelated to tax policy such as trust law for the definition of income[8] or vicarious liability tort law for the definition of an employee,[9] provide general guidance, a starting point for determining their application to particular circumstances. Taxpayers and tax administrators then draw on the judicial guidance to reach an understanding acceptable to both, with courts resolving the issue in the rare cases in which the parties cannot agree on a position.

On its face, a tax law that is applied by way of negotiation between taxpayers and tax administrators appears difficult to reconcile with rule of law principles. And yet, as noted, observers never question tax law itself as inconsistent with the rule of law, whatever criticisms there may be over particular uncertain measures such as the general anti-avoidance provision. How is it that a law based on negotiation between the subject of the law and the body administering the law is accepted as a law consistent with the rule of law principles of legislation by Parliament, certainty and consistency?

[7] See eg, Australia's fringe benefits tax, applying to non-salary remuneration, with separate valuations for all three of these benefits: *Fringe Benefits Tax Assessment Act 1986* (Cth) ss 9 (car benefits), 18 (loan benefits), 39C–39DA (parking benefits).

[8] J Prebble, 'Income Taxation: A Structure Built on Sand' (2002) 24(3) *Sydney Law Review* 301; R Parsons, 'Income Taxation: An Institution in Decay' (1991) 13(3) *Sydney Law Review* 435, 436–43; R Krever, 'Interpreting Income Tax Laws in the Common Law World' in M Achatz, T Ehrke-Rabel, J Heinrich, R Leitner and O Taucher (eds), *Steuerrecht Verfassungsrecht Europarecht: Festschrift für Hans Georg Ruppe* (Vienna: Facultas Verlags- und Buchhandels AG, 2007) 354, 357–59.

[9] Brooks, n 5 above, 123–24.

The answer to this question may lie with other areas of law seemingly unrelated to tax law. If uncertainty and undefined terms were hallmarks of departures from the rule of law, tort law based on the undefined concept of negligence, contract law based on the undefined concept of consideration, and statute laws such as company law based on undefined fiduciary obligations or criminal law based on factors such as mens rea and causation would fall equally afoul of the rule of law test. The fact that most cases outside the criminal law field and many in that area are resolved by negotiation would seemingly reinforce this conclusion. They are never viewed that way, however, because of the foundation principle in the common law that judicial precedents will provide sufficient guidance to administrators of a law and the persons subject to the law faced with the task of finding the optimal interpretation of a term or phrase in the law for a particular fact situation.

Available interpretations admittedly span a range of meanings, but sufficient guidance is available for targets of the law and administrators to negotiate an outcome consistent with the broad policy aims supported by precedents. Indeed, a general theory of tax practice might well conclude a central role for the tax practitioner is that of negotiator,[10] with negotiation emerging as a ubiquitous element of tax administration and compliance. The view that the application of tax law by negotiation is consistent with the rule of law is only possible, however, if the underlying premise, that precedents showing how judicial doctrines and concepts applying to specific fact situations arising in decided cases provide the guidance needed for tax negotiators to agree on an interpretation consistent with rule of law principles, is satisfied.

International Tax and the Allocation of Multinational Profits

Without doubt, the most ironic phrase in international tax law is 'international tax law', a concept that exists neither in practice nor conceptually. Tax law is domestic law and inevitably references to 'international tax law' actually refer to the manner in which domestic tax law applies to foreign source income derived by residents and domestically sourced income derived by non-residents.[11] To the extent there is any apparent 'international' element to tax law, the concept only refers to bilateral or even, and far more rarely, multilateral agreements that modify domestic tax law generally or insofar as it applies to residents of a treaty partner.

The development of international tax law and the principles that govern it arose over a remarkably short period. Commencing a few years prior to the First World War and largely concluded within a few years after the armistice, almost all developed countries that did not have an income tax in place moved to adopt one, leaving profits from much of the world's investment and business subject to income taxation.

[10] J Frecknall-Hughes and E Kirchler, 'Towards a General Theory of Tax Practice' (2015) 24(2) *Social and Legal Studies* 289.

[11] R Mason, 'The Transformation of International Tax' (2020) 114(3) *American Journal of International Law* 353.

The post-war period saw the growth of multinational enterprises operating through subsidiaries and branches, with single economic enterprises comprised of many parts in different countries. While multinational enterprises operated as a single integrated economic entity to build on the synergies of self-supply insulated from the market,[12] the parts stood as separate entities or operations in a strict legal sense.

The duplication of income tax systems across the western world in the first decades of the twentieth century meant every jurisdiction in which a multinational had a presence could claim a right to tax a share of the multinational's profits but the question remained what share. Fearing inconsistent and overlapping claims of taxation, the International Chamber of Commerce asked the newly formed League of Nations to recommend a global solution to the question of profit allocation and the League's Financial Committee acted quickly to appoint a group of experts to consider the issue.[13] While the United States was not a member of the League of Nations, it was the world's most important economy and US foundations funded much of the League's important work.[14] It was thus not surprising when the Finance Committee agreed to the appointment of an American expert to the four-member expert group.

The American, Edwin Seligman from Columbia University, brought to the group the approach adopted by US states with company income taxes in place when allocating the profits of US enterprises operating across state borders. The US states had adopted a 'formulary apportionment' system for allocating the profits of multistate enterprises, calculating profits of the group as a whole and then allocating it to states on a pro rata basis calculated by reference to each state's relative contributions to profits based on inputs (the share of capital and labour used to create goods and services) and subsequent sales for a price exceeding cost.[15]

While the group of experts' report[16] was widely respected and influential within a circle of tax experts,[17] Seligman's enthusiasm for formulary apportionment was not shared by all US academics, at least in the context of the inspiration for his views, the state income tax system in the US. Thomas Adams, the Yale University economist credited with the design of the modern foreign tax credit regime and, by Americans, with the idea of a value added tax, conceded that separate accounting for each part

[12] In effect, the success of multinational firms is merely an international extension of the synergy benefits first articulated by Robert Coase. See RH Coase, 'The Nature of the Firm' (1937) 4(16) *Economica* 386. For a discussion of the importance of these synergies for multinational enterprises see K Sadiq, 'The Traditional Rationale of the Arm's Length Approach to Transfer Pricing – Should the Separate Accounting Model Be Maintained for Modern Multinational Entities?' (2004) 7(2) *Journal of Australian Taxation* 196.

[13] For a comprehensive review of the League's contributions to international tax law, see S Jogarajan, *Double Taxation and the League of Nations* (Cambridge: Cambridge University Press, 2018).

[14] See L Tournès, *Philanthropic Foundations at the League of Nations: An Americanized League?*, trans A Gharibian (Abingdon: Routledge, 2022).

[15] N Foran and D Gray, 'The Evolution of the Unitary Tax Apportionment Method' (1988) 15(1) *Accounting Historians Journal* 65; S Sicilian and J Huddleston, 'The US States' Experience with Formulary Apportionment' in R Krever and F Vaillancourt (eds), *The Allocation of Multinational Business Income: Reassessing the Formulary Apportionment Option* (Alphen aan den Rijn: Kluwer Law International, 2020) 41.

[16] League of Nations, *Report on Double Taxation*, League of Nations Doc. EFS 73 F 19 (1923).

[17] MJ Graetz and MM O'Hear, 'The "Original Intent" of US International Taxation' (1997) 46(5) *Duke Law Journal* 1021; RS Avi-Yonah, 'All of a Piece Throughout: The Four Ages of US International Taxation' (2005) 25(2) *Virginia Tax Review* 313.

of a multinational enterprise was open to 'real abuse'[18] but remained quite sceptical of formulary apportionment.[19] Also unenthusiastic were multinational companies and more importantly the home for the most important of these, the United States. The US had adopted the foreign tax credit designed by Adams that reduced US tax revenue from multinational enterprises based in the US by any foreign taxes paid on their offshore income and, not surprisingly, preferred to see the world adopt an allocation system that could be used by multinational enterprises to reduce foreign taxes.

The US influence on the tax work of the League was reinforced when the League agreed to the appointment of Thomas Adams, who had already expressed his scepticism of formulary apportionment as a model for allocating profits, as chair of the Fiscal Committee responsible for preparation of a model tax treaty. The impact of that influence was compounded when Adams had the League's Fiscal Committee commission prominent US tax attorney and Chief of the Tax Section at the US Department of Commerce, Mitchell B Carroll, to prepare a study of global practice on the allocation of multinational profits. The study was seen as the starting point for the development of recommendations on a model profit allocation regime. Carroll was subsequently appointed 'Director of the Study of Allocation Methods under the Fiscal Committee, League of Nations' and promised a study that would consider all options.[20]

At the time, it was clear that some member states were leaning towards a formulary apportionment regime as the basis for allocating profits of multinational enterprises and had adopted treaties that reflected this approach,[21] a factor noted in the final report which was, as promised, a comprehensive survey of practice. In the final chapter of the report, however, were a set of what were described as 'prerequisites for a regime of allocation' that included some uncontroversial assertions and one that, in retrospect, may be seen as quite controversial. The prerequisites first suggested that parts of a multinational enterprise should be treated as separate taxpayers and the income attributed to each part should be determined separately with respect to each part.[22] It then addressed the key question of how the income should be calculated for each part of a multinational enterprise, bypassing entirely consideration of a formulary apportionment system and instead offering what had been until that time a far from universally accepted agreed assertion that profits should be calculated looking at transactions with 'outsiders and other corporate units of the enterprise'.[23] The conclusion was consistent with accounting practice in the US with the profession preparing

[18] TS Adams in 'Discussion on Business Income' (1931) 24 *Proceedings of the Annual Conference on Taxation under the Auspices of the National Tax Association* 348, 351.

[19] TS Adams, 'Allocation vs Apportionment' (1931) 24 *Proceedings of the Annual Conference on Taxation under the Auspices of the National Tax Association* 345.

[20] MB Carroll, 'Observations on Report of the Committee of the National Tax Association on Uniformity and Reciprocity in State Tax Legislation, Especially with Regard to the Allocation of Income of International Enterprises' (1931) 24 *Proceedings of the Annual Conference on Taxation under the Auspices of the National Tax Association* 333.

[21] See further SI Langbein, 'The Unitary Method and the Myth of Arm's Length' (1986) 30 *Tax Notes* 623, 632.

[22] League of Nations, *Taxation of Foreign and National Enterprises* (Geneva, 1933), vol 4, 176.

[23] ibid, 177.

books of accounts and tax returns respecting allocations within a group as chosen by the multinational.[24]

Recognising the likelihood that this separate accounting system would result in profit shifting, the report indicated tax authorities would be given the right to restate income to an entity 'on the basis of what it would have earned had it been dealing with an independent enterprise' and that this could be determined 'by comparison with independent companies engaged in similar activities under similar circumstances'.[25] This is, of course, a concise description of what is now known as arm's-length methodology. Outside of international income tax, the rule had been explicitly embedded in excise tax[26] and implicitly included in regulated utility pricing rules.[27]

The sleight of hand slippage in the League of Nations report from support for formulary apportionment to a recommendation for separate accounting and arm's-length pricing was surprising to an extent, given the scepticism some of the individual players had regarding the arm's-length methodology. As Ralph Jones, an academic from Yale University and a contributor to the 1933 report, put it, an 'attempt to base a tax on figures so determined is almost as futile as to try to tax transfers of money from one pocket to the other'.[28] Separate accounting and arm's-length pricing nevertheless was adopted as the recommended approach to profit allocation.

The shift to separate accounting and allocation of profits based on notional arm's-length pricing was subsequently reinforced by Carroll when, in parallel with his work writing up the allocation report, he prepared a draft model treaty.[29] The arm's-length system advocated in his report subsequently made its way into early US tax treaties, the League and subsequently OECD model treaties and, eventually, more than 3,000 bilateral tax treaties and the domestic tax laws of almost all nations.[30]

Constructing a Legal Rule on a Foundation of Myths

As a single integrated economic entity, a multinational enterprise is indifferent as to where its profits are allocated within the enterprise for legal (and accounting) purposes, particularly if there is a benefit to shifting profits to a lower tax jurisdiction.[31]

[24] Special Committee on International Double Taxation of the American Institute of Accountants, 'International Double Taxation, Statement' (1931) 9(10) *Tax Magazine* 366.

[25] League of Nations, *Taxation of Foreign and National Enterprises*, n 22 above, vol 4, 177.

[26] See eg, *Revenue Act 1932*, US Public Law 72–154, 47 US Statutes at Large, ch 209, s 619(b)(3) (manufacturers' excise tax): 'If an article is (1) sold at retail; (2) sold on consignment; or (3) sold (otherwise than through an arm's-length transaction), at less than the fair market price; the tax under this title shall (if based on the price for which the article is sold) be computed on the price for which such articles are sold, in the ordinary course of trade, by manufacturers or producers thereof, as determined by the Commissioner.'

[27] See eg, *Western Distributing Co v Public Service Comm'n*, 285 US 119 (1932) (US Supreme Court).

[28] RC Jones, 'Present Problems of the Consolidated Return' (1929) 22 *Proceedings of the Annual Conference on Taxation under the Auspices of the National Tax Association* 414.

[29] MB Carroll, *Global Perspectives of an International Tax Lawyer* (New York: Exposition Press, 1978).

[30] The transfer from Carroll's report to international treaties is described in E Baistrocchi, 'The International Tax Regime and Global Power Shifts' (2021) 40(2) *Virginia Tax Review* 219, 282.

[31] RM Bird, 'The Interjurisdictional Allocation of Income' (1986) 3(3) *Australian Tax Forum* 333.

By treating each part of a multinational enterprise as a separate entity and recognising all intra-group transactions provided they were priced on an arm's-length basis, the system opened the door to wholesale profit shifting. A multinational enterprise can easily establish a subsidiary in a tax haven and then transfer any type of intellectual property or company know-how to the subsidiary, use the subsidiary as a financial arm of the company, lending to other parts, or have the subsidiary carry out notional responsibilities such as intermediary marketing of the goods or services produced by the enterprise. The multinational enterprise can then shift profits to the low- or no-taxed entity through intra-group payments for the use of intellectual property, for on-lent funds, or intermediary services.

The solution to the problem of tax minimisation by way of profit shifting offered by the proponents of separate entity profit taxation is the continued use by tax authorities of the twentieth century's arm's-length rules to establish the value for tax purposes of intra-group pricing used by multinational enterprises to shift profits to lower-tax jurisdictions. The notion of an 'arm's-length' relationship has a long history in Western law, originating in equity law to protect vulnerable parties from exploitation by persons purporting to be acting in their interests[32] and has proven to be a useful tool to achieve equitable outcomes between parties outside of tax contexts.[33] While the application of the concept faces uncertainties at the margins, in ordinary circumstances the value by reference to comparable transactions can be found elsewhere in the economy.

At first look, the resolution of arm's-length pricing disputes does not seem dissimilar from other tax disputes that are viewed as entirely consistent with rule of law principles. The taxpayer opens with a bid towards one end of a spectrum and the tax authority counters with another towards the other end and the two parties move towards a compromise or they fail to and an adjudicator is called upon to choose the acceptable point between the two competing views. Risk-averse taxpayers who wish to avoid uncertainty will opt for negotiations before lodging a return, possibly seek an advance pricing agreement, and likely trade off some further profit shifting potential to avoid possible penalties from overly audacious claims.[34]

There is one crucial difference between resolution of a transfer pricing dispute and those arising in other fields of law where the liability threshold or test is uncertain and open to alternative interpretations. In areas such as tort law, contract law, criminal or company law, when arguing for their preferred interpretations of ambiguous terms, the parties rely on precedents based on actual fact situations. Drawing analogies to known facts is the basis for continuity and consistency, foundational inputs to the application of rule of law principles.

[32] *Parfitt v Lawless* (1872) LR 2 P & D 462.

[33] See eg, *Gibson v Jeyes (1801)* 6 Ves 266; 31 ER 1044; *Cane v Allen* (1814) 2 Dow 289, 3 ER 869; *McPherson v Watt* (1877) 3 App Cas 254.

[34] AAT Rathke, AJ Rezende, C Watrin and RM Antônio, 'Profit Shifting and the Attractiveness of Advance Pricing Agreements' (2023) 93(5) *Journal of Business Economics* 817; S Picciotto, 'Indeterminacy, Complexity, Technocracy and the Reform of International Corporate Taxation' (2015) 24(2) *Social and Legal Studies* 165; H Rogers and L Oats, 'The Use of Advance Pricing Agreements in Transfer Pricing Management' (2013) 1 *British Tax Review* 76.

A similar process is used in tax law whenever transactions arise in the grey area between certain points on a spectrum. A revenue expense such as a simple repair is deductible when incurred. An expenditure for the acquisition of a long-life asset is capitalised and recognised by way of ongoing capital allowance deductions. Looking at the precise facts of the actual transactions that have taken place, courts (and consequently subsequent taxpayers and tax administrators) are able to understand how the law will apply to these situations. For example, if the repair is made to a property that was in disrepair when acquired, a key factor might be how long it is used prior to the repair. If the repairs are needed before the asset can be used, the expenditure is likely to be characterised as a capital outlay, implicitly integrated into the acquisition cost.[35] If the newly acquired asset can continue to be used for a period before repairs are made, the repair expenditure is more likely to be characterised as a deductible revenue expense.[36] If, however, the part in disrepair needs to be replaced with a substitute material, the expense will be considered a capital outlay,[37] although a combination of some repairs and replacements can tip the characterisation back to a revenue nature.[38] To be sure, some precedents may be difficult or even impossible to reconcile,[39] but the guidance from earlier cases provides a template that can be used to resolve the majority of cases. The crucial element of all decisions is a foundation based on actual facts that can be evaluated. The process is one of characterising known facts.

In contrast, in the case of arm's-length determinations, it is impossible to develop precedents based on the application of tests to actual fact situations because the entire structure is built on a façade of artificiality, hypothetical arrangements that would never exist in the real world. No global multinational enterprise would develop a proprietary mobile phone system compatible only with its own phones, tablets, and computers and then transfer the intellectual property to an independent third party while agreeing to pay the outside party for sole use of its intellectual property.[40] No food or drink company would transfer its unique and unequalled proprietary recipe to an independent third party and then pay royalties for sole access to the recipe[41] or the main ingredient in their product offering.[42] No mining company would establish solid ties with customers around the world and then hand over all marketing responsibilities to an unrelated marketing company.[43] No multinational group would require a subsidiary to borrow on

[35] *Law Shipping Co, Ltd v Commissioners of Inland Revenue* [1923] 22 TC 621.

[36] *Odeon Associated Theatres Ltd v Jones* [1973] Ch 288.

[37] *FCT v Western Suburbs Cinemas Ltd* [1952] 86 CLR 102.

[38] *Conn v Robins Bros Ltd* [1966] 43 TC 266.

[39] Inland Revenue Department (NZ), 'Repairs and Maintenance' (1994) 5(9) *IRD Tax Information Bulletin*, 4.

[40] This is the hypothetical arrangement on which the profit-shifting arrangement in the *Apple* case (CJEU, *European Commission v Ireland and Others* (Case C-456/20 P, ECLI:EU:C:2024:724, 10 September 2024)) was based.

[41] *Coca-Cola Co v Commissioner*, 155 TC No 10 (2020): see RS Avi-Yonah and G Mazzoni, '*Coca-Cola*: A Decisive IRS Transfer Pricing Victory, at Last' (2020) 169(11) *Tax Notes Federal* 1739.

[42] ECJ, General Court, *Netherlands v Commission* (Case T-760/15) and *Starbucks Corp and Starbucks Manufacturing Emea BV v Commission* (T-636/16) ECLI:EU:T:2019:669.

[43] *BHP Billiton Ltd v Federal Commissioner of Taxation* (2020) 270 CLR 60; a similar dispute involving Rio Tinto Ltd was settled in 2022: see Australian Taxation Office, 'ATO Secures Settlement of Marketing Hub Tax Dispute' *Media Release*. Available at: www.ato.gov.au/Media-centre/Media-releases/ATO-secures-settlement-of-marketing-hub-tax-dispute/, last modified 20 July 2022.

the open market with no guarantee by the parent company or group as a whole, incurring substantially higher interest rates to cut into group profits more than necessary.[44] No drug company would transfer its lucrative patents acquired at significant research and development cost to an independent third party and then pay for exclusive use of the patents.[45] While these transactions may be hypothesised as 'arm's-length' scenarios by taxpayers and tax authorities based on 'arm's-length' prices,[46] in reality they will only exist between parts of the same entity.[47]

Several consequences follow from the application of a rule based wholly on artificial hypotheses. The first is a practical consideration – taxpayers can almost never lose from the resolution of a transfer pricing dispute. Whether a court decides in favour of the taxpayer[48] or tax authority,[49] some level of profits will be shifted[50] as the final price must sit between no profit shifting and full profit shifting, an inherent feature of a system that allocates profits from arrangements that would not have happened between genuinely unrelated parties. Following from this, the rule encourages taxpayers to engage in profit shifting transactions, an activity quite inconsistent with the policy objective of the income tax to allocate profits and consequent taxing rights to the jurisdiction in which profits are sourced.

A tax rule based on myths is incapable of yielding a single correct answer. Rather, as the OECD's guidelines for applying the arm's-length rule suggest, there may be a range of methodologies and consequent answers with no one method holding the mantle as the preferred method.[51] Tax administration optimists might hope that the strategic use of tax law uncertainty might pressure risk-averse taxpayers to report higher tax liabilities, but it turns out the uncertainty and consequent opportunity it opens for taxpayers leads to precisely the opposite behaviour.[52] At the same time, the bias in the legal rules in favour of profit shifting activities rewards those governments friendly to transfer pricing schemes that facilitate the arrangements to attract diverted profits[53]

[44] This is the hypothetical arrangement on which the profit shifting arrangements in *Singtel* and *Chevron* were based: see *Singapore Telecom Australia Investments Pty Ltd v Federal Commissioner of Taxation* (2021) 114 ATR 51; *Chevron Australia Holdings Pty Ltd v Federal Commissioner of Taxation* (2017) 251 FCR 40.

[45] See, eg *Roche Products Pty Ltd v Federal Commissioner of Taxation* (2008) 70 ATR 703. Other profit shifting drug companies include Merck and Eli Lilly. See further Avi-Yonah and Mazzoni, n 41 above.

[46] In the *Apple* and *Starbucks* cases, nn 40 and 42 above, the tax authorities had abandoned their attempts to dispute transfer pricing and the cases arose when the European Commission intervened to argue the profit shifting arrangements violated the state aid rules aimed at securing a neutral market in the European Union.

[47] R Baker and D Baker, 'The Pricing of Goods in International Transactions between Controlled Taxpayers' (1958) 10(3) *The Tax Executive* 235, 247–48.

[48] *Federal Commissioner of Taxation v Glencore Investment Pty Ltd* (2020) 281 FCR 219.

[49] *Chevron Australia Holdings Pty Ltd v Federal Commissioner of Taxation* (2017) 251 FCR 40.

[50] In *Chevron*, for example, the court allowed Chevron, which had borrowed funds at 1.2% to on-lend them to its Australian subsidiary at 8.97%, to claim successfully an interest rate far higher than that at which the subsidiary could have borrowed: see further K Sadiq and R Krever, 'Anatomy of Transfer Pricing: Lessons From Australia' (2020) 100(5) *Tax Notes International* 679.

[51] OECD, *OECD Transfer Pricing Guidelines for Multinational Enterprises and Tax Administrations* (Paris: OECD Publications, 2022).

[52] L Osofsky, 'The Case Against Strategic Tax Law Uncertainty' (2011) 64(4) *Tax Law Review* 489.

[53] B Huesecken and M Overesch, 'Tax Avoidance through Advance Tax Rulings – Evidence from the LuxLeaks Firms' (2019) 75(4) *Finanzarchiv* 380; O Marian, 'The State Administration of International Tax Avoidance' (2017) 7(1) *Harvard Business Law Review* 1; O Zhen Li, SJ Lusch and F Murphy, 'Tax Planning Through Advanced Tax Rulings – An Exploratory Analysis Using the Luxembourg Tax Leaks', (2024) 33(4) *European Accounting Review* 1431.

and punishes those that adopt clear and unavoidable rules that limit opportunities for profit shifting.[54]

The Arm's-Length Pricing and Rule of Law Schism

International tax law and, in particular, its most important element, the allocation of profits across jurisdictions in which multinational enterprises have interests, is based on actual transactions that trigger tax liabilities – sales and purchases of trading stock from related parties, loans extended to other members of the same group, royalties and licence fees paid for the use of intellectual property, and so on. The transactions not only yield profits and trigger tax liabilities, but also form the basis for allocation of the profits for tax purposes. The notional profit allocated to source countries under current international rules is calculated using an invented arm's-length price based on a hypothetical comparable that will never exist. If the task of interpreting tax law were simply a matter of ascertaining the legislative intent, judicial decision-making would be an easy task. The interpretation process starts with words in the law and the task of the legislative drafter is to put into those words the policy intent of the legislators.

Completing this task, however, assumes there is a discernible intent that can be uncovered with due diligence by the drafter.[55] If the legislature adopts language that has no objective meaning (a reference to the price in a hypothetical transaction that does not exist)[56] and provides no guidance in debates, committee reports, explanatory memoranda, or other possibly relevant sources, the task of the courts is not simply herculean, it is impossible.[57] The adjudicators are left with the bare words of the statute, directed to decide tax liability on the basis of a mandated hypothetical. The use of a mandated hypothetical per se is not a cause for alarm; so many areas of our law require adjudicators to consider a hypothetical alternative – the profits that would have been derived had a contract not been breached; the tax that would have been paid had the taxpayer not engaged in a transaction stopped by the general anti-avoidance provision, and so forth. It is a serious concern, however, if adjudicators are directed to find a tax liability by reference to a wholly imaginary hypothetical that can never exist.

In some jurisdictions, a gap in the law will be filled by the executive, drawing on their preferred interpretation of the policy goals of the law.[58] In 'Anglo' jurisdictions tax administrators and taxpayers when faced with a legislative abdication and consequential definitional lacunae in the law can draw on precedents and concepts from other

[54] R de Mooij and L Liu, 'At a Cost: The Real Effects of Transfer Pricing Regulations' (2020) 68(1) *IMF Economic Review* 268.

[55] VCRAC Crabbe, 'The Ethics of Legislative Drafting' (2010) 36(1) *Commonwealth Law Bulletin* 11.

[56] See, eg Taxation (International and Other Provisions) Act 2010 (UK) s 147, mandating the use of an arm's-length price.

[57] L Eisenstein, 'Some Iconoclastic Reflections on Tax Administration' (1945) 58(4) *Harvard Law Review* 477.

[58] LA Zelenak, 'Leaving It up to Treasury: Congressional Abdication on Major Policy Issues in the Early Years of the Income Tax' (2018) 81(2) *Law and Contemporary Problems* 137.

areas of law to fill in the gaps – the well-known transplanted category approach to interpretation of tax law noted earlier. However, if the language of the law provides little guidance, taxpayers and tax administrators have only two options. One is to wait for judicial resolution of disputes in these circumstances on a case-by-case basis. The other is to resolve the uncertainty through negotiation. The first is an intolerable option in a legal regime that relies on self-assessment and certain outcomes. The default position – negotiation – quickly emerges as the only workable option. Is there a difference between negotiation in this instance and all other tax law negotiations?

Limited uncertainty is a feature of tax law where key terms are undefined in the legislation and instead understood by reference to judicial doctrines and concepts. In each case, the judicial interpretations span a spectrum, identifying examples at either end – amounts that are clearly income at one end and capital gains at the other; outgoings that are clearly revenue in nature or capital in nature; and so on – while providing guidance on tests that can be applied to characterise cases that fall between the two. Crucial to the application of precedents to current interpretation disputes is the fact that past decisions are based on actual transactions. Taxpayers, tax administrators and tax adjudicators can start with real facts and compare the facts of the current transaction with those of the precedents to obtain an acceptable degree of certainty and consistency, hallmarks of a legal system consistent with rule of law principles. This cannot be said of transfer pricing disputes based on the application of an arm's-length price determined by reference to hypothetical arrangements that will never occur. In this environment, the role of the courts is not adjudicating a dispute through legal interpretation to achieve the rule of law goal of consistency in application of the law, but rather to act as an arbitrator between parties in a commercial dispute.

Viewed closely, international tax law based on arm's-length prices might be best characterised as an ironic oxymoron. Outcomes are not only inconsistent with the fundamental features of a legal system based on the rule of law, but arguably are not even based on law. The negotiations and even adjudication that resolve profit shifting disputes are based not on principles or precedents but rather compromise between assertions based on imaginary arrangements. The system undermines a core goal of international tax, allocating the profits of a multinational enterprise to its sources, by enabling some profit shifting whatever the outcome of a transfer pricing dispute. It discourages tax morality by legitimising tax minimisation arrangements.

In other areas of tax law, judicial doctrines and tests set limits to negotiated outcomes – the law is set out in precedents and disputes turn on the application of the law to particular fact situations. There is no law for transfer pricing, however, where there are no boundaries to the value of a wholly unreal hypothetical transaction. The question with transfer pricing arrangements is not whether profit shifting is possible, but rather how much is possible. Wherever the price is set, it is not based on the process used to reach decisions in the context of a justice system based on the rule of law. There are no precedents that provide tests and doctrines that can be used to characterise a transaction in light of guiding principles. Instead, an agreement is struck or decreed to set the price of a hypothetical transaction somewhere between the more extreme prices hypothesised by the two parties. In contrast to other areas of law, this is negotiation in its purist form, without reference to legal principles; it is making law wholly outside the constraints of rule of law.

A profit allocation system based on treating parts of a single economic enterprise as separate taxpayers and determining the allocation of the enterprise's profits to its parts using hypothetical prices for the transactions between those parts amounts to an invitation to transfer price and consequent loss of tax revenues.[59] The alternative approach entertained by the League of Nations a century ago, allocating profits to their actual source using a formula based on each jurisdiction's share of the factors that give rise to profits, would yield a result far better aligned with rule of law principles. The formula system has long been used successfully to allocate the profits of national enterprises to states for the purpose of state income taxation in the United States and to provinces for the purpose of provincial income taxation in Canada. A shift to this system would involve few operational or administrative challenges, as shown by the experience of California, which extended its formulary apportionment rules to multinational enterprises.[60] The efforts of reformers to combat transfer pricing-enabled tax avoidance through replacement of arm's-length pricing with a formulary apportionment regime should be applauded by advocates of the rule of law.

[59] P Sikka, 'Accounting and Taxation: Conjoined Twins or Separate Siblings?' (2017) 41(4) *Accounting Forum* 390.

[60] W Hellerstein, 'The Application of Formulary Apportionment to Related Entities: Lessons from the US Experience' in R Krever and F Vaillancourt (eds), *The Allocation of Multinational Business Income: Reassessing the Formulary Apportionment Option* (Alphen aan den Rijn: Kluwer Law International, 2019) 137.

INDEX

www.ingramcontent.com/pod-product-compliance
Ingram Content Group UK Ltd.
Pitfield, Milton Keynes, MK11 3LW, UK
UKHW021036150926
475561UK00003B/139

9 781509 977796